THE PUCCINI PROBLEM

The first detailed investigation of the reception and cultural contexts of Puccini's music, this book offers a fresh view of this historically important but frequently overlooked composer. Alexandra Wilson's study explores the ways in which Puccini's music and persona were help up as both the antidote to and the embodiment of the decadence widely felt to be afflicting late-nineteenth- and early-twentieth-century Italy, a nation which although politically unified remained culturally divided. The book focuses upon two central, related questions which were debated throughout Puccini's career: his status as a national or international composer, and his status as a traditionalist or modernist. In addition, Wilson examines how Puccini's operas became caught up in a wide range of extra-musical controversies concerning such issues as gender and class. This book makes a major contribution to our understanding of both the history of opera and of the wider artistic and intellectual life of turn-of-the-century Italy.

ALEXANDRA WILSON is Lecturer in Musicology at Oxford Brookes University. Her work has appeared in *Cambridge Opera Journal* and *Music & Letters*, and she is a regular contributor to BBC radio programmes. This is her first book.

CAMBRIDGE STUDIES IN OPERA
Series editor: Arthur Groos, Cornell University

Volumes for *Cambridge Studies in Opera* explore the cultural, political and social influences of the genre. As a cultural art form, opera is not produced in a vacuum. Rather, it is influenced, whether directly or in more subtle ways, by its social and political environment. In turn, opera leaves its mark on society and contributes to shaping the cultural climate. Studies to be included in the series will look at these various relationships, including the politics and economics of opera, the operatic representation of women or the singers who portrayed them, the history of opera as theatre and the evolution of the opera house.

Published titles
Opera Buffa in Mozart's Vienna
Edited by Mary Hunter and James Webster
Johann Strauss and Vienna: Operetta and the Politics of Popular Culture
Camille Crittenden
German Opera: From the Beginnings to Wagner
John Warrack
Opera and Drama in Eighteenth-Century London: The King's Theatre, Garrick and the Business of Performance
Ian Woodfield
Opera, Liberalism, and Antisemitism in Nineteenth-Century France: The Politics of Halévy's *La Juive*
Diana R. Hallman
Aesthetics of Opera in the Ancien Régime, 1647–1785
Downing A. Thomas
Three Modes of Perception in Mozart: The Philosophical, Pastoral, and Comic in *Così fan tutte*
Edmund J. Goehring

Landscape and Gender in Italian Opera: The Alpine Virgin from Bellini to Puccini
Emanuele Senici
The Prima Donna and Opera, 1815–1930
Susan Rutherford
Opera and Society in Italy and France from Monteverdi to Bourdieu
Edited by Victoria Johnson, Jane F. Fulcher and Thomas Ertman
The Puccini Problem: Opera, Nationalism and Modernity
Alexandra Wilson

The Puccini Problem

Opera, Nationalism and Modernity

Alexandra Wilson

CAMBRIDGE UNIVERSITY PRESS

CAMBRIDGE UNIVERSITY PRESS
Cambridge, New York, Melbourne, Madrid, Cape Town, Singapore, São Paulo, Delhi

Cambridge University Press
The Edinburgh Building, Cambridge CB2 8RU, UK

Published in the United States of America by Cambridge University Press, New York

www.cambridge.org
Information on this title: www.cambridge.org/9780521106375

© Alexandra Wilson 2007

This publication is in copyright. Subject to statutory exception
and to the provisions of relevant collective licensing agreements,
no reproduction of any part may take place without the written
permission of Cambridge University Press.

First published 2007
This digitally printed version 2009

A catalogue record for this publication is available from the British Library

ISBN 978-0-521-85688-1 hardback
ISBN 978-0-521-10637-5 paperback

Cambridge University Press has no responsibility for the persistence or
accuracy of URLs for external or third-party Internet websites referred to in
this publication, and does not guarantee that any content on such websites is,
or will remain, accurate or appropriate. Information regarding prices, travel
timetables and other factual information given in this work are correct at
the time of first printing but Cambridge University Press does not guarantee
the accuracy of such information thereafter.

CONTENTS

List of illustrations | *ix*
Acknowledgements | *x*
Note on translations | *xii*

Introduction | 1

1 Inventing an Italian composer | 11
2 *La bohème*: organicism, progress and the press | 40
3 *Tosca*: truth and lies | 69
4 A frame without a canvas: *Madama Butterfly* and the superficial | 97
5 Torrefranca versus Puccini | 125
6 The Italian composer as internationalist | 155
7 A suitable ending? | 185

Epilogue | 221

Appendix 1: selected newspapers and journals | *229*
Appendix 2: personalia | *237*
Notes | *254*
Bibliography | *292*
Index | *310*

ILLUSTRATIONS

Fig. 1.1. Puccini at the wheel (Archivio Storico Ricordi. All rights reserved. Reproduced by permission) | 35
Fig. 1.2. 'Maestro Puccini's motoring catastrophe', *Musica e Musicisti*, March 1903 (Archivio Storico Ricordi. All rights reserved. Reproduced by permission) | 36
Fig. 1.3. Puccini departs for Buenos Aires in 1905 – the banner bears the word 'speed' (Archivio Storico Ricordi. All rights reserved. Reproduced by permission) | 37
Fig. 1.4. Puccini the huntsman (Archivio Storico Ricordi. All rights reserved. Reproduced by permission) | 38
Fig. 3.1. Hariclea Darclée as Tosca, January 1900 (Archivio Storico Ricordi. All rights reserved. Reproduced by permission) | 78
Fig. 4.1. Rosina Storchio as Madama Butterfly, February 1904 (Archivio Storico Ricordi. All rights reserved. Reproduced by permission) | 99

ACKNOWLEDGEMENTS

I began writing this book as a Junior Research Fellow at Worcester College, Oxford, and completed it during my tenureship of a one-year Randall-MacIver Junior Research Fellowship at St Hilda's College, Oxford. I am extremely grateful to both colleges for electing me to these posts and for providing not only material support but congenial and intellectually stimulating environments in which to work. Research in Italy was essential to investigating 'the Puccini problem', and I am indebted to Worcester and St Hilda's as well as to the University of London Scholarship Fund and the *Music & Letters* Trust for awarding me grants that made this possible. I also benefited greatly from travel grants awarded by the British Academy, the American Musicological Society, and Oxford Brookes University, which allowed me to present conference papers based upon my research to an international audience.

I should like to acknowledge the assistance given to me by the staff of the following libraries: the Music Faculty Library, the Bodleian Library, and the Taylorian Institute Library, University of Oxford; the British Library and the British Newspaper Library; the Music Library at Royal Holloway, and Senate House Library, University of London; the Biblioteca Braidense, the Biblioteca Livia Simoni, and the Biblioteca del Conservatorio Giuseppe Verdi, Milan; the Centro studi Giacomo Puccini, Lucca; the Centro internazionale di ricerca sui periodici musicali, Parma; the Biblioteca del Conservatorio Arrigo Boito, Parma; la Biblioteca Nazionale Centrale and the Biblioteca Marucelliana, Florence; and the Biblioteca Nazionale Centrale, the Biblioteca e Raccolta Teatrale del Burcardo, and the Biblioteca del Conservatorio di Musica Santa Cecilia, Rome.

I should like to thank Arthur Groos and my anonymous readers for their helpful suggestions, and Victoria Cooper and Rebecca Jones of Cambridge University Press for their assistance during the production of the book. I am extremely grateful to the Modern Humanities Research Association for awarding me a subvention to fund the illustrations, and to Maria Pia Ferraris of the Archivio Storico Ricordi in Milan for granting permission to reproduce them. An earlier version of chapter 5 appeared as 'Torrefranca vs. Puccini: Embodying a Decadent Italy', *Cambridge Opera Journal* 13/1 (March 2001), 29–53, and an earlier version of chapter 7 appeared as 'Modernism and the Machine Woman in Puccini's *Turandot*', *Music & Letters* 86/3 (August 2005), 432–51. I gratefully acknowledge the permission granted by Cambridge University Press and Oxford University Press to reprint excerpts from these articles.

Many friends and colleagues took an interest in my work on Puccini, passed on references, read sections of the book or offered valuable advice and suggestions. In particular I would like to express my appreciation to Richard Bosworth, Ruth Clayton, Christopher Duggan, Linda Fairtile, Andreas Giger, Helen Greenwald, James Hepokoski, Julian Johnson, Roger Parker, Julia Prest, Annie J. Randall and Emanuele Senici. I would also like to thank my colleagues at Oxford Brookes University for their support during the period when this book was in production. I must offer special gratitude to Katharine Ellis, who supervised the doctoral dissertation from which this book originated, who offered her time and advice generously, and who has been a staunch source of encouragement from start to finish. On a personal note, I would like to thank my parents, who supported me throughout what must have seemed a bewilderingly long apprenticeship into academia. Most of all, I am more grateful than I can say to Andrew Timms, for accompanying me to Italy on my final review-finding expedition, for reading several drafts of this book, and simply for being there for me. This book is for him.

Oxford, May 2006

NOTE ON TRANSLATIONS

Translations from Italian into English are my own unless otherwise stated. Because of the extensive amount of cited journalistic material, I have not, as a rule, reproduced the original Italian texts. However, in cases where the original is particularly striking or ambiguous, it is given in the notes.

Introduction

Today there seem to be few composers as central to the popular operatic repertory as Puccini. A perennial favourite of audiences the world over, his most enduring works are staples of opera companies from San Francisco to Sydney. Puccini is, to put it bluntly, a safe bet: at a time when adventurous productions of new works pose considerable financial risks for state-subsidised theatres, even a very run-of-the-mill production of *La bohème*, for instance, can be relied upon to bring in the mainstream operatic audience and, in the process, balance the books. Puccini also represents to a perhaps unrivalled extent the very essence of Italian opera, at least as it is popularly imagined: tuneful, passionate and emotionally direct. At first glance, then, there would seem to be no composer less problematic than Puccini.

A closer inspection of the reception of this intriguing figure's music, however, reveals a far more complex situation. While Puccini's audiences surely still view him as the Italian opera composer *par excellence*, his reputation among today's critics and academics is – to say the least – mixed. A long-held cultural distrust of overt, comprehensible artistic sensuality seems to relegate Puccini to the second-class carriage of music history. Puccini, one might speculate, is too popular, too unchallenging, too conservative to win the respect that mainstream modernism has long enjoyed. Joseph Kerman's notorious jibe – that *Tosca* is a 'shabby little shocker' – can stand as emblematic of the hostility that Puccini's operas can provoke.[1]

None of this would have surprised the composer, however, for he always polarised opinion. In the words of early-twentieth-century conductor and critic Vittorio Gui, Puccini was 'the most beloved and most despised' of composers,[2] while the modernist critic Guido M. Gatti noted in 1927 that 'there has perhaps been no example, in the history of Italian music of the last fifty years, of an œuvre that has provoked as much praise and as much hostility as that of Giacomo Puccini; that has had idolisers and detractors in such equal measure, all of them impassioned and resolute'.[3] Indeed, Puccini's status was anything but assured in his own time. He was, of course, a famous and popular figure, enjoying a degree of international superstardom possibly hitherto unfamiliar to any composer in the history of Western music. Initially, however, this was precisely the problem with Puccini: for critics at the turn of the twentieth century, the question of the composer's Italianness – versus his 'international-ness' – was a matter of fraught debate. The arguments raged with a vehemence that today seems almost unbelievable: his music was simultaneously held up as a symbol of cultural strength and derided as a manifestation of decadence. The sharp divide between critics who viewed his works as 'a constant sigh of pure, uncorrupted, unadulterated Italianness',[4] and those who castigated them as 'the collaboration of two impotents'[5] mirrored wider ideological rifts in a society increasingly beset with dissatisfaction and disunity. Responses to score and libretto were at times almost drowned out, as Puccini became caught up in a crossfire of polemics concerning the contested question of what it really meant to be Italian. The first aspect of the Puccini problem thus becomes clear: how could he be secured as a fundamentally Italian composer, and what was at stake in this process?

This problem lay at the heart of a broader crisis of national identity that gripped Italy at the turn of the twentieth century. The nation, although politically unified, remained culturally divided, and the debates surrounding Puccini's operas illustrate the existence of many different, competing visions of national identity. Furthermore, there was a widely shared belief in turn-of-the-century Italy that the nation was in a period of social and moral decline, and the arts could not remain aloof from such concerns. Music critics of all political persuasions shared similar anxieties about the state of contemporary Italian society; where they diverged was in the contradictory solutions that they proposed. Puccini's music and persona were presented as both the antidote to and the embodiment of the degeneration widely felt to be afflicting contemporary Italy.

That a composer should fall victim to such politicisation was unsurprising, for opera had long been a vehicle in Italy for the dissemination of nationalist messages to a wide audience. Verdi was, of course, the most prominent among the politically active Italian opera composers, although his reputation as the 'bard of Italian nationalism' has come under some scrutiny in recent years, as we shall see shortly. Puccini, on the other hand, has repeatedly been presented by recent commentators as apolitical, both personally and musically.[6] He certainly had few aspirations to emulate Verdi's political activity, though he undoubtedly craved his musical prestige, and there are few references to current affairs in his published correspondence, at least until the First World War. Yet as the leading exponent of the Italian art form most closely linked to the national self-image, Puccini and politics became inextricably intertwined. Critics of Puccini's own time pointed again and again to the connections that they perceived between his operas and developments in contemporary society: the works thus became political – and involved in the nation-building process – irrespective of their composer's own degree of personal commitment.

This politicisation responded to a wide variety of musical concerns that can be provisionally unified in the notion of anxiety. First, the time of the premières of some of Puccini's most lasting works was also the time when the full force of Wagner's operatic reforms was felt in Italy. The insecurity of the critics in the face of the German is telling: as the debates discussed in chapter 2 show, the reception of *La bohème*, for instance, was significantly coloured by concerns as to whether a Teutonic notion of compositional organicism was compatible with the fabric of Puccini's scores, and whether Puccini's style had developed since *Manon Lescaut*. The superficial concern of the critics was obvious: was Puccini as adept or modern a composer as Wagner? However, underpinning this question was a more intensely troubling anxiety: to what extent was a crucial ingredient of Italian opera, its more modular yoking together of memorable arias for star singers, compatible with the modernity of the (supposedly) artistically unified *Musikdrama*? The second aspect of the Puccini problem thus emerged: to what extent was Puccini's Italianness reconcilable with an equally vital notion of modernity?

Faced with this challenge, Puccini's critics initially responded with a whole host of interesting arguments designed to address the first aspect of the problem – how to underwrite the composer's Italianness. Questions of gender, for instance, became intimately connected to the nationalising discourses that surrounded Puccini, as his supporters attempted to portray him as the ideal Italian male. This endeavour and the motivations underpinning it are crucial themes running throughout this book, for the notion of manliness was intrinsic to the pan-European *fin-de-siècle* imperialist mentality. For a new nation struggling to define itself, questions of gender and the cultivation of suitably 'masculine' behaviour were particularly necessary and urgent. However, as will become apparent, the most extreme anti-Puccini rhetoric also hinged upon images of gender, inverting the manly metaphors employed by Puccini's admirers. Considerations of gender led in turn to discussions of class, as contemporary intellectuals opposed Puccini's music as the embodiment of the vulgar, 'feminised' bourgeois culture represented by Prime Minister Giolitti's *Italietta*. Carducci, for example, argued that the rise of the bourgeoisie after 1860 'completed the emasculation of Italy'.[7] Puccini's status as 'the mouthpiece of middle-class sentiment', as one of his obituarists would later put it,[8] was far from unproblematic.

These controversies reached their high-water mark in a fascinating, savage study that will serve as the centrepiece of this book – Fausto Torrefranca's *Giacomo Puccini e l'opera internazionale*, written in 1910 and published in 1912. In order to belittle the composer and his music, Torrefranca charged him with 'effeminacy', which had a number of related connotations: sickness, weakness, intellectual incapacity and lack of originality. If we delve into wider contemporary discourse we can see that these tropes were also attached to other 'outsider' groups, most notably homosexuals, foreigners and Jews. As Puccini was the leading exponent of an art so intimately linked to the national identity, such labels were profoundly troubling. Puccini was here being quite deliberately marginalised: one of the critic's concerns was precisely the extent to which Puccini's operas were international but not Italian. And while Torrefranca's book may nowadays seem a crazed one-off attack, it is more accurately viewed as a culmination and synthesis of arguments that had already been expressed about Puccini's works during the 1890s and 1900s. As one might deduce from the title of the book, such concerns about internationalism and its political and aesthetic implications had reached a decisive point.

Surprisingly, however, Puccini's critical fortunes after Torrefranca's attack are much more difficult to assess. The 1910s brought *La fanciulla del West*, *La rondine* and *Il trittico*, all of which were premièred abroad, and all of which – with the exception of *Gianni Schicchi* (the third panel of the *Triptych*) – were largely disappointments. Ironically, Puccini's musical style had probably never been more self-consciously – if problematically – modern and adventurous, particularly in *Fanciulla*, but the continuing concern about the composer's internationalism increasingly had to be reconciled with his considerable fame abroad. The view that Puccini's music represented a debasement and cheapening of 'pure' Italian values had long been fermenting in the critical dialogue surrounding the composer, and it would come to form an important part of his reception from 1910 onwards. But increasingly this first aspect of the Puccini problem was displaced by its second dimension: what price this Italianness if it came at the cost of Puccini's modernity? Or, looked at in another way, what if Puccini's international success and eventual historical greatness were to come at the expense of a contemporary sense of *italianità*?

In other words, the Puccini problem became a problem of progress and reaction, of modernity and tradition. As with the issue of the composer's Italianness, this reflected broader aspects of the cultural moment: fears of a profound crisis of modernity – prompted by the threats posed at the turn of the twentieth century by urbanisation, industrialisation and technology – were widespread, and they came to be filtered through criticism of Puccini's music. At a crucial moment of self-definition in Italian history, coinciding with a pan-European period of radical upheaval across the arts, Puccini became caught between those who strenuously sought to defend the old order and those who sought radical cultural regeneration. Indeed, the two perhaps structurally incompatible dialogues – how to be Italian and how to be modern – were inextricably linked, and would be negotiated and renegotiated throughout Puccini's career. They come to their head in the responses to *Turandot*; by this stage, Puccini's status inside and outside Italy was fairly secure, but this time his music provoked critical responses from those conservative commentators worried by the comparative adventurousness of the score and a seeming retreat from 'Italian' emotion.

Puccini's career was thus marked by popular success and critical doubt; in the years since his death, these motifs have remained central to his musical and musicological reputation. Indeed, while the first aspect of the Puccini problem – the composer's national identity – has receded somewhat, the second – his modernity – has continued to cripple his reception history. The composer's popularity has only added to the problem: crowd-pleasing Italian operas were not valued particularly highly by the modernism that is typically supposed to have ruled the musicological academy for much of the later twentieth century. As the boundaries between popularity and artistic achievement have blurred, however, scholarly attitudes towards Italian opera have changed. By the 1980s Verdi's music had begun to gain critical respectability, but this process did not achieve as much for Puccini. For some time his works remained objects of contempt, and even when he was not openly derided, he was often conspicuous by his absence, failing to merit more than a cursory mention in many supposedly 'comprehensive' studies of twentieth-century music.[9]

The radical transformation of the musicological discipline in recent years, however, has altered this situation: Puccini's suitability for scholarly treatment is no longer in doubt, as has been demonstrated by the publication of several new critical biographies (including the first 'Master Musicians' study devoted to the composer[10]), a Puccini research guide,[11] a critical catalogue of his works,[12] Puccini-focused journals such as *Studi pucciniani* (the first issue of which included a bibliography comprising some 1,500 items on the composer[13]), and articles approaching his life and works from a variety of different perspectives. The more pluralistic approach taken by many current musicologists means that they are untroubled by previously vexing issues such as Puccini's almost unsurpassed ability to straddle the divide between art and entertainment. However, although Puccini's popularity may no longer be an overt problem for musicologists, to say that one can now respectably study Puccini is not to say that he is now valued particularly highly.

Unlike several of the recent studies of Puccini's life and works, this book has not been conceived as a revisionist history seeking primarily to legitimise Puccini's place in the canon. It concerns itself not so much with the aesthetic worth of Puccini's music *per se* (however that might be defined) as with the ideologies that shaped the many divergent responses to it in Puccini's own time. However, it does so from the basic premise that rather than being dismissed as an insignificant throwback to the nineteenth century, Puccini deserves recognition as a profoundly modern figure: he raises provocative questions about how, precisely, we should define the modern in music. Puccini was indisputably one of the key cultural players of his age, both in Italy and abroad, and the influence of his music and the repercussions of the debates that it prompted were widely felt both in Europe and across the Atlantic. Although this book deals primarily with the Italian reception of Puccini's works, aesthetic debates elsewhere are also considered in some detail, because foreign influences had a profound impact upon Italian thought and culture of this era, and because Puccini was an unashamedly international figure, ever eagerly responsive to the most modern of foreign trends.

This book is both the first in-depth investigation of the critical reception of Puccini's operas and the first serious attempt to contextualise Puccini within his political, aesthetic and intellectual milieu. The sources I have examined in writing this book include monographs, musicological journals, popular music reviews, daily newspapers, and magazines devoted not only to music, but to arts and culture in general. Appendix 1 gives further information about these publications: places and dates of publication, periodicity, circulation and important contributors. In certain cases background information is also provided on the newspaper or periodical's particular political or musical stance. Appendix 2 provides biographical details about the principal critics and writers – as well as singers, artists, theorists, politicians and members of Puccini's circle – mentioned in the book, where these are traceable and, in the case of those writing under assumed names, identifiable. Unfortunately – yet inevitably – some critics remain elusive.

The findings presented in this book open our eyes to the different but equally valid possibilities offered by 'high-', 'middle-' and 'low-brow' publications as historical documents. Debates about Puccini's contribution to the health of the nation permeated all levels of review, and I seek to highlight the important but all too often overlooked role played by popular journalism in communicating ideas of nationhood to a wide audience. Even the most impressionistic of reviews – and there were many, for the development of what we might term 'musicology' came late to Italy – have their uses. Critics were often reiterating long-standing clichés, but the subtle transformation of such rhetorical tropes in each new era can be extremely illuminating to the historian.

Although this study is broadly chronologically ordered, it is not a linear life-and-works study, and makes no pretence at comprehensiveness. My aim has not been to produce an exhaustive catalogue of everything written about Puccini in his own time, for such a study would be unrealistic in scope and limited in value. Rather than chronicling Puccini's critical fortunes, individual chapters concentrate on core themes that emerge from the reception documents in order to illuminate specific areas of Italian *fin-de-siècle* debate. Each opera thus becomes a lens through which to consider a particular facet of the contemporary Italian nation-building process, and Puccini's role in that process. However, thematic continuity between chapters with different perspectives results from the emergence of recurring rhetorical themes during the course of Puccini's career. These included debates surrounding the succession to Verdi, the question of whether true art could flourish in the absence of political struggle, Italian responses to the rise of modernism, and the perceived 'death' of opera. Organicism, progress and sincerity (or, more commonly, their antonyms) were further topics that emerged powerfully and repeatedly from the Puccini reviews; all were related to wider philosophical concerns about progress and decline. Critics' quests for coherence and unity in contemporary Italian music had resonance for their aspirations for the nation.

In chapter 1, I explore tensions in Italian society around the turn of the twentieth century that prompted the politicisation of Puccini's works, and examine the inflated terms in which Puccini was lionised as a 'national composer'. Subsequent chapters then reveal how the Puccini myth established at the beginning of his career began to crumble. Chapters 2 to 4 examine the reception of *La bohème*, *Tosca* and *Madama Butterfly*, operas which, despite being adopted swiftly into the performing canon, prompted mixed responses at their first performances. All three works provoked the expression of profound insecurities about the future of Italian music and the nature of opera criticism itself. Chapter 2 focuses upon the idea of progress, with regard both to music (specifically *La bohème*) and to music criticism, while in chapter 3 the theme of insincerity and its worrying nationalist implications are explored in the context of *Tosca*. Chapter 4 provides new perspectives on the ill-fated première of *Madama Butterfly* by highlighting a current of press criticism focusing upon the supposedly superficial aspects of Puccini's opera – a dialogue in which the work was criticised for being too international and too feminine.

The notion of Puccini as a 'feminised' composer introduced in the context of *Madama Butterfly* emerges more vehemently still in the following chapter. Providing a sharp counterbalance to the hagiography presented in chapter 1, chapter 5 takes as its focus Torrefranca's *Giacomo Puccini e l'opera internazionale*, contextualising the book alongside contemporary fears about the feminisation of Italian culture, and considering the implications for Puccini's status as national composer of the rise of an increasingly aggressive, proto-Fascistic Italian nationalism in the lead-up to the First World War. Chapter 6 focuses upon the reception of Puccini's works of the 1910s: Puccini's commitment to continuing the Italian operatic tradition was questioned repeatedly in these years. *La fanciulla del West* (1910) was seen as a botched experiment in being modern that pleased nobody, failed to fulfil the criteria for a genuinely 'Italian' opera and was widely regarded as representing a 'crisis' in Puccini's career. *La rondine* (1917) was seen as a lightweight quasi-operetta, condemned as a hybrid work and even an 'enemy opera' in a time of conflict. Finally, just as Puccini's status as national composer seemed to be in profound danger, *Gianni Schicchi* (1918) was hailed as the ray of light Italy needed as it emerged from the First World War. This chapter also discusses a second literary assault on Puccini, this time by his fellow composer Ildebrando Pizzetti, and a political demonstration against him and his music by Marinetti's Futurists.

Puccini died unexpectedly in 1924, three weeks before his sixty-sixth birthday. The tributes paid to him by his obituarists were grandiose – his status as national hero seemingly beyond dispute – and the première of *Turandot* took on the aura of a highly charged memorial service, marking the passing not merely of a composer but of an entire tradition. Yet although the opera was hailed as a triumph by Ricordi, critical responses were in fact mixed, often verging on the hostile, with few critics apparently genuinely believing *Turandot* to be the monument to Puccini for which the nation had so desperately longed. In chapter 7, I focus in detail upon the press's adverse response to the opera's eponymous heroine, widely regarded as a sterile machine woman symbolising what reviewers interpreted as Puccini's attempt to turn his back on 'Italian' sentiment. This chapter also grapples with the complex, ambivalent reception of Puccini's music in Fascist Italy, considers how the challenges posed by modernism were confronted within an Italian context and posits *Turandot* as a work that engages in a reflexive dialogue about the merits of the old and the new. At this point we seem at a very distant remove from the Italy of the *fin de siècle*, politically, socially and aesthetically. However, this book reveals surprising points of continuity in the ways in which Italians invented and reinvented their collective identity between the Risorgimento and the Fascist era. Puccini's music was fundamental to this process.

1 | Inventing an Italian composer

Italy at the turn of the twentieth century could be said in many respects to be a figment of the imagination. When the disparate states of the Italian Peninsula were brought together as a nation in 1861, statesman Massimo d'Azeglio is famously reputed to have said, 'we have made Italy; now we must make Italians'. But by 1900 his ambition had yet to be fulfilled, and creating a culturally homogeneous nation would remain a matter of pressing concern well into the new century. From the 1880s onwards the high hopes of the Risorgimento had been replaced in the minds of Italian intellectuals by a pervasive sense of anticlimax and disillusionment with the new state. Rather than narrowing regional, social and cultural divisions, the much-yearned-for unification had merely served to make them deeper. The north and south of Italy were, to all practical intents and purposes, separate countries, the economic inequalities between them having been exacerbated by rapid industrial modernisation in such northern cities as Milan and Turin. Regional allegiances remained stronger than national pride, emigration was rising sharply and unrest among new, disaffected social groups was on the increase. Creating a strong sense of shared identity and a unified, prosperous, modern Italy was therefore imperative, both in order to maintain stability at home and in order to present a united front to the rest of the world.

But how was this sense of common origins to be created in a country not united since Roman times? The initial phase of fostering allegiance to the state during the decades following Unification focused upon endorsing the use of a common language. During this period, 'standard' Italian was routinely presented as the God-given tongue of all Italians since time immemorial. Luigi

11

Rava, Minister for Public Instruction, declared in a speech given in 1909 that

> [Italian] is the language of Dante ...; it is the language of thinkers, artists and poets from the Renaissance and the Risorgimento; it is the language – in a word – of the Italian nation, created by the people, maintained with heroic tenacity, reconsecrated by plebiscites and with faith in the same principles that inspired the unification of Italy.[1]

However, such comments were wishful thinking, seemingly blind to the fact that even in the first decade of the twentieth century the use of local dialects was still widespread, especially in the south. Moreover, a common language alone was not sufficient to create a national consciousness: the new Italy needed shared myths and memories. Thus programmes of patriotic education aimed both at schoolchildren and adults celebrated the social and economic progress made by Italy since 1861, in an endeavour to foster a *religione della patria* that might substitute the nation for the (declining) Church as the object of the population's loyalty and affection. Statues and memorials were erected to great Italian heroes of the past, and each Italian city was given its Via Cavour.

It was widely recognised that the arts could also be useful in providing patriotic symbols around which the nation might rally. Artworks from the past could provide a sense of shared heritage; contemporary ones on the other hand could actively help to create a spirit of *italianità* and demonstrate the good health of the new nation. Works of art of all genres were subject to nationalist appropriation in the last decades of the nineteenth century, with Dante being the figure most frequently exploited for political ends. Large-scale festivities in Florence in 1865 marked the six-hundredth anniversary of his birth while simultaneously celebrating the achievements of the newly unified nation. In 1889, Dante lent his name to a proto-nationalist cultural organisation in Rome, the Società 'Dante Alighieri', an organisation that sought to promote 'Italianness' both in contested areas of Italy and among Italian emigrants through its endeavour to 'defend the Italian language and culture wherever conflicts of nationality threaten them'.[2] Some decades later a Dreadnought battleship was even named in Dante's honour (along with a 'Giulio Cesare', a 'Leonardo da Vinci' and a 'Conte di Cavour'). But if the Trecento offered nationalist myth-makers rich pickings, the modern age boasted few literary figures who could be held up as national icons, with the notable exception of Manzoni, author of *I promessi sposi* (1827), which was celebrated as a patriotic tract. This was in part attributable to the fact that the prevalence of regional dialects and widespread illiteracy meant that a strong tradition of novel writing had failed to develop in Italy during the nineteenth century – approximately half of the Italian population was still unable to read in 1900, although this statistic masked dramatic regional variations. In the final decades of the century D'Annunzio's works received acclaim from intellectuals, but they were too verbose and cerebral to hold the wide popular appeal necessary in order to become truly national monuments. Even the works of Carducci, Italy's most eminent contemporary poet, were read by only a small educated élite and were little known outside Italy.[3] Fine art, similarly, tended to rest on the laurels of a more glorious past. In the period immediately following Unification a number of major touring exhibitions celebrating the Renaissance masters were organised to remind the world of Italy's great artistic heritage. But contemporary art was at a low ebb, as the prevalence of mediocre, conservative Salon paintings at the early Venice Biennale exhibitions illustrates – and this despite the fact that the Biennale had been conceived at its foundation in 1895 as a monument to the artistic endeavours of the new nation.

Opera, however, was different. Not only was it *the* supremely Italian art form – invented in Italy by Monteverdi and his contemporaries and in time exported with phenomenal success to the rest of the civilised world – but it remained a flourishing living tradition with sufficiently wide popular appeal to be exploitable for nation-building purposes. No other art form was so powerful and so effective a patriotic tool. Music's capacity to have a bearing upon every aspect of public life was recognised by Cavour, who is reputed to have said, 'I can't tell a violin apart from a drum ... but I know very well that for our nation music is not merely a source of glory, but also a genuinely great industry, which has ramifications everywhere.'[4] Recent scholarship has cast doubt upon the credibility of the claim that Verdi was spontaneously proclaimed by the Italian people as the Bard of the Risorgimento and voice of their collective patriotic aspirations in the 1840s.[5] This was undoubtedly a myth constructed to a large extent in retrospect by Verdi's biographers, but it was propagated so effectively as to be widely accepted as fact by the final decades of the nineteenth century. Thus at a time when it was becoming apparent that political unification had failed to instil a sense of Italianness, opera seemed to be the best cultural medium through which a sense of shared Italian identity might be created.

This chapter is concerned with the ways in which the reception of Puccini's operas became entangled with the making of the new Italian nation. Both endeavours were, to an extent, carefully constructed fictions. National identities operate on the basis of seeming to be intuitive and pre-existing, but they are in fact shaped according to political, essentialising agendas. Puccini's reputation was equally carefully moulded: reading the early biographical and critical profiles of him and scrutinising what commentators emphasised and what they played down provides a fascinating opportunity to consider the ways in which public figures' reputations are manipulated for ideological ends. Puccini's operas do not tell epic stories about the foundation of the nation; indeed, their subject matter is rarely Italian. They were not in themselves vehicles for the diffusion of patriotic ideals, yet Puccini was elevated to the status of a national composer through rhetoric and iconography selected by his supporters, and most especially by his publishing house, Ricordi. The image portrayed of Puccini in the daily and musical press and the values attached to his music and his persona contributed to a sense of communal belonging fundamental to the creation of the Italian nation. As well as considering the ways in which this reputation was constructed, this chapter will also consider how Puccini's works were charged with a second task: to provide an antidote to the sense of social, political and aesthetic crisis widely perceived to be afflicting the new nation.

ITALY'S SENSE OF DECADENCE

Italy's sense of its own weakness was a long-standing problem. Intellectuals had for many centuries expressed concern that their native culture had peaked during the Renaissance, and had since the mid-sixteenth century been in a phase of progressive decline. Centuries of foreign domination were felt to have adversely affected the national character, rendering it apathetic and subservient to other nations, despite the fact that other European countries had enthusiastically embraced Italian art, culture and manners from around the time when this decline had supposedly set in. This feeling of cultural and political inferiority was self-perpetuating and propagated more by Italians than by foreign observers. Giacomo Leopardi, for example, wrote a discourse on Italian mores in 1824 entitled *Discorso sopra lo stato presente dei costumi degl'italiani*, although the pamphlet was not published until the turn of the twentieth century, when (significantly) it attracted much interest.[6] Focusing upon the difficulties of modernisation, Leopardi warned of the spiritual death of 'Italia' (at this stage a literary term rather than a political reality, of course), claiming that the advent of modernity had stripped Italy of its moral foundations and ideals. During the mid-nineteenth century, Cesare Balbo, Vincenzo Gioberti and Massimo d'Azeglio were among the prominent figures to write about the reasons for Italy's historical decline, with the latter admitting that 'the most dangerous enemies of the Italians are not the Germans, but the Italians themselves'.[7] Moral regeneration was therefore as much an aim of the Risorgimento as political unification. The new nation had to be restored to its former greatness and rediscover what was widely referred to as its lost sense of *virtù*. Unification had given Italy a chance to reassert its prominence, and yet the moment had been lost. After an initial post-unitary period of optimism, Italy's perception of its own shortcomings was not lessened but aggravated, with commentators including Carducci, D'Annunzio, Capuana and Verga returning obsessively to the old theme of Italy's lost greatness as the twentieth century approached. In Richard Drake's words:

> The sense of loss, of decadence, of failure in living up to the country's highest ideals was ubiquitous. ... This unsparing self-critical assessment, which eventually resulted in a quixotic nostalgia for the

vanished heroism of Italy's Risorgimento and classical past, became the distinguishing characteristic of the Umbertian mind, or at least of most Umbertian intellectuals and artists who have left us their impressions of the period.[8]

The crisis of confidence that hit Europe in the last decade of the nineteenth century, with aftershocks radiating out from London and Paris to Vienna and Milan, compounded Italy's historical consciousness of its own perceived shortcomings. Underpinning the superficial prosperity of the *belle époque* was the omnipresent spectre of 'decadence' – a sense that civilised society was entering a period of moral and cultural decline, despite rapid urbanisation and technological development. This was part of the backdrop of modernism, with many viewing progress itself as an inevitable precursor to decline, with too much comfort inevitably leading to spiritual and physical laxness. Countless books and articles were published in which social commentators identified manifestations of 'degeneration' in all aspects of modern life. Prophesies of impending doom became a veritable industry, as editors in the burgeoning press realised how effectively they boosted sales. The most important and influential scaremongering tract was unquestionably the German writer Max Nordau's *Entartung* (*Degeneration*) of 1892, which was a best-seller in Italy, as elsewhere in Western Europe and the United States.[9] Imitations of *Degeneration* sprang up in book and article form all over Western Europe, their common aim being to warn that the modern age was divorcing itself from tradition – in art, literature and music as much as in social mores – and that the consequences would be grave.

This common sense of unease and inferiority was exacerbated by contemporary evolutionary, racialist and proto-eugenicist theories. Italian thinkers were prominent in this movement, with scientists such as Cesare Lombroso (to whom Nordau had dedicated *Degeneration*), Alfredo Nicefero, Giuseppe Sergi and Paolo Mantegazza leading the way in promoting apocalyptic theories of biological degeneration that seemed to point to the ineluctable decline of the Latin race. Such concerns prompted nations to assert their cultural identities aggressively. Contemporary thinkers, many of them influenced by Herder, codified physical and cultural characteristics that were felt to define a particular race. The following words from an anti-Wagnerian article published in an Italian music review of 1896 were typical of such rhetoric: 'every people has its habits and its customs, and its art is always related to these customs, to the education and manner of feeling of the people'.[10] This was a period in which cultural 'traditions' were consciously invented in response to the growing need to assert a national identity. For example, the sudden drive from the 1880s onwards to create a national music in England, a nation neither occupied nor oppressed, is indicative of a profound sense of self-doubt. Previously untroubled by its reputation as 'the land without music', England felt the need to define its cultural identity actively through the establishment of a national music at the point when Germany began to pose a threat to its political and military supremacy.[11]

This flight towards essential characteristics of given races was highly defensive: the cross-fertilisation of cultures that resulted from late-nineteenth-century improvements in communications led to fear of a bland internationalism that threatened to eclipse distinctive national characteristics. Carducci, for example, lamented the fact that 'today we are too French, too English, too German, too American; we are individualists, socialists, authoritarians – everything except Italians'.[12] This paradox – the tension between the national and the international – was a theme that, as we shall see, would emerge repeatedly throughout Puccini's career, even while he was being vaunted as the greatest living composer in Italy.

A TRADITION IN DECLINE?

Rather than fostering its native talent, the new Italy was increasingly receptive to imported foreign culture, a tendency that was common to all the arts. Few readers of the cultural review *La lettura* (edited by Puccini's librettist Giacosa and distributed as a supplement to the *Corriere della sera*) would have been surprised to read the journal's assertion in 1901 that 'the public doesn't go to the theatre unless the production is French'.[13] The theatrical repertory in *fin-de-siècle* Italy was dominated by translations of crowd-pleasing French boulevard dramas that were merely vehicles for individual star actors and actresses, or second-rate imitations of such works by Italian authors. Literature fared no better: French popular novels were so popular and Italian novels so derivative that Carducci went so far as to write in 1894 that 'in literature we have become a French *département*'.[14]

In music, too, there was a mass influx of foreign works onto Italy's stages from the 1860s onwards, and because opera was the nation's strongest art form the consequences of importing music were even graver than those of importing novels. Most prominently, the Sonzogno company saw the financial potential in promoting the music of French composers, in whom its rival firm Ricordi, which virtually monopolised the market, had demonstrated little interest. The Sonzogno gamble paid off, and by the end of the decade works by Halévy, Auber, Gounod and Meyerbeer had become staples of the La Scala repertory. Works by Lalo, Thomas, Bizet, Berlioz, Saint-Saëns and Massenet swiftly followed, to great popular acclaim, along with operettas by Hervé, Lecocq and Offenbach. Even more threatening to the indigenous operatic tradition was the arrival of Wagner's works in Italy; as we shall see in the next chapter, Wagner's reception had a profound and at times surprising bearing upon responses to Puccini's operas. In 1850 the repertory at La Scala had consisted almost exclusively of operas by native composers, with occasional performances of works by Meyerbeer and Mozart. Half a century later, foreign works dominated the repertory to such an extent that Italian operas were regularly outnumbered by foreign imports. In the 1896 season, for example, only three Italian operas (Mascagni's *Guglielmo Ratcliffe* and *Zanetto*, and Giordano's *Andrea Chénier*) were staged at La Scala out of a total of ten productions.[15] The other works were all French (although performed in Italian translation): Saint-Saëns's *Henry VIII* and *Samson et Dalila*, Berlioz's *La Damnation de Faust*, Massenet's *La Navarraise*, Bizet's *Carmen* and *Les Pêcheurs des perles*, and Thomas's *Hamlet*.

Even German instrumental music was perceived as a threat by the end of the nineteenth century. Viennese Classical works were held in high regard in Milanese intellectual circles as early as the 1830s, and would have been readily available to the student Verdi, but were not widely disseminated.[16] The first quartet society was established in Milan in 1864, and Italy heard its first Beethoven symphony in Turin in 1873. By the final decades of the nineteenth century, Italian conservatoires were even allotting an increasing portion of the curriculum to training young composers in techniques of writing for orchestra, leading the composer and theorist Cesare Dall'Olio to announce in 1897 that 'melody has been dethroned, song has been relegated to a purely declaimed genre; symphonic music dominates exclusively, blocking the path of countless composers'.[17] The policy of cultural 'splendid isolation' that Italy had long attempted to assert was, by the final quarter of the nineteenth century, no longer possible to sustain. Italian intellectuals became increasingly preoccupied by a hitherto unthinkable prospect – that Italian operatic hegemony was no longer guaranteed.

In response, contemporary music critics used emotive words such as 'contamination' and 'pollution' to protest at what they depicted in no uncertain terms as the quasi-militaristic 'invasion' of foreign operas. But in truth such works had not been foisted upon Italian audiences against their will. Leaving aside Wagner's œuvre, whose reception in Italy was complex, the Italian public embraced foreign operas enthusiastically. Even more troubling than this ready acceptance of non-Italian works by the public was the eagerness of young Italian composers to imitate them, motivated by a desire to be seen as 'modern'. Paradoxically, the price that had been paid for Italy's political independence seemed to many to have been a growing artistic enslavement to other nations; political struggle had been, it seemed, a necessary stimulus for the creation of true art. In a speech given in 1884 on the dangers of musical cosmopolitanism, subsequently published in the *Gazzetta musicale di Milano*, the musicologist and composer Riccardo Gandolfi stated: 'it is truly curious to observe that Italy, whilst under foreign domination, possessed a genuinely national art, whereas now that she is politically liberated, we see her morally subjected to German influence'.[18] Gandolfi claimed that whereas a spirit of heroic self-abnegation had stimulated the imagination of composers such as Verdi, the current generation was cynical, egotistical and motivated only by material gain. This was a reflection of a wider tendency felt to be afflicting the Italian national character: too much comfort and prosperity led inevitably to a lack of discipline and a decline in morals. Thanks to an absence of lofty ideals, Gandolfi wrote, young composers were more than content to imitate foreign music slavishly, to the detriment of the distinctive qualities that had marked Italian music for centuries. His choice of vocabulary reflects the contemporary obsession with codifying essentialist racial characteristics, and in particular with the fashionable science of physiognomy, which had been coopted into cultural criticism.

The extent to which Italian composers ought to look to their northern neighbours for inspiration was, however, a long-standing, and contentious, issue. Despite Verdi's undisputed status by the late nineteenth century as the supreme master of Italian opera, his career had also been dogged by debates about the ideal future of the art form, with critics pointing to supposedly 'French' and 'German' traits in his later works. Doubts had been growing since the mid-nineteenth century as to what constituted a 'national' work of operatic art, but by the turn of the twentieth century all certainties seemed to have been swept aside. The trend towards internationalism was such by this time that the growing domination of foreign music became an almost obsessive issue for the music press. Italy must revivify and reassert its musical culture and find – come what may – a new and distinctively Italian musical voice to resist the much-feared 'eclipse' of Italian culture. The *Cronaca musicale* called in January 1897 for a return to a musical training and production that corresponded 'to Italian feeling, to the race's genius, to our great traditions'.[19]

One of the pressing concerns of such criticism was, of course, the question of who would succeed Verdi. In 1884, a few months before Giacomo Puccini first came to the nation's attention with *Le villi*, the Ricordi house journal, the *Gazzetta musicale di Milano*, placed a picture of the seventy-one-year-old Verdi on the front cover of its first issue of the year. The accompanying text issued a challenge to young Italian composers.

> In publishing this picture of Verdi today, we want to say to young composers: look into this prolific force, this spotless conscience, this noble will; remember our greatnesses, and endeavour to be great, remaining Italians.[20]

Although Verdi was at the peak of his talents in 1884, with *Otello* and *Falstaff* still ahead of him, the need to line up his successor was acutely felt in contemporary musical circles. Indeed, Verdi himself was concerned about the future of Italian music after his death, writing to Hans Bülow in 1892 that Italy used to have a great tradition but 'now it has become bastardized and ruin threatens us'.[21] Whereas Verdi's works were by this time enjoying enormous international acclaim, the operas by younger Italian composers of the 1880s enjoyed only limited and ephemeral success even at home and were almost totally ignored abroad. As the new century approached, the pages of contemporary music journals were filled with ominous warnings of the imminent death of Italian opera. New journals were founded explicitly to respond to concerns about the lamentable state of both contemporary Italian music and music criticism. Tancredi Mantovani, one of the first Italian musicologists, opened the inaugural issue of his *Cronaca musicale* in 1896 with a stern call to attention:

> Our musical art, everybody will probably agree, has been in a period of transition – from which we all hope it will soon escape – for more than a few years. ... In terms of artistic output our era is almost prolific, but it is less happy and clear in its aims: artists produce a lot, they work at high speed through a mad desire to reach their goal quickly, and in general they produce work that is lacking in assurance of method and clarity of artistic conception.[22]

Musical decline was seen by many as a reflection of the wider social and political anxieties that Italy seemed to face: artistic productivity was regarded as intimately connected to the 'health' of the nation. In a book of 1897 specifically devoted to this issue, Enrico di San Martino attributed the current 'impotence of Italian musical genius' to a wider social malaise and most notably a decline of faith in the 'high ideals of religion, fatherland [and] love' in the modern age.[23] Progress in certain areas of Italian life had led to the deterioration of others. In an attempt to revive itself politically and militarily, the nation had diverted its energies away from culture, to the extent that Michele Virgilio was driven to write in 1900: 'unfortunately the new Italy is preoccupied solely with cannons and barracks, forgetting to protect and encourage music, which was one of the nation's most vibrant and thriving activities'.[24] The problem was obvious: Italy needed a national composer to succeed Verdi who would produce a music that was wholeheartedly and indisputably 'Italian'; that would give the disparate peoples of Italy a sense of shared identity; that would not be derivative of foreign styles; and that would be an antidote to the nation's cultural 'decadence'. This was a weighty responsibility indeed.

PUCCINI'S EARLY FORTUNES

'Finally we seem to have found the maestro that Italian art needs so badly,' wrote the music critic for *La Lombardia* after the première of *Le villi* in 1884[25] – this despite the fact that the work had failed to merit even a commendation by the judges of the Sonzogno competition for which it had been written, and despite the reportedly lukewarm response from the public at early performances. Similarly, Marco Sala wrote in *L'Italia*: 'Puccini's opera is – in our opinion – a small but rich masterpiece, from beginning to end. ... A great success; a great composer emerges!'[26] Despite such gushing words, Puccini's status as national composer was by no means assured from the outset; indeed there were several potential candidates for the position during the 1880s and early 1890s. Probably the strongest contender poised to inherit the Verdi mantle around this time was Mascagni, whose *Cavalleria rusticana* was greeted ecstatically at its première in 1890. Mascagni seemed to offer a new and distinctive path for the operatic genre, in a work that fused impassioned music with a work of contemporary – and genuinely popular – Italian literature. Certainly, *Cavalleria rusticana* struck a chord with audiences; Guido Pannain, looking back at the work's première on its fiftieth anniversary, attributed its tremendous success to the fact that 'the audience, the people, felt that it was their voice, and were overwhelmed by it'.[27] However, within a month of the première, critics had reverted to their customary pessimistic tone, with Francesco D'Arcais asking in the *Nuova antologia*, 'To what state will our musical theatre be reduced on the day that Verdi abandons the stage for good, if, indeed, he has not already done so?'[28] When Mascagni's subsequent works failed to live up to the early promise of *Cavalleria rusticana* – a work Pannain referred to with hindsight in the 1940s as 'more an ending than a beginning'[29] – fickle critics and audiences swiftly turned to other potential musical 'Messiahs' who would bring about the much-needed 'redemption' of Italian opera. In response to D'Arcais's question 'With which new works will we counter the foreign repertory? With which arms will we fight?' (typical of the militaristic rhetoric of the day),[30] Lorenzo Parodi suggested Sgambati, Mancinelli, Martucci and Franchetti along with Puccini as a 'phalanx' of young Italian composers poised to lead Italy to new musical conquests.[31] Interestingly, the journal in which Parodi was writing, *Il teatro illustrato e la musica popolare*, was owned by Sonzogno; this apparent irony demonstrates the existence of a deeply entrenched musical nationalism even on the part of those who stood to profit financially from the promotion of foreign works.

Puccini would soon emerge as the front-runner of this group, thanks in no small part to the weight lent to him by his publishing house, Ricordi. Reading the early reviews of Puccini's operas it becomes apparent that he was effectively shoehorned by Ricordi into the role of national composer before he had had a chance to prove himself or consolidate his style. As early as 1889 a disillusioned Alfredo Catalani testified to a powerful publicity machine backing Puccini: 'I am terrified of the idea of what might be my future, now that there's only one publisher and that publisher doesn't want to hear of anyone but Puccini. ... Now there are "dynasties", even in art, and I know that Puccini "must" be Verdi's successor.'³² In that same year the Ricordi-sponsored *Gazzetta musicale di Milano* declared Puccini's new opera, *Edgar*, to be 'a work of genius',³³ which was 'fundamentally melodic, fundamentally Italian' (presumably in contrast to *Le villi*, in which Verdi himself had discerned a worryingly foreign 'symphonic' quality).³⁴ However, critics from other, more impartial newspapers were less enthusiastic, and some were even acerbic; *La Lombardia*, for example, accused the young composer of 'great sins against art, lack of faith, conviction, and well-defined ideals'.³⁵ According to Ildebrando Pizzetti, looking back more than twenty years later, '*Edgar* was not successful, not even with the masses: one might even call it a fiasco.'³⁶

In 1893, however, *Manon Lescaut* succeeded in being what *Le villi* and *Edgar* had in all truth failed to be – a genuinely popular success. The work was a triumph with audiences and critics alike, and sumptuous banquets were held in Puccini's honour, something that the surprisingly publicity-shy composer must have hated. (Five years later he would write in a letter to Giulio Ricordi: 'An invitation to lunch makes me ill for a week. I was made that way and I haven't changed at almost forty! It's useless insisting; I wasn't born for a life of salons and receptions.'³⁷) The *Gazzetta musicale di Milano* published extensive coverage of performances of the opera in every major Italian city, and its impact is illustrated by the fact that it swiftly reached the far-flung Italian diaspora in Argentina and Brazil. Puccini was hailed as 'one of the strongest, if not the strongest of the young Italian composers',³⁸ and 'a maestro who brings honour to his nation'.³⁹ 'All discussion ends at this point,' wrote the reviewer for *Il parlamento*, 'whatever the question, whatever the reply, there is only one conclusion: we have a maestro!'⁴⁰ Already Puccini was being vaunted as the answer to Italy's perceived moral, social and aesthetic crisis, with Giuseppe Depanis writing in *La gazzetta del popolo*: 'Amid so much that is hysterical, Byzantine and decadent, this is healthy music.'⁴¹

Manon Lescaut seemed decisively to confirm Puccini's status as the heir to Verdi, with the admittedly biased Giovanni Pozza (who had taken a hand in crafting the opera's libretto) declaring in the Milanese daily the *Corriere della sera*: 'if, amongst young composers there is one who has understood [Verdi's] famous motto "torniamo all'antico", it is Puccini'.⁴² Here Pozza was referring to the comment 'Torniamo all'antico, sarà un progresso', made by Verdi in a letter of 4 January 1871 to Francesco Florimo (archivist at the St Pietro a Majella Conservatoire in Naples) about the training of young Italian composers, in which he advocated the study of Palestrina and Marcello.⁴³ Pozza's assertion is an odd one, because all evidence would seem to suggest that Puccini tended to look more outwards than backwards for inspiration; yet the suggestion that Puccini was continuing a time-honoured tradition was crucial for nation-building purposes. The timing for comparisons with Verdi was particularly fortuitous in 1893, with *Manon Lescaut* making its début only a week before the première of *Falstaff*. The two operas were often hired out as a pair, at a discount, and Ricordi presented them as a double triumph – the latest (and most likely last) work by the nation's greatest maestro, alongside a work by 'the young man in whom our highest hopes for our art are now placed'.⁴⁴

MAKING A MAESTRO

It was not merely Puccini's music that triggered debate in the press. In an age that witnessed the beginnings of the cult of celebrity and the first widespread use of photography in the mass media, Puccini's personality and physique drew as much press attention as his operas. The late nineteenth century witnessed an upsurge in interest in popular biography and the day-to-day lives of public figures, and was an era in which a composer's temperament was presented to readers as indicative of the qualities that were to be found in his music. Thus, critics intent upon mythologising Puccini made such grandiose declarations as 'man and maestro merge in him in the most perfect harmony'.⁴⁵ This close association of man and music would run throughout Puccini's career, and one of the earliest Puccini biographies, published in 1925, was entitled *Giacomo Puccini: l'uomo – l'artista* (*Giacomo Puccini: The Man – The Artist*).⁴⁶ Alas for Puccini, those who were less enamoured of his music also made their attacks personal, as subsequent chapters will reveal.

Certain myths about Puccini's 'Italianness' were established in the very earliest reviews and reiterated virtually unchanged until his death, suggesting that critics were approaching the works with a predetermined agenda far removed from musical concerns. The first detailed article to appear about Puccini was a short biographical sketch by his librettist, Ferdinando Fontana, published in the *Gazzetta musicale di Milano* in 1884. This profile established a nexus of motifs concerning Puccini's personality that would recur throughout his career: his glorious family lineage, his struggle against poverty – a classic tale of rags to riches – and his unquantifiable natural musical talent. Music was claimed to be in Puccini's blood to the extent that he had not even needed to study; Fontana claimed that 'Puccini learned music without noticing, one might say, drinking his mother's milk. ... The air [in his home] was saturated with musical notes', as Puccini's widowed mother 'struggled courageously' against poverty to support her gifted son.[47] Sanctifying an artist's birth and early childhood in this way is a common biographical motif; we see a similar process in action in Giorgio Vasari's claim of 1550 that Michelangelo 'sucked in the attraction to hammer and chisel with the milk of his wet-nurse'.[48]

From the outset critics employed a mythologising rhetoric that emphasised Puccini's links with a noble musical past. Fontana went on to pronounce that 'Giacomo Puccini ... is 172 years old ... since he is in fact simply the latest flowering of a branch of musicians planted in Lucca in 1712'.[49] Establishing the new national composer-elect as a figure who belonged to a tradition was important in fostering the myth that Italy had been spiritually united for centuries prior to political unification: it was imperative to emphasise a sense of historical continuity, of dynastic succession. The fact that some critics even brazenly likened the 'Puccini dynasty' – a phrase present-day biographers do not flinch from using, despite the fact that all Puccinis other than Giacomo have long since passed into musical oblivion – to the Bachs demonstrates an awareness of the threat of foreign repertories and a hope that Italian music could compete.[50] Similarly, Puccini's youthful walk from Lucca to Pisa in an evening to hear a performance of *Aida* in 1876 – an anecdote of questionable plausibility imbued by biographers with the aura of a sacred pilgrimage – was frequently compared to Bach's famous 260-mile walk from Arnstadt to Lübeck to hear Buxtehude, or Wagner's journey to hear Beethoven's *Eroica* symphony.

Topographical references are also fundamental to standard nation-building rhetoric. Although the association of geography and race dates back to classical antiquity, such correlations were particularly prominent in *fin-de-siècle* discourse. Throughout Puccini's lifetime his works would be depicted as the embodiment of the Italian climate and landscape, shaped by and inseparable from them. 'Light, heat, radiation, ardour': these were the qualities that, for Alessandro Cortella, a writer and librettist employed for many years at Casa Ricordi, marked Puccini's *Edgar* as a wholeheartedly Italian work, supposedly untainted by French or German influences.[51] In 1896, Giulio Ricordi described *La bohème* in terms of 'pure glowing colours, in perfect unison with our land, with our sky: art designed along simple lines perhaps, but that wells up sincerely from the heart'.[52] Likewise, the critic 'A', of the *Rivista politica e letteraria*, employed the standard references to climate with regard to *Tosca*: 'in you is the reflection of the radiance and warmth of our southern sky. ... *Tosca* is therefore an essentially Italian opera'.[53] Such references were calculated to suggest in an emotive way that the composer was rooted to a land and to a past, but were rarely qualified by reference to specific aspects of the score.

The fact that the turn of the century witnessed an intensification in attempts to link composers with their respective landscapes was doubtless motivated by a nostalgia for the pastoral in the face of relentless urbanisation. Similar associations were constructed a little later between the music of Elgar, Vaughan Williams and Finzi and the English pastoral landscape, Elgar being described in the *Musical Times* in 1900 as 'one who habitually thinks his thoughts and draws his inspiration from [the] elevated surroundings' of Worcestershire and the Malverns.[54] In the case of Italian rhetoric, references to climate were frequently underpinned by an anti-German subtext. The blue skies and warmth of Italy and Italian music were often contrasted explicitly with the cold and fog north of the Alps, in an attempt to highlight the superior clarity of thought and emotional honesty that characterised Italian art and were deemed to be lacking elsewhere. Simply being born in Italy was enough to turn a modest composer into a genius, as the following picturesque comments, which appeared in the *Cronaca musicale* in 1912, illustrate:

> For those who are destined for art, and most especially for music, being born in Italy is no small advantage. To open one's eyes for the first time to such wondrous delights of nature; immediately to feel oneself enveloped in the sweet warmth of our spring; always to have before your eyes the purest blue of the sky and the sea illuminated by the brightest sparkling sun; to breathe an air balmy with the perfume of flowers that sprout up everywhere spontaneously as though in an immense and delightful garden; always to have the chirruping of birds in your ears, the sweet song of the nightingale; to hear the thousand *canzoni* in which the people express their joy, their pain, their soul; to find oneself at every step in front of masterworks of architecture, sculpture or painting; to hear, almost suffused in the air, the themes from our musical masterworks; to read Dante, Petrarch, Foscolo, Leopardi: all this cannot fail to make the soul resound of those who will one day become artists.[55]

Local variations in the Italian landscape and climate went unnoticed as contemporary nation-builders attempted to depict a homogeneous state unsullied by regional diversity. And just as there was apparently only one Italian climate, so too was there only one Italian music. Commentators claimed that despite centuries of political division, the various Italian cities shared a distinct national musical style. Gandolfi argued:

> If modern Italian music is a fusion of the Roman, Venetian, Lombardian, Bolognese and Neapolitan schools, this is not the product of eclecticism but rather the fact that all these schools

belonged to one people, who lived off the same soil, warmed by the same sun, with the same religious, philosophical, moral principles, with common idioms, literature and poetry. There were merely technical and didactic variations.[56]

However, there were times when it could be useful to dwell upon local variations, and critics made much of Puccini's Tuscan origins as well as emphasising his generic 'Italianness'. This was not a conscious exercise in regional reaffirmation, as may be witnessed in late-nineteenth-century France, where artists such as Cézanne began deliberately to abandon Paris in favour of the hitherto deprived and marginalised provinces.[57] Such an endeavour would have seemed perverse in a new nation that lacked a clear focal point, its capital having moved from Turin to Florence to Rome within the space of only a decade. Rather, the emphasis upon Puccini's regional origins was an attempt to present the customs and identifying features of a particular area as typical of an entire nation, another common technique of the nation-building process. Critics might have been rather reluctant to emphasise Puccini's place of birth and ongoing attachment to his home town had he been from marginalised Calabria. As it was, Puccini's regional roots enhanced rather than compromised his position as the ideal patriot, for Tuscany occupied a privileged place in the contemporary Italian imagination, being regarded as emblematic of the 'real Italy'. The Tuscan dialect – the language of Dante – formed the basis of the standard Italian language, and the unification project further embraced Tuscany as the cradle of Italian civilisation. Other artists and intellectuals around the turn of the twentieth century would draw upon their Tuscan origins as a badge of prestige. Most notable of these were *i vociani*, the editors of the radical Florentine cultural journals that appeared in the early 1900s, who fostered a cult of *toscanità*, although, as we shall see in chapter 7, their aspirations were diametrically at odds with those of Puccini's promoters.

Puccini's *verismo* contemporaries, however, often looked to the southern regions of Italy for inspiration (for example, Mascagni's

Sicilian *Cavalleria rusticana* and Giordano's Neapolitan *La mala vita*), in an age when such places were regarded by north Italian audiences as being almost as exotic as India or Japan. Despite his interest in creating 'local colour', and despite toying for some time with the idea of setting Verga's *La lupa* – the story of a Sicilian peasant woman who falls for a young olive crusher – this was not a path Puccini would ultimately choose to follow; nor would he look to his local roots and set an opera in Tuscany until *Gianni Schicchi* in 1918. Puccini wrote his operas for a pan-European, and very soon a global audience; his prestige and international prospects might to some degree have been devalued by a turn towards an overly folkloristic aesthetic. Indeed, Guido Pannain argued in the 1940s that it was Puccini's interest in the universal rather than the local that guaranteed him the international success that latterly eluded Mascagni.[58]

Nevertheless, the Tuscan landscape was often presented as Puccini's muse by his patrons and supporters. In a supplement to the *Gazzetta musicale di Milano* published in 1900 and entitled *La Tosca* to coincide with Puccini's latest work, Eugenio Checchi (writing under the pseudonym 'Tom'), recalled a visit to the composer at his country home. Checchi described the area around Torre del Lago as 'a landscape of combined majesty and grace, of fine and soft lines, with a certain indeterminacy, evanescence, tremulousness, precisely that which is needed for the imagination of a dreamer, for the soul of an artist, for the inspired vein of a musical maestro'.[59] Checchi explicitly linked the qualities of the Tuscan landscape to Puccini's music, claiming that Puccini was so at one with his rural surroundings that he was incapable of composing in any other location: 'composing in the countryside is an inescapable necessity for him: in the hubbub of Milan, during the harsh winter months, he is incapable of doing anything'.[60] Checchi depicted Puccini's frustrated city existence thus:

> [Puccini] thinks, ponders, makes sketches in his imagination, and spends entire sleepless nights in bed tossing and turning, tormented, encircled, and caressed by the winged apparitions of characters from his previous operas. If, however, it occurs to him to sit at his desk or

the piano, he cannot even write two consecutive bars, come up with a chord, an arpeggio or a phrase.[61]

Checchi contrasted this scene of urban unproductiveness with a rhapsodical description of Puccini's return to Torre del Lago, a locus of fertility that allowed Puccini to compose without apparent effort:

> But at the first flowering of the almond trees, at the first spring breezes, at the first blue skies, he runs to the station, having stuffed a vast quantity of manuscript paper into his trunk. Upon descending at Torre del Lago he is reanimated, exalted, and inspired; he turns to the lake and the mountains, plunges into the woods that lead down to the sea, and once there imagines, and creates, and writes.[62]

Checchi's affectionate depiction of Puccini, who was a close personal friend, may be in part attributable to an attempt to romanticise his own upbringing: like Puccini he was born in Tuscany, lost his father at an early age and experienced straitened economic circumstances. However, his hymn of praise to the composer was not inspired by personal motives alone, for Checchi undoubtedly had an ideological agenda. Born in 1838, he had lived through the Peninsula's struggle for liberty, was a devoted admirer of Verdi and Manzoni, and was staunchly committed to Italian cultural independence. Noted as the author of historical books for children on the Risorgimento, he was well known for his sentimental nationalist proselytising.

Similar motifs can be discerned in the tribute to Puccini by Edmondo De Amicis (1846–1908), famed as the author of *Cuore* (1886), a patriotic tale aimed at schoolboys that was the best-selling Italian novel of its era. Set in a Turin school in the 1880s, it extolled the virtues of honesty, courage, loyalty and brotherhood, and was given state approval as a key pedagogical text for promoting a sense of mass national identity. De Amicis's endorsement of Puccini in 1900 in the newspaper *La prensa* is a marker of the high esteem in which the composer was held by the turn of the century. In styling Puccini as 'erect and strong like one of the pillars of the celebrated cathedral of his native Lucca', De Amicis testified to the composer's regional roots, his manly potency and the timeless, enduring qualities of his music.[63]

Such nostalgic images of Tuscany as motherland, calculated to promote ideas of collective homecoming, would have held particular significance for the readers of La prensa. The newspaper was published in Buenos Aires, where a large community of Italian migrants had made their home – including Puccini's own brother, Michele, who settled there in 1890 and died of yellow fever in Rio de Janeiro a year later – and where there was an enthusiastic following for Puccini's operas. This article was an overt manifestation of the project to maintain a sense of 'Italianness' in 'exiled' Italians, as espoused by patriotic organisations such as the Dante Alighieri Society.

ANCIENT AND MODERN

In his profile of Puccini, De Amicis alluded to a hallowed period in Italy's history – ancient Rome. The language used to describe Puccini's physical appearance accorded the composer the characteristics of an athlete, an emperor or even a god. He depicted Puccini as a statue, describing his face as 'sculptural', and 'bronzed', bearing the mark of the health-giving Italian sun. De Amicis wrote of Puccini possessing

> the stature of a grenadier; the head of a Roman emperor, crowned with thick black hair, very slightly grizzled at the top of the forehead; the frame of an athlete. . . . To sum up, he is a fine Tuscan of the ancient type, his sculpted, bronzed face overflowing with health, his features regular and firm, his expression open and tranquil.[64]

But just as he steered clear of subjects set in the Italian regions, Puccini would avoid setting an opera in ancient Rome (ignoring his friend Sybil Seligman's suggestion that he set *The Last Days of Pompeii*[65]), unlike his contemporary Mascagni, whose career would end with his opera *Nerone*. Yet Classical allusions would, as we shall see, serve Puccini's biographers well.

The exploitation of Classical images as part of the process of nation-building was a widespread nineteenth-century conceit, as they could be used to evoke what historian of nationalism Anthony D. Smith calls 'an idealized golden age and a heroic past that serve as exemplars for collective regeneration in the present'.[66] Readers of Puccini's time would have been familiar with such classicising discourse, which had by the turn of the century become part of a standard journalistic vocabulary. Academic art of the nineteenth century had long celebrated the muscular bodies of classical statues, and the idealised physique of the ancient athlete was accompanied in the late-nineteenth-century mind by the attendant spiritual values of strength, discipline and self-improvement. This tendency was appropriated in diluted form by a *fin-de-siècle* popular culture that celebrated circus strongmen, wrestling and the growing cult of body-building, and close links were fostered between physical exercise, politics and patriotism. By the late nineteenth century, France, Germany, England and Italy were all actively engaged in the promotion of sport in order to build up military and moral strength, in the belief that such an endeavour could counter the 'degeneracy' with which modern men were widely held to be afflicted.

Italian attempts to bring about regeneration in the present through recourse to selective, idealised models from the past were marked by a special claim to authenticity that Italy's neighbours could not match. Risorgimento activists, early-twentieth-century aspiring colonialists and Fascists would all in turn seek historical legitimacy for their ambitions in the precedent of the Roman Empire. The self-conscious promotion of a cult of *romanità* in early-twentieth-century Italy encompassed the widespread use of Classical themes in both popular fiction and in the burgeoning film industry, which provided the perfect vehicle for presenting the spectacular glories of Italy's past to a mass audience. The ancient world offered precisely those characteristics that the present age appeared to lack: national unity, cultural supremacy and empire. Italy's decision to enter the race for colonial expansion in the 1880s and 1890s, previously an issue that had preoccupied Italians less than the unification of their own country, was intimately connected with attempts to regain past imperial greatness and prompted by unease about Italy's diplomatic and military dependency upon its stronger allies in the Triple Alliance.

Manly descriptions of Puccini and their accompanying photographic images were therefore a politically charged act of confidence-boosting in an era of uncertain identity. At the *fin de siècle*, Puccini's association with prototypically ancient ideas of health, fitness and regeneration were encapsulated in an early photograph that depicts him wrestling among the ruins of Pompeii.[67] Alas for Puccini, his paunchy and less than godlike physique exposes a yawning gulf between fact and fantasy. And there is a further irony to the photograph, beyond Puccini's implausibility as a physical icon. While Puccini's patrons who released the photograph presumably sought to evoke memories of the glorious Roman empire, the backdrop of Pompeii is of course unfortunate because it stands for a civilisation that had claimed to be almighty but that was ultimately unable to withstand a more powerful force. It was precisely the cultural decay represented by ancient remains that attracted many foreign aesthetes or 'decadents' to make pilgrimages to the ruins of ancient Rome – something that later prompted the Futurists to call for them to be removed. Thus Puccini struggles in front of a symbol of civilisation in decay – a fitting, if unintentional, metaphor for *fin-de-siècle* Italian society.

Journals depicted Puccini on the one hand as a Classical hero and on the other as the embodiment of everything modern and forward-looking about contemporary Italy. Images of Puccini engaged in musical activities were comparatively rare, and in the few carefully posed photographs at the piano that Ricordi published he appears more apathetic than inspired. The image Puccini's patrons created is not that of the closeted, hot-house composer, but of the ebullient Italian who happens to compose. The visual images of Puccini and articles that underplayed his creativity are telling, revealing much about a certain suspicion in contemporary Italian society of the notion of genius, prompted by the widespread dissemination of Cesare Lombroso's *Genio e follia*. In this highly influential study, the prominent psychologist and criminologist drew comparisons between artists of outstanding ability and the lunatics whom he had treated at his clinic in Turin, and argued that artistic creativity was the product of hereditary insanity.[68]

Fig. 1.1. Puccini at the wheel (Archivio Storico Ricordi: All rights reserved. Reproduced by permission).

The Ricordi publicity photographs more often depicted Puccini enjoying what had been one of his most cherished pastimes since 1901 – driving fast cars (Figure 1.1).[69] The composer's 1903 automobile accident inspired as many column inches as his operas, and, indeed, was whipped up into a drama of operatic proportions. The first page of the report published in the Ricordi journal *Musica e musicisti*, entitled 'Maestro Puccini's motoring catastrophe', showed the dramatically subtitled 'luogo del disastro' ('scene of the disaster' – Figure 1.2), and four pages of photographs followed, depicting Puccini on a stretcher at various stages of his journey home after his brush with death.[70] Puccini's taste for boats was another topic that garnered detailed media coverage, and would have been of particular interest to the readers of Ricordi's journals, which by the early 1900s capitalised upon the increased leisure opportunities of the growing middle classes by publishing articles on travel, sport and such

Fig. 1.2. 'Maestro Puccini's motoring catastrophe', *Musica e musicisti*, March 1903 (Archivio Storico Ricordi. All rights reserved. Reproduced with permission).

glamorous aspirational objects as the latest cars and boats. Here, too, the press sought to emphasise Puccini's position at the cutting edge of taste and technology. The May 1909 issue of Ricordi's *Ars et labor*, for instance, depicted Puccini in his ultra-modern and high-speed boat 'Ricochet', declaring: 'thirsty for movement, air, light, ... he was and

Fig. 1.3. Puccini departs for Buenos Aires in 1905 – the banner bears the word 'speed' (Archivio Storico Ricordi. All rights reserved Reproduced by permission).

still is a passionate pioneer of every sport. As well as being the top motorist in Italy, today he is equally successful as a yachtsman'.[71] Even when Puccini was photographed boarding the transatlantic liner the 'Savoia' for a publicity trip to Buenos Aires in 1905, he was shown ascending a ramp adorned with a banner bearing the words 'LA VELOCE' ('speed' – Figure 1.3).[72] Thus Puccini could be presented as all things to all people: not merely a link to Italy's glorious past but an emblem of the dynamic modernity of Italy's future.

Other favoured poses included Puccini wielding a large gun (Figure 1.4). Checchi's profile of Puccini in La Tosca prioritised the composer's interest in shooting above his music: 'his houses are two, his operas are five, but the coots he's killed, at the maestro's own confession, are as innumerable as they are foul tasting'.[73] An early English biography of the composer by Wakeling Dry (1906), meanwhile, reproduced images of the composer as a man of leisure engaging in equally fancy-free activities: throwing snowballs in Sicily and descending Mount Etna on a mule.[74]

Fig. 1.4. Puccini the huntsman (Archivio Storico Ricordi: All rights reserved. Reproduced by permission).

The depiction of Puccini as an 'everyman' figure was by no means incompatible with his mythologisation. Roland Barthes, in an essay on Gide entitled 'The Writer on Holiday', argues that 'the singularity of a "vocation" is never better displayed than when it is contradicted – but not denied, far from it – by a prosaic incarnation: this is an old trick of all hagiographies'.[75] But what we have in Puccini's case is not an example of what Barthes calls the 'proletarianization of the artist'.[76] Rather, the composer was held up by the press as representing Italy's collective ambitions for the future: wealth, success and a leading role in Europe and beyond. Puccini was portrayed both as a glamorous international star – enjoying luxury transatlantic travel, sumptuous hotel rooms and the trappings of celebrity on his visit to Buenos Aires – and as a humble man of the people. Thus he both represented the common man and showed what the middle classes might aspire to.

Numerous photographs showed Puccini in domestic situations and engaged in leisure activities that played up his ordinariness, his ever-present cigarette in mouth, which features even today on a statue of him next to the house of his birth in Lucca. Such images of the composer engaged in everyday activities provided an ostensibly exclusive insight into the private life of a public man. The depictions of Puccini engaged in trivial occupations were calculated to heighten, rather than to banish, the mystique that surrounded him, and throughout his life, commentators would continue to stress his humility and lack of pretension. In 1884, at the very outset of Puccini's career, Fontana presented him as 'a fine young man, with polite manners, but who likes the simple life and has a certain aversion to frequenting the so-called salons',[77] while almost forty years later the journalist Ugo Ojetti would write that Puccini's most endearing quality was that he 'does not dress like a genius, does not talk like a genius, has neither the aspects nor the looks of a genius'.[78] Such questions would have been just as pertinent in the 1890s: as Wagner's shadow lengthened across the Italian operatic tradition, it would soon become contentious whether Puccini could compose like a genius.

2 | La bohème: Organicism, progress and the press

La bohème is nowadays one of the best-loved and most frequently performed of all Puccini's operas. After its première in February 1896 it was swiftly adopted into the repertory of all the major theatres across Italy, and performances soon followed in such diverse cities as Buenos Aires, Alexandria, Moscow, Lisbon, Manchester, Berlin, Rio de Janeiro, Mexico, London, Vienna, Los Angeles and The Hague. However, the response of the audience that listened to its first performance at Turin's Teatro Regio was subdued, and that in Rome a short time later little more enthusiastic. Critical responses were polarised (one commentator referred to them as either *di cotte* or *di crude* – burnt or raw[1]) and coloured by a significant event that had taken place in Turin a little over a month earlier – the first Italian production of *Götterdämmerung*. In a city where many critics were relatively tolerant of forward-looking musical tendencies, La bohème was not judged on its own terms but became caught up in heated arguments about the merits of Wagner's music and ideas. Two key themes emerged from the comparison with Wagner: the issue of organic wholeness in music and the separate but related issue of organic growth, or how Italian music ought to progress. Thus, despite the subsequent popular success of La bohème, its initial critical reception was dominated by anxieties about the vitality of contemporary Italian music and its ability to keep pace with musical developments elsewhere in Europe. The Italian intelligentsia was caught between its desire for a decisively Italian music (and discouragement of the imitation of foreign models) and a nagging concern that Italian opera was not sufficiently 'modern'.

Wagner's operas arrived only slowly and belatedly in Italy: *Lohengrin* was the first to be performed, in 1871, but others arrived much later – *Tristan und Isolde* not until 1888, *Die Meistersinger von Nürnberg* the following year, *Das Rheingold* in 1903, and *Parsifal*, for reasons of copyright, in 1914. However, Wagner's name was already something to be feared, for news of the controversy that had surrounded the premières of his works in France had reached the Italian press much earlier, with many critics pronouncing them, sight unseen, to be the pernicious antithesis of the Italian operatic tradition. The first performances in Italy were greeted by near-riots (such as when *Lohengrin* was staged at La Scala in 1873) and cries of 'viva Verdi!' (heard at performances of *Die Walküre* in Naples). Critical responses to the works, as elsewhere in Europe, were sharply polarised. The popular music press and the majority of daily newspapers were initially extremely hostile to the German composer. A prominent example was the *Gazzetta musicale di Milano*, which in the early 1880s expressed out-and-out contempt for Wagner's operas, the scores of which Giulio Ricordi referred to as 'hieroglyphs full of science and poison'.[2] (He would keep quiet about his views on Wagner after 1888, when the firm took over the Italian rights to Wagner's works on purchase of the Lucca publishing house.)

Hostility to German music was frequently expressed via physiological metaphors to demonstrate its incompatibility with the Italian spirit. Italian critics had long characterised Italian music as healthy, wholesome and life-affirming, and Teutonic music as unhealthy, indigestible and sterile. Filippo Filippi, an eminent critic and pro-Wagnerian, commented in 1876 on the metaphors of sickness employed by most of his contemporaries when writing about the German composer:

> Wagnerphobia has reached the state of a paroxysm in some: not only do they claim that his music (that they never even know) is the negation of art, of melody, of common sense, but that listening to it brings veritable bad fortune; and serious newspapers don't hesitate to assert that listening to a Wagner opera can cause jaundice, smallpox, cholera, and goodness knows how many other diseases![3]

The Wagner furore reached its peak in Italy around the turn of the twentieth century, coinciding with the first performances of Puccini's middle-period operas, when Michele Virgilio argued that Wagner's works represented 'an artistic form that is in absolute contradiction with our nature'.[4] In the view of the unnamed anti-Wagnerian writing in *La lanterna* in 1896, Wagner's music prompted a physical discomfort in Italian listeners for which a cure would never be found:

> The abstruseness, the difficulties, the nebulousness of the Music of the Future grates on the nerves of those who listen to it today, as it grated on those who listened thirty years ago; and it will grate on the nerves of those who will listen in the future.[5]

This critic explained that Italians had grown to accept *Lohengrin*, *Tannhäuser*, selected parts of *Die Meistersinger*, the 'Ride of the Valkyries', and a few other pieces, 'but we haven't been able to digest the rest; the rest is too repulsive, too hard, too indigestible'.[6] Wagner's music was, for this critic, part of 'a genre of art that has nothing to do with our traditions, with our sentiment, with our past, with our environment, with a future that we dream will be less gloomy, less eccentric, but clearer and fresher with more health-giving, pure, genial melody'.[7] Moreover, the sheer length of Wagner's works came as a considerable shock to the Italian constitution, and in order to make them more palatable they were often shortened; indeed, Puccini himself was consulted by the Ricordi firm in 1889 on suitable cuts to *Die Meistersinger*.[8]

However, certain sectors of Italian cultured society welcomed Wagner's works: they were embraced during the 1860s and 1870s by Arrigo Boito and other members of the *scapigliatura* movement, as an expression of their dissatisfaction with the conservative tastes of the new, bourgeois Italy as much as out of admiration for Wagner's music itself. Italian literary enthusiasm for Wagner reached its apogee in the 1890s, epitomised most notably in the works of D'Annunzio, who would write novels such as *Il trionfo della morte* (1894) and *Il fuoco* (1898) – Wagnerian in subject matter, replete with references to Wagner's operas and written in prose designed to recall Wagner's compositional style. In the early twentieth century many disaffected young proto-nationalists would also turn to Wagner's works and ideas, distilling from them an advocation of elitist aesthetic ideals that they believed would go hand in hand with a return to Italian greatness.

Furthermore, music criticism was changing around the turn of the twentieth century, with the emergence of a new breed of critics (discussed in detail later in this chapter) who were passionate about Wagner's music and gave it great prominence in the pages of their journals. Wagner's works were therefore the subject of so much topical debate that even the most hostile critics found them impossible to ignore. In 1896 'Diapason' reported in the *Fanfulla della domenica* that Wagner's name was now regarded by some as 'the touchstone against which it is obligatory to judge any given musical work', a state of affairs that had serious nationalist implications.[9] The responses that greeted *La bohème* show that it seemed to Puccini's contemporaries that Italian works could never again be heard on their own terms; rather, they had to be compared with the works of a foreigner, with which they inevitably shared little common ground. Suddenly, for the first time in Italian opera's history, foreign music threatened to set the terms by which it was judged, a tendency that was to intensify as the twentieth century progressed. Shifting patterns of expectation on the part of reviewers meant that hitherto unquestioned assumptions about the very nature and purpose of Italian opera were suddenly open to challenge.

The Turin staging of *Götterdämmerung* on 22 December 1895 seemed to some commentators to represent an important turning point in the reception history of Wagner's works in Italy. The work had in fact already been staged in Italy, but in German and by a German company: Angelo Neumann's touring Richard-Wagner Theater had performed the complete *Ring* in Venice and Bologna in April 1883. However, this was a mere curiosity, whereas a performance in Italian to mark the reopening of a major Italian theatre was a highly significant event. Ippolito Valetta, a rare example of a critic who was both a Wagnerian and a Puccini supporter, reported in the *Nuova antologia* that even the most 'alien' of Wagner's operas had now achieved success in one of the most important Italian theatres:

> In Turin, *Götterdämmerung* – that had seemed to the national taste to be the most repulsive of Wagner's dazzling works and the staging of which in Italy was prophesied as impossible – was a triumph.[10]

Valetta regarded the acceptance of Wagner into Italian theatres outside of Bologna – the Italian 'capital' of Wagnerism – as a positive development, and his fellow Torinese critics also responded warmly to *Götterdämmerung*. Reports of the public's reaction, on the other hand, varied. Valetta pointed to a paradigm shift in national sensibilities:

> This episode now incontrovertibly affirms a real change of taste, or at least a greater seriousness on the part of our public. ... The overwhelming success of *Götterdämmerung* at the Regio in Turin, affirming that we can now produce the rest of the Wagner cycle with full confidence in the result, is a positive gain for the future of our theatre.[11]

However, *La lanterna*, a more popular agency journal based in Milan, told a very different story, reporting that the public 'screwed up their noses', got bored and walked out, leaving only those who had gone to hear 'a demonstration in algebra and trigonometry' in the theatre.[12]

Whatever the response of ordinary listeners, the many Turin critics who had been impressed by *Götterdämmerung* were unable to eradicate memories of it from their minds when judging *La bohème*, which seemed lightweight in comparison. 'Diapason' of the *Fanfulla della domenica* objected to a plot that lacked substance, particularly the episode in which Mimì is preoccupied on her deathbed by thoughts of how to warm her hands, 'a subject one cannot imagine Bellini, Verdi or Wagner bothering to set':

> Opera should not simply depict atmosphere; it should represent man's strongest affections, like love, hate and jealousy, not the insignificant psychological expressions of everyday life.[13]

The score of *La bohème* seemed to many critics to be as insubstantial as the plot; Carlo Bersezio wrote in *La stampa* that 'the music of

Bohème is light, very light, too light, not only in the lively parts but in the dramatic and passionate moments too',[14] and damned *La bohème* as a hastily written and ultimately shallow piece:

> Puccini has called upon his innate aptitude for invention and a great fluency of ideas to write his music with much haste (or so it seems) and with little hard work in terms of selection and refinement. He has sought the maximum effect with the maximum simplicity, without noticing that he often falls into vacuity and sometimes into puerility. To obtain the original and the new he has now and then given in to the artificial and the baroque.[15]

Even critics writing in journals one would have expected to have spoken highly of *La bohème* could not get Wagner's opera out of their ears. For instance, 'Leporello' (Achille Tedeschi) of the *Illustrazione italiana*, whose readership was made up predominantly of the bourgeoisie who frequented La Scala, evidently found it impossible to give Puccini's opera his wholehearted endorsement, not least because, after Wagner, the criteria for evaluation had changed:

> The impressive polyphony of *Götterdämmerung* meant that some judged Puccini's orchestral simplicity with unfounded severity. I overheard a good many Torinesi repeating the words: 'it no longer seems like the same orchestra'. And it wasn't, and it should not have been. Even leaving this inopportune comparison aside, [*La bohème*] contains many weak points, and it isn't difficult to attack.[16]

Thus Wagner's legacy became a crucial factor in shaping the way in which Puccini was regarded by his contemporaries. Interestingly, Puccini's own attitude towards Wagner's music was far from antipathetic. He had studied Wagner's works, attended the Bayreuth Festival in July 1888 and again in August 1889, and even initially had a reputation as a 'Wagnerian'.[17] Certain aspects of his compositional style bear a Wagnerian influence: the descriptive orchestral passages; the adoption of a more through-composed approach than his *verismo* contemporaries; the quasi-symphonic organisation of certain scenes; and a use of motifs that, although certainly not full-blown leitmotifs, perhaps owed more to Wagner than to Verdi. Nevertheless, the proximity of the two premières served to highlight the perceived limitations of *La bohème* as a result of the comparisons that were drawn between Wagner's music and his own. Puccini was not the only composer to suffer in such a way: in Rome, Gounod's *Roméo et Juliette* had been the victim of a similar accident of timing, being deemed 'pale and anaemic' by the Rome press after they had heard the 'sparkling' *Die Walküre*.[18] But the implications were graver for Puccini, as a native Italian composer, than for Gounod: the criticisms levelled at him were not merely to his personal detriment but also raised wider questions pertaining to the fundamental aesthetics of Italian music.

Virtually all the critics – even those sympathetic towards Puccini – felt compelled to define their position vis-à-vis the Wagner question. Arguably the Wagner camp won, because of the extent to which discussions about the German composer dominated the reception of *La bohème*. Perversely, however, this was in large part due to Puccini's own supporters, who kept the issue alive, at times almost sidelining *La bohème* from the debate. Perhaps unsurprisingly, given the perceived power of the Wagnerian threat, it seems that the German composer's opponents were more obsessive about the issue than those they labelled 'Wagner fanatics'. It is plausible that the Puccinians played up the Wagnerian prejudices of their opponents in order to conceal problems they perceived in Puccini's score, an opera whose success was politically imperative. They realised that the issue of Wagnerism was a highly emotive one that could be counted upon to prompt a nationalist, anti-German response from most bourgeois readers. However, as we shall see, Wagnerian priorities had begun to permeate the mindset of even those critics who believed themselves to be defiant supporters of the Italian aesthetic.

ORGANIC WHOLENESS

The theme to emerge most forcefully from the reviews of *La bohème* was the perceived lack of organic wholeness in Puccini's music, a problem that was exacerbated in critics' minds after hearing

Götterdämmerung. Crucially, however, fragmentation and stylistic incoherence were issues that preoccupied *all* critics, not merely those who had responded favourably to Wagner's opera. The idea of organic unity as a marker of beauty – and the analogy between organicism and the state – dates back to the ancients, most notably Plato, but was taken up with renewed vigour in the late-eighteenth and nineteenth centuries by such figures as Kant, Herder, Coleridge, Goethe and Spencer. At the *fin de siècle*, prompted by Darwin-inspired fears of physical and cultural degeneration, cultural commentators applied biological and evolutionary metaphors to all aspects of modern life, including music. Ruth Solie, writing in 1980, points to the historical longevity of this idea:

> The characteristic of biological systems most commonly invoked in aesthetic evaluation is their 'organic unity', a notion which lies at the center of a whole network of related ideas. The use of such unity as a primary criterion for excellence in works of art is hallowed by time and tradition.[19]

The idea that an artwork must form a homogeneous unit, from which no parts can be removed without detriment to the whole, was of course problematic in the case of Italian opera, a genre in which arias were routinely added or removed, certainly until Rossini's time, and the sense of musical continuity was constantly interrupted by audience applause. However, as the nineteenth century progressed, Italian composers began to demonstrate greater concern for unity, and to write operas more as a continuous line than as a set of disjointed numbers. This was an approach of which increasingly organically minded critics approved, as Michele Leoni's assessment of *Nabucco* in 1843 illustrates:

> In this work it is fair to say that one fragment may prevail over another, but not that one can shine just as brightly without the other. This is so because the harmony among the various parts is deliberately so complete and continuous that, if one point is lacking, the whole would suffer as a consequence.[20]

The idea of a unified musical conception was to become increasingly important to Verdi over the course of his career, arguably reaching its peak in *Otello*. Thus, by the turn of the twentieth century, a work perceived to be lacking in unity not only failed to meet the new demands of post-Wagnerian opera, but was also a retrograde step in terms of the Italian tradition itself.

It is perhaps surprising that the Italian critics writing in daily newspapers and popular music reviews should have become so concerned about the organic unity of a composition. For decades the slightest suspicion of what was termed a 'scientific' approach to composition had prompted anti-German vitriol. The abundant derogatory references in the Italian press to 'science' or a 'system' – deemed contrary to the simple 'purity', spontaneity and emotion of Italian music – were invariably intended as swipes at Wagner. Italian critics generally borrowed their terms of reference from French anti-Wagner rhetoric: just as the French press frequently made 'references to German long-windedness and opacity in contrast to French "concision" and "clarity"',[21] Italian critics drew the self-same distinction between the supposed 'Germanic' manner of thinking, writing and composing and their own. In 1896 the passionate Wagnerian Enrico Thovez wrote *La leggenda del Wagner*, a study of the reception of Wagner's music in Italy, in which he observed that in the eyes of most Italian critics (himself of course excluded) 'German music was *science*, constructed laboriously on paper, rather than art that gushes forth from poetic inspiration: feeling, heart and melody were completely absent from it'.[22]

However, despite an ongoing hostility towards German music, by the turn of the twentieth century organic metaphors had found their way into the pages of the popular Italian music press as the chief criterion of artistic excellence, and fragmentation was becoming a term of abuse. Artworks were commonly cited as evidence of the good health of the nation, and the 'wholeness' and goal-oriented development of the work of art was supposed to mirror the same qualities nationalists aspired to find in the body politic. Just as society was frequently depicted in physiological terms, opera was referred to as a body undergoing a process of growth, renewal and perfection. As Italy's national composer elect, therefore, it was essential that Puccini should display appropriate organic qualities in his music; yet, as will become apparent, reviewers of *La bohème*, and later of *Tosca* and *Madama Butterfly*, failed to find the unity, sincerity, naturalness and progress they so fervently sought. Metaphors of physical weakness and atomisation recurred obsessively throughout the reviews of these works, with many critics perceiving his operas as being composed of a series of disjointed parts, which failed to coalesce into a coherent whole.

The most forward-looking Italian critics of Puccini's day increasingly looked to Wagner's music as a model of organic wholeness, and complained that unity – which they saw as paramount on the grandest scale in Wagner's aesthetic – was an area in which Puccini's latest work was deficient. For instance, E. A. Berta, the correspondent of the Turin newspaper the *Gazzetta del popolo*, who called *La bohème* 'commercially successful but artistically deplorable', wrote that 'the principal sin is the work's lack of unity; unity has been sacrificed to variety, sought, like popular approval, too eagerly'.[23] In particular, Act II, referred to by the correspondent for the *Corriere di Napoli* as 'the Achilles heel of the opera',[24] was almost universally panned for its lack of cohesion. Colombani, for example, wrote: 'in this part one does not succeed in finding the cohesion and unity that one finds in the first act. The music is less sparkling and somewhat disconnected'.[25]

In part the opera's problems were deemed to be the fault of Giacosa and Illica rather than Puccini. 'Veritas' of the Milanese *Il secolo*, a Sonzogno-owned newspaper rarely well disposed to works from the Ricordi stable, wrote: 'Murger's *La bohème* is an episodic novel but it has a strong backbone that keeps the action on the straight and narrow. The libretto of *La bohème* exaggerates the episodic weakness, exacerbating the lack of unity.'[26] Such claims are rather hard to swallow. Murger's tale had a huge cast of characters – from which Puccini's librettists picked only a select few – and was little more than a series of incidents, a structure that was acceptable in its first incarnation as a collection of serialised magazine stories, and relatively untroubling as a novel, but more problematic when the tales were adapted for the stage. Thus, in drastically simplifying Murger's text, Giacosa and Illica produced a libretto that was patently more homogeneous. Yet reviewers repeatedly blamed the 'fragmented' libretto for causing Puccini to compose a score that was disjointed at both macro and micro levels – that is to say, in terms of the overarching structure of the opera and of the individual melodic lines.

'Diapason' in the Rome-based *Fanfulla della domenica* objected to Murger's tale as an operatic subject, for it had encouraged discontinuity in the music, resulting in an opera in which 'there is no dominant and continuous plot'.[27] For this critic the libretto was simply not suited to musical treatment: 'the nature of the *Bohème* libretto leads inevitably to situations that cannot be set to music; it merely suggests words and phrases, which are badly suited to melodic expression'.[28] Indeed, according to 'Diapason', melody, that defining characteristic of Italian music, was sadly lacking in Puccini's latest work:

> Speaking with sincerity, there is little 'melody' in *Bohème*, in the highest sense of the word, and that little that there is is fairly colourless. Here and there detached phrases or movements caress the ear in a pleasing way, but you will search in vain across the entire four tableaux for one of those thoughts that unwinds in its fullness, in a broad and complete development, that constitutes a 'beautiful passage of music'.[29]

This charge seems incredible to modern ears, yet 'Diapason' was not the only critic to make the point. Hanslick observed that 'on the whole melodic invention is extremely scanty' in *La bohème*.[30] Such a claim was damning: to accuse Puccini of renouncing melody was to undermine his status as national composer. Critics such as 'Diapason' viewed Puccini's flexible, through-composed arioso style, with its constant juxtapositions and deviations that mimic the patterns of casual speech, as short-windedness, a retreat from the purer lyricism of Verdi and his predecessors. However, such commentators failed to note that the score's spontaneity and quasi-improvisatory quality were entirely appropriate to the opera's subject matter. Morandi of the popular music

La bohème: Organicism, progress and the press | 51

magazine the *Frusta teatrale* rushed to Puccini's defence, pointing to *La bohème*'s 'divine pages, with melodies that are truly ingenious, inspired and rich with *italianità*',[31] yet even this staunch supporter of Puccini was forced to note the work's 'deficient unity'.

Thus, even critics writing in newspapers customarily supportive of Puccini could not disguise their concern about the lack of organicism in *La bohème*. Colombani, of the conservative *Corriere della sera*, was confident that the work's shortcomings would not prevent it from enjoying long-lived popular success. Nonetheless, he highlighted what he perceived to be the work's incoherence when he lamented the fact that '*La bohème* is interesting in its details ... but not in its entirety'.[32] Such comments would set the tone not only for the contemporary reviews of Puccini's next two operas, particularly *Madama Butterfly*, but also for much late-twentieth-century criticism of Puccini, which chided him for his prioritisation of impassioned moments, not necessarily set within the context of a grand overriding plan, and his concentration upon the musical surface – melody and orchestration at the expense of harmony, an aspect that lends itself more readily to graphic analysis.

Why though, one might ask, should Puccini be chastised for revelling in the moment? Indeed, the impassioned utterances, the instances of melodic and harmonic intensity that stand out from the surrounding texture (for example, the moment in Act III when Rodolpho confesses his love for Mimì and his fear that she is close to death[33]) would seem to be what gives his music its distinctive appeal. But the most serious music critics of Puccini's time problematised these ardent moments. In 1914 the composer Ildebrando Pizzetti wrote they were not 'the consequence of an organically developed feeling reaching its maximum ardour, but ... expressions of accidental and superficial and fleeting impressions'.[34] The criticisms frequently levelled at Puccini in implicit comparison to Verdi, both during his own time and today, are strikingly similar to those levelled at Schubert in comparison to Beethoven. As Lawrence Kramer has observed:

> Schubert is a wonderful melodist but he is structurally 'weak'.
> Schubert repeats himself too much. Schubert substitutes sensuousness

for forward momentum. Schubert loses himself in the pleasure of the part and neglects the discipline of the whole. Each of these defects corresponds to a virtue traditionally ascribed to Beethoven: structural integrity, economy of expression even in large-scale works, purposeful drive, mastery of organic form.[35]

Although the repeated insistence upon organicism by Puccini's contemporaries might seem old fashioned by postmodern standards, the fact that his music (and that of composers such as Schubert) is still implicitly or explicitly criticised today for prioritising 'the parts over the whole' reveals that large-scale structural coherence remains for many musicologists a fundamental criterion of musical excellence.

Some critics seeking to praise Puccini in 1896 found a way of turning a potential weakness into a strength by stressing his skill as an able 'miniaturist'. Reviewers of *La bohème* – and, as we shall see *Madama Butterfly* – stated that Puccini was adept at bringing out the lustre of the work's details through a use of musical 'varnish'. But according to the rhetorical conventions of the time, to highlight the 'details' of Puccini's music, however beautiful, was to emphasise its superficiality, and would come in time to be understood as code for the 'femininity' of the composer's music, as will be discussed in more detail in chapters 4 and 5. Thus what appeared to be a compliment in fact revealed an opinion held even by Puccini's patrons that he lacked a sense of compositional control over broad expanses of music. In the hands of less well-disposed critics, such as Gustavo Macchi of *La sera*, the term 'varnish' was used explicitly as an insult. This critic acknowledged that Puccini's style had matured in *La bohème*, that he had succeeded in moving the audience, and that his writing for the orchestra was here much improved.[36] Yet as a scholar acquainted with foreign musical developments, who would later write studies of Wagner's *Ring* and Beethoven's symphonies, Macchi left his readers in no doubt that Puccini's attention to detail was to the detriment of the organicism widely accepted as a marker of musical quality:

> But often he stopped to paint, to varnish almost, the plot of the libretto with graceful and light music, scene by scene, episode by

episode, sometimes losing sight of the overall whole. ... The music had the task of bringing all these details together, of making a living organism out of these dead organs. In truth it hasn't succeeded; the elegant details, the expressive musical meanings of the episodes follow one another ... but ... do not come together.[37]

Puccini's most determinedly loyal supporters leapt to his defence with a torrent of scornful anti-Wagner invective. However, rather than attempting to divert attention away from an aspect of Puccini's work that was deemed by general consensus to be flawed, they simply inverted the attacks levelled by his detractors and waxed lyrical about Puccini's success in creating an integrated work. An anonymous telegram published in the *Perseveranza di domenica* after the Turin première called Act I of *La bohème* 'a jewel of unity' and Act IV 'admirable in its unity'.[38]

Similarly, Gino Monaldi, who, as we shall see, was a master of hagiography, challenged those critics who had accused Puccini of creating a fragmented, mosaic-like work by praising his 'fine organic unity of thought and style'.[39] Monaldi seized upon the qualities that other critics attributed to Wagner and transplanted them onto Puccini, but his comments in *Il popolo romano* about the homogeneity of *La bohème* suggest a defensive tone:

> Such a system as Puccini employs is one consisting of a compact, solid, organic edifice constructed on equally large, homogeneous passages that often cover an entire act and are never, in any way, the assemblage of small detached pieces, skilfully superimposed and cemented together.[40]

Monaldi's compliments were generally so hyperbolic that it is difficult to take them seriously. However, on this point his claim seems justified: there is indeed a high level of recurrence of musical material in *La bohème*, and it ranks today as one of Puccini's best-integrated scores. The opera's dramatic structure is symmetrical, with the first and final acts both taking place in the same location, and both dividing into two contrasting portions, the first light-hearted or comic and the second reflective. Furthermore, musical connections are drawn between the two acts in order to produce pathos-laden reminiscences of happier times. However, most critics failed to notice these features on a first hearing, perceiving instead an impressionistic approach to compositional organisation, and interpreting Puccini's clever creation of a distinctive mood for each act, set in contrast with what has come immediately before, as a tableau-like design that seemed to have little in common with the traditional construction of Italian opera. Some of those critics of Puccini's time who commented later upon his use of recurring motifs deemed them to be of little consequence. Ildebrando Pizzetti argued that Puccini's motifs did not express deep impressions or emotions, but rather 'superficial, fleeting, forgettable' impressions,[41] and that Puccini had adopted a quasi-leitmotif technique without understanding its possible value, simply in a spirit of 'mechanical imitation'.[42]

ORGANIC GROWTH AND PROGRESS

In addition to organicism, improvement was another crucial late-nineteenth-century credo: the entry on 'progress' in the 1875 *Larousse* dictionary states, 'Faith in the law of progress is the true faith of our century.'[43] Evolutionary thinking demanded that art, like society, develop in a teleological manner, and the reviews of *La bohème* illustrate that organic growth, like organic unity, was becoming an issue of profound concern to Italian music critics at the *fin de siècle*. Increasingly, as Italian reviewers became familiarised with the distinct 'sound worlds' Wagner had created in each of his operas – something to which the later Verdi had also aspired – they were less prepared to tolerate operas that they perceived to be composed after a type. Critics thus began to demand that Puccini's style should also develop and 'improve' from opera to opera, each work making a significant contribution to the evolution of Italian opera as a whole. Carlo Bersezio argued in the Turin daily paper *La stampa* that *La bohème* had been deficient in this regard:

> Just as *La bohème*, I believe, left no great impression on the hearts of the listeners, nor will it leave a great mark on the history of Italian

opera; and it would be a good thing for the author – considering it (if you will permit the expression) as a momentary error – to attempt vigorously to regain the right course, and to persuade himself that this was a brief deviation from artistic progress.[44]

Bersezio's words suggest that there was a single 'right course' that Italian opera ought to follow in order to reach perfection. However, as the trajectory of Puccini reception illustrates, there was in fact little consensus among critics as to what might constitute the correct direction for Italian opera.

The principal reason Puccini's style was deemed not to have evolved in *La bohème* was what struck critics as the disconcerting similarities in musical language between this opera and *Manon Lescaut*. Even in the broadly positive reviews carefully selected by Ricordi for reproduction in the *Gazzetta musicale di Milano* as evidence of *La bohème*'s triumphant success, some commentators could not conceal their concerns about the opera's apparent lack of originality. The recycling of musical material was a long-established practice in Italian opera; as Fabrizio della Seta points out, 'in the history of Italian operatic conventions, shared codes and repetition of formulas often prevailed over the search for novelty'.[45] Yet by the later nineteenth century self-borrowing had become problematic, with critics adopting an increasingly organicist mindset that dictated that it was impossible to remove a passage of music from one work and graft it onto another. Originality had become the prime indicator of artistic value, even within Italian opera, yet concurrently, and perhaps somewhat paradoxically, a composer was also expected to maintain a defined musical 'physiognomy' that would make his works instantly recognisable: thus, his output should be homogeneous but with subtle variations from work to work. The fine line between unoriginality and the reaffirmation of a personal aesthetic was a matter that would be debated throughout Puccini's career, and would rear its head particularly forcefully when critics assessed the unity of his entire œuvre in the reviews of *Turandot* some thirty years later. In 1927, for example, the modernist critic Guido M. Gatti would argue that

Puccini's melodies 'did not originate from an original cell, were not matured slowly in the artist's heart, but were formed from diverse, pre-existing elements, by an almost mechanical process of welding and repetition'.[46]

However, the physiognomy argument gave Puccini's supporters ammunition to rebut charges of compositional laziness with claims that any similarities between his works were in fact deliberate. For them, Puccini's reliance on what his detractors labelled overworked formulae was positive evidence of the fact that his music had not been distorted, corrupted or rendered 'foreign'. In his review of the Rome production of La bohème in the Gazzetta ufficiale del regno d'Italia, Leone Fortis drew his choice of words from the fashionable school of physiognomy, which regarded external expression as an index of inner character:

> Now, for us, Puccini's principal merit is that he has never sacrificed his own artistic originality to the prejudices and impositions of modernity; has never subscribed to the dominant Wagnerian confraternity; has conserved his own physiognomy, his own character; has remained Puccini.[47]

Other critics sat on the fence: Ippolito Valetta of the Nuova antologia, for example, acknowledged that 'in La bohème it is difficult to defend Puccini wholeheartedly against a general indictment of self-plagiarism'.[48] However, he praised the fact that the work 'harmonises fundamentally with the Italian tradition', its simplicity and clarity marking it out from the hotch-potch of quasi-Wagnerian works being produced by many young Italian composers, and his overall assessment of the work was that Puccini had made 'not one but many steps forward in Bohème'.[49]

The composer's champions argued that there was a distinctly 'Italian' manner of composing that Puccini was aspiring to resurrect. The presence of a hallmarked Puccini style was a positive attribute, for the great Italian composers of the past had each written in their own recognisable musical idiom. Rocco Pagliara of Il mattino asserted: 'think back to how Bellini was always Bellini, Donizetti was always Donizetti,

Verdi was always Verdi, and so forth',[50] while the ever hyperbolic Eugenio Checchi wrote that reminiscences of earlier works were only natural – a virtue, indeed – as Puccini composed according to his 'heritage', thus dubbing patriotism that which others labelled plagiarism.[51] While for some critics Puccini's self-repetition was indicative of the failure of his aesthetic to evolve, for others self-borrowing and progress were not regarded as mutually exclusive. Colombani of the *Corriere della sera*, for example, wrote that 'the melodic material bears evidence of having sprung from the same source, but here it is purer, more noble'.[52] Using similar imagery – and likewise refraining from supporting his claim with any reference to the specifics of Puccini's music – the unsigned reviewer for the *Corriere di Napoli* cited the opera as 'indisputable proof of the fact that a wonderful purification has taken place in the mind and art of the young *maestro*'.[53]

Critics were therefore divided over the issue of whether or how Puccini's music had progressed. The *idea* of progress, however, mattered to them all, although subsequent chapters will reveal that Puccini was at times paradoxically criticised for going too far. But what did critics in the 1890s actually understand by the term 'progress'? Certainly, imitating foreign music was not to be condoned. Gino Monaldi was unreservedly hostile towards the attempt by many young Italian composers to imitate the modern style of much German and French music:

> The 'modern manner' essentially signifies the exclusion of the purely lyrical, means the substitution of melodic declamation for melody, of workmanship for form, of ornamental detail for the grand architectural lines of true and genuine art. ... Therefore the 'manner' begins precisely where creativity ends.[54]

For Monaldi, *La bohème* had transformed Italian opera and pointed the way forward:

> Now ... that the Maestro has triumphed, the Italian artist should follow his lead. Letting things stay as they are would have meant no success for him, no honour and glory for us and would not have set a

positive example to our young musicians. And Puccini understood this and thought ahead to the future.[55]

Crucially, Monaldi insisted that Puccini had brought about progress along *Italian* lines, referring in another review to 'a personal and distinct organism' brought to life with a 'warm wave of youthful Italian blood'.[56] However, he failed to be any more specific about what, precisely, the Italian characteristics of *La bohème* were, other than by drawing vague and unsubstantiated comparisons with late Verdi: 'Puccini, more than any other composer, comes close to Verdi and to the model of classic instrumentation that is *Falstaff*.'[57] But this compliment merely serves to emphasise how infrequently Puccini's supporters explicitly appealed to the shadow of Verdi. The rarity of such comparisons suggests a tacit acceptance of Puccini's inferiority to Verdi, even on the part of those who strove to depict the younger composer as a national icon.

E. A. Marescotti, writing in *Il palcoscenico*, took a different view from Monaldi of Puccini's relationship to modern composition. Both critics attempted to bolster Puccini's reputation but in contrasting ways. Where Monaldi represented the old school, which prioritised the composer's ability to move the listener over all other considerations, Marescotti, while defending Puccini, believed it was important to stress that Puccini was technically innovative. Where Monaldi poured scorn upon the 'modernists', Marescotti tried to claim that Puccini was their technical equal, even writing: 'Puccini has shown himself to be in many respects superior to the modern masters.'[58] Contrary to the opinion of those who claimed Puccini's music to be regressive, Marescotti believed it to lead the way forward, while still maintaining fidelity to Italian traditions. Thus Puccini had solved the difficult problem of reconciling progress with accessibility:

> In this score too, then, those of a technical bent cannot fail to admire the inventive and elegant harmonist; the refined, skilled, enchanting orchestrator; and finally – and this is the greatest honour – the refreshed, impassioned and irresistible melodist. In *Bohème*, the scholar can treasure the most original vocal writing, rhythms and elegant

tonal method, and above all can educate his own taste to clear ideals that will exert a regenerative power on our art.[59]

Many contemporary commentators disagreed with Marescotti's assessment, but what is striking here is how his review reflected a growing concern with technical sophistication amongst Italian critics. The very fact that he considered the opinion of 'those of a technical bent' is surprising. Previously Italian critics would have had sufficient confidence in the superiority of Italian music not to have been troubled by such matters; on the other hand there would also have been fewer 'scholars' around to complain.

THE EVOLUTION OF MUSIC CRITICISM

The contrasting views expressed by Monaldi and Marescotti illustrate the fact that music criticism was itself metamorphosing at the *fin de siècle*, to the consternation of the dilettante writers who had long presided over the field. At the beginning of the twentieth century we witness the belated development of serious music criticism in Italy, partially in response to the arrival of Wagner's works. This was a double-edged development: the resulting theoretical knowledge of course increased the musical penetration of such criticism, but the need for it came, problematically, from a feeling that Wagner's music demanded such responses; the historical significance of the latter's music was thus explicitly acknowledged. The reviews of *La bohème* reveal a growing schism between those fearful of a compositional 'system' and those who demanded that Italian opera composers also adopt a 'modernist' mode of composition: the two groups had very different ideas about what constituted musical progress. Furthermore, the writers who challenged the accepted conventions of Italian opera also began to re-evaluate their own role as critics, and with this reassessment of the role of the critic came a questioning of the 'correct' relationship between the audience and post-Wagnerian opera.

Opera-going was enjoying a boom around the time of the *La bohème* première, as is illustrated by the number of singers in employment: in 1897, Milan alone was able to sustain a workforce of

1,106 singers.[60] And as opera attendance increased, so too did the demand for literature about music. Numerous popular periodicals concerned with singers and operas appeared on a weekly or monthly basis, in many of which the level of analysis was at best superficial or, more often, totally absent. These journals were little more than society magazines, with the critics paying more attention to the attire of the ladies in the audience than the opera being performed on stage, the quality of which was typically assessed simply by the number of curtain calls its composer and performers received. Such publications employed critics whose music education was often fairly scant, with some unable even to read music. A commentator in the *Gazzetta musicale di Milano* identified only as 'Dottor Libertà' wrote in 1886 that even a schoolboy ignorant of the basic rules of music could pass himself off as a critic,[61] a state of affairs that led Michele Virgilio to lament: 'unfortunately, music criticism does not exist in Italy'.[62] Journals with a slightly more sophisticated remit, such as *La lanterna*, *La frusta teatrale* and *Il mondo artistico*, provided long articles and reviews that attempted to analyse the music and libretto, although in language designed for a lay readership.

As a general rule, the popular music press was happy to swallow and regurgitate Ricordi-sponsored propaganda about Puccini. Of course, the strongest support of all for Puccini came from the Ricordi house journal itself, which appeared in various incarnations: the *Gazzetta musicale di Milano*, *Musica e musicisti*, *Ars et labor* and latterly *Musica d'oggi*. While the inevitable partiality of these journals means that caution should be exercised in using them in order to assess Puccini's critical fortunes, they are nevertheless a valuable resource in allowing us to observe how the 'Puccini myth' was constructed and fuelled. At the beginning of Puccini's career, the *Gazzetta*, which dated back to 1842, was a serious music periodical, publishing numerous substantial reviews of new works and revivals of established repertory, discussing issues of contemporary musical debate and music history, and demonstrating a commitment to music education. Contributors employed a fair level of technical detail, albeit tailored to a non-specialist readership. However, in 1903 Ricordi replaced the

Gazzetta musicale di Milano with a small-format, lavishly illustrated journal entitled *Musica e musicisti*, itself superseded in 1906 by the broadly similar *Ars et labor*, which sought to capitalise upon the current vogue for illustrated magazines such as the *Illustrazione italiana* and Giacosa's recently established *La lettura*. Now a monthly rather than a weekly publication, the Ricordi house journal was unrecognisable in its new guise, and undoubtedly sacrificed intellectual credibility. The eventual eradication of 'music' from the title was significant, as detailed music reviews were replaced by brief listings, serialised stories, and articles on sport, leisure pursuits, travel, painting, current affairs and fashionable ideas from the burgeoning sciences of psychology and criminology.

Inasmuch as newspaper production as an industry developed much later in Italy than in other European countries, the Italian market for newspapers and periodicals was far smaller than that for French or British publications, although it began to grow from 1866 with the launch of *Il secolo*, the first newspaper aimed at a broad middle-class readership. Towards the end of the nineteenth century daily newspapers began to devote increasing space to arts coverage, with the growing importance of the 'terza pagina' – the third page, devoted to the arts – while the foundation of the *Fanfulla della domenica* also encouraged other newspapers to produce cultural and literary supplements. Reviews in newspapers tended to follow the same format as those in popular music journals, providing a catalogue of notable audience members; a summary of the plot; some generalised comments about the music; an indication of the number of curtain calls; and an assessment of the singers. Naturally, criticism in the daily press was limited by its very nature: the copy had to be prepared at speed; the reviewer was often forced to base his review on first impressions without access to the score; and the review had to capture the interest of a browsing reader. Sometimes, however, opera criticism in the daily press probed more deeply than reviews published in many of the popular music journals, suggesting a fairly musically literate readership.

A good example of one of the most extreme members of the dilettante school of music criticism (although he did occasionally write for more sophisticated publications such as the *Rivista musicale italiana*) was Gino Monaldi, whose colourful prose we have already encountered. Monaldi had written a biography of Verdi in 1878[63] that was to influence generations of later writers, in which he was guilty of what John Rosselli terms a 'cavalier misuse of evidence'.[64] Frank Walker is even more damning of the 'gossipy' Monaldi's credentials as a biographer:

> What are we to say of Gino Monaldi, another 'eye witness', except that his innumerable shallow publications have been responsible for half the apocryphal stories current about Italian composers of the last century? He had an Olympian disregard for awkward facts, habitually touched up the texts of any original documents he had occasion to quote, and almost invariably misread or misprinted their dates.[65]

Walker writes with a modern historian's view of the responsibilities of the biographer, and his criticisms of Monaldi could be justifiably applied to many of Puccini's other supporters, whose scholarly credibility is equally questionable. Yet Walker's criteria would have been alien to these writers, who saw no problem in sacrificing accuracy for a good narrative in the cause of patriotic propaganda.

The dilettante writers allowed themselves to be led by public taste when judging a work of art, claiming that unschooled audiences were the best critics: they knew what they liked and they recognised 'pure' Italian music. At first only a few critics took a different view. Going against the common Italian consensus that music should be immediately accessible to all, Filippo Filippi had argued in the 1870s that an understanding of music was the product of hard effort and advocated the sort of serious musical appreciation cultivated in Germany:

> We should educate the public, make them patient and diligent, aware of the fact that music is an art, and that a taste for it and particularly an understanding of it develops only with patience, and involves overcoming the initial tedium, casting prejudices aside, taking it seriously, as they do in Germany, where everyone who listens appreciates it, because they understand it, and because the education of the public takes place everywhere, in squares, in homes and in the

theatres, where people listen to great music, classical music, real music. I don't hold the view that music is art for the masses, for the people. No, my good sirs: music is written for educated people, for those people who, when listening to a music drama, know and appreciate its entire historical and aesthetic discourse.[66]

By the last decade of the nineteenth century, the first generation of professional Italian musicologists began to take up Filippi's call to arms. A dissatisfaction with the poor state of existing Italian music criticism stimulated the establishment of a number of serious musicological journals around the turn of the twentieth century. Pre-eminent among these was the *Rivista musicale italiana* (*RMI*), founded in Turin in 1894 by Luigi Torchi (1858–1920), a critic, musicologist, historian, teacher and librarian who promoted knowledge of Wagner's ideas in Italy. He translated Wagner's prose works and was the author of the most important Italian book devoted to the German composer to be published in the nineteenth century, a magisterial tome of some 610 pages.[67] The *RMI* represented an entirely new departure in Italian journalism: no other music periodical approached it in terms of scope, sophistication or seriousness. Its principal areas of interest were the current decline of Italian music, the revival of early Italian instrumental works, and the promotion of the most progressive foreign works, by Wagner, Strauss, Debussy and their contemporaries. Torchi detested contemporary Italian opera – even Verdi was ignored, with the exception of a special issue marking his death in 1901 – and sought the creation of a new Italian 'opera nazionale'. During Torchi's ten-year editorship of Italy's most serious musicological journal Puccini's operas would scarcely merit a mention – an omission that must surely call into question his status as 'national composer'. The only piece devoted to Puccini during this period was a hostile review of *Tosca* in 1900 (discussed in detail in the next chapter), which prompted G. Conrado to respond in the *Gazzetta musicale di Milano* with the following sarcastic words: 'Oh illustrious Minos, how have you become so Germanised as even to forget your own language? So why don't you just write in German, then?'[68]

It was in keeping with the *RMI*'s remit that reviewers should consider works in substantial detail and provide music examples in order to show readers the main musical motifs under consideration. This sort of analysis was in general not valued by Italian critics. As Conrado's comment reveals, dilettante critics derided the sort of technical music criticism favoured by the new musicological journals as 'German', and, like German music, portrayed it as unhealthy. Giulio Fara, in an article on Wagner and Verdi serialised in the *Cronaca musicale* in 1912, referred to serious-minded, pro-Wagner critics as 'sterile, malignant and pedantic'.[69] However, it was not only dilettante critics who regarded technical music criticism with suspicion in Italy. Benedetto Croce believed analysis was inimical to organicism, writing: 'the fact that we divide a work of art into parts, a poem into scenes, episodes, similes, sentences, or a picture into single figures and objects, background, foregrounds, etc. ... annihilates the work, as dividing the organism into heart, brain, nerves, muscles and so on turns the living being into a corpse'.[70]

Eugenio Checchi, Puccini's staunch supporter, contrasted the foolishness of the erudite critics with the wisdom of the people, who had recognised in *La bohème* 'an air more suited to Italian lungs':

> Of the two litigants, I think the public is right. Free from preconceived ideas and a system, from methods and from a 'school', and from all the other scientific devilries that have nothing to do with imagination and inspiration, the public of the Teatro Regio applauded Puccini's new opera warmly and enthusiastically yesterday (as I reported in my telegram), and today huddled together to read the ridiculous, incomprehensible things written by the critics.[71]

The critic for *La tribuna* was equally scathing of the 'intellectual' stance of the Turin press, which he regarded as both out of step with public opinion and a desperate measure on the part of critics who could find no other fault with Puccini's work:

> In fact in the Turin newspapers, which arrived today, we see that in order to criticise Puccini's latest score, the critics, unable to deny the incontrovertible success of *Bohème*, have been forced to come out with

references to 'thirds and fifths', successions of 'forbidden fifths' and a whole host of other technical terms, ignored by the good public who look for nothing else in a piece of music than sweet melodies to entertain and move them.[72]

This critic responded to the Wagnerian critics who derided Puccini for 'writing more for the public than for musical science' with the following catalogue of *La bohème*'s attributes:

> Writing music that is clear, comprehensible, moving, of immediate effect and above all that does not fall into the slightest vulgarity (a difficult thing to avoid in this case) could be a weakness to those for whom Wagnerian systems have become an exclusive religion. But for the mass public, who hear music in an Italian way, who do not have a musical education, but who are impressed by that which the music – expression of the characters' feelings – has wanted to say and succeeded in saying to their hearts and brains, Puccini's music has the great merit of bringing pleasure.[73]

For this critic, 'writing for the people' was not only a positive attribute but an act of patriotism; furthermore, he made much of his own position as an uneducated listener, calling himself 'nothing but an impressionist'.[74] Thus, it is clear that those critics who pilloried learning and idealised the 'pure' way in which a public liberated from the constraints of an education listened to music were motivated by a personal agenda: it was in their interests to maintain the public's ignorance of musical technicalities in order that their own lack of training should not be noticed. At their most extreme, critics were prepared to denigrate the intelligence and the attention span of Italian audiences in order to deride German opera. 'Quirite', writing in *La lanterna*, would proudly contrast Puccini's concision in *Tosca* with Wagner's long-windedness, which, he claimed, was enough to make one run from the latter's music as a hydrophobic dog might flee from water.[75]

Dilettante criticism remained alive and well throughout Puccini's lifetime, as is exemplified by the publication in the early 1920s of Monaldi's overtly nationalistic biography of the composer, to which we shall return later, in which he continued to demonstrate a disdain for 'elitist' foreign music and for those who appreciated it, an extremely conservative stance for the time.[76] However, as we have seen, some forward-looking critics at the turn of the century began to question whether the audience – and the dilettante critics who spoke for them – really did 'know best'. The public should henceforth be guided by the critics rather than the other way around. Michele Virgilio, later to become the author of a damning pamphlet on *Tosca*, turned on the audience in his review of *La bohème* in the *Gazzetta teatrale italiana*, mocking them for their unsophisticated taste and writing that 'there are ears that aren't accustomed to other, more refined, melodic sounds'.[77] Virgilio depicted what he perceived to be the work's fundamental weakness – its lack of originality – as a source of comfort to an uneducated public who had failed to notice that Puccini's musical devices had been 'abused' and 'diluted' to the point where they had become 'colourless'.[78]

Thus, around the turn of the twentieth century, Italian critics began to debate whether composers ought to write for the people, one of the fundamentals of Italian opera composition and production. Should opera be mere entertainment, or should it have higher artistic aspirations? To what extent were entertainment and art incompatible? Italian opera had traditionally been a populist art form and its practitioners felt no shame at working more or less within the horizon of expectation of their audiences. But a greater exposure to German music led Italian critics to question long-standing assumptions about the relationship between composer and audience; as Jim Samson writes: 'the rise of the Romantic aesthetic, German in origin and nature, was profoundly threatening to the prestige of Italian opera, inimical to its entertainment status, to its approach to text and authorship, and even to its performance conditions'.[79] Traditionally, the view that accessibility constituted a positive Italian attribute would have been beyond challenge. However, some critics contemporary with Puccini began to regard the act of writing for the people not as Italian opera's greatest strength but as its greatest weakness. Luigi Alberto Villanis of the *Gazzetta di Torino* put his finger on the paradox when he described *La bohème*'s 'music designed for instant pleasure, intuitive music' as being 'both to Puccini's commendation and his condemnation'.[80] This was a problem for Italian opera that was both new and highly disconcerting.

Puccini was judged on different terms from his predecessors because of a growing exposure to foreign repertories – particularly the music of Wagner – and because of a burgeoning historicist mindset and faith in the importance of musical progress on the part of contemporary critics. Suddenly it was not enough to be a composer who 'wrote for the repertoire' rather than the canon,[81] despite the fact that this was what composers of Italian opera had always done. Concerns about the perceived lack of organicism in *La bohème* permeated reviews in all levels of publication, with serious nationalist implications in an age in which not even opera was immune from fashionable Darwinian notions of the survival of the fittest. Italian and German music were depicted as pitted against one another in an evolutionary struggle. The debates that *La bohème* prompted emphasised the widespread perception that Italian music was going through a transition phase and struggling to redefine itself in the face of foreign challenges. A few reviewers pronounced *La bohème* to be an indisputable national triumph from the start, *La perseveranza* confidently declaring the opera to be a 'precious document that affirms that the ancient, glorious flag of our art still flies high'.[82] Most Italian critics, however, forced for the first time to reassess their music in terms set by a foreigner, evidently feared that German culture would triumph.

After hearing Wagner's operas, and whether they liked them or not, most critics had come to expect a more organic approach to composition. But although Wagner had readjusted Italian critics' perception of the roles of composer and listener, few advocated that Puccini actually imitate Wagner. Critics with a more modernist viewpoint such as Torchi were prepared to admit their respect for German music as the pinnacle of well-organised art but stopped short of advocating Wagner as a model, for to do so at this time would strike too harsh a blow to long-cherished Italian traditions. Critics repeatedly called for a return to a truly 'Italian' music, but were uncertain what this might be. Verdi might plausibly have provided a more acceptable model of 'organic' composition, and yet advocating that composers on the brink of the twentieth century imitate Verdi, sat at odds with the critics' need for progress. For all their preoccupation with the idea of goal-oriented development, therefore, critics at the turn of the century were profoundly confused as to what Italian music was actually striving towards. If the challenges posed by Wagner were what critics saw as progressive, it was difficult to see how a composer could be both Italian and modern. With all these competing strings tugging at him, Puccini could not win; indeed, his music could not be perceived as anything other than a 'problem'. The complex tropes that appeared first in the reviews of *La bohème* – a lack of organic wholeness, insincerity, a preoccupation with insignificant 'small things', a failure to 'evolve' – are issues that continue to be debated today. But first they would re-emerge vehemently in the reviews of *Tosca* and *Madama Butterfly*.

3 | *Tosca*: Truth and lies

Tosca is an opera caught between truth and lies. Set in real places, at real times, it is probably the opera Puccini researched most scrupulously in order to ensure historical accuracy. Yet insincerity is its main theme: the opera's principal events are structured around a series of deceptions that intensify in dramatic power and consequence over the course of the work. Act I: Cavaradossi lies to Tosca in order to conceal the fact that he is sheltering Angelotti, the political prisoner. Act II: Tosca makes a false bargain with Scarpia, agreeing to succumb to his lustful advances and then stabbing him as he is about to claim his prize. Act III: Scarpia's deceit is revealed when the 'fake' execution he has arranged for Cavaradossi turns out to be for real. Furthermore, *Tosca* is a performance about performance, with its fictional characters constantly donning masks: Tosca is a singer and actress by profession; Cavaradossi prepares to feign his own death; Scarpia conceals his malevolent nature behind a clerical façade. With its strains of *verismo* and *Grand Guignol*, *Tosca* is arguably Puccini's most self-consciously 'theatrical' opera, its high drama epitomised most vividly at the moment when Tosca places a crucifix on Scarpia's chest and floodlights his corpse by surrounding it with candles. Beyond the basic level of plot, contemporary spectators perceived yet further layers of insincerity in *Tosca* that, as we shall see, permeated through the libretto and into the music itself. Responses to *Tosca* were dominated by the idea that the opera – with its obvious dramatic deceptions, its wooden characters, its music contaminated by a surfeit of foreign influences, its cheap melodrama posing as high art – was fraudulent at all levels. Puccini's perceived insincerity in this opera stood at odds with the claims of compositional sincerity upon which his career had been built.

Tosca is an opera that permits no neutral responses. Later-twentieth-century musicologists, favouring the Austro-German canon, have in many cases recoiled from Puccini's work, and singled this opera out for particular censure.[1] In Puccini's own time, too, *Tosca* made people sit up and listen, but rarely for positive reasons. By 1900, those progressive critics who lamented the ongoing primacy of what they regarded as an increasingly backward-looking operatic culture in Italy and advocated artistic regeneration through other genres no longer felt able simply to ignore Puccini's works, but increasingly made their voices heard. Thus, in addition to being reviewed in all the customary daily newspapers and mass-market music journals, *Tosca* attracted attention in unusual quarters. Of particular note were two rather unprecedented extended articles, both of which will be considered in some detail in this chapter. The first was a review by Luigi Torchi in his *Rivista musicale italiana*, striking because, as we have already seen, Italy's most serious musicological journal deliberately set out to ignore Puccini and his operas. Torchi made an exception for *Tosca*, not because he felt it to be a work of particular merit (although he was reasonable enough to approach the work with an open mind, praising Puccini for his skills as a melodist and orchestrator[2]), but because he wished to single it out as representative of a number of worrying tendencies in contemporary Italian opera. Torchi acknowledged the difficulties in criticising the composer upon whom the nation's hopes rested, arguing that no critic had so far been prepared to tackle the 'vexatious, uncomfortable and highly controversial' problems that characterised the work of this 'talented and successful young man'.[3] Less forward-looking journals mocked the *RMI*'s sudden interest in Puccini, G. Conrado casting scorn upon Torchi as 'the most determined and relentless demolition worker', who had 'not wasted two words' on Puccini's previous operas and had now gone to town in attacking him.[4] The second particularly notable essay was Michele Virgilio's *Della decadenza dell'opera in Italia: a proposito di 'Tosca'*, one of the first explicit counter-responses to the claim disseminated by Puccini's patrons that his music was the antidote to the nation's 'decadence'.[5] In this thirty-page pamphlet, Virgilio denounced *Tosca* as representative of the current decline of Italian music, linking it to ominous trends in Italian society as a whole.

The decision on Puccini's part to set Victorien Sardou's *La Tosca*, which he had watched in 1889 and 1895, raised eyebrows in Italy from the outset. Puccini's librettists were initially unwilling to adapt such material; Giacosa voiced his reservations about it to Giulio Ricordi as early as 1896, anticipating many of the objections later levelled by the press:

> I am profoundly convinced that *Tosca* is not a good subject for operatic treatment. On first reading it seems to be, thanks to the fast pace and the obviousness of the dramatic action. ... But the more one gets inside the action and penetrates each scene to draw out lyric or poetic life from it, the more one is convinced of its absolute unadaptability for music theatre. ... The first act is all duets. It's all duets in the second act (except for the brief torture scene, and even there there are parts when the audience sees only two characters). The third act is one interminable duet. ... This eternal succession of scenes for two characters cannot fail to come across as monotonous. ... It is a drama of coarse emotional events, without poetry.[6]

Ricordi shared Giacosa's negative opinion of the material, expressing to Puccini as late as October 1899 – the month in which the opera's composition was completed – his fear that the consequences of setting Sardou's work would be 'disastrous for my publishing house! ... And terrible for you financially'.[7] Yet Puccini, ignoring the advice of his closest collaborators and mentors, was determined to make a success of his latest work, and was eager to try his hand at setting a *verismo*-esque subject, despite the fact that the *verismo* craze had arguably passed its peak.

By 1900 Puccini bore the full weight of the nation's musical expectations, rather like a queen expected to produce an heir. Audiences had waited almost four years for a new opera from their foremost composer; Puccini's publishers had been promoting *Tosca* for almost as many years. Following the international success of *Manon Lescaut* and *La bohème*, the publicity accompanying the new opera virtually guaranteed it commercial success. Michele Virgilio, who had mocked Puccini's 'uneducated' followers four years earlier in his review of *La bohème*, noted that the people had once again pinned all their expectations on Puccini as the nation's musical saviour:

> Immense was the hope invested in the success of Maestro Puccini's work by art and by the Italian public. For two years, from one end of the Peninsula to the other, high hopes had been invested in this Messiah, who should have been able to reaffirm once more the supremacy of Italian genius.[8]

As far as the musical establishment was concerned, the need for a 'saviour' who would put Italian music back on course was still acute; critical responses to *La bohème* had been mixed, and hopes were high that Puccini's next work would be more successful. Ricordi was pedalling the sort of nationalistic propaganda that those who hoped Puccini would be the next Verdi were eager to hear. The firm stated in a special supplement to the *Gazzetta musicale di Milano* to mark the première of *Tosca* that the new work would consolidate the illustrious musical tradition of a nation that was a 'glorious standard-bearer' among the world's nations. Ricordi confidently declared:

> From Donizetti, Bellini, Verdi and Ponchielli to Mascagni, Leoncavallo and Puccini: here is the resplendent past and the no less splendid present of our lyric art! The future will be equally luminous![9]

The première of *Tosca* on 14 January 1900 was a predictably lavish event, with all fashionable society converging upon the Teatro Costanzi in Rome, including the usual throng of politicians, royalty, writers, painters, composers (Mascagni, Cilea and Siegfried Wagner among them), and representatives of the Italian, European and American press. A rather jittery mood descended on the theatre when the orchestra had to be silenced by the conductor, Mugnone, after only a few bars, following a disturbance outside that prompted fears of a possible bomb explosion; the atmosphere at the theatre was already apprehensive because of a recent spate of political demonstrations in

Rome. However, even this could not detract from what was a glittering social occasion. The critic of *Il messaggero* described the evening thus:

> All intellectual Rome wanted to attend this artistic event, which had been the most fascinating subject of conversation for so long, and all elegant society, crammed into the boxes, stalls, parterre, the foyer of the theatre and above all in the amphitheatre and the galleries, yearned for the moment when maestro Mugnone would ascend onto his podium, and were anxious to acclaim with sincere and enthusiastic applause the brilliant author of *La bohème*, on whom opera has rightly pinned so many hopes.[10]

Ultimately, of course, *Tosca* was far from being the box office disaster that Ricordi had predicted, and audiences responded enthusiastically to the opera from the outset. The *Gazzetta musicale di Milano* published lengthy reviews of the performances in Rome, Turin and Milan, reprinted numerous reports from the French and British press after the premières in Paris and London, and devoted much space throughout 1900 to regional performances around Italy. The index to the 1900 volume lists forty-nine separate references to the work, averaging almost one report per weekly issue. Despite the ongoing public love affair with Puccini, most critics who took the time to analyse Puccini's score in detail were unconvinced of his success in writing an opera that would reinvigorate Italian music. Using the language of organic development so favoured by progressive critics of the day, Virgilio deemed Puccini not to be a musical 'Messiah' who could carry Italian music forward into the future, but to have produced a work that 'in form and in content, represents a great step backwards in the evolution of opera'.[11]

Sex, violence, politics and lies: such universal themes are the ingredients of Sardou's *La Tosca*, and, one might think, the ingredients of great theatre. However, after the first performance of Puccini's *Tosca*, critics from daily newspapers, popular reviews and scholarly journals alike put on a rare show of unanimity over one issue – the composer's unfortunate choice of subject. The opera's 'depraved' elements provoked discomfort in many, with critics balking at its violence and – although few made direct reference to it – the erotic aspect. Although early audiences seemed to respond to *Tosca* with enthusiasm, critics writing in many different types of publication expressed their concern for the nation's moral well-being. Alfredo Colombani wrote in the staunchly bourgeois *Corriere della sera* that 'in *Tosca* everything is black, tragic, terrible', while Virgilio in his more intellectual pamphlet expressed distaste for the opera's 'atmosphere tinged with blood that pervades and overwhelms everything'.[12] Macchi of *Il mondo artistico*, an illustrated journal run by a Milanese theatrical agency, called Sardou's drama 'one of the least agreeable, most violent and most artificial' of works, which heaped intense sensations one on top of another, to the extent that the audience lost sight of the characters.[13] Thus critics regarded the subject Puccini had chosen as being essentially superficial – all gratuitous sensationalism with little of substance beneath, something that, as we shall see, had implications for the way in which Puccini was perceived to have set the work.

This was only the first of several ways in which the opera's scenario was judged by the Italian reviewers to be intrinsically insincere. Sardou's play was, at root, perceived to be passing itself off as something it was not – cheap melodrama posing as high art, or 'counterfeit tragedy', in the words of Giovanni Battista Nappi of *La perseveranza*.[14] Furthermore, one could never create an honestly Italian opera out of a subject such as this, critics argued, for it summed up all the worst excesses of French decadent literature – sadism, wanton violence, depraved sexuality, murderous women, artificiality, gratuitous sensation – phenomena that Italian critics were eager to depict as incompatible with the national character. The Italian taste around the beginning of the twentieth century for French novels and plays was noted in chapter 1; the tendency for contemporary composers to choose 'lurid' French prose works over Italy's rich heritage of indigenous poetry, as Virgilio put it, was more troubling still.[15] Puccini's persistent avoidance of subjects by Italian writers (in contrast to his contemporary Mascagni, who had made a patriotic choice in his decision to set Verga's *Cavalleria rusticana*) was beginning to attract notice and be deemed unfitting for a national composer. Such concerns pointed the way forward to a concern about Puccini's perceived internationalism that would intensify over the years to come.

Thus, Puccini had chosen a subject widely regarded as insincere in its own right; moreover, it was one perceived to be profoundly unsuited to his personality, leading him to compose in a style that did not strike critics as heartfelt. 'Strong subjects like *Tosca* do not suit Puccini's talent or temperament,' Luigi Torchi wrote in the *RMI*, suggesting that Puccini stick in future to topics of a soft, sentimental character.[16] Such criticisms were levelled not only by Puccini's detractors but also by his supporters and later biographers, although this apparent condemnation of Puccini's sense of judgement by his patrons is not as surprising as it might at first seem. In an essentialist age in which everything from national identities to gender roles was depicted as and widely accepted to be immutable, composers were expected to speak in a recognisable personal 'voice'. This tendency was particularly pronounced in Italy, a country where audiences enjoyed a certain amount of predictability in their operas, and the fact that a sentimental work such as *La bohème* and a violent one such as *Tosca* should have sprung from the same pen seemed to many of Puccini's contemporaries inconceivable. (Ironically, of course, a composer could also be deemed too predictable, and Puccini was accused of 'self-plagiarism' on more than one occasion. The fine line between maintaining a distinctive musical idiom and 'repeating himself' was one that he would have to steer with caution throughout his career.)

Naturally, critics of different persuasions had different agendas in claiming that Sardou's violent work was at odds with Puccini's disposition. For his supporters, *Tosca* was not a subject with which they wanted their great white hope to be associated; rather, they sought a national composer who would produce inoffensive works of soft bourgeois sentimentality. For Puccini's detractors, on the other hand, there were mocking overtones to the charge that Puccini was unsuited to 'strong' subjects: they sought to depict him exclusively as a sentimentalist, incapable of handling 'masculine' scenarios. Virgilio, for example, sought to undermine Puccini's standing both as a composer and as a man when he argued that, when Puccini attempted to set works that were not sweetly sentimental, 'his lyre becomes cold and sterile; it neither convinces nor moves the listener!'[17]

MUSICAL MARIONETTES

Puccini's special appeal to his audience was widely deemed to rest upon his ability to create characters with whom they could empathise. La bohème had found favour with middle-class listeners because they saw in Mimì, Rodolfo and their friends – Bohemians in little more than name – a romanticised version of themselves, their values and their aspirations. Puccini's obituarists and early biographers made much of how, during his impoverished student days at the Milan Conservatoire, he had lived the existence of a 'real life Bohemian', subsisting on meagre diet of beans.[18] Such accounts were doubtless to a large extent embellished, but well into middle age Puccini enjoyed playing at a Bohemian lifestyle: he and several friends had their own 'Bohemian club' in Torre del Lago from 1892, the activities of which seem to have consisted primarily of drinking, playing cards and gossiping about women. If the characters in La bohème were really Puccini and his friends, it would seem that, at the end of the day, the composer was capable only of playing himself, and floundered when faced with the more sharply drawn characters of Sardou's La Tosca.

Whereas La bohème was resolutely opera for a democratic age, such humanity was absent in Tosca, and for many critics the opera's lack of agreeable characters also contributed to the overall sense of insincerity and falseness that it provoked. Virgilio argued that the personalities depicted on stage were depraved: 'Tosca and Scarpia are people created by a sick imagination in a moment of aesthetic aberration.'[19] Far from being even credible, the characters were dishonest creations – puppets masquerading as living and breathing human beings. Virgilio continued: 'All the principal characteristics of the protagonists in Tosca are altered, falsified: they are robots, moved around at the whim of Victorien Sardou without an ounce of logic. From beginning to end we see nothing more than absurd puppets and repugnant situations.'[20]

Although softened somewhat in the hands of Puccini and his librettists, Sardou's characters remained a fundamentally problematic aspect of the opera, for which even a first-rate performance could not make amends. Hariclea Darclée's interpretation of the title role was widely praised, even by critics otherwise hostile to the opera, many commenting upon how her acting skills were on a par with those of the celebrated Sarah Bernhardt, for whom the original spoken version had been a vehicle (Figure 3.1). 'Quirite' in *La lanterna*, for example, praised Darclée's ability to express the most subtle nuances of emotion with a movement, a modulation of the voice, a flick of the eye.[21] This notwithstanding, critics continued to note that the opera's characters were somehow not quite human, for Puccini had been incapable of empathising with them sufficiently to bring them to life. Giorgio Barini – a composer and teacher who reviewed music for many newspapers and journals – wrote in the *Fanfulla della domenica* that Puccini's lack of imagination in this opera (surely criticism enough) offended less than the absence of strongly drawn characters, which rendered the opera insipid and feeble.[22]

For Torchi, meanwhile, Scarpia and Tosca were mere pastiches – a pantomime villain and a cardboard cut-out leading lady, expressing no feeling that was credibly their own:

> And Scarpia – what characterises him musically? Only his motif, the thematic motif that takes its name from him. In his sentimental and erotic outbursts, always expressed with exaggerated pomposity, he is nothing more nor less than the usual lyric baritone, just as Tosca is merely the usual prima donna.[23]

Torchi argued that Scarpia did not sing in the right 'voice', claiming that 'Scarpia uses a language that is too lofty and passionate' and that his love music is 'too lyrical, too sweet' for his personality.[24] He pointed to the 'musical impossibilities' presented by Sardou's drama and its multifaceted levels of deception. A composer such as Verdi

Fig. 3.1. Hariclea Darclée as Tosca, January 1900 (Archivio Storico Ricordi: All rights reserved. Reproduced by permission).

might have been capable of bringing out the necessary contrasts between Scarpia and the lovers, but Puccini had proved himself incapable of shifting between the two worlds:

> To be realistic the musical expression must be two-sided. It must occupy itself simultaneously with both Scarpia and with Cavaradossi and Tosca and it cannot do so. It must be sincere and strong and healthy on the one side and simulated, indifferent and lustful on the other. The drama can be all of this, but the music cannot follow it. ... Musically speaking, Tosca cannot lie.[25]

However, in Torchi's view, Tosca's music did indeed 'lie'. Calling her jealousy motive 'bland, placid, reserved', he argued that the music was not suited to the drama: an expansive hymn of tenderness was, in the context of the character's state of mind at this point in the drama, 'a musical anachronism and a dramatic falsehood'.[26]

To be fair, Torchi was not unremittingly hostile towards Puccini's music in his review. He felt that the composer had found an appropriate musical vein for certain key moments of the drama, such as when Scarpia's motif returns slowly and softly as Tosca arranges the candles around his corpse, writing of this scene: 'It is a genuine, beautiful piece of art, a scene in the background of which still move the shadows of an erotic dream; and a great passion and a mournful misery invade the soul. It works.'[27] Yet effective moments here and there could not compensate for the many deficiencies that Torchi perceived in the opera, and his overall assessment of Puccini's music was that it fitted the dramatic material poorly. Ildebrando Pizzetti, assessing *Tosca* fourteen years later, would be far less generous about the murder scene, calling it 'a rhetorical, false, ridiculous gesture, because it lacks in the music the expression of the character's internal passion required to justify it'.[28]

Even 'Vissi d'arte', destined to become a staple of divas' greatest hits albums, failed to impress many of the first-night critics. Torchi wrote that the aria, although perhaps beautiful in its own right, was in this context 'a curious dramatic improbability of no musical significance',[29] while Virgilio considered it to be musically inspired but dramatically absurd – 'silly, insipid twaddle' at a moment that demanded high drama[30] and Nappi criticised it in the *Perseveranza di domenica* for being 'in the form of a sentimental academic arioso'.[31] Thus even the aria in which Tosca seemingly bares her soul was interpreted by the critics as colourless, academic and utterly unsuited to its context, and Cavaradossi's victory cry was, for many critics, equally unpersuasive.[32] The lovers' plight ultimately failed to stir the listeners' emotions; Virgilio wrote that the majority of the third act 'neither convinces nor moves, since it is the artful product of a cold, insincere music'.[33]

The perception of the characters as musical marionettes would re-emerge in considerations of Puccini's music in later years. In an article published in the serious music review *Musica* in 1911, bluntly entitled '"Brutality" in Puccini', Mario Thermignon objected to Puccini's obsession with physical suffering as a purely sensational effect. As a prime example he pointed to the moment when Cavaradossi comes onstage to show off his bleeding limbs, and dismissed Cavaradossi's death as *burratinesca* – 'puppet-like'.[34] References to Puccini's puppet-like characters would re-emerge a quarter of a century after the composition of *Tosca*, as we shall see, when Puccini set *Turandot*, another 'strong' subject. The connotations of such rhetoric would by then have taken on a rather different twist, but references to musical 'puppets' in Puccini's works around the turn of the twentieth century were calculated to raise two key concerns. The first was primarily aesthetic – Puccini's compositional 'insincerity', and apparent desire to manipulate his audience's emotions cynically with characters who were false rather than genuinely felt (with little success, if the critics were to be believed). The second concern had wider cultural and social ramifications: *Tosca*, with its puppet-like characters, was depicted by critics as symbolic of what seemed to many to be an age in Italy's history profoundly lacking in heroes.

AN AGE WITHOUT HEROES

A new mood descended upon Italy in the early years of the twentieth century – one that placed the concept of heroism at its heart. This was in part a reaction against the fact that, from the 1890s, the middle classes were coming to dominate Italian society, both materially and socially. This group, who read the *Illustrazione italiana* and enjoyed Puccini's operas, have consistently been characterised by historians as epitomising the spirit of the Italian *fin de siècle* and the Giolitti regime. For them, the start of the new century marked the onset of a more prosperous era, which would bring with it electricity, cars, foreign holidays and hitherto-undreamed-of leisure opportunities. But Italy in 1900 was a place of paradoxes: the nation that enjoyed genteel afternoon teas in the Milan Galleria was a very different one from the nation of growing agrarian unrest and urban uprisings. Far from consolidating itself as a homogeneous country, Italy's internal difficulties had intensified by 1900, as the gap between rich and poor grew ever wider, a tendency that was increasingly difficult to ignore as the workers began to mobilise. The profound dissatisfaction that many of the disenfranchised poor felt would reach a peak with the assassination of King Umberto I by an anarchist in July 1900, six months after the première of *Tosca*.

Added to this, a further backlash against the bourgeoisie came from a young generation of intellectuals that reached maturity around 1900, bored with their lack of a heroic cause for which to fight and craving a 'Risorgimento' of their own. Over the coming years, this group would promote a new and aggressive style of nationalism, which would have ramifications for cultural criticism as much as for politics. This new nationalism, which will be considered in more depth in chapter 5, would pave the way to the confrontational posturing of the Futurists, and ultimately to Fascism. Although *Tosca* predated the founding of the first radical journals in which the young intellectuals' ideals were expressed (such as Corradini's *Il regno*, 1903–1906), the seeds of this new mood were already growing by 1900. Throughout the 1890s, Gabriele D'Annunzio had promoted a quasi-Nietzschean vision of a *superuomo*, who would bring about Italy's redemption – a vision embraced enthusiastically by the young nationalists. They believed that heroism was what was needed to bind the people together at a time when the nation was beginning to fragment; this sense of heroism was profoundly lacking in the comfortable complacency of the Giolitti era. For the middle classes, heroism was something unrelated to their everyday lives, a mere game at which one might play. For everybody else, whether intellectuals seeking a new model of Italian nationalism or disenfranchised workers seeking rights, a heroic cause was something that they desperately craved, and that should be transmitted as much through the nation's culture as through foreign policy or social action. In this new political mood, characterised by stark social tensions, *Tosca* – an opera that lacked both a heroic style of music and a heroic plot (or, rather, whose characters merely feigned heroics) – was a deeply problematic work.

SIMULATED PASSIONS

For those music critics attuned to this new mood, the vivid subject matter of *Tosca* demanded to be set to music of an equivalent boldness. Unfortunately, despite Puccini's reputation as a 'man of the theatre', *Tosca* also disappointed on this count, with many critics complaining that he had removed the hard edges from Sardou's play, which, although perhaps disagreeable, were an inextricable part of it. Giorgio Barini carped in the *Fanfulla della domenica* that the work contained two or three strong dramatic moments, but that these had been set to music with insufficient vigour.[35] Apparently cautious about alienating his listeners, Puccini had been unable to find an appropriate musical idiom for the events on stage. Vincenzo Morello of *La tribuna* (a friend and patron of D'Annunzio's, and the founder of the lavishly illustrated *Tribuna illustrata*, who wrote under the pseudonym 'Rastignac') scorned the timid and insipid opera that had resulted: 'Out of fear, perhaps, of falling into vulgarity; out of fear of being less elegant or less correct than he has been, Puccini has sought to soften all the work's angles, to put a brake on its impetuosity, to suffocate, as far as is possible, all its boldness.'[36] The torture scene, in particular, was an episode Puccini had set with excessive timidity, as Torchi explained:

> Moreover [the scene] contains no original, penetrating music, underlining the tragic violence of such a cruel event: the musical language doesn't become sublime with the pain and heroism of the torture victim. There are no notes that bleed, no groans, cries of agony, no howls of the most savage human protestation.[37]

Gushing as ever, the *Gazzetta musicale di Milano* called the torture scene 'tremendously moving',[38] but for many critics this intensely dramatic episode was precisely the moment that failed to move the audience. Torchi and others argued that Cavaradossi's victory cry was dramatically implausible in the character's torture-weakened state. The critic for *Il secolo* reported that the music of Act II made little impression and was more 'coldly received' than that of the other two acts, and correspondents for *La nazione* and *Il messaggero* also reported that this act left the audience cold.[39] Virgilio simply called it 'ugly and anti-aesthetic'.[40] The critic of *Il mondo artistico* wrote that 'the second [act] seems to mark a considerable drop in temperature',[41] while Mascagni wrote in a letter to Illica of the 'icy coldness' that greeted it – not forgetting to add that hostility to Puccini was natural in Rome, where his own work *Iris* was 'more popular than any other opera'.[42]

What a subject such as *Tosca* demanded was a bold, impassioned, 'masculine' music. Indeed, these were qualities that ought to characterise *all* modern Italian opera, as the critic for *Il mondo artistico* argued in an article published in advance of the first performance of *Tosca*, stipulating what Italy's artistic establishment demanded of Puccini's work:

> Art demands a work of value and of substance from the young Lucchese composer; one that is moving but enduring; one that has both geniality and solidity; and that has blood and muscles under the glamour of its trappings and the charm of its ornamentation.[43]

For many critics, however, *Tosca* was a work devoid of 'blood and muscles'; it was in fact *nothing but* 'trappings' and 'ornamentation', terms loaded with gendered associations that would pave the way to the more vicious attacks on Puccini's masculinity that we shall encounter in the next two chapters. Playing upon the same theme, Morello portrayed the opera as anodyne, likening Puccini's art to a 'feminine' needle where it should have been a 'masculine' arrow:

> Art should be an arrow of gold or lead, like those of mythological love or hate, but that goes straight to its target and strikes hearts and excites imaginations. Last night the arrow's point was covered with cotton wool and flew through lace. The public made a great effort to catch sight of it in the air. And remained bewildered in the search.[44]

It is evident from such comments that there was considerable concern among the more serious contemporary music critics that Italian opera had lost its heroic bite, become softened, neutered even, as composers pandered to the tastes of the ever-more-influential bourgeoisie. This idea that Puccini prioritised only the 'superficial' elements of composition at the expense of a more profound depth, that his works were at their core somehow devoid of meaning, was a criticism that had begun to gain ground, as we have seen, in the reviews of *La bohème*, and that critics would utter even more vocally in the reviews of *Madama Butterfly*, many of which were organised around the metaphor of the 'over-decorativeness' of the opera.

At the crux of many critics' objections to *Tosca* was the idea that it was a work fundamentally lacking in drama, foreshadowing Kerman's central objection to *Tosca* half a century later – that its music often seems extraneous and that 'a work of art in which music fails to exert the central articulating function should be called by some other name than opera'.[45] For instance, Primo Levi (an early-twentieth-century music critic rather than the better-known novelist of the same name) reported that many in 1900 were calling Puccini's opera 'a situation rather than a drama' and claiming that 'in *Tosca* there are no feelings, but merely the reflection of feelings', although this was not a view that Levi himself shared.[46] Such claims may seem surprising, but *Tosca* struck many critics more as a half-baked display of theatrical effects than as the sincerely felt human drama it ostensibly claimed to be. An opera that might seem at first glance to be all flaming passion, was, according to Torchi, profoundly lacking in genuine emotion:

> There is no real, strong, overflowing passion – whether sorrow, love, disdain or prayer – in Puccini's melody. Tosca is without tragic force; hers are not the notes of a desperate passion, not the frenzies of jealousy, not the shattering of an abused soul, not the scheming of vendetta, not the flames that galvanise heroes. Puccini's music has no nerves, no jerks, no shudders.[47]

This fundamental 'falseness' in *Tosca* was encapsulated in Morello's claim that where there should have been passion there was mere 'simulation'.[48] Morello questioned Puccini's status as national composer by drawing direct comparison with Verdi, in whose hands even a subject such as *Tosca* would have attained the status of a great work of art.[49] Morello's choice of imagery here is striking, particularly his reference to 'knives sparkling in a brawl', which conjures up images of duels to the death in defence of family honour, still very much a part of life in some poorer areas of Italy at the turn of the twentieth century (as vividly brought to life in recent *verismo* works such as *Cavalleria rusticana*). His message is clear: Verdi knew how to write 'manly' music and how to transport the listener to the realm of the sublime, pre-empting Kerman's later claim that 'Verdi aimed for something deeper in his operas than Puccini did':[50]

> We have in Italy, alive and still fresh in his almost divine old age, the grand maestro of dramatic music: Giuseppe Verdi. When a drama made up of limping verses or disconnected strophes appears on the stage, the genius that is Verdi takes it over and brings it to life, and the very essence of Italian passion constantly explodes in the notes and musical phrases, like knives sparkling in a brawl, and blood flows from lacerated hearts. Everything is hot and smouldering in the Verdian expression of dramatic passion, and quivers and shakes and writhes, as if in life's harshest torments, before pain and death, and the soul weeps, and the voice cries out, and the being rises upon wings of flame above all society's conventions.[51]

PSEUDO-MUSIC

Seemingly lacking in sincerity at every dramatic level, Puccini's opera was even perceived by critics as not containing 'proper' music. Many shared Giacosa's opinion that Sardou's story lent itself poorly to musical treatment. Alfredo Colombani, critic for the *Corriere della sera* and also the author of a book on nineteenth-century opera, regarded the problems in Sardou's work to be so fundamental as to be insuperable: 'the original weakness of the drama – its excess of sensationalism and absence of any psychological element – remained a visible obstacle to the free development of Puccini's musical imagination'.[52] Most crucially, Sardou's plot had a dramatic structure that discouraged the inclusion of prolonged passages of extended lyrical writing, and those that Puccini strove to include were, as we have seen, regarded largely as dramatically unjustified. In the entire first act Virgilio could detect no continuity of style or thought; the concerns about organicism that many critics had expressed with regard to *La bohème* had clearly not disappeared:

> The ideas, the episodes are disconnected. ... The whole of this first part of *Tosca* makes me feel as though I am looking at a mosaic made by a craftsman without a pre-arranged design![53]

Giorgio Barini, writing in the *Fanfulla della domenica*, noted an overabundance of scenic effects in Giacosa's and Illica's libretto that followed on from one another incessantly, and a series of small episodes that lent themselves to what he called 'acoustic' rather than musical setting.[54] Giacosa and Illica had presented Puccini with a fragmented libretto, which he had matched with an equally fragmented musical score ('short, fragmented and brief phrases, adapted to a fractured, rapid, agitated dialogue', according to Colombani of the *Corriere della sera*[55]) incorporating 'mere noise': bells, gunshots, *verismo*-esque shouts and cries. Barini lamented the fact that 'there is no doubt that the maestro often wanted to exclude music, considering the incredible number of "parlato" sections, which we meet constantly throughout this lengthy score, even in the chorus parts!'[56] The claim that Puccini's score was essentially 'lacking in music' was reiterated by most of the more serious critics who reviewed the opera. According to Virgilio:

> Everything is artificial: not one note is truly felt. They are sounds that follow on one from the next; effects that attempt to mask the lack of passion of the scenic moment; deafening sonorities that are inappropriate to the dramatic situation; styles and cadences cobbled together at random, unsuited to the general character of the music that clothes the drama![57]

For many critics, *Tosca* epitomised all the worst tendencies of Italian music of the turn of the century, as young composers turned their back upon the Italian tradition of melody and lyricism, which even progressive critics such as Torchi wished to maintain. He lamented the substitution of veristic 'effects' for melody, writing: 'Today in the lyric theatre, [the singer] makes noises, recites, declaims, and shouts rather than singing – and the system, so I am told, will be extended – that is to say, the essential element of opera, the singer's voice, will be renounced altogether.'[58] Morello's impatience with Puccini's 'dishonesty' is palpable in his grumpy rebuke that 'musical "intent" is not enough: we want music'.[59] He depicted Puccini's opera as a grotesque, distorted charade:

> For half an hour we listened to two characters singing in monosyllables, exclamations, swear words, short phrases and truncated words. ... How is it possible to prolong this fragmented dialogue for so long? ... Musical characters need to have something to say, need the words to express their own thoughts and feelings: gestures and grimaces are not enough![60]

If the voices were treated in a clumsy manner, the use of the orchestra was deemed little better, with several critics, including Virgilio, Morello and Torchi, commenting upon Puccini's unimaginative orchestral palette. Particularly offensive was the horn theme at the beginning of Act III that is repeated unaccompanied and in unison by Tosca and Cavaradossi, a passage Torchi labelled 'pseudo-music', writing: 'of all the dusty junk, the composer has really chosen a rancid flower'.[61]

With this, Puccini's third major commercial work, concern began to grow about his ability to generate original ideas, as critics chastised him for his lack of imagination and tendency to rely upon a small number of hackneyed conventions. The opera's perceived lack of emotional credibility was in part blamed upon Puccini's use of a consistently similar melodic contour throughout, irrespective of dramatic context. Torchi's assessment of the originality of *Tosca* was unguarded and damning:

> This opera does not reveal the development of new qualities in the musician, but shows him to be excessively stuck in his ways and, unfortunately, those resources that brought him glory and fortune appear to have been exhausted. ... Puccini, with his new music, has not said anything new to us.[62]

Torchi developed this objection more fully in his final assessment of the opera; here he pre-empts the charges of self-plagiarism that would be so central to the *Madama Butterfly* fiasco, and the objections to Puccini's 'internationalism' that would gather pace over the next decade:

> Puccini, in *Tosca*, has not composed an original work. He has run into a kaleidoscopic manipulation of styles, covering the full gamut from Wagner to Massenet. He has said nothing new, perhaps because he too has nothing new to say in this genre; ... he has merely repeated that which we already know.[63]

Torchi's words here about *Tosca* illustrate a fear shared by many contemporary commentators that the national art was becoming unrecognisable because it was losing the very features that had made it Italian. Rather than listening to the words of Verdi, who had exhorted young composers to study the great Italian works of the past, master their technique and 'put a hand on their heart and write down what is dictated to them from within',[64] the younger generation had looked instead to other sources of inspiration.

Several critics objected to the 'fact' that Puccini was not merely being unoriginal but was also undermining Italian traditions by emulating harmful foreign styles. This amounted to charlatanism, a serious offence in an artistic tradition in which sincerity was judged to be paramount. Giorgio Barini argued that Puccini had adopted a clumsy Wagner-inspired style in *Tosca* but that his motives merely assumed a 'remembrance' function, without the more subtle power of suggestion of Wagner's leitmotifs.[65] For Torchi, Puccini's attempt to write leitmotifs was misguided, unconvincing and 'un-Italian'. Again, it is interesting to note that, although Torchi was an ardent Wagnerian, he did not believe that Italian composers should attempt to follow Wagner's model; for him, as for most other critics of his time, the need to preserve a distinctively Italian music was imperative:

> The first of [Puccini's] peculiarities is the use of thematic motives that, with the exception of two cases (Scarpia's and Angelotti's themes) are the products of instinct, of vague impressions, but not of clear ideas. Adopted without circumstantial elaboration or symphonic drama, the thematic motive is a simple reminiscence device and swiftly becomes tiresome. It is out of place, like a cabaletta in a work by Wagner.[66]

Barini also noted a superficial appropriation of mawkish and affected techniques borrowed from French music (presumably he is referring to Gounod and Massenet), such as liberal use of the harp and muted strings, which gave his music an overly 'sugary' air. Moreover, Barini claimed Puccini's avoidance of Italian characteristics to have been wilful rather than naïve: 'Puccini seems knowingly to avoid the hallmarks of the Italian school.'[67] This was not acceptable Italian music.

THE MALADIES OF ITALIAN MUSIC

In Torchi's view, Puccini was not entirely to blame for the deficiencies of his work, for he was merely a representative of his time: 'as an artist he is suffering from a common malady'.[68] Other young composers were equally at fault, but Puccini, as the most prominent, fashionable and commercially successful composer of his day, was targeted for particular condemnation. Virgilio went further in his elaboration of the implications of *Tosca*'s deficits. In his view the opera was more than a passive manifestation of societal decadence; it contributed actively to a crisis in Italian opera and in Italian culture more generally. He used *Tosca* as the basis of a thesis about the intrinsic degeneration of the Italian nation.

Virgilio's pamphlet argued explicitly that Italian composers were losing their ability to compose 'Italian' music, which had entered a period of decline: 'Our artistic life feeds only on lies and shallow hypocrisy, to hide, under false blandishments, the canker that has gnawed at our art for some time.'[69] It was crucial for this individual racial stamp to be expressed through the art of each nation:

> Every people, every race, has its own art, which is the ethnic product of the external conditions of life, of climate, of light and of temperature in which the population is compelled to live and think. ... The endeavour of the chosen minds, of the men who honour their land, was and will always be to synthesise in their work the qualities of the race and also, sometimes, those of their region.[70]

Virgilio argued that Dante, Michelangelo, Raffaelo and Poliziano had, through their respective arts, been profoundly expressive of the Latin soul during the Renaissance, just as Goethe, Schiller, Schopenhauer, Beethoven and Bach had all conveyed a clear sense of Germanness in their works. Modern Italian artists, however, whether composers, writers or painters, expressed nothing of the Italian spirit, largely thanks to their embracing of foreign influences. The characteristics of one national style, critics agreed, could never be successfully transplanted onto the artworks of another nation; thus, any Italian composer who attempted to emulate German or French music would inevitably produce a work that was at its core soulless, empty of true meaning, a lie.

The 'dilution' of Italian music had serious political implications, as opera had long been a form of culture that Italy exported to the rest of the Western world. Virgilio pointed to Italy's past artistic superiority: 'Italy was the cradle of all forms of music; ... the blue sky and the sweet climate made pure and simple melody spring naturally from the soul of the people.'[71] In the modern age, Italian artistic superiority was under threat, as he explained:

> Italian music is going through a truly unhappy phase! This fact is of very great importance for our national life, if you consider that until a few years ago our country occupied the first rung in the artistic field, and if you consider the not insignificant benefit we received from exporting our artistic production abroad.[72]

Not only did Italy lack a physical empire, but it was now allowing its cultural and artistic 'empire' to fall into decline. For Virgilio, works such as *Tosca* represented a threat to the very identity of the Italian race and the national temperament. He issued an apocalyptic warning: artists' increasing inability to express the identity of the race through culture spelled 'the beginning of the end for the existence of that race in terms of artistic production'.[73] Pointing out that the culture of a nation required constant regeneration and renewal in order to remain in good health, Virgilio provided a historical precedent for Italy's plight: that of the ancient Greeks. Through this reference to a noble empire that had ultimately succumbed to decline, he sought both to allude to Italy's own glorious Classical empire and to pose a dire warning for the future; the Greeks, content to rest upon their laurels in the shadow of the Parthenon, had allowed all the artistic qualities that had made them great to wither.[74]

Yet despite his thoroughly damning assessment of *Tosca*, Virgilio maintained a somewhat desperate optimism that Puccini would indeed prove himself to be a 'Messiah' at some point in the future, perhaps resigning himself to the lack of any more promising alternative. He concluded his pamphlet with an expression of hope that Puccini would find a stimulus for his next work that would allow Italy to resume its 'rightful' place in the world:

> I believe that Puccini must now understand the inanity of this attempt at dramatic opera, and, for the good of art and of our Italy, will be able to find verse adapted to his exquisite artistic nature, and that as soon

as possible he will give us the work of art that is so greatly anticipated and so greatly desired. ... I hope that *Tosca* will be a salutary example for young composers, to make them return to pure sources of poetry and art, because only thus can we reoccupy the position in the world that is due to us.[75]

AN ITALIAN OPERA?

Despite the damning criticisms levelled at *Tosca* by critics such as Torchi and Virgilio, Puccini's staunchest supporters rushed to his aid with their customary nationalist propaganda. They proclaimed that there was in fact much evidence of 'Italian' qualities in *Tosca*, although their argument was flimsy because it hinged largely upon the customary hagiographic compliments ('in you is the reflection of the radiance and warmth of our southern sky'[76]), often unsubstantiated by reference to specific aspects of the opera. The *Gazzetta musicale di Milano* announced that the Rome newspapers had unanimously declared *Tosca* a triumph and cited *Il popolo romano* as calling the new work an 'unquestionable, impressive success for Italian music'.[77] The *Gazzetta* also quoted critic 'A', of the *Rivista politica e letteraria*, as having said that *Tosca* contained the necessary lyricism – something found to be lacking by those critics who analysed the score in depth – to be deemed a genuinely Italian opera:

> Oh melody, old friend of ours, how very welcome it is to see you fresh, innocent, sincere and ever adorable in an Italian work of art, after having digressed so far away from us ... , to find you in such a work, not disguised in the foreign fashion, as is normal, but once again delineated according to the national character.[78]

Nasi, writing for the *Gazzetta musicale di Milano*, claimed that Puccini's latest work had fulfilled 'Italian' criteria admirably with its 'evocativeness, elegance, penetration, persuasiveness, effectiveness'.[79] The critic for *Il messaggero* (probably Primo Levi), meanwhile, recognised the foreign influences in the opera, but argued that Puccini had maintained an 'Italian' identity throughout, and even attempted to posit Puccini's music as the perfect amalgam of foreign and indigenous, masculine and feminine characteristics, writing: 'Within his music he condenses and sums up all the elegance of Massenet and the vigour of Berlioz, but he always remains Italian in character, in design, in inspiration. His music is both a sweet web of lace and a torrent that rushes impetuously; it has both the softness of velvet and the majesty of infinity.'[80]

For 'Quirite', reviewing the opera in *La lanterna*, Puccini's work confirmed both his stylistic continuity and his status as Italy's great hope:

> Puccini continues clearly and boldly along the bright path that he laid in his previous operas and the new success that he has received with *Tosca* demonstrates even to those who didn't wish him that success that he ranks as number one amongst our young modern composers.[81]

'Quirite' attacked the pomposity of contemporaries who dictated that a work should be constructed in a certain way. Having overheard an 'ardent Wagnerian' pondering what, in terms of artistic progress, Puccini could have hoped to accomplish with this opera, 'Quirite' responded with a catalogue of the composer's achievements. For him, Puccini was a 'born melodist' who had put passion, elegance and 'all his heart' into the work.[82] Puccini had created 'pleasing music, which is clear in [its] melodies, pure in inspiration, sincere in sentiment, simple and effective in orchestration, and above all interesting'.[83] In contrast to Torchi's comments about the disappearance of lyricism from Puccini's music, this critic emphasised the profusion of lyrical moments, including, most surprisingly, Act II (the act other critics had found particularly objectionable), which he referred to as 'so charged with, so heavy with, so rich with melodic sweetness'.[84] More explicitly, he noted that '[Puccini] wanted to create an opera in which there were also human parts, in which the singer is not sacrificed or overwhelmed or relegated to the status of an onlooker'.[85] 'Quirite' applied the impressionistic language of Puccini's hagiographers, drawing upon references to health, purity and honesty, to the Act III invocation

'O dolci mani', which, he claimed, 'wells up from the soul as a spring of restorative and beneficial water gushes from a rock' and 'is already on everybody's lips'.[86] Finally, 'Quirite' boldly asserted that the work was a victory for the Latin over the Teutonic, paradoxically positing Italian opera as Siegfried, come to liberate the world:

> A pure, solemn, vibrant, total and utter triumph: a triumph as music, as a performance and above all a triumph of Italianness, of that Italianness that all the warped novelty-hating Mimes would like to suffocate in the hearts and minds of our young composers, but that to their vexation continues to reveal itself and to shine in the bold and ardent rhythms of the new melodies.[87]

Continuity of tradition, originality, primacy of melody, sincerity of sentiment, purity, health and well-being? Was 'Quirite' really listening to the same opera as the other critics? For him, Puccini's new work contained the full range of positively Italian features: he inverted the very objections expressed by the majority of his contemporaries. Although many present-day listeners would agree that there are moments of sublime lyricism in *Tosca*, this critic's overblown praise fails to convince; the anti-Wagner reference and the use of stale clichés suggest that he was assessing *Tosca* according to a pre-set agenda rather than on its own terms. It is hardly surprising that he should have come out with bland, patriotic praise in a conservative and intellectually undemanding publication such as *La lanterna*, an agency magazine that contained only one detailed article per issue and whose readers expected musical gossip rather than music criticism.

For the most part, Puccini's supporters heard what they wanted to hear in *Tosca*, and their assessments of this work were near identical to their comments about all of Puccini's other operas. While those journals whose interests depended upon Puccini's success continued to surround him with grandiose nationalist imagery, the majority of critics expressed profound concern about Puccini's status as a supposed national idol. The composer vaunted as an emblem of national culture had failed to produce a work that could fruitfully be employed for patriotic instruction. Close analysis of the

Tosca reviews reveals recurring anxieties that connected to more fundamental concerns in Italian society. Many of these objections would re-emerge a decade later in Torrefranca's monograph *Giacomo Puccini e l'opera internazionale*, but this time with an overtly politicised and gendered twist.

Although *Tosca* swiftly gained popular support after a shaky first night, with theatres the length of Italy clamouring to produce the work, it did not provide the feeling of well-being that the serious Italian musical establishment sought; in fact, it further accentuated existing feelings of cultural malaise. In composing an 'insincere' opera, Puccini was deemed by many to have betrayed himself, his operatic heritage, and even his nation. Puccini's reputation depended upon his continuing to display certain highly prized qualities, yet most critics believed him to have abandoned them in his new work. The critical 'failure' of *Tosca* – the latest much-hyped work by Italy's national composer – represented much more than a personal embarrassment for Puccini and his librettists: it hammered a further nail into the very coffin of Italian music. Virgilio wrote: 'So many truly talented young men, led astray by a false desire for popularity, squander their intellectual powers on an artistic form that, over the long term, will be the death of Italian opera and of Italian art!'[88] Just as Tosca the character acts out a role, so too did *Tosca* the work: it acted out the role of an 'Italian opera'. For Giorgio Barini of the *Fanfulla della domenica*, Puccini's operas had never been properly 'Italian' but his latest work was a deliberate renunciation of national values: 'Puccini, whose *Le villi* showed the influence of Ponchielli, whose *Manon Lescaut* and *La bohème* still presented some small residue of *italianità*, seems to have renounced it in *Tosca*.'[89]

Tosca had a particularly symbolic status: its performance date in 1900 made it the last significant Italian opera of the nineteenth century, and the expectation that it would bridge the gap between two centuries intensified the anticipation surrounding the première. But *Tosca* failed to fulfil the hopes invested in it; the following words, written in the journal *Ars nova* in 1903, reveal that the sense of profound dissatisfaction many contemporary critics felt with Italian music continued into the new century:

> We might well say that nobody, or almost nobody, has been successful in adequately continuing an era of great and undisputed glory for our nation. In passages here and there we find a fleeting throb of enthusiasm, but immediately a great silence descends, the heavy torpor of death.[90]

Tosca was not regarded by the majority of critics as either an honourable tribute to the nineteenth century or a fitting way forward to the twentieth. However, it certainly merited the label of the ultimate *fin-de-siècle* opera, containing as it did all the hallmarks of turn-of-the-century decadence: fragmentation, falsification, immorality and a nexus of pleasure and pain. It was with trepidation that musical Italy looked forward to the twentieth century.

4 | A frame without a canvas: *Madama Butterfly* and the superficial

'*Madama Butterfly* flopped, flopped irredeemably. Last night's performance at La Scala was not just a failure; it was what one might frankly call a disaster, a catastrophe.'[1] Of all operatic fiascos, the first performance of *Madama Butterfly* at La Scala on 17 February 1904 ranks among the most notorious. The ominous silence that greeted much of Act I was replaced in Act II by contemptuous grunts, bellows, guffaws and even bird and animal noises. The rumpus was so loud that the voices and instruments were inaudible, to the point that the leading lady, Rosina Storchio, was reduced to tears when she could not hear her cues. The principal reason for this near-riot was the audience's impatience with a work that seemed excessively long by the customary standards of Italian opera, consisting of a first act of an hour and an interminable second act of ninety minutes.

However, the swiftness with which the disruption spread through the auditorium led to conspiracy theories, with Puccini's supporters immediately declaring foul play. The Ricordi journal *Musica e musicisti* discreetly relegated news of the disastrous première to a brief statement, claiming that the audience had been ill disposed to the opera from the moment the curtain rose, had gone on to create a pandemonium and had 'left the theatre as pleased as Punch!'[2] The use of a hostile claque to disrupt an opera by a rival was not an uncommon practice at this time, although the *Madama Butterfly* première was an extreme case. It is certainly plausible that Puccini's contemporaries and the Sonzogno publishing house, Casa Ricordi's arch-rival, would have felt jealous of the composer's international success, celebrity status and top billing by 1904, although it has never been possible to establish with any certainty the precise culprits responsible for the fiasco. However, the theory put about by Ricordi that the performance had been deliberately sabotaged conveniently

| 97

deflected attention away from the shortcomings critics perceived in the opera.

Naturally, the failure of the opera came as a huge blow to Puccini. He and his close coterie of collaborators were convinced that the new opera would be a sensation: rehearsals had gone well, and the run looked set to be a sell-out. Moreover, Puccini felt confident in his cast (especially Storchio, whom he had hand-picked two years earlier – Figure 4.1), and the set designs realistically representing the interior of a Japanese house looked stunning. And as we have already established, Puccini was by 1904 an international celebrity, and a new Puccini opera was guaranteed to make headlines not only in Italy, but all over Western Europe, and even in the United States. Huge hype surrounded the première, as it had for the composer's previous two works, and all Milanese high society rushed to buy tickets. But although the world was shocked by the opera's failure, it was in fact no bolt from the blue. Rather, it was part of a trajectory of criticism, with reviewers reiterating and building upon concerns already expressed about *La bohème* and *Tosca*, and pointing the way forward to Fausto Torrefranca's devastating attack on Puccini in 1912. What made the hostile reaction to the première so worrying was the fact that ordinary audience members – Puccini's supposedly loyal public – had now become aware of troubling aspects of his music that had concerned critics for some time.

Although the criticisms levelled at the opera by the press were seemingly diverse, a single idea recurred persistently – that the opera was all surface and no substance. This notion was often expressed using metaphors from the visual arts that suggested that Puccini's music was overly 'decorative'. Such figures of speech might seem to be fitting, given Puccini's keen interest in the minutiae of stage design, costume and movement, and his efforts to 'compose the décor into the music', as David Kimbell puts it.[3] However, when critics made reference to 'lacquer', 'resin' and 'varnish', they intended it as no compliment, as we shall see. It is important to note at this point that when critics talked about 'decoration' with regard to Puccini's operas they were not referring to the melodic writing. Indeed, given his

Fig. 4.1. Rosina Storchio as Madama Butterfly, February 1904 (Arichivio Stonico Ricordi. All rights reserved. Reproduced by permission).

tendency for predominantly syllabic text setting and the striking lack of vocal embellishments and decorative cadenzas in his scores, references to 'decoration' seem at first sight to be nonsensical. This is something of which his music is practically devoid, in comparison with, say, that of Rossini, which has sometimes been described as being little more than embellishment.[4] When art critics condemned ornament they were referring to an abundance of meaningless curlicues and arabesque-like figures,[5] but music critics discussing *Madama Butterfly* did not draw a direct parallel between these and any vocal or instrumental equivalent: the contemporary visual arts were cluttered with ornament in a way Puccini's music certainly was not. Rather, music critics drew analogies with the decorative arts to indicate what they perceived to be a shallowness common to modern art forms – superficially attractive surfaces masking the absence of deeper structures.

In the case of *Madama Butterfly*, references to 'decoration' or 'detail' were an oblique metaphor used to articulate many subtle, complex and mutually entangled anxieties about the opera, some concerned with its formal and technical aspects (building upon criticism of *La bohème* and *Tosca*), others connected to its social role. Critics detected parallels between Puccini's opera and the contemporary decorative arts in terms of function and intended audience (both regarded as somewhat superficial). As we have seen, the reception of Puccini's operas was guided to such a degree by extra-musical agendas that critics frequently disregarded the music itself. The seemingly paradoxical attack on *Madama Butterfly* for being too 'decorative' was often simply a way of signalling some sort of excess that the critics perceived in the opera: it was too international, too feminine, too frivolous, too bourgeois – issues central to 'the Puccini problem'.

A FRAME WITHOUT A CANVAS

'And so in place of the opera we have the cornice, the frame, the decoration; but we have no substance – that is to say ideas, thought, imagination.'[6] Thus wrote an anonymous critic reviewing *Madama Butterfly* in the popular Milanese theatre magazine the *Frusta teatrale* a few days after its première. One would not expect profound analytical comment from a periodical such as this, a middle-brow publication featuring only one detailed review per issue (followed by shorter reviews and listings), which assumed relatively little musical literacy on the part of its readers. However, its critic's curious image of the opera as a 'frame without a canvas' was no mere throwaway remark but encapsulated widespread objections to *Madama Butterfly*. This unknown and long-forgotten reviewer was perhaps unable to articulate his objections to Puccini's opera in technical terms – or avoided doing so for the sake of the journal's lay readership – but nevertheless found an evocative way of signalling a growing discontent with the 'superficial' nature of contemporary Italian opera, which many shared, including those ostensibly well disposed to the composer.

This metaphor merits closer scrutiny. The purpose of a frame is to support, flatter and complement the painting it surrounds. However ornate a frame may be in its own right, its function is ultimately to draw the viewer's attention to something beyond itself. One could well imagine a canvas without a frame, for frames may be substituted and photographic reproductions of paintings rarely show the frame. A frame without a canvas, however, would be inconceivable, disorientating, redundant, at least in Puccini's time – a very odd figure of speech indeed, then. However, although the *Frusta teatrale* critic may not have known it, this was a metaphor with a history.

In a discussion with Toni Gallo of a performance of *La forza del destino* in Vicenza, Verdi wrote in 1869 that 'everything has been turned upside down. The frame has become the canvas!!!'[7] Verdi's comment formed part of a contemporary debate about the desirability of operatic reform along French or German lines; *La forza del destino* was an opera that included a number of 'modern', French-inspired *scene di azione*. Verdi noted in his letter that the audience members in Vicenza had applauded these only half-heartedly, as if such scenes were merely the 'frame', whereas what really interested them (and also the singers, who had performed the tableaux with little enthusiasm) were the old-fashioned, indisputably Italian arias and duets. Thus Verdi pointed out that the audience's demands were at odds with those of the reformers. In saying that 'the frame has become the canvas' Verdi was noting that the reformers' demands had come to prevail, but it is uncertain whether he regarded this as a positive development, despite the presence of 'modern' action scenes in his own opera. The tone of the letter is so ambivalent that it is not clear whether he intended to chastise the public for its resistance to modernisation or was using the audience's reaction in order to vindicate the adverse comments about reform that he had himself expressed elsewhere, often contradicted by his music. Regardless of Verdi's personal view of 'progress', the metaphor of a frame without a canvas was a useful way of talking about a freer approach to composition towards the end of the nineteenth century.

Debates using the metaphor of decoration were therefore part of an intense battle that had raged amongst Italian musicians and critics for several decades about the true essence of opera: what was fundamental to its aesthetic and what was mere inessential detail? In Puccini's case, the critic seems to have been using the frame/canvas image (read: the prioritisation of inessential details over substance) to complain that the opera was long; boring; constructed from small, disconnected pieces of music; overpreoccupied with subplots; and above all relatively lacking in what most critics regarded as the essence of an Italian opera – arias. Certainly, the audience had reacted negatively to the relative lack of arias for the tenor lead, Lieutenant Pinkerton. This was something that Puccini would remedy for the second production of *Madama Butterfly* in Brescia in May 1904, adding a remorseful aria for Pinkerton near the end of the opera ('Addio, fiorito asil'), which satisfied the audience's desire for vocal display, softened his previously thoroughly unsympathetic character and was an important factor in the success of the opera in its revised state.

But it is worth remarking that if Puccini had indeed emphasised 'surfaces' over 'substance' he was very much in keeping with the spirit of his time, for a prioritisation of detail for its own sake was a pan-European marker of the modern in the early 1900s, common to all the arts. For example, Puccini's contemporaries in the visual arts were exploring the genre of Divisionism, characterised by the separation of colour into individual patches or dots. Exponents of this technique in Italy in the 1890s and early 1900s included Giovanni Segantini, Gaetano Previati, Angelo Morbelli and Giuseppe Pellizza da Volpedo.

In the decorative arts, meanwhile, art nouveau and its sister movements (the Jugendstil, the Secession movement and the Italian *stile liberty* or *stile floreale*) took the attractive but ultimately inessential details that had traditionally adorned picture frames – carvings, twists and arabesques – and turned them into objects of aesthetic contemplation in their own right. The new style was seemingly inescapable, for it was not confined to art galleries but impinged upon all areas of everyday life, adorning everything from architecture to armchairs.

Fin-de-siècle literature was no less attentive to details. D'Annunzio, whose works bear the clear influence of the French symbolist and decadent writer Joris-Karl Huysmans,[8] was obsessed with decoration both in terms of subject matter (vivid depictions of colours; precious stones) and in compositional approach (an ultra-refined, hyperbolic prose style). Exaggerated embellishment was the defining hallmark of artistic decadence; Paul Bourget codified what it meant for literature to be decadent in an 1883 essay on Baudelaire:

> A decadent style is that where the unity of the book breaks down to give way to the independence of the page, where the page breaks down to give way to the independence of the sentence, and the sentence to give way to the independence of the word.[9]

Detailed description was no longer something disposable that could be skipped over with no injury to the plot, then, but had become the very essence of literary composition. Such *fin-de-siècle* art, in a sense, aimed precisely to be all 'surface'. Moreover, life also imitated art, for excessive detail was a key factor in styling a decadent personality. The most fashionable artistic figures of the moment surrounded themselves with meaningless clutter, such as D'Annunzio, who wrote: 'My spiritual education draws me irresistibly to the desire for and the acquisition of beautiful things ... divans, precious fabrics, Japanese china, bronzes, ivories, knickknacks, all those useless and beautiful things which I love deeply and passionately.'[10]

All of these innovative art forms came under attack from conservative commentators, who feared them to be signals of the breakdown of traditional aesthetic forms and techniques. But the castigation of decoration as decadent, deceptive and effeminate dates back to ancient rules of rhetoric; the idea that ornament, whether literary or visual, could have a corrupting effect upon both mind and body continued to be a powerful force throughout the Middle Ages and into modern times. Moreover, a peculiarly Italian hostility to ornament emerged around the turn of the twentieth century, largely attributable to the widely disseminated theories of influential criminologist Cesare Lombroso, who identified bodily embellishment in the form of tattoos as signs of an innate criminal disposition, a marker of atavism. Lombroso's theories were diffused not only through his own voluminous published writings, but also through summaries in popular journals, and would have a profound impact upon foreign thinkers. The most famous of these was the Viennese modernist architect Adolf Loos (1870–1933), who built upon Lombroso's theories about tattooing, arguing in a manifesto of 1908 that ornament had no place in modern art or architecture: 'Ornament is no longer a natural product of our culture, but a symptom of backwardness or degeneracy. ... *The evolution of culture is synonymous with the removal of ornamentation from objects of everyday use.*'[11] For Loos, ornament was antithetical to genius in all areas of the arts, including music; he argued that 'Beethoven's symphonies would never have been written by a man who had to dress in silk, velvet, and lace. ... Lack of ornamentation is a sign of intellectual strength.'[12]

Puccini's detractors were merely reiterating an age-old cliché, then, but at a time when extravagant decoration seemed to be impinging upon all aspects of life. Critics drew upon a long tradition of rhetoric positing decoration as something incidental and 'added on' which ostensibly enriches a structure but actually brings about its fragmentation. Ornament signifies overindulgence, digression, fetish, superfluity, immoral luxury, unbridled freedom: all disturbing tropes that seemed to many observers to have taken on heightened significance at the start of the twentieth century. As Rae Beth Gordon observes in her study of ornament in nineteenth-century French literature, 'virtually every definition of ornament connotes the inessential, the superfluous, or the superficial, the "merely" decorative. Ornament, as commonly understood, is an accessory designed simply to please and is therefore fundamentally without meaning, if not morally reprehensible.'[13]

SELF-REPETITION

But how, in stylistic terms, were the 'over-decorative' qualities that marked the contemporary visual arts and literature perceived to be manifested in Puccini's opera, if not in the form of embellished vocal lines? Comments about the over-decorativeness of *Butterfly* were a new way of articulating concerns that had emerged in earlier reviews about Puccini's inability to control large-scale musical and dramatic structures. The anxieties about fragmentation that had emerged persistently from the reviews of *La bohème* were reiterated more vehemently eight years later in the reviews of the first version of *Madama Butterfly*.

The critics' complaints about the opera's supposed emphasis upon surface details were multifaceted. At the most simplistic and immediate level they can be read as a comment on the libretto, which seemed to critics to be preoccupied with lives so trivial that they did not merit setting to music; Cio-Cio-San's status as a 'little person' is confirmed in the Act I love duet, when she sings: 'Noi siamo gente avvezza alle piccole cose, umili e silenziose' ('We are people accustomed to small things, humble and silent'). Puccini's interest in 'little things' was something of which he often boasted, reportedly remarking to a journalist during the later 1900s:

> What tragedies or historical dramas? What heroes, what great memorable figures? I'm not cut out for that sort of thing. I am not a composer of great things; I feel the little things and don't like to set anything other than little things. ... I loved Butterfly because she is a dear little woman who knew how to love so much that she was willing to die for it, and although she knew how to die like a "great historical figure", is still a dear little woman, fragile and beloved like a Japanese doll, without pretensions.[14]

However, Puccini's choice of subjects that tended to concentrate on the plight of humble individuals (metaphorically speaking, the isolated 'detail') rather than the collective experience would be injuriously compared to Verdi from his own time to the present. To extend the critics' own visual imagery: Verdi's operas seemed the history paintings to Puccini's lesser genre pieces. Even after cutting the proposed consulate episode,[15] the *Madama Butterfly* story, particularly the first act, seemed to many critics to be overburdened with superfluous digressions and secondary characters, a point summed up by the critic for *Il marzocco*, identified only as 'Mos':

> The libretto seemed to be so fragmented, so episodic, so overburdened with hollow characters and useless scenes that even Puccini's famous balance and theatrical know-how could not succeed in giving it unity, in bestowing upon it the solidity of a well-proportioned and logical organism.[16]

In their eagerness to create a Japanese ambience – or what they perceived to be a Japanese ambience from their second-hand knowledge of Eastern culture – Puccini and his librettists were deemed to have laid too much emphasis upon inactive, picturesque, over-fussy tableaux, which detracted from the opera's musical and dramatic essence. The same problem would arise some fourteen years later in *Suor Angelica*, also faulted by critics for being overly static.

Musically, too, *Madama Butterfly* seemed to critics to be characterised by a profusion of redundant detail for its own sake, appearing to be an amalgam of styles rather than a homogeneous work. Italian opera had traditionally been a 'fragmentable' genre, in the sense that arias were frequently cut or substituted, and although this was widespread and largely unquestioned by audiences, even Rossini had come under attack for this practice by critics from as early as the 1810s.[17] A different expectation had certainly come to prevail in post-Verdian Italian opera, as the idea of homogeneity became fundamental to perceptions of what constituted a good Italian work of music. Verdi wrote to Du Locle in 1869 that the French style was 'not a work that gushes forth, but a mosaic, as beautiful as you like, but always a mosaic', and added, 'I believe in *inspiration*; you others in *manufacture*' and 'I want art ... not the *arrangement*, the artifice, the *system*, that you prefer.'[18] Puccini's operas were, of course, strongly indebted to French influences, especially the works of Massenet, and *Madama Butterfly* did not seem to have been composed seamlessly, but rather had been compiled precisely in mosaic-like fashion, drawing together a combination of phrases highly reminiscent of those already heard in his earlier works. The opera had scarcely commenced when a murmur of surprise passed through the auditorium as the audience noticed a melodic passage strikingly similar to one from *La bohème*,[19] and others would follow. G. B. Nappi of *La perseveranza* went so far as to call Puccini's latest work 'no more than an encore of *La bohème*, with less freshness and abundance of melodic ideas', claiming the characters in the two operas to be 'almost all the same'.[20]

The suspicion that Puccini was lazily repeating himself was a key factor in the failure of *Madama Butterfly* at La Scala, for although similar charges had been made in the reviews of *La bohème*, the problem was – crucially – by now obvious to ordinary audience members as well as critics. 'Max' (Mario Roux) of *La tribuna* commented upon the poverty of melodic inventiveness in the opera and the hackneyed orchestration, notably the 'saccharine' strings and the incessant abuse of muted trumpets.[21] The critic for *Il secolo*, meanwhile, wrote:

> The treatment of the voice is always the same; the melodic contour is similar to that in his other operas; we still sometimes have the voice in octaves with the syncopated accompaniment; always the continual use of ninths and again the chains of fifths. In short, Puccini repeats himself because he doesn't distance himself from those formulae that he himself has rendered conventional.[22]

One might expect this sort of less-than-enthusiastic response from *Il secolo*, sponsored by Ricordi's publishing rival Sonzogno. But even the customarily gushing Giovanni Pozza of the *Corriere della sera* was forced to concede Puccini's 'obstinate insistence ... on a single melodic effect' to be 'unwise', 'dangerous' and 'not pleasing', although he did not deem the sin so grave as to merit the contempt levelled at the opera by the public.[23] Other critics were more outspoken in their condemnation: for the *Frusta teatrale* critic, *Madama Butterfly* was 'new clothes made with old cloth; economical art', while Nicola D'Atri of *Il giornale d'Italia* noted that 'the entire work is of a wearying uniformity'.[24] 'Max' in *La tribuna* articulated the point using imagery drawn from the visual arts:

> In *Madama Butterfly* ... Puccini has maintained – and rightly so – his artistic temperament, his character, but all the truth and the force of passionate sentiment of *Manon* has become worn out in the process of watered-down reproduction.[25]

Thus stylistic traits that had earlier been praised as evidence of a clearly defined personal style now seemed hackneyed. Rather like art nouveau design, which used excessive ornamentation to mask its uniformity, Puccini's music was instantly recognisable, and characterised by monotonous repetition of particular motifs. In his comment about a 'watered-down reproduction', 'Max' also implied that Puccini's operas were cheap, mass-produced commodities, outwardly distinct but essentially all the same. And in allying Puccini with the decorative rather than the fine arts, critics called into question the composer's aesthetic credentials, depicting him as more artisan than artist.[26] Although the art nouveau movement beautified candlesticks and vases, such everyday objects, affordable by the middle classes, could never transcend their utilitarian, commercial status and attain acceptance as proper art. Similarly, *Madama Butterfly* was attacked by the critic Camaroni of *La lega lombarda* as 'a work that cannot be taken seriously because neither in conception nor in practice does the artist's honesty preside, but rather the criterion of easy and immediate success'.[27] In a book of 1914 devoted to key musical figures of the day (discussed in more detail in chapter 6), Ildebrando Pizzetti would write that the only good parts of *Madama Butterfly* were those Puccini had 'borrowed' from his earlier operas, and his final assessment of the work left the reader in no doubt of his opinion that Puccini was a spent force:

> If *Butterfly* had been produced before *Manon* and *Bohème* perhaps it would have given the impression of containing the signs and the expressive accents of a personality in formation. But if one considers that *Butterfly* is a work of mature intellect and experience and that *Manon* and *Bohème* were written ten or eight years earlier, one is almost forced to see in the most recently composed work the signs of a personality that is by now declining if indeed not already dissolving.[28]

Much later, in 1924, Gino Monaldi – a writer ever adept at turning what other critics regarded as faults into virtues – would desperately attempt to redeem Puccini's reputation:

> In this score Puccini has, in my view, attained a homogeneity and a simplicity of melodic pacing, more convincing than in the other operas. The Puccini style, in *Butterfly*, establishes itself more constantly and decisively than elsewhere: I've expressly said *style* and not *manner*, for the first is quite different from the second. A manner is an expedient for repeating what has already been said, without making it obvious; a style on the other hand is the precise and sincere expression of oneself.[29]

Few commentators in 1904 seem to have shared his view.

SIMULATED EMOTIONS

Puccini believed the *Madama Butterfly* story to be the most poignant subject he had set: when he saw David Belasco's play in London on 21 June 1900, he claimed that 'the drama was so self-explanatory and evocative that I was immediately moved',[30] despite the fact that he had at best only a cursory knowledge of English. Puccini wept openly at the heroine's unhappy plight and decided that the story of Madam Butterfly would make the perfect subject for his next opera. This cruel tale of crushed hopes and innocence betrayed seemed to contain all the ingredients required to create the most poignant of operatic tear-jerkers, and setting it to music could surely only intensify its emotive power. In the eyes of the critics, however, the work had no emotional heart and genuine passion had been replaced by affectation. Altini wrote in *Il tempo*:

> Maestro Puccini's languid sentimentalism seemed this time to the listener to be vacuous, and perhaps it was. . . . The Maestro, who was himself moved and knew how to move us with the sorrowful lament of Manon, with the romantic story of Mimì, did not know how to touch the public this time, perhaps because the emotion that he aspired to translate into notes eluded even him.[31]

Most critics reported that the public had remained distinctly impassive at the first performance; 'Mos' went so far as to write in *Il marzocco* that 'the truly excessive repetition of one of the soprano's phrases made them rude to the point of violence, the prolixity of the orchestral interlude tired them and Butterfly's death passed without communicating the slightest emotion'.[32]

'Max' used another metaphor drawn from the visual arts to illustrate the deceptiveness of Puccini's apparently 'suggestive' yet in fact emotionally vacuous work, explicitly arguing that the opera was all surface:

> All that has remained of passion and feeling is a painted varnish exterior: a varnish that is always attractive, perhaps, but, unfortunately, varnish nevertheless.[33]

Thus the opera seemed lacking in feeling, yet was overly preoccupied with technique. Many of the critics who commented upon this aspect of Puccini's opera would doubtless have been aware of the ideas of the philosopher Benedetto Croce, highly influential in Italy at this time. Croce proposed that an artwork's content and technique were inextricably bound together: the work and the technique of the work were one and the same, and if the two could be separated then the artwork was flawed. Croce wrote in his *Estetica* (1902): 'It is impossible . . . to distinguish intuition from expression. The one issues forth in the same instant as the other, because they are not two but one', and 'the technique of a playwright is one and the same with his dramatic conception'.[34] Thus, the artwork and what it hoped to express ought to be the same thing. But in Puccini's latest opera content and technique had seemingly become dislocated: contrary to Croce's principle, the opera had become all expression and no content, in other words, all surface detail. Fausto Torrefranca – to whose stinging attack on Puccini we shall turn in the next chapter – would later draw upon Croce's theories when he identified the separation of technique and content as a fundamental manifestation of the 'decadence' inherent in Puccini's works, writing: 'Now decadence can signify only this: that art, from being spontaneous, becomes forced; from being a complete expression, shrinks back towards that which is no longer expression but merely the desire to express.'[35]

Madama Butterfly was also perceived by critics as 'all surface' in the sense of being too stylised. Ippolito Valetta, a forward-looking critic with an interest in foreign instrumental music, observed in the *Nuova antologia* that in the public's opinion, Puccini had written 'almost exclusively in what one might call a "manner", more with the brain than the heart, more with the calculation of theatrical experience than the anguished fever of inspiration'.[36] Thus the opera seemed insincere (and as we have already seen, emotional honesty and directness were the key assets upon which Puccini's reputation as national composer had been built), a charge that Puccini vehemently refuted: 'I swear to God and to his angels that this is my most heartfelt and sincerely written work, and he will make today's denigrators swallow green bile – you will see – and soon. God is just!!!'[37] But the architecture or skeleton of *Madama Butterfly* seemed all too easily discernible, to the extent that Valetta announced that 'the public, who have declared themselves by now satiated with artificial processes, feel the need to breathe with full lungs'.[38] Valetta pointed out that although the public lacked the technical knowledge to allow them to analyse the score, they were capable of recognising a compositional 'system' that displeased them:

> Naturally the public has not, this time more than at any other time, analysed the Puccini 'manner'. They have not discussed it from the

rhythmic nor the harmonic point of view. They have simply protested against a new case, if you will permit me the expression, of concentration on emptiness and have candidly said: 'I know this manner, I have also enjoyed it, now I have had enough of it.'[39]

INTERNATIONALISM

Like the comparisons drawn with Wagner in the hostile reviews of *La bohème*, the concerns about formal ambiguity and technique in *Madama Butterfly* were shot through with nationalist anxiety. As we have already seen, references to a 'manner' or 'system' were consciously anti-German; Italian music, in contrast, ought to be spontaneous. As with *La bohème*, critics detected a pseudo-German aspect to the opera: Valetta expressed his concern that Puccini had succumbed to the allure of Wagnerism when he observed that 'the orchestral commentary [is] continually in direct opposition to the national tradition of simplicity of line'.[40] But Puccini was not the only composer of his day to be attacked for an overly 'heavy' orchestral accompaniment: works by his contemporaries, including Leoncavallo, Mascagni, Catalani and Franchetti, were similarly disparaged for adopting 'foreign' stylistic tendencies. It is noteworthy that orchestral complexity should have continued to strike listeners as 'contrary to the national tradition' even at this late date: little had changed since the late operas of Verdi, in which the orchestra had been given considerable prominence and which were thus criticised in many quarters as too 'German'.[41] Furthermore, *Madama Butterfly* began with a *fugato* introduction, with regard to which Ildebrando Pizzetti would note in 1914 that 'in [Puccini's] music counterpoint is therefore often an element of decoration, of embellishment, appropriate to varying degrees, but it cannot be an element of real expression; and in fact it is never beautiful'.[42] Other foreign influences were also at play: the tableaux-like nature of the opera, as already noted, seemed French. Moments of impulsive 'Italian' vocal expression remained, although not in abundance, for these had largely been crowded out by the more 'modern' (which was to say foreign) techniques. Thus the form seemed confused, neither properly Italian, nor German, nor French: audiences no longer knew what they ought to be listening for, as a range of different aesthetic ideologies seemed to compete simultaneously with one another.

There is a powerful sense in the *Madama Butterfly* reviews of the purity of Italian music being contaminated, pre-empting Torrefranca's diatribe on the dangers of Puccini's internationalism a few years later. The many comparisons that critics drew with art nouveau highlighted the hybrid, international nature of the opera, for art nouveau was itself an eclectic foreign import to Italy regarded with suspicion. Furthermore, it was chastised for its artifice; its alliance of high and low art; its appeal to the middle classes (and, by default, its cheapness); and its perceived 'femininity' – charges strikingly similar to those levelled at *Madama Butterfly*. The Italian hostility towards the style is illustrated by the responses that greeted the Esposizione Internazionale d'Arte Decorativa Moderna, the first international exhibition devoted to the decorative arts, hosted in Turin in 1902. This was organised by a group of young artists and art critics, led by Enrico Thovez, as a consciously self-aggrandising gesture, calculated to demonstrate the new Italy's artistic and industrial credentials to the rest of the Western world. Italy was not yet noted for having a distinctively national school of modern decorative art; its contribution in the field of the decorative arts to the 1900 Paris Exposition Universelle had been deemed unremarkable, bordering on the disastrous, and this was Italy's chance to prove itself to be at the cutting edge of artistic developments.

The exhibition drew crowds in their thousands, and press coverage was extensive, both in Italy and abroad. However, despite the interest that the event stimulated, responses among the critics and members of the public who attended the exhibition were on the whole unfavourable. The *Corriere della sera* reported that Italians were 'indifferent' to the new style displayed at the Turin exhibition, whereas 'everybody was talking about it' abroad.[43] Certainly the style seemed alien to Italian taste; one art critic, unimpressed by the exhibition, called for 'a form of art that, while responding to the needs and tendencies of the new times, is genuinely, decisively Italian'.[44]

The founding of a *lingua franca* of modern European culture was an explicit goal of the art nouveau movement, a key marker of its modernity. By assembling *objets d'art* from all corners of the globe for the Esposizione Internazionale, Italy's most forward-thinking visual artists played a deliberate role in fostering the internationalism of art nouveau, despite the fact that this was profoundly problematic for Italy, as a new nation trying to assert an identity. Rather like the Turin Exhibition (which a reviewer for the English art journal *The Studio* likened to 'a huge bazaar, rather than an exhibition of artistic work'[45]), *Madama Butterfly* put on display an eclectic selection of national styles. In preparation for composing *Madama Butterfly*, Puccini had read voraciously about Japanese culture, had several meetings with the wife of the Japanese Ambassador and attended performances by the Imperial Japanese Theatrical Company (led by the actress Sadayakko) on its tour of Italy in 1902.[46] He incorporated a number of authentic Japanese folk songs into the finished score, made liberal use of the pentatonic scale and employed exotic percussion instruments, including the tam-tam and Japanese bells. However, the exotic local colour that Puccini had researched so scrupulously was attacked as indistinguishable from the ambiences of his earlier operas. *Madama Butterfly* seemed neither authentically Japanese nor credibly Italian, but, rather, struck listeners as a tribute to bland internationalism.

Romeo Carugati of *La Lombardia* – a conservative nationalist who expressed his opposition to most of the key foreign artistic figures of the modern age – posited this as further evidence of the insincerity of Puccini's music; once again the vocabulary chosen by this critic was drawn from the visual arts and suggests the prioritisation of false surface detail, and the idea of the cobbling together of pre-existing elements:

> *Madama Butterfly* is certainly framed with Japanese lacquer and held together with American resin, but does its core really give the sensation of the Far East seen through Butterfly's little house? In appearance we seem to be in Japan but in substance Puccini has returned to the Parisian atmosphere of *Bohème*, the Roman atmosphere of *Tosca*, the Franco-American atmosphere of *Manon*.[47]

However, it is unclear to what extent this should be viewed as a legitimate criticism. Puccini may have claimed, or even genuinely believed, *Madama Butterfly* to be 'authentic', but in many ways it would not have been surprising if the opera had instead foregrounded its own construction of an imagined East. Such themes were very much part of the decadent aesthetic, as is exemplified by a particularly striking passage in Huysmans's *A rebours*. The novel's central character, le duc Des Esseintes, moves away from Paris to live in isolation, surrounding himself with beautiful objects. His obsession with artifice reaches a remarkable extreme when he decides to travel to London. He makes it no further than Paris, because, on finding an English tavern where he can have his dinner, he decides that the actual reality of England can only spoil his imagined fantasy:

> I would be insane to risk losing, by an ill-advised journey, these unforgettable impressions. After all, what kind of aberration was this, that I should be tempted to renounce long-held convictions, and disdain the compliant fantasies of my mind, that I should, like some complete simpleton, have believed that a journey was necessary, or could hold novelty or interest?'[48]

Puccini was perceived by some of his critics precisely as a kind of Des Esseintes: someone who had been seduced by his own imagined construction of a foreign land to the point at which he no longer felt it necessary actually to travel there and verify his fantasy. (Although well travelled, Puccini never visited Japan.) This criticism, however, is rather puzzling; after all, if *Madama Butterfly* was being criticised for seeming to be part of the decadent aesthetic that privileged artifice and ornamentation over depth and substance, then it is hardly surprising that the composer would be viewed as constructing an inauthentic image of Japan. And, crucially, this criticism in any case now seems almost untenable, for there is little evidence to suggest that Puccini did, in fact, view his orientalism in this way: on the contrary, all the evidence signals that he felt the Japan of *Butterfly* to be a real Japan (no matter how astonishing this may seem to the modern observer), and most members of the audience would have been none the wiser.

However, the very presence of so much local colour in *Madama Butterfly* – authentic or otherwise – seemed to critics more threatening than picturesque. The recreation of such colour, whether in literature, painting or opera, inevitably forced the artist to linger upon minute details at the expense of the compositional whole. There was undoubtedly a fad for *japonisme* in turn-of-the-century Italy but it was less pronounced than in France or England; indeed the Italians gained much of their knowledge of Japanese culture second-hand, largely through contact with French sources. (For instance, several members of the Macchiaioli movement had studied in France and been influenced by the Japanese techniques fashionable among Impressionist painters.) Journals such as *La lettura* sought to educate the Italian middle classes with articles about Japanese costumes, religion, culture and women, many of which were translations of articles previously published abroad. John Luther Long's *Madame Butterfly* was serialised in the journal in February and March 1904, to coincide with the first performance of Puccini's opera. *Musica e musicisti* also sought to open the world to readers, publishing numerous photographs of members of foreign races, particularly Japanese and Egyptian women, as objects of curiosity. This voyeuristic element indicates a fascination with exoticism and a wishful colonialism, revealing much about the society to which Ricordi spoke through its journalism and the target audience for Puccini's operas.

However, apart from the interest that surrounded the tour of Italy by Sadayakko's troupe, most ordinary Italians' first-hand contact with Japanese culture in 1904 would have been limited primarily to imported decorative objects such as vases and ornaments. Such items were much in vogue, but were regarded by the serious art establishment as little more than colourful knick-knacks. In fact Western audiences had a false perception of the 'over-decorativeness' of Japanese art and culture more generally: as Helen Greenwald has observed in her consideration of the staging of *Madama Butterfly*, contemporary European presentations of *japonaiserie* were disfigured by inauthentic clutter.[49] Thus the Japanese subject matter of *Madama Butterfly* intensified the view that the opera was overly ornamental.

Puccini's collage of pre-prepared musical gestures seemed akin to Japanese enamelled or lacquered objects with raised surfaces that appeared to have been applied externally.

Another opera that had exploited the contemporary taste for all things Japanese was Mascagni's *Iris* (1898), in which the composer had painstakingly attempted to recreate the sound of authentic Far Eastern instruments in his orchestration.[50] The similarities in the reception of the two operas are striking (some critics even complained that *Madama Butterfly* reminded them too much of the earlier work). Luigi Torchi in the *Rivista musicale italiana* called *Iris* 'a work in which action and drama are things of secondary importance', peopled by 'stunted mummies' and 'straw characters'.[51] Torchi maligned the opera's 'episodic, disjointed scenes' and lack of solid design. Mascagni had suspended vaporous 'ornamental chattering' and inert, quasi-Wagnerian motifs above a series of overstrained modulations. In short, the opera was artificial, mannered, inexpressive, insincere; the composer had, in Torchi's words, 'sketched, coloured, but depicted nothing'.[52]

In *Madama Butterfly* Puccini was also perceived to have prioritised 'colour' for its own sake, dramatically, musically and visually. Ildebrando Pizzetti would later depict *Butterfly* as an opera in which Puccini had merely followed the fashion of the moment, in which the use of Japanese motifs in order to produce local colour seemed cold, forced and pasted on.[53] In his view, indeed, an opera on an exotic subject could never be anything other than skin-deep, since 'a composer cannot express anything but himself, his own soul' and 'the particular sentiments of men, for example of the Japanese or Indian or American, can never be expressed, even artistically, except by Japanese, Indian or American men'.[54]

Ten years later still, one of Puccini's obituarists would rebut the accusation that Puccini's evocation of atmosphere was merely simulated, once again using the metaphor of canvas and frame: 'Puccini, in other words, feels the atmosphere of his dramas as an essential element, not as a pretext, not as a cornice.'[55] Such views, however, were not widely shared in the immediate aftermath of the *Madama Butterfly* première. At the purely scenographic level, this was Puccini's most 'colouristic' opera to date, culminating in the lengthy unsung vigil scene in Act II. In Belasco's play the vigil scene had been a brilliant show of modern lighting technology, taking place in complete silence and lasting fourteen minutes, during which coloured lights were manipulated to represent the transition from dusk to dawn. This was one of the aspects of the play that had most enchanted Puccini in London and he was eager to recreate the same effect in his opera by accompanying the scene with an extended passage of instrumental music with simulated birdsong. However, the scene failed to mesmerise the audience; indeed this was to prove to be the part of opera during which they became most restless.

The Japanese subject matter of *Madama Butterfly* seemed to some to have had a direct bearing upon the artistic technique that Puccini had employed in the opera. The techniques used in Japanese art seemed an echo of everything that concerned critics about the musical and dramatic techniques used in *Madama Butterfly*, particularly his apparent preoccupation with aspects of the musical 'surface': colour and texture at the expense of the all-important arias. Japanese art was regarded as a powerful element of modernity, having influenced virtually every artist of the Impressionist, Post-Impressionist and Symbolist movements – Manet, Monet, Degas, Cassatt, Van Gogh, Toulouse Lautrec, Whistler, Rennie Mackintosh and Klimt included.[56] Furthermore, Japanese art, as one of the most important influences on the art nouveau aesthetic, could be held in large part responsible for the pretty but threatening 'over-fussiness' of the contemporary decorative arts. Japanese art was regarded by Western commentators as inherently 'fragmentary' and unity was not seen to be a governing factor in its compositional technique. James Jackson Jarves, an American art historian who resided in Italy for many years from the mid-nineteenth century as United States vice-consul and acting consul in Florence and established several important art collections, wrote in 1871: 'Japanese pictorial art has a fragmentary aspect in the mass. It is better pleased with strong bits than whole pictures. . . . In dealing with colour the artist can employ it either as an accessory to form or wholly independent of it.'[57] Other ways in which Japanese approaches to compositional organisation differed profoundly from those of Western artists included the use of flat surfaces of bold colour; a disregard for perspective and the three-dimensionality of objects; a stacking up of compositional elements; and a lack of light and shade. All of these tendencies were features of the increasingly abstract visual arts of the West, and music critics detected parallels between the characteristics of Japanese painting and Puccini's generically experimental opera.

In the *Madama Butterfly* revisions for Brescia, and for the subsequent Albert Carré production in Paris in 1906, the Japanese ambience was much reduced. Over the course of the three versions, Puccini cut a lengthy (157-bar) scene from Act I, which involved the introduction of Butterfly's family to Pinkerton; cuts for Brescia also included Yakusidé's drinking scene later in Act I,[58] an episode the audience found particularly tiresome. Another important change was breaking up the vigil scene as Puccini split the second act in two, eventually conceding defeat in his earlier aim to 'hold the audience riveted for an hour and a half' with no entr'acte.[59] The eradication of what seemed to critics to be overdone, superfluous decoration – a hindrance to the opera's essential drama and lyricism – was one of the factors in the revised opera's success. After hearing the Brescia version, Pozza of the *Corriere della sera* evidently felt that enough of the 'ornamental' aspects had been removed in order to enable him to turn earlier charges of fragmentation on their head:

> The unity is admirable. The action unfolds across a continuous web of recurring themes that the Maestro transforms in a thousand ways without effort and without abstruse polyphonic complications, indissolubly binding together the most meaningful moments of the drama.[60]

GENDER

Perhaps the most troubling subtext implied by the depiction of *Madama Butterfly* as cluttered with useless details was that detail was commonly understood as synonymous with the feminine – again, an ancient trope.[61] As an art form that prioritised ornament for its own sake, impinged upon household objects and used the sinuous female body as its most prominent motif, art nouveau was devalued because of its perceived 'femininity'. Similarly, references to Puccini's tendency to pay most attention to aspects of composition perceived to be superficial were tacitly gendered.

Shortly before the première of *Madama Butterfly* Luigi Alberto Villanis wrote an article in *Musica nuova* that explicitly identified the 'femininity' of Puccini's musical style; like critics' comments about internationalism, this also pre-empted the more vehement criticisms that Torrefranca would issue a few years later.[62] Villanis (1863–1906) was a musicologist who taught music history and aesthetics at the Liceo Rossini, Pesaro (1891–1892), at Turin University (1894–1896), and at Pesaro Conservatory (from 1905). As well as writing for *Musica nuova* he was the music critic for the *Gazzetta musicale di Milano* and *La stampa*, and his writings included works on aesthetics and Beethoven.[63] Attempting to account for Puccini's popularity (naturally assuming that *Madama Butterfly* was guaranteed to be a hit), Villanis wrote that his operas 'respond to the almost unconscious needs of the current hour'.[64] He posited Puccini's works as a mirror image of a 'feminised' society, writing: 'the spirit of the masses in our time is singularly impregnated by those sentimental tendencies and that rhythmic fever that warm the depths of Puccinian opera'.[65] Drawing upon ideas developed in Max Nordau's *Degeneration*, Villanis attributed the current mood to the restless pace of modern life. Exhausted by long hours and heavy work (arguably even more disorientating in a still predominantly agrarian society such as Italy than in the northern European nations observed by Nordau), audiences disdained 'intellectual' art and favoured instead works with immediate emotional appeal:

> The restless pace of modern life, long working hours and the same heavy use of energy drive the audience to avoid entertainments that demand the hard work that oppresses them for the whole day. And

since what we might call the 'intellectual' orientation of contemporary great art tires them because they are obliged to indulge in deep reflection, the audience rushes out of preference to pure and simple scenes of passion and love that provoke spontaneous emotion.[66]

Thus Puccini's operas were perfect, because, to quote Villanis, 'everything in him converges in a single aim, ... everything is summed up in the fascinating enchantment of a caress, where deep thought vanishes in the flowering of emotion'.[67]

Villanis used gendered critical references very much like Altini's comment, cited above, about Puccini's 'languid sentimentalism'. Among the 'feminine' attributes that characterised Puccini's style, he listed the 'insinuating and sensual sweetness' of his harmonies, the voluptuous instrumentation and – crucially – the prioritisation of suggestive moments at the expense of an overriding structure. Here Villanis drew upon a long tradition of disparagement of 'feminine' creativity when he referred to Puccini's inability to handle large-scale scenes effectively. Furthermore, for this critic, it was not only modern music that was breaking down (Nordau, doubtless influenced by Nietzsche, levelled this accusation at Wagner), but also the modern way of listening. Modern life, with its accumulation of detail and its exhausting excesses, had had an enervating, feminising effect on audiences and encouraged a passive, atomised manner of listening. Audiences could cope only with small chunks: modern music, of which *Madama Butterfly* was a prime example, responded precisely to this need.

Villanis drew a comparison between Puccini's works and the operas of Massenet, which had been widely characterised as 'feminine' by French critics.[68] Villanis likened Massenet's musical discourse to the charm of 'a beautiful woman adorned by the seductive rustling of silk and exciting and suggestive perfume', which appealed to a public 'who abhor the merest hint of a deep or demanding concept'.[69] Puccini's operas had similar appeal and a similar surface sensuality; Villanis cited the composer's ability to 'spread a veil of subtle poetry over the facts of everyday life'.[70]

The metaphors chosen by this critic – silk, perfume, veils – once again emphasise the idea of inessential self-adornment, here explicitly feminised. Although such images may at first sight seem innocently picturesque, Villanis played upon widespread contemporary fears, discussed in chapter 1, that the Italian character was weak and in need of reform when he wrote that 'the flabby virility of the moment prefers the seduction of lace and silk to the living call of strong passion'.[71] As we have already seen, in the first decade of the twentieth century a new brand of increasingly bellicose nationalism was beginning to emerge in Italy that would pave the way to the belligerent posturing of the Futurists (who would call for war as the answer to Italy's moral and social problems), and ultimately to the Fascists. Villanis's remark hints at this new mood: Puccini, strongly linked in the minds of critics with the middle classes and the ideals of Giolitti's regime, is here implicated as a pacifist, a frivolous materialist. Villanis's article thus strikes at the heart of 'the Puccini problem'. Critics were using Puccini's music to express their fears of modern life itself, which seemed to be lived entirely on the surface; Puccini was singled out for censure not because he went against the grain but because he seemed to typify a prevailing set of values that angry commentators such as Villanis had come to detest. In depicting the 'details' of Puccini's opera as threatening, critics signalled their unwillingness to engage with the challenges posed both by modern life and by modern music.

Comments about Puccini's supposed emphasis upon meaningless 'surfaces' were near ubiquitous in the reviews of *Madama Butterfly*, and the metaphor signified many different things: the internationalism, commercialism, effeminacy and fragmentation of Puccini's music. Thus *Madama Butterfly* brought together a constellation of ideas that conflated the oriental with the ornamental, the decorative with the decadent. References to ornament and surfaces were a way of suggesting that Puccini's opera lacked meaning, or that its meaning was distorted by fussy details – ornamental overburdening seemed actually to signify a void. The foregrounding of 'details' compromised what was commonly understood to be the proper hierarchy of periphery and centre. Furthermore, references to surfaces were used as a way of expressing broader ideological concerns, of articulating fears that the modern age was divorcing itself from tradition, musically, visually and in terms of social mores.

Although contemporary audiences certainly found *Madama Butterfly* challenging and bewildering on first hearing, we should not necessarily read a supposed excess of decoration as an indictment of a 'bad' opera. While comments about fussy details might at first sight simply be interpreted as an attempt to depict Puccini's opera as poorly written, critics were in fact signalling their own unwillingness, or inability, to engage with aspects of the work that struck them as troublingly modern. The music of Puccini's foreign contemporaries such as Richard Strauss and Maurice Ravel was similarly chastised as fragmented and ornamental,[72] and in criticising the 'surfaces' of Puccini's work, Italian critics signalled their reluctance to engage with such an aesthetic. The hostile reviews perhaps say more about this mindset than about the shortcomings of Puccini's opera.

The reviews of *Madama Butterfly* reveal a modern approach to organising a score that we tend to overlook in Puccini's work today. The juxtaposition of musical styles that struck his contemporaries simply as 'fragmentation' may be viewed, in a different light, as a stylistic eclecticism that is perhaps more adventurous than it seems. A preoccupation with surfaces is a fundamental marker of the modern: many literary and art theorists have noted the increasing – and deliberate – flatness of twentieth-century artworks. (This tendency has perhaps reached its peak in postmodernism, which disdains depth and depends upon a play of meaningless surfaces.[73]) Seen in this perspective, our image of a frame without a canvas becomes a metaphor for the modern, something that seemed to many contemporary commentators to be unworkable within the traditional paradigms of Italian opera. As the natural rite of passage for a modern artwork, a riot was therefore perhaps the appropriate reception for Puccini's opera, although this would have been of little comfort to an Italian composer reared in a system in which success was measured almost entirely by audience enthusiasm.

The critics who chastised Puccini so harshly upon hearing *Madama Butterfly* were in the main not musicologists (the *Rivista musicale italiana*, for instance, did not give Puccini's opera space in its pages). Rather, with the exception of those writing in *Il marzocco* and the *Nuova antologia*, which targeted a more élite audience, they were critics employed largely by newspapers and popular journals aimed at ordinary members of the bourgeoisie – Puccini's supposed natural allies. The comments gathered together here were scattered across a large number of different publications – a remark here, a comment there – although these were in large enough quantities to add up to a sustained chorus of disapproval. A few years later the whispers would become a shout when Fausto Torrefranca took up the ideas often merely hinted at by other critics – internationalism, commercialism, effeminacy and fragmentation – and made them the basis of a thesis that attempted to codify Puccini's decadence decisively. The ultra-nationalistic spin that Torrefranca put on arguments expressed by earlier reviewers, and the relentless and overt connections he drew between Puccini's music and the ills of contemporary society, afford us an opportunity to trace changing perceptions of Italian identity during the course of the first decade of the twentieth century. It is to this assault that we now turn.

5 | Torrefranca versus Puccini

'Puccini ... embodies, with the utmost completeness, all the decadence of current Italian music, and represents all its cynical commercialism, all its pitiful impotence and the whole triumphant vogue for internationalism.'[1] Thus was the project to promote Puccini as a national hero checked in 1912 when the Turin-based academic publishing house Fratelli Bocca released a vitriolic monograph entitled *Giacomo Puccini e l'opera internazionale*. Fausto Torrefranca, the book's twenty-nine-year-old author, made no attempt to disguise his contempt for the composer promoted by Ricordi as Verdi's successor, and his assessment of Puccini stood in stark contrast to the idolatry of the popular musical press. Nominating himself as the only critic courageous enough to stand out against the current artistic climate of vulgarity and insincerity, Torrefranca wrote his book as a call to arms to his dissatisfied peers, encouraging them to rise up against an older generation characterised by 'spiritual mediocrity'.

Torrefranca organised his 133-page assault on Puccini into four sections. The first ('Psicologia dell'opera pucciniana') considers the decadence of Italian opera and of Puccini's personality, while the second ('La vita artistica del Puccini e l'ambiente') is a caustic biographical profile and commentary on Puccini's operas up to 1910. The third, entitled 'Puccini uomo di teatro', examines Puccini's attitudes towards dramatic structure and characterisation, and the final section (provocatively entitled 'Puccini musicista?') is an assessment of Puccini's musical style and influences. Although familiar to music historians, Torrefranca's book has not been considered in terms of its cultural significance; yet to read the Puccini monograph simply for its musical observations, as most critics have done, is to neglect the social and political discourses central to its thesis. As the title indicates, the book's principal preoccupation is Puccini's internationalism, the way in which Puccini's music 'defames Italian culture abroad because it ... reveals an intellectual wretchedness' – an astonishing claim to make about a composer widely held up as a national treasure.[2] But the gendered subtext that underpins Torrefranca's condemnation of Puccini's internationalism has been largely ignored, despite the fact that it lies at the core of the author's thesis. For Torrefranca, Puccini was anything but the epitome of masculinity; rather, Torrefranca regarded him as emblematic of the most effete and decadent tendencies of the *fin de siècle*.

Torrefranca's publishing house, Fratelli Bocca, had provided a platform for the burgeoning disciplines of psychology, sociology, criminology and sexology in the late nineteenth century, publishing the first Italian translations of Krafft-Ebing's *Psychopathia Sexualis* (1887) and Nordau's *Degeneration* (1896), along with the major works of Lombroso, Sighele and Mantegazza, all of whom we shall encounter later in this chapter.[3] Torrefranca drew upon contemporary medical and anthropological discourses in order to depict Puccini as a 'feminised' composer, a label with harmful political implications. He launched a series of insults at Puccini – weakness, sickness, intellectual incapacity, lack of originality – all of which centred on the notion of the composer's 'effeminacy'. As similar accusations were also contemporaneously attached to other 'outsider' groups, Torrefranca was able to use gendered references to undermine Puccini's status as national composer. This chapter situates Torrefranca's accusations within the context of early-twentieth-century Italian debates over gender, race and decadence, issues crucial to the contested question of 'Italianness'.

Despite the fact that Torrefranca's book was written in 1910 and published in 1912, its terms of reference looked back consciously to the *fin de siècle*. He built upon the full panoply of clichés of decadence inherited from previous critics but took them to vitriolic extremes. The perceived equation between Puccini and women had been hinted at some time earlier, as we have seen in chapter 4, but in Torrefranca's assessment it became central. Furthermore, whilst earlier critics had used 'femininity' as a dismissive label, Torrefranca's comments about women and female creativity are more overtly misogynistic. Arthur Groos and Roger Parker have commented that 'the book's anti-feminism is laughably extreme',[4] and by modern standards this may be the case; but it was intended by Torrefranca in all seriousness, and I propose that we ought not to dismiss his rhetoric so swiftly. Within the context of the present study, his vitriolic hatred of women allows us to trace a fundamental paradigm shift in the years around 1910, not only in attitudes towards Puccini, but in contemporary thinking about the equation between gender and national identity.

Torrefranca did not merely build upon earlier rhetorics about Puccini; he invented new ones, as exemplified most notably by his veiled anti-Semitism. These rhetorics, together with his misogyny and imperialism, will doubtless seem alien and abhorrent to the modern reader, yet for all that the book's value as a historical document remains undiminished. Torrefranca's obituarists, writing not long after the celebrations to mark Puccini's centenary, played down the significance of the Puccini book within his œuvre, some claiming that the author himself later dismissed it as an ill-judged error of youth.[5] But the author's impetuous spirit gave the book a rare honesty, with the consequence that it offers a window onto a specific moment in Italian history and onto the ideals of a generation. Torrefranca was not in fact the isolated extremist he might seem at first sight to be. The product of a well-established intellectual lineage, he engaged in topical debates that crossed disciplines and national boundaries, and played upon the neuroses of a society in which any deviation from the 'norm' provoked panic. His discourse is indicative of deep and widely held concerns about the state of contemporary Italy, and many of the objections he made to Puccini's music are found in diluted form in the writings of more moderate critics. Thus, in order to further our understanding of how Puccini's works were evaluated in their own time, it is necessary to confront the discomfiting issues that surrounded them.

THE NEW NATIONALISM

Before examining Torrefranca's charges against Puccini in detail let us consider his ideological background and the intellectual circles in which he moved. The scion of a noble, patrician family of Sicilian descent, Fausto Acanfora Sansone dei duchi di Porta e dei duchi di Torrefranca was born in Monteleone Calabro (now Vibo Valentia) on 1 February 1883. After an itinerant childhood moving around Italy with his prefect father, Torrefranca settled in Turin to study engineering at the Politecnico, and was awarded his degree in 1905. A musical autodidact, he taught music history at conservatoires and universities in Rome, Naples, Milan and Florence, and was an ardent campaigner for the creation of music professorships, later becoming the first holder of such a post in Italy.

Torrefranca's aristocratic origins predisposed him to believe that art was for the delectation of the privileged few rather than the edification or entertainment of the masses, as evidenced by his remark that opera and *Lieder* catered to the taste of 'commoners' whereas instrumental music could be understood only by an 'intellectual aristocracy'.[6] The ideal vehicle for his exaltation of high art, which he expressed in distinctively florid and inaccessible language, was the *Rivista musicale italiana*, Italy's most serious musicological journal (also published by Fratelli Bocca), which was dedicated to the revival of early Italian music and to detailed analysis of the most avant-garde foreign works. But it is also imperative to consider his wider network of influences: most notably, the fact that he would become music critic for Enrico Corradini's far-right nationalist newspaper the *Idea nazionale* from 1914 to 1915 situates him within a far more militant camp. His promotion of particular genres of music was ideological rather than purely aesthetic, his rhetoric invariably suffused with the political. The Puccini monograph was no exception.

During the first decade of the twentieth century a new brand of bellicose nationalism was beginning to gain ground and supplant the old model of Risorgimento patriotism. The generation born, like Torrefranca (and, not insignificantly, Mussolini), around 1880 was too young to have lived through the battles for Italian independence, and craved a heroic cause for which to fight. Hostile to Giolitti's liberal reformist government, and disillusioned, directionless and plagued by ennui (a mood they caught from the slightly older generation of *scapigliatura* artists), they were increasingly vociferous in their aspiration to bring about radical change in all spheres of life. They protested against what they regarded as the effeminacy, lack of high ideals and comfortable complacency of Giolitti's regime, which they blamed for the humiliating military defeat at Adua in 1896, and in place of the status quo they promoted an aggressive, expansionist nationalism, taking the French Action Française as a model. In 1910 a formal nationalist movement, the Associazione Nazionalista Italiana, was established, bringing together as a coherent body the various disparate proto-nationalist factions of the early 1900s, and the *Idea nazionale* was founded in March of the following year as the mouthpiece of the disaffected young.

Authoritarianism, action, imperialism and opposition to parliamentary democracy lay at the heart of the new nationalist movement's credo, and the 'passive' middle classes were regarded by the young avant garde as an internal enemy. The sociologist, psychologist and criminologist Scipio Sighele drew connections between crowds and criminality in his *La folla delinquente* in 1891, and scientists such as Gaetano Mosca and Vilfredo Pareto used quasi-Darwinian theories to argue that the bourgeoisie's ascendancy would be short lived. Within such a context, Torrefranca's hostility towards a composer widely promoted by his patrons as 'the voice of the people' is unsurprising. His ideas were also in keeping with the rejection of liberal values that characterised contemporary developments in the field of literature and philosophy. The dissatisfaction of the young nationalists found its expression in the avant-garde journals that flourished in Florence in the first decade of the twentieth century: *Leonardo*, *Il regno* and, most important the Crocean, anti-positivist *La voce*, founded in Florence in 1908. While not pre-eminently musical in focus, these periodicals included music reviews and articles by such figures as Pizzetti and Bastianelli, along with Torrefranca, in which they outlined their plans for a redefinition both of Italian art and of the very nature of Italianness itself.

The most prominent figures in this movement, Giuseppe Prezzolini, Giovanni Papini, and Ardengo Soffici, styled themselves as an intellectual 'aristocracy' and, like Torrefranca, consciously advocated elitist values. They loudly voiced their opposition to a bourgeoisie they regarded as materialistic and superficial, with Prezzolini writing in 1908 that 'Italy doesn't lack a brain, but she errs by making use of it for frivolous, vulgar and base ends'.[7] Thus those who defined themselves as the most serious arbiters of taste in Italian society approached their task with an anti-democratic agenda that made no pretence at social unity. While the Risorgimento had depended upon cooperation across social classes in pursuit of a common goal, by the turn of the century the intelligentsia had become disillusioned, and increasingly sought to set themselves apart from the masses. This aspiration had profound consequences for the sorts of music and culture that they sought to promote, and was one of the motivating factors in the critical reaction against Puccini's music. Giuseppe Prezzolini, the founding editor of *La voce*, expressed his explicit disdain for contemporary Italian opera in a letter of 1908 inviting Romain Rolland to contribute to the journal:

> As our aim is to be open to all general trends and to inform readers of what is taking place beyond the Alps, we ask you to be so kind as to send us some piece of writing from your pen, however brief. We would value greatly some article on contemporary music in France, some violent attack on our horrible and effeminate Puccini, Leoncavallo, etc.[8]

The anti-democratic ideals of the new nationalists went hand in hand with a misogynistic rhetoric. Manliness was central to nineteenth- and early-twentieth-century pan-European concepts of nationalism. Channelling male energies into sport – a useful peacetime substitute for military pursuits – the German and English bourgeoisie manipulated gender roles as a means of effecting social control. Whereas southerners were characterised in the eyes of northern observers by an inability to curb their passions, the ideal northern European man was depicted as strong, forceful, yet emotionally restrained.[9] To disillusioned young Italians like Torrefranca, the Anglo-German archetype of manliness had produced enviable results both on the battlefield and in the colonies and might be emulated as part of their vision of a reinvigorated Italy. Many activists held the view that war was the only way in which Italy could heal its wounded self-esteem, achieve its 'rightful' glory and, crucially, restore the 'correct' balance of power between the sexes. This was the era of F. T. Marinetti's Futurist movement, whose manifesto declared: 'we want to glorify war – sole cleansing of the world – militarism, patriotism ... and contempt for women'.[10] Ever self-contradictory, Marinetti envisaged a prominent role for female artists within the Futurist movement and aided the careers of various women. He was also later to call for reforms that would improve the lot of Italian women, including easier divorce and equal pay,[11] and yet organised feminism was one of the demons that his movement wished to exorcise. In common with other Italian nationalists of this period, the Futurists promoted a vision of a reinvigorated Italy led by a strong man of action, with heroism and virility as its core values, inspired by the idea of the Nietzschean superman that had been Italianised by D'Annunzio. Marinetti's words signal the difficulties for the new manly nationalism of supposedly 'feminine' elements in Italian culture. The Futurists were a separate movement from *i vociani*, but they shared certain common aspirations, most notably a nationalist vision that was inextricably bound up with issues of gender: the eradication of what they perceived to be an effeminate, passive status quo and the desire to 'masculinise' the Italian race.

A few years later, the ultra-nationalist writer Giovanni Papini – whom Torrefranca would undoubtedly have known personally through his involvement with Papini and Prezzolini's *La voce* – would call for Italy to enter the First World War as a cure for the nation's 'emasculated' state. Drawing upon images of sexual and physical incapacity, he derided Italy as 'a great power, but the weakest of all; armed, but incapable of waging war; conservative, but spineless whenever there was a hint of threat to stability', and a country where power had been allowed to fall into the hands of 'the impotent ... those without backbone'.[12] The vocabulary chosen by Torrefranca to describe Puccini's music and persona was strikingly similar.

MASCULINE WOMEN AND FEMININE MEN

Giacomo Puccini e l'opera internazionale must surely be a contender for the most unremitting character assassination in the history of music biography. '[Puccini] is the perfect womanly musician,' wrote Torrefranca.[13] Under a subheading 'Femminilità del Puccini' he took a swipe at Puccini's status as a 'real man' by noting his 'poor fecundity'.[14] Torrefranca portrayed Puccini not merely as a woman but as a lower-class woman, proclaiming him to be the little seamstress rather than the aristocratic lady, 'ignorant but content to be so; poor but elegant; of easy virtue but romantic; silly but wilful; venal but concerned to keep up appearances as far as possible'.[15] In short, for Torrefranca, Puccini was Mimì. The composer's admirers regarded his female characters to be among his greatest achievements, but Torrefranca considered them a negative reflection on the composer because, to borrow from Otto Weininger, 'those men who claim to understand women are themselves very nearly women'.[16]

Weininger's misogynist tract *Geschlecht und Charakter*, published shortly before his death in 1903, provides a useful frame within which to consider Torrefranca's attack on Puccini. At once attracted towards and obsessively repulsed by the bisexual character that he detected to be present in all humans, and driven to suicide by his own homosexuality, Weininger initially seems an improbable character to have appealed to Italians of masculinist and nationalist inclinations. However, his anti-feminism – which depicted women as an obstacle to humanity's attainment of moral, intellectual and spiritual enlightenment – was embraced wholeheartedly by the flowering nationalist movement and would later endear him to the Fascists. Weininger argued that men should liberate themselves once and for all from sexually predatory women, who were fundamentally without souls;

the extreme outcome of this project – the end of the human race – was in his view a price worth paying. He wrote, 'Every form of fecundity is loathsome, and no one who is honest with himself feels bound to provide for the continuity of the human race.'[17] Papini, following Weininger's lead, would publish an article in *Lacerba* in 1914 advocating the massacre of women as the only solution to the fundamental incompatibility of the sexes.[18]

It was probably through his involvement as an occasional contributor to Papini's *La voce* that Torrefranca first became aware of Weininger's ideas. Articles about Weininger appeared in *Leonardo* in 1906 and *La voce* in 1910; the latter was part of an entire issue devoted to 'La questione sessuale' that also contained discussions of the writings of Freud and Mantegazza and a lengthy bibliography of foreign books on the flourishing science of sexology.[19] Even if Torrefranca had not read the book in its original German – which he is likely to have done – Weininger's thesis had been the subject of such intense debate in the circles in which Torrefranca moved that it could hardly have escaped his notice. For example, Scipio Sighele's lengthy critique of the book in *Eva moderna*, two years before its publication in Italy, demonstrates how readily pan-European ideas on fluid gender boundaries were taken up in Italy.[20] (Sighele was sympathetic to Weininger's criticism of the notion of sexual equality, but stopped short of accepting the proposal to suppress sexual relations, an idea he derided as 'preposterous'.) When Weininger's book was translated into Italian as *Sesso e carattere* in 1912 – almost exactly contemporaneously with Torrefranca's book and by the same publishing house – it became one of the most talked-about publications of the year.[21] A best-seller from the outset, the book went through a prodigious number of reprints, and remained influential in Italy long after its fame had faded elsewhere.

Weininger's ideas found an enthusiastic following in a country whose intellectuals had led the way in investigating the boundaries of physical and behavioural 'normality'. In the late nineteenth century Cesare Lombroso and his disciples had pioneered the positivist study of criminality and crowd psychology. Lombroso's *La donna delinquente*, co-authored with his son-in-law Guglielmo Ferrero, presented a statistical analysis of the facial and bodily measurements of female criminals in order both to prove links between physical traits and misconduct and to produce a scientific definition of the 'normal' woman.[22] Women who possessed male physical features were not merely oddities but criminals: the female offender was thus characterised as having a large jaw and generally 'masculine aspect'.[23] In 1898 Lombroso went so far as to found a Museum of Criminal Anthropology in Turin specifically devoted to deviancy. Nominally intended in the spirit of advancing scientific knowledge, this monument to freakishness put on public display not merely the skulls of delinquents, but babies preserved in formaldehyde, pornographic drawings and – most ghoulish of all – Lombroso's own pickled head following his death in 1909.[24]

By 1912, in a climate of increasingly bellicose nationalism, fear of what Weininger referred to as the modern excess of 'sexually intermediate forms' – narrow-hipped, flat-chested women and dandified men – was intensifying.[25] Thus Torrefranca was able to draw upon a set of clichés about the 'effeminate man' in order to disparage Puccini to maximum effect and to call into question his status as national composer. Not averse to adopting a fashionably pseudo-scientific tone, he claimed that Puccini belonged to a 'cultural demi-monde': a group predominantly made up of women, but also including biological males who by rights belonged to the female sex.[26] It was not by chance that Torrefranca chose to categorise Puccini alongside Oscar Wilde.[27] Whatever Puccini's actual sexual behaviour – and there is no reason to suspect that the womanising composer had homosexual leanings – Torrefranca knew that the merest taint of 'inversion' was sufficient to stigmatise him. Homosexuality had recently, thanks to the writings of contemporary psychologists and physiologists and a number of very public scandals, become an issue of topical debate. And morality was not all that was at stake: the idea of homosexuality also carried darker political implications, as contemporary discourse linked it to secrecy, insanity and conspiracy theories, all of which were thought to affect the security of the state.[28]

WOMANLY WEAKNESSES

To associate Puccini with women was to demean his talents, since women were still widely believed at the turn of the twentieth century to be incapable of any form of significant artistic endeavour. The notion of the uncreative woman had a long patrimony across Europe, with the French socialist Proudhon claiming that 'no woman will ever come anywhere near the great artists, nor the great orators and the great poets'.[29] The influence of Proudhon is evident in the writings of Italian intellectuals such as Paolo Mantegazza, Professor of Physiology at the University of Florence and Italy's foremost early-twentieth-century anthropologist, who wrote: 'the small number of great artists among women is enough to prove their intellectual inferiority'.[30] Weininger proposed that, while women might dabble in painting or writing, they were particularly unsuited to musical composition because they depended upon external stimuli in order to be creative, and music bore no relation to sight, sound or smell.[31] Women's art could by its very nature be nothing other than insubstantial, for 'woman's thought is a sliding and gliding through subjects, a superficial tasting of things that a man, who studies the depths, would hardly notice'.[32] Similarly, Torrefranca expressed his hostility towards women in the hitherto exclusively masculine field of criticism by arguing that 'what women do is still not much more than a "translation" of elements of art and thought already worked out by the male brain'.[33] He thus implied that the men he labelled as 'feminine composers' were inert and empty vessels incapable of creativity without assistance from others, drawing upon Proudhon's idea – itself inherited from Rousseau – that 'woman is a receptacle. Just as she receives the embryo from man, so too does she receive her spirit and conscience from him.'[34] Thus Torrefranca's criticism of Puccini's 'intellectual mediocrity' and 'weakness' would have been obvious to a contemporary reader as a code for 'womanliness'.[35]

Puccini's commercial success at home and abroad – regarded by his supporters as a matter of national pride – was for Torrefranca both a marker of his vulgarity and yet another indicator of his effeminacy. By

1912 Puccini led a life of considerable luxury, owned several homes and was able to command extremely high fees and favourable terms for his works. Torrefranca's apparently complimentary reference to Puccini as the ultimate 'hero of fashion' was in fact highly derogatory; he observed that Puccini was like 'the woman of today. ... The type of woman eager for experiment' (a remark suggesting disapproval of women's supposedly increasing appetite for adventure in both the workplace and the bedroom).[36] More prominent and influential than ever before, fashion was considered inherently ephemeral, frivolous and attention-seeking: a metaphor for woman herself. In the era that witnessed the development of mass advertising and in which the first great department stores opened in Europe's capital cities to cater to woman's every trivial desire, femininity became intimately associated with materialism. Not only were women exploited as a useful marketing tool, their sinuous naked bodies adorning countless art nouveau posters, candelabras and items of furniture, but their importance as consumers was also recognised.

For Torrefranca, Puccini's 'simpering sentimental' works aroused the same sort of interest as gossip columns and fashion reports.[37] This appeal to women demoted his operas to the status of a commodity being fed to the bourgeoisie. Here a parallel may be drawn with the French reception of Massenet, the composer considered by many contemporary critics to have provided Puccini with his strongest stylistic model. Massenet's capacity to delight women, like Puccini's, was constructed by his detractors as an indicator of his own lightweight 'femininity', as Steven Huebner explains:

> Wagnerians doubtless perceived [Massenet's] operas in the same general category as quintessentially feminine commercial products such as crinolines, fashion magazines, cheap sentimental novels – cultural artefacts not amenable to nationalist boasting about progress. ... He could not escape his image as a colossal representative of the age of nascent mass-market commercialism.[38]

Whereas Torrefranca commented explicitly on Puccini's 'effeminate' character, his analysis of the music hinged upon a more subliminally feminine imagery. Branding Puccini's music as 'not art but artifice',[39] he drew upon the well-worn cliché of the decadence of the merely decorative, as discussed in chapter 4. In contrast to the many critics who applauded Puccini for his ability to express honest, authentic feeling, which they constructed as a particularly Italian virtue, Torrefranca depicted Puccini's supposed passion as an act of simulation, writing of Puccini's style, 'even in the best parts, it is sincere only moment by moment. ... But momentary sincerity is, in fact, absolute impotence.'[40] If one wanted to put together a synthetic, composite artist, assured of success, he argued, Puccini's music would contain all the requisite ingredients, but would be characterised by a 'spiritual void.'[41] He drew the reader's attention to Puccini's propensity to borrow the music of others as a marker of the composer's dishonesty. It was hardly coincidental that the composers whom he accused Puccini of crudely attempting to imitate – Massenet, Debussy and Strauss – were 'decadent' figures in their own right who had themselves, to varying degrees, also been tarred with the brush of effeminacy.

Given his supposed 'womanliness', it was only natural, according to the prevailing value system, that Puccini should turn to external influences for inspiration. According to Torrefranca the effeminate artist was bereft of an individual voice, unable to leave an imprint upon the era in which he lived, instead merely subsuming cultural tendencies and reproducing them. Torrefranca wrote that 'the insincere artist is almost always a monotonous artist, a tedious composer, even if he makes the effort to dress up his mode of expression in a thousand different guises. And Puccini is certainly monotonous.'[42] Thus Puccini's music was, like a vain woman, dressed up as something that it was not, seeking to mislead the listener. Disguise and deceit were inextricably associated with women during this period; Weininger, for example, wrote that 'organic untruthfulness characterises ... all women'.[43] Even seemingly innocuous discussions of make-up carried a nationalistic subtext: cosmetics were viewed with suspicion in late-nineteenth-century Italy as a French import, a dangerous threat to the Italian taste for natural, virtuous beauty.[44]

Lombroso expressed concern that prostitutes seduced men with make-up that concealed their 'virile' nature beneath an attractive feminine exterior. Torrefranca deemed Puccini's sale of his operas – like the prostitute's sale of her body – both fraudulent and gender-problematic.

Puccini's purported lack of originality was also gendered. Imitation was regarded as 'female', and Torrefranca's disparagement of Puccini's music as 'reflected art' imbued it with a narcissism constructed by contemporary culture as feminine.[45] In *Fisiologia della donna* Mantegazza identified man's predominant characteristic as ambition and woman's as vanity,[46] while Weininger proposed that men were so afraid of the *Doppelgänger* – a figure used repeatedly in Romantic literature to symbolise threatened subjectivity – and of being thought a 'mere echo' that they feared mirrors. Women, on the other hand, were content to receive their opinions 'ready made'.[47] The woman contemplating her image in a mirror or pond was a favourite subject of *fin-de-siècle* painters; a particularly censorious twist was put on this popular theme by the Italian painter Giovanni Segantini in *La vanità (La fonte del male)* (1897), in which an unabashed naked woman gazes at her image in a snake-filled pool that represents evil.

Torrefranca's next charge was that of Puccini's supposed childishness. He claimed that, in a culture in which men increasingly sought to emulate small children, 'Puccini remained a baby, never reached manhood' (or, to translate more literally from the original Italian, 'did not attain virility').[48] Using infantilism as a stick with which to beat Puccini was the logical extension of Torrefranca's misogyny, for the woman–child association was deeply ingrained in the culture of the *fin de siècle*. In Italy a widespread intellectual conservatism, influenced by German theories on women's mental inferiority, amalgamated women and children as similarly ingenuous, irresponsible and simple-minded. Mantegazza wrote that 'in woman we find a character that is childlike and above all atavistic' and that 'woman was and is and always will be less intelligent than man; and her thoughts are generally infantile'.[49] Lombroso and Ferrero provided 'scientific' justification for the subjugation of women by suggesting that their infantile and immoral tendencies could be 'neutralised by piety, maternity, want of passion, sexual coldness, by weakness and an undeveloped intelligence'.[50] As mother and child were regarded as one and the same, it would have come as no surprise to the book's readers to discover Torrefranca likening Puccini to a 'little mother' who soothes her baby to sleep with a monotonous lullaby of caresses and kisses because she cannot express herself in any more coherent manner.[51]

References to disease abound in Torrefranca's monograph. He described Puccini as 'a symptom of decadence', 'anaemic and emaciated', 'a neurasthenic' and 'a third-rate physiological product of Italian culture'.[52] Such insults stood in marked contrast to the rhetoric of health and the heroic imagery of statuary employed by Puccini's supporters, and further undermined claims that he was a full-blooded Italian male. The legacy of such remarks has been long lasting and one hears their echo in many later writings about Puccini: Arnold Whittall, for example, writes that, in comparison with Verdi, 'Puccini inevitably seems more neurotic, a pampered bourgeois rather than a national hero active in politics'.[53] Torrefranca also applied metaphors of sickness to the music, observing that Puccini's themes were inert to the point of death, while *Tosca* represented 'the sublimity of decay'.[54] In effect Torrefranca posited Puccini's works as embodying the *malaise* of the era that produced them, but was infinitely more caustic than earlier critics who had pointed to connections between Puccini and the spirit of the age.

Contemporary readers would immediately have recognised the rhetoric of disease as feminine, the equation of masculinity with health and femininity with sickness being a common topos in late-nineteenth-century European culture. In the decadent literature of the *fin de siècle*, peopled by legions of pale, consumptive heroines, women were presented as agents of disease by whom innocent men ran the risk of contamination. Italian theorists in the late nineteenth century went so far as to claim that ill health was abnormal for men, but represented women's natural state.[55] Tapping into fears about female contamination and impurity, Torrefranca depicted male culture and thought as an ancient tree being maliciously sabotaged by women and, by extension, 'womanly' men such as Puccini:

> Female endeavour ... springs up and spreads as a parasite on the ancient trunk of culture which, through natural selection, has fed upon that which it knew to be virile and strong rather than on that which was soft and light in character .... Now, if female culture – or at least what we have seen of it so far – is a parasitic culture, it cannot but depress the sap's vitality and richness, even sucking the life from the last remaining branches. And indeed this is what happens, and in this environment the de-nourished masculine culture finds nothing better to do than to incline towards femininity and start living a parasitic existence itself.[56]

The image of women sucking sap from the strong 'trunk' of masculine culture – at once abhorrent yet titillating – reveals Torrefranca's anxieties about the existence of a female plot to enfeeble men. The metaphor of the parasite resonates with the widespread contemporary fear that, at the same time as having to contemplate its relationship with its external neighbours, the Italian state was also under attack from a number of enemies within. Once again, Torrefranca played upon the association between physical anatomy and the political corpus, recalling Proudhon's vision of the French nation as a body attacked by gangrene.[57] The implication that Puccini was a parasite associated him with attempts to weaken the national moral fibre, as well as casting doubt upon his sexuality.

PUCCINI AS 'JEW'

In the cultural rhetoric of all West European cultures during the late nineteenth and early twentieth centuries, charges of sickness were regularly applied to 'outsider' groups such as Jews and foreigners.[58] Like women, Jews were frequently depicted as parasites, infiltrating society and attacking it from within. Again, it is profitable to turn to Otto Weininger in order to illustrate the close connection between misogynist and anti-Semitic rhetoric: 'Judaism is saturated with femininity' and 'like women, because they are nothing in themselves, [Jews] can become everything'.[59] It should be remembered that Weininger was himself Jewish and his attack on the Jews, like his attack on homosexuals, was to a large extent an expression of his own self-loathing. Italian critics, including those who were themselves Jews, appear to have accepted this aspect of Weininger's thesis without reservation. The persistent intersection of misogyny and anti-Semitism is further demonstrated by the fact that Lombroso – also Jewish – followed *La donna delinquente* with *L'antisemitismo e le scienze moderne* (1894), a book that purported to defend the Jews but in reality vilified them, employing similar rhetoric to that used in his condemnation of women.

Anti-Semitic stereotypes also informed Torrefranca's attack on Puccini; while he never explicitly referred to the composer as Jewish, his subtext is clear. Torrefranca's seemingly bizarre disparagement of 'Jewish' traits in a non-Jewish composer gains a certain perverse 'logic' in the context of Weiningerian thought. Weininger wrote in *Geschlecht und Charakter*:

> I must, however, make clear what I mean by Judaism; I mean neither a race nor a people nor a recognised creed. I think of it as a tendency of the mind, as a psychological constitution which is possible for all mankind, but which has become actual in the most conspicuous fashion only amongst the Jews.[60]

Such thinking was fairly commonplace in early-twentieth-century Europe; in France, for example, Vincent d'Indy was similarly prone to attacking non-Jewish composers for possessing 'Jewish' characteristics, which he defined as superficiality, greed and, most important, a derivative artistic style cobbled together from a variety of national schools.[61] Thus, the fact that Puccini was not Jewish was no hindrance to highlighting the purportedly 'Jewish' characteristics of his music. Torrefranca stated that 'in Puccini, a truly personal quest for the new is absent'[62] and argued that when borrowing traits from French, German and Russian composers, Puccini 'never succeeds in enlarging upon that which he has learned from others but makes use of it to form a "cliché" of modern music, blessed by success and acclaimed by fashion'.[63]

Not only did Torrefranca chastise Puccini for the very act of attempting to imitate foreign composers; he also blamed him for the fact that the results were unconvincing. In his view, Puccini lacked the breeding or aptitude for study and thought that would equip him to understand or attain 'fluency' in foreign musical styles.[64] 'Ignorant of foreign languages', Puccini was nevertheless the international composer *par excellence*, adept at creating works that were not Italian, Russian, German or French, but that had all the easy syntax and commercial advantages of Esperanto.[65] He could only pick at them, lifting the crudest features of foreign music and rearranging them in ad hoc fashion, and the result was a style that was fragmented and dismembered, hardly a fitting national music. Torrefranca was not the only commentator to warn of the political dangers of writing 'derivative' music in an age of easy international communications; the phenomenon was of concern to conservative commentators across Europe. In a nationalist tract published in London contemporaneously with Torrefranca's book, the English writer on music and composer Cecil Forsyth, for example, warned how dishonest, imitative music could lead to spiritual decay and be unpatriotic. He wrote: 'We have, unfortunately, always had the imitator with us, and he has produced for us endless imitations of Handel, Haydn, Beethoven, Mendelssohn, Wagner, and Tchaikowsky. Now he is beginning to turn his attention to Richard Strauss and Claude Debussy; but however clever his imitations may be – and they are often diabolically clever – there is in them all a seed of death. It is dishonest music; or worse, it is treacherous.'[66]

Ironically, given Torrefranca's chastisement of Puccini for being too international, his rhetoric was highly derivative of Wagner's. He was surely familiar with that composer's 'Das Judentum in der Musik' since the original essay, translated as 'Il Giudaismo nella musica', was published in full in the *Rivista musicale italiana* in 1897 in response to reader demand.[67] Torrefranca's attack on Puccini's desire and efforts to compose in 'foreign' styles paraphrases Wagner's theories about

Jewish attempts to speak foreign languages, which he then extended to their efforts in musical composition:

> The Jew converses in the tongue of the people amongst whom he dwells from age to age, but he does this invariably after the manner of a foreigner. . . . The general circumstance that a Jew speaks his modern European language only as if acquired and not as if he were native to it shuts him out from all capability of full, independent and characteristic expression of his ideas.[68]

According to Wagner, therefore, a Jew's inability to understand foreign languages properly meant that he remained perpetually incapable of expressing himself coherently. Wagner referred to Jews using a 'confused heap . . . of words and phrases' and to Jewish composers likewise making 'a confused heap of the forms and styles of all ages and masters'.[69] Wagner's theories were, of course, far from new, and drew upon the well-established myth of the rootless wandering Jew, which was exploited with new vehemence in the nineteenth century across Europe in order to use the Jews as scapegoats for wider cultural concerns.

Italians prided themselves upon being immune to anti-Semitism, and it was a commonly held conviction in the early twentieth century that as a result of successful assimilation there was no 'Jewish problem' in Italy, in contrast with neighbours such as France. Following unification, Jews ostensibly enjoyed complete emancipation, held prominent positions in society and, having been resident in Italy for many centuries, were not regarded as foreigners. In reality, however, Italy had a long history of characterising the Jew as an outsider, at all levels from popular fiction to highbrow literature.[70] Furthermore, at the turn of the twentieth century, anti-Semitism was becoming more widespread among the artistic avant garde, who regarded Jews as the personification of the much-detested bourgeoisie, whom they saw as materialistic, cowardly, pacifist supporters of internationalism.[71] Seeking to stoke subconscious prejudices, Torrefranca could be sure that the metaphors that he employed were familiar to his readers, however blind to racial difference they might outwardly claim to be. That the analogy of the rootless Jew struck a smarting chord with contemporary Italians is illustrated by Sighele's warning against cultural internationalism: 'races ... that cast aside or forget their duty, that have no roots and that are not attached to memories ... are ... dispersed races like the Jews'.[72] Sighele had perhaps been inspired in turn by the great Italian patriot Mazzini, who had written: 'without a fatherland you ... are the bastards of humanity. Soldiers without a flag, the Israelites of nations'.[73] In an era in which Italy wanted to shout more loudly on the international stage, the charge that its foremost composer was a speaker of foreign tongues, diluting Italian culture from within, suggested that, in reality, the nation had no voice of its own.

AN AMPUTATED ART

In much the same way that Chopin's contemporaries labelled him 'effeminate' because he specialised in small-scale works for domestic or salon consumption,[74] Torrefranca drew a connection between Puccini and the 'feminine' genre in which he composed. Torrefranca described opera as an incomplete art, devoid of true content, and the opera composer as nothing more than 'a failed musician, an incomplete artist'.[75] Once again, he could not resist the temptation of making mocking reference to Puccini's virility, calling opera the collaboration of 'two impotents', and 'an amputation' – surely a barely disguised reworking of the hysterical castration imagery that haunted the *fin de siècle*, especially in the vogue for plays, operas and paintings based upon the story of John the Baptist and Salome (by Wilde, Strauss, Massenet, Moreau and others).[76]

For Torrefranca, Puccini's *demi-monde* heroines mirrored opera's own wantonness.[77] Here again is evidence of a selective reading of Wagner: in this instance the claim in *Opera and Drama* that Italian opera is a harlot, a degenerate woman who gives herself to lovers indiscriminately with no worthier motivation than a desire for money.[78] Attacking what most Italians considered to be a proud and glorious tradition, Torrefranca implied that it was shameful that, for centuries, an art form that he considered to be corrupt and emasculated should have represented Italy. For him the opera composer was the result of 'a degeneration of ancestral lineage' – a threat to pure Italian blood – and the public's predilection for opera indicative of a weak and submissive national character.[79] Torrefranca exploited images of hazy sexual identities to strike at the heart of a nation that associated opera closely with its sense of self. That jealous foreigners might deride Italian opera as effeminate was perhaps only to be expected, but for an *Italian* musicologist to do so was alarming indeed. In a pre-emptive strike against possible charges of disloyalty, Torrefranca argued that it was not he but those who listened to and enjoyed contemporary opera who were unpatriotic.

What, then, did Torrefranca see as the alternative to opera's stranglehold on Italian musical life? His manifesto for artistic reform was two-pronged. On the one hand he championed the careers of the avant-garde composers whom he saw as representing the new voice of Italy: Ildebrando Pizzetti (1880–1968), Gian Francesco Malipiero (1882–1973) and Alfredo Casella (1883–1947). Simultaneously, he was an active member of the circle calling for the revival of early Italian music, which included the playwright D'Annunzio, the composer Malipiero, the composer, lecturer and critic Giacomo Orefice and the librarian and archivist Angelo Solerti among its numbers.[80] The movement was a politically charged one, analogous to similar endeavours in France, such as those of Vincent d'Indy (a member of the *Ligue de la patrie française*), who promoted early music as the starting place for French cultural regeneration in his teachings at the Schola Cantorum. This group of artists, scholars and librarians were driven by nationalist fervour as much as Puccini's supporters, but for them, capturing the essence of Italianness meant looking back to an earlier age and renouncing the current vogue for sentimental realist opera, which they saw as having bastardised and emasculated the Italian musical tradition. Many of the Italian early music revivalists transcribed, edited and promoted the works of early opera composers such as Monteverdi. Torrefranca, however, renounced opera altogether, damning the fact that Italy was 'a nation that still does not know the history of its own music', arguing that 'the history of Italian music is not the history of opera' and seeking to create a new national artistic aesthetic through the promotion of *musica pura*.[81] For Torrefranca, Italian music had been in a state of decline since the late seventeenth century,[82] and the current musical establishment sought deliberately to perpetuate ignorance of Italy's non-operatic musical past.

Torrefranca approached his task with quasi-religious zeal, calling for 'the spiritual regeneration of musical Italy',[83] and his endeavour to rewrite musical history was strongly nationalistic in tone. In addition to denigrating opera as the bearer of Italian culture it also reveals the anti-German prejudices for which he was well known. He envisioned a situation whereby Italy might compensate for its military inferiority to its northern neighbour by attempting to usurp German cultural dominance. In common with many young Italian critics and composers who had received their musical training abroad, Torrefranca was uncomfortably aware that German instrumental music occupied a position at the top of the European artistic hierarchy, a position he hoped to reclaim for Italy. Alleging that Italian composers had sown the seeds of the most highly revered music of the past 150 years – the symphonic tradition – he appropriated Mozart, Haydn and Beethoven as honorary Italians, and promoted the music of such composers as Corelli, Veracini, Vivaldi, Vitali, Pasquini and Platti.[84] Torrefranca sought to claim that it was the sonata – characterised by order, logic and the predominance of the masculine according to theorists from A. B. Marx to Vincent D'Indy – rather than opera that was the truly Italian national music.[85]

MALE MEDUSAS

As the products of a feminised composer working in a feminised genre, it was only natural that Puccini's male characters should seem unmanly. In typically purple prose, Torrefranca portrayed them as sexually ambiguous sea creatures:

> Des Grieux and Marcello, Rodolfo and Pinkerton belong to the world of what could be termed invertebrate men, which is also the world of neurasthenic lovers and frenzied hypochondriacs. They are the

molluscs of literature, hydras and light and transparent medusas, which, suspended in the gentle water of the poetic pond that produced them, have a form that can be graceful and wandering, while, when they are removed from their natural environment – and artificial ponds are dried out every so often by temporary droughts or through the need to be cleaned out – they become little more than a shapeless blob of gelatine.[86]

This description is replete with *fin-de-siècle* indicators of femininity: sickness, fluidity, formlessness and dependency. Puccini's characters as portrayed here are more evocative of the watery women of Gustav Klimt's paintings or sinuous art nouveau women mutating into plants and fishes than fitting models of Italian masculinity. Again, in characterising Puccini's men as 'invertebrates' Torrefranca creates an image not merely of metaphorical spinelessness, but of impotence and of possible homosexuality, for to call a man an 'invert' at this time was to cast doubt upon his sexual preferences.

But Torrefranca's rhetoric was not merely zoological: his mythological references reversed the classical images used by the pro-Puccini camp. As well as denoting an amorphous primitive life form that it is impossible to kill, the hydra was the many-headed snake killed by Hercules, whose heads grew as fast as they were cut off. More striking still is the allusion to the Medusa, the woman turned into a Gorgon with venomous snakes for hair as punishment for boasting of her beauty, and who turned all those who looked upon her into stone. Omnipresent in decadent iconography, the Medusa represented the ultimate *fin-de-siècle* nightmare of unrestrained female sexuality and evil: having appropriated male power, she was vain, destructive towards men, but also tempting.

FEARS OF A FEMINISED CULTURE

To appreciate the damaging implications of Torrefranca's depiction of a feminised Puccini it is crucial to understand both the intensity of misogynist feeling that developed in Italy in the years preceding the First World War, and its close association with nationalist ambition.

As elsewhere in Europe at the turn of the century, feminism provoked a violent backlash on the part of male commentators. The Italian women's emancipation movement began to stir in Milan in the 1880s with the foundation of several organisations devoted to the cause of women's suffrage, such as Anna Maria Mozzoni's Lega Promotrice degli Interessi Femminili. The socialist Anna Kuliscioff gave a speech in 1890 entitled 'Il monopolio dell'uomo' in which she spoke of the serious and widespread demand for emancipation that she detected among Italian women.[87] Despite the efforts of a few notable individuals such as Kuliscioff, feminist Teresa Labriola and novelist Sibilla Aleramo, and the foundation of women's journals such as *La donna* and *La cornelia*, the women's movement was impeded by low levels of literacy and was at first slow to develop beyond the salons of privileged gentlewomen. In 1908, however, 1,400 women attended the first congress of the Consiglio Nazionale delle Donne Italiane in Rome.[88] Most male critics reacted to the suggestion of female emancipation with frenzy, despite Italian feminism's relative restraint and prudence compared with its British counterpart.

The vast number of texts on the 'woman question' published in Italy in the first years of the twentieth century challenge any notion that Italy remained immune from the pan-European debate over feminism. Italian men – and some women – were suspicious of the developments taking place abroad and hoped to quell feminism in Italy by ridiculing it as a foreign import.[89] Around 700 titles were listed under the subject heading *donne* in the general catalogue of Italian books published during the 1900s, 1910s and 1920s, representing one of the longest entries in the inventory.[90] Alongside comportment manuals, books on women's health and beauty, and the predictably large body of literature on women and Catholicism were to be found many works on women's education and entry into the professions. A large number of titles reflected upon contemporary social issues such as divorce and female suffrage, and there was even a category devoted to 'women's shortcomings': intellectual inferiority, infantilism, degeneracy, alcoholism, criminality and neurasthenia.

Some thirty titles listed in the catalogue included the phrase *la missione della donna*, reinforcing the need for women to devote their energies fully to motherhood. Predictably, writers exploited the politics of reproduction in order to raise the Italian anti-feminist consciousness, a discourse into which Torrefranca tapped with his reference to a 'de-nourished culture'.[91] These years witnessed widespread anxiety at declining birth rates (which still seem astonishingly high by our standards): of the generation of Italian women born between 1871 and 1886, only 25 percent produced seven or more children as opposed to 40 percent of the previous generation.[92] In Italy, as in France, fear of declining fertility rates became intertwined with Darwin-inspired anxieties about the proliferation of the weak at the expense of the élite, with consequent military implications.[93]

Such concerns even permeated the fine arts. When Torrefranca described parasitic women in trees, he may well have been recalling Giovanni Segantini's 1894 canvas *Le cattive madri*, inspired, ironically, by a poem of 1889 entitled 'Nirvana' by none other than Luigi Illica, one of Puccini's librettists. The painting depicts a woman in a state of sexual ecstasy suspended in a tree, holding a dead or dying baby. Segantini thus presented modern women's rejection of motherhood as the selfish exercise of personal choice at the expense of duty to others; the punishment for their lustful ways was banishment to the icy mountains, where, in return for repentance, they would be reunited with the children who might have been. Here is the stereotypical woman-as-nature trope gone wrong: the trees are gnarled, the background is a cold, barren wasteland, a metaphor for the subject's own sterility. It is unclear whether Segantini's censure of self-indulgence at the expense of procreation was targeted specifically at Italian women. The painting exploited pan-European anxieties, yet the painter's depiction of women here and elsewhere seems harsh even by the standards of customarily misogynist *fin-de-siècle* art. No attempt was made to coat the women in a seductive gloss for the delectation of the viewer: they are angular, tormented and ugly, and Segantini's titles are always bluntly moralising. The painting was exhibited at the second Milan Triennale, an important showcase for the latest Italian art, attended by politicians and royalty, its warning to modern women thus implicitly being given official state approval.[94]

The creation of a 'symbolic code of national femininity', centring on a quasi-religious idolisation of women, was part of the post-1861 project of cultural unification.[95] Italy had the reputation of being a fiercely matriarchal society that 'made the nineteenth-century cult of motherhood into a national devotion';[96] Mantegazza called woman 'the vestal virgin of morality and human idealism'.[97] However, by the 1910s, a far more virulent strain of anti-feminism had developed, in which 'feminine' culture represented a significant threat to the fabric of the nation. The depraved model of womanhood presented by Torrefranca contradicted the Catholic view of woman as a morally civilising force that had prevailed only a few decades earlier, and is indicative of a dramatic paradigm shift in Italian culture, attributed by many contemporary commentators to the corrupting influence of French literary models.[98] Torrefranca's book demonstrates that the notion of Puccini's operas as national art came to be increasingly at odds with a culture of intensifying aggression, which opposed all remnants of what it saw as the effeminate, bourgeois *belle époque*. Just as thinkers such as Weininger and Papini believed that only by annihilating women might humanity attain fulfilment, Torrefranca suggested that culture too must liberate itself from all traces of the feminine.

AFTERMATH: CRITICAL RESPONSES

What, then, were the critical reactions to Torrefranca's monograph? The response of the official Puccini machine was silence. As the biggest player in a large, commercially successful industry – of which Torrefranca had declared himself contemptuous – Ricordi could perhaps afford to ignore the young musicologist's opinions. And Puccini himself, unsurprisingly, declined to comment in public. At times his letters betray a tendency towards profound self-pity in reaction to the mildest of negative press reports, yet on other occasions he claimed to take no interest in the views of critics, writing to his confidante Sybil Seligman after a performance of *Manon Lescaut* in Paris in 1910, 'Those pigs – the gentlemen of the press – were full of bile against me, and who cares a fig, if the public takes my side in this way?'[99] Similarly, on another occasion he was quoted by his biographer Dante del Fiorentino as having said:

> They [the critics] are absolutely useless, and they do so much harm. It is very amusing to hear them telling me how to compose. I write as my heart dictates. If I do not produce the music that pleases them, then it is either because I do not want to produce that music or because I am incapable of producing it. I must express my own ideas – nothing else matters.[100]

Yet Torrefranca's comments must have been devastating. There is only a single reference to the book in Puccini's published correspondence, in which the composer remarked in a letter dating from 1915 to Alfredo Vandini, a childhood friend, that 'dear Torrefranca ... could do with a good cudgelling',[101] revealing that the wounds had not healed even three years after the book's publication.

An absence of reviews of Torrefranca's book in the lightweight music periodicals that saturated the market is not surprising. As glorified listings magazines or publicity vehicles run by theatrical agencies, in which the level of criticism did not extend beyond reporting how many curtain calls a performance received, theirs were not the pages in which to discuss a monograph of this kind. In a country in which literacy levels remained low outside of the affluent north, print runs and sales figures for serious books on music were small.[102] Moreover, as a critical text on a contemporary composer, Torrefranca's book was something of an oddity. Hence there was little point in the popular music periodicals reviewing a book that was unlikely to reach the average bourgeois opera-goer. One critic, seeking to cast aspersions upon both Puccini and his audiences, remarked acidly, 'the person who loves Puccini would certainly never read a book on him: they would merely go and hear his operas'.[103]

However, it is unlikely to have been of concern to Torrefranca that his monograph was read only by an élite, for it encompassed the crucial intelligentsia that he wished to address. Moreover, the impressive coverage that Torrefranca's book gained in serious musicological or cultural journals published in Milan, Turin, Rome and Florence – and the fact that it attracted attention abroad – should be regarded as exceptional, particularly given the writer's youth. The chorus of approval that greeted the book from critics such as Mario Ferraguti in *Vita musicale* and the unsigned reviewer in the *Rivista teatrale italiana* would appear to substantiate Torrefranca's claim that he was voicing a widely shared opinion.[104] Indeed, Domenico De Paoli would write with hindsight in 1939, 'Nobody, until then, had spoken out with such frankness against the dominant art, but the words of Torrefranca – tone apart – revealed the thought that many young people, whether musicians or simply music lovers, had not dared to express.'[105]

In 1912 the monograph attracted praise for its prose style, its incisiveness, and its 'tastily satirical' metaphors.[106] Critics who endorsed the book lingered approvingly over its most damning – and most feminising – accusations: Puccini's artificiality, insincerity, monotony, emptiness, laziness and uniformity. The charge that Puccini was 'not a real musician' found wide support, while Ferraguti borrowed Torrefranca's metaphor of the parasite to argue that Puccini was 'a weakling', 'a woman', because he always hung off someone else's arm rather than offering his own.[107] Since there were no written reactions to Torrefranca's depictions of women, homosexuals and Jews as harbingers of social disintegration, we can speculate that they were accepted as given.

At the opposite end of the critical spectrum, other critics seemed to leap to Puccini's defence. Foreign observers looked on with horror as Puccini was attacked by one of his own kinsmen: in an extravagantly entitled article in the *Cleveland Leader*, for example, Raymond O'Neil depicted Puccini as a betrayed Caesar.[108] O'Neil called Torrefranca a 'traitor ... who does not let patriotism stand the least in the way of his consigning Puccini and several other Italian composers to oblivion', and reported that a 'violent newspaper controversy' had arisen in Rome, with 'protests and congratulations and satirical letters' being published by the dozen.[109] When Torrefranca complained to the editor of the *Tribuna* about the newspaper's criticism of his book, the editor reportedly replied:

> Has Torrefranca desired or has he not to proclaim the baseness of our national opera, excoriating the group which includes the composer of the *Matrimonio segreto*, the *Vestale*, *Guglielmo Tell*, *Favorite*, *Cavalleria rusticana*, etc., and offending all who feel the highest admiration for these great artists? Has Torrefranca used or has he not language of the most outrageous kind, exercising a criticism which may well be called homicidal, since it tends in the manner of a principle of art to destroy a composer dear to the public of two hemispheres – namely Giacomo Puccini?[110]

However, close analysis of Italian reviews ostensibly hostile to Torrefranca reveals a greater degree of consensus among critics on both sides than is initially apparent. Ferruccio Vecchi, writing in the lightweight *Il trovatore*, believed Torrefranca's attack upon Puccini's character to be exaggerated, and ridiculed his diatribe against opera *per se*.[111] However, such comments were a smokescreen: he could find few concrete words of praise for opera's leading contemporary exponent, and tellingly the grandiose declarations about Italian passion and inspiration with which his review closed referred to Verdi rather than to Puccini. Even reviewers who were sufficiently hostile to Torrefranca to dismiss him as a 'pseudo-critic' and 'dilettante' conceded that nobody would attempt to exalt Puccini to the level of a Verdi or a Wagner.[112] But Vecchi went further, implicating Puccini in the current trend towards decadence and admitting that his works were frequently far from original. Thus, a review that purported to defend Puccini effectively reinforced many of Torrefranca's accusations.

Torrefranca's book was reviewed in *Il mondo artistico* by Silvio Benco, one of the most cultured journalists of his age, a specialist in politics, history, art, theatre and music, who also provided libretti for the operas of Smareglia and Malipiero. Benco made much of the fact that although he was personally indifferent to Puccini's music, he felt obliged to shield the composer from an attack of such severity.[113] However, any compliments that he hoped to pay were distinctly double-edged: he 'defended' Puccini by arguing that the composer had never expressed aspirations to great art, as was obvious from his setting of works by 'facile' and 'insincere' writers. Moreover, Benco, a passionate Wagnerian, accepted all of Torrefranca's basic premises: Italian music's descent from glory, the self-evident inferiority of opera to absolute music and the noxious influence of uniform 'international' opera. Benco wrote disparagingly of music that pandered to 'men of the lower classes and women' and observed that the real artist did not concern himself with the emotional needs of 'ignorants and little women'.[114]

Even those reviews that expressed outraged claims of foul play, then, were nevertheless underpinned by an implicit groundswell of support for Torrefranca's general claims. Critics may have challenged Torrefranca over technicalities, but not one of them felt able to express wholehearted support for Puccini. The charge of 'effeminacy' struck a chord among reviewers: of those who did not explicitly applaud Torrefranca's assessment, several showed tacit support by reporting the accusation without comment, whilst others tactfully ignored a sensitive issue. Why Puccini's supporters did not try to refute Torrefranca by reference to the standard Classical images that accompanied popular perceptions of the composer (see chapter 1) is unclear; it would seem that such rhetoric was drowned out, at least temporarily, by the polemic presented in Torrefranca's book. In fact the seeds of Torrefranca's apparently extreme rhetoric were present in countless earlier reviews of Puccini's works, including those written by the composer's own allies, and the aspects of Puccini's work to which he objected would continue to trouble later commentators. In many ways, Puccini's detractors and defenders did not disagree over the traits they perceived in his works; rather, they presented differing evaluations of these characteristics. Torrefranca's polemic, by far the most critical attack, would cast a long shadow over Puccini's reputation in the years to come.

6 | The Italian composer as internationalist

The 1910s were, on the whole, unhappy years for Puccini. It is hard to imagine how his reputation as national composer could have withstood the blow dealt to it by Torrefranca's book, which had denounced his music so explicitly and publicly as unoriginal, artificial, merely decorative, effeminate and diseased. Unfortunately for Puccini, the reviews of his operas of the 1910s, and particularly of *La fanciulla del West* and *La rondine*, did little to refute Torrefranca's objections, and the charges of insincerity and fragmentation in his music that critics had been pressing for near on two decades merely grew louder. Of particular concern was the issue of internationalism, which emerged prominently at this stage in Puccini's career for a number of reasons: because it had been problematised so stridently in Torrefranca's book, because received notions of Italian national identity were being vociferously challenged by the new nationalists during the 1910s and because Puccini's operas of this period were all first performed in front of foreign audiences. For many observers this last trend raised questions about Puccini's commitment to carrying on the Italian tradition, at a time when the long-standing anxieties about what constituted 'Italian music' were intensifying. As Francesco Balilla Pratella, a member of the Italian musical avant garde, observed in Verdi's centenary year (1913): 'A great preoccupation for all musicians, whether old or young, is that of the question of *italianità*. Our musicians are no longer sure of their Italianness.'[1]

The Italian 1910s ostensibly got off to a patriotic start, for 1911 was *giubileo* year, marking the passing of fifty years since the foundation of the Kingdom of Italy in 1861. Numerous festivities were held to mark the anniversary and the extravagant Vittorio Emanuele Monument in Rome was completed, making a bold statement about Italy's national greatness to the rest of the world. It should by rights have been a moment of unsullied glory, the whole nation rallying round in joyous celebration, yet despite Prime Minister Giolitti's democratising measures and claims of a united society, the splits between various political factions and ideological groupings were growing ever deeper: socialists, republicans and Catholics abstained from and protested against the *festa della nazione* on the grounds that it did not represent 'their' Italy. Another group who resolutely refused to toe the party line was the nationalist right discussed in chapter 5: the invasion of Libya in September 1911 was in part intended to placate this fractious group, but would, of course, backfire, turning into yet another imperialist miscalculation. Half a century after the unification of Italy, there continued to be little shared sense of what it meant to be Italian, as Benedetto Croce observed in the same year, extending familiar arguments about organicism to the social corpus:

> I believe that every alert and unbiased observer of the present Italian spiritual life cannot fail to be struck by the decadence that one notices in the idea of social unity . . . . Individuals no longer feel linked to a greater whole, part of a greater whole.[2]

The nationalist celebrations of 1911 also prompted Scipio Sighele – an activist for the Associazione Nazionalista Italiana in its early years – to voice the anxiety that many Italian nationalists felt about the growing vogue for internationalism:

> Weak individuals and communities – those who lack an awareness of their own nationality – are not merely content to reduce themselves to that common denominator that is international uniformity . . . , but spontaneously 'denationalise'. They make a show of their denationalisation, believing it to be a sign of good taste to denationalise. They only appreciate and buy foreign clothes; dress themselves and decorate their homes in the foreign manner; educate themselves chiefly from foreign books; only draw upon foreign examples in politics, art and science; and are unwittingly happy to appear completely detached and almost uprooted from their Italian roots. In this way they believe themselves to have arrived at the apex of civilisation, modernity and superiority.[3]

Italians were, as we have seen, highly susceptible to the spell of internationalism: it was therefore perhaps only natural that they should be easily 'detached and uprooted from their Italian roots' when such a sense of common origins had not yet been firmly established. Mindful of this state of affairs, Sighele urged Italians to assert their culture more strongly:

> We are slaves of foreign culture: we have subjugated our spirit to foreign culture. Is it not perhaps time to tear ourselves away from this slavery, and to seek to subjugate the foreign spirit to *our* culture?[4]

For Puccini's supporters this was precisely what his operas could achieve. They asserted that the international appeal of his music was attributable to what they claimed to be its strong national character. From their perspective, Latin civilisation encompassed values that could be universally understood, and just as the Romans had exported their beliefs and art to the rest of the world, so too might the new Italy; thus the fact that Puccini's operas were successfully produced abroad was proof of the health or even the hegemony of Italian culture. In 1910, Eugenio Checchi, whom we encountered in Chapter 1, continued to portray Puccini as the embodiment of Italian art, and rejoiced in the fact that he was exporting it to the New World. In an article about *La fanciulla del West* he wrote: 'Italian art, harbinger and herald of liberty when we were oppressed and humiliated by despots both domestic and foreign, continues its noble mission today, and helps to create brotherhood between peoples much more effectively than pedantic protocol and diplomatic absurdity ever could.'[5]

For Puccini's adversaries, however, his music was attractive to foreigners for precisely the opposite reason: because it had no significant national character and was not firmly rooted in a tradition. In the eyes of Torrefranca and other earlier commentators who had expressed concern at Puccini's apparently wilful renunciation of national traits, the composer's internationalism signalled the decisive loss of an Italian musical identity. Puccini's global appeal was proof, for Torrefranca, of his cheap opportunism. The composer's eye for commercial exploitation meant that his operas were necessarily reduced to the lowest common denominator, no better than the plays and novels that pandered to frivolous francophile tastes. Moreover, Torrefranca accused Puccini of deliberately writing music that sought to distance itself from Italian traditions and a distinctive national character:

> Puccini, then, represents, better than other musicians, the progressive *denationalisation* of the Italian lyric theatre. And for this reason he succeeded in being the international opera composer *par excellence* at a time in which – except for the brief *Cavalleria* episode and the isolated case of *Falstaff* – the national art had not even one word to say to the world that was truly its own, truly characteristic, a profound expression of its historical moment.[6]

For Torrefranca, then, Puccini's music was the emblem of a nation that had lost its voice, that seemed on the point of being culturally eclipsed, a tendency Sighele had lamented when he wrote in 1910:

> The bell tolled to signal the imminent funeral of the Latin race, while the fanfares blared of the victorious and invading German race. The light, it was said, comes from the north. We, the Mediterranean peoples, condemned ourselves to retreat fatally into the shade.[7]

Puccini's operas drew censure not only from critics, however, but also from his fellow composers. By the second decade of the twentieth century members of the Italian musical avant garde, known as the *generazione dell'ottanta*, were beginning to express profound dissatisfaction with what they regarded as the uniform, reactionary and purely crowd-pleasing nature of contemporary opera. In 1910, when he was on the point of becoming an active member of the Futurist movement, Francesco Balilla Pratella noted 'the intellectual mediocrity, the commercial baseness and the hatred of anything new that reduces Italian music to a single and almost unvarying type of vulgar melodrama, which leads to our total inferiority in comparison with the forward-looking development of music in other countries'.[8] It is small wonder that Busoni was led to observe in 1912 that 'at the present time, Puccini is the sole Italian opera composer with an international reputation – and his countrymen do not like him at all'.[9] Nor, it seemed, did many of his foreign contemporaries. Puccini's absence from a list of noteworthy contemporary foreign composers that Vincent d'Indy sent to his friend Gabriel Marie in 1911 illustrates the low esteem in which Puccini's music was held by some foreign composers and critics. Marie was planning to put on a season of international music, and d'Indy recommended, amongst others, Strauss, Mahler and Bruckner as German composers of distinction, and Rimsky-Korsakov and Rachmaninov as illustrious Russians whose music might be included in the programme. However, he also suggested some less familiar names, including the Spaniard Mareira and the Norwegian Sinding, and even identified the now-forgotten Gilson, Vreuls and Dupuis as up-and-coming Belgian composers. Astonishingly, in the case of Italy he wrote simply: 'I've looked hard; I've found: o.'[10]

PUCCINI'S AMERICAN EXCURSION

Amid the heated discussions in 1911 about internationalism and the state of Italian culture, audiences had their first opportunity to hear an opera that struck to the heart of such debates: Puccini's *La fanciulla del West*. The first Italian performance took place at the Teatro Costanzi in Rome on 12 June 1911 and was a much-hyped event, as the first hearing of a new Puccini opera since the ill-fated *Madama Butterfly* seven years earlier. The Rome audience was eager to hear a work that had already achieved what the reporter for the *Nuova antologia* had called 'a triumph of American proportions' at its première proper on 10 December 1910 at the old New York Metropolitan Opera House, where it had been greeted by some fifty-five curtain calls.[11]

The Metropolitan Opera had never previously staged a world première, and this was New York's chance to establish itself as a major operatic centre. The staging on American soil of a new work by Italy's pre-eminent composer was a huge coup for a nation that felt inferior to Europe in terms of artistic achievement. This time, the Met's publicists assured New Yorkers, the European audiences would be jealous of them, and the opera house spared no expense in turning the première into a glittering social occasion, granting the press 'exclusive' advance interviews with Puccini and Toscanini. Tickets went on sale for twice their usual price, with individual seats selling for as much as $150 on the black market, a huge sum in 1910. As Annie J. Randall and Rosalind Gray Davis have shown in their recent study of *La fanciulla del West*'s American reception, the symbolism and sums of money invested in the opera's première were such that it could not afford to be anything less than a sensation and the opera's triumph was to a large extent engineered.[12]

The Met publicists emphasised the fact that *La fanciulla del West* was 'the perfect blend of two worlds', old and new, and the theatre was decked out in Italian *tricolores* and American stars and stripes for the occasion. The opera brought together the cream of artistic talent from both sides of the Atlantic: an Italian composer, librettists and conductor; a popular American playwright; and a cast including Italian, French, Spanish and Polish singers, headed by the Czech star Emmy Destinn. No less cosmopolitan were the audience members: the great American nouveau riche families filled the boxes, while the cheap seats were packed with Italian immigrants who had come to hear their idol Enrico Caruso, a working-class Italian boy made good. Puccini's 'internationalism' had, it seemed, become a positive selling point. The reviewers, on the other hand, almost without exception contested the authenticity of the opera's 'American' atmosphere, gestures and music.[13] This was an issue of obvious interest in America, a nation arguably even less confident about its cultural identity than early-twentieth-century Italy, and where the question of what might constitute American music was being fiercely debated following Dvořák's suggestion in the 1890s that African-American spirituals be used as the starting point for a new American musical style.

The accuracy of the aspects of American life depicted in *Fanciulla* and the authenticity of the music were of less interest to the Italian press, which concentrated for the most part upon other issues. Nevertheless, Puccini must surely have felt aggrieved by the reception his work received in the New York press, for it bolstered the criticisms

Italian reviewers had been levelling at him for years about the uniformity of the local colour in his works. In calling *Fanciulla* a 'synergy of old and new, European and American', the Met publicists sought both to stimulate American interest in the work and to confer upon it the cachet of having been composed by the most prestigious of European opera composers.[14] However, this 'synergy' would later be interpreted by many Italian commentators as yet further evidence of Puccini's rootless internationalism, and *Fanciulla* was widely depicted as an unsatisfactory hybrid work, an unsuitable opera for a national composer to have written.

Somewhat vexed that the opera had been performed abroad first, both in the United States and also in England (where it received a mixed reception at Covent Garden on 29 May 1911), the Italian press in June 1911 made much of the fact that Puccini's opera had now 'come home'. The Italian première also had patriotic significance: the new work by the nation's pre-eminent composer was presented as the cultural centrepiece of the *giubileo* festivities, a demonstration to the many foreign visitors and Italian senators and deputies in the audience of the good health of contemporary Italian music.[15] Paradoxically, then, whereas the American press had expected an American opera, the Italian musical establishment were determined that *Fanciulla* should be an *Italian* masterpiece.

With the world's eyes upon it, Puccini's opera could not afford to be anything other than a national triumph, and predictably it was reported as such by his most determined supporters, writing in the contemporary music magazines aimed at a popular readership. The critic for the *Frusta teatrale* reported the work to be 'a new, powerful manifestation of Puccini's musical genius', demonstrating the composer to be a master of musical technique and colour,[16] while *Lirica* declared that there were passages in Puccini's new work (especially the nostalgia song) that were destined to become as memorable as 'E lucevan le stelle' from *Tosca*.[17] For *Il trovatore*, the work marked 'a great step forward' for Puccini, and was 'a jewel box full of precious gems'.[18] Some open-minded critics saw Puccini's move to a more adventurous harmonic and orchestral palette as the next logical step in his career; the *Illustrazione italiana*, for example, reported that Puccini had remained recognisably himself in his new work but had also 'perfected himself'.[19] However, as we shall see, there was considerable resistance from other quarters to the more adventurous harmonic language Puccini had used in his new opera.

Fanciulla, which Puccini called 'the best opera I have written',[20] was reportedly received with genuine enthusiasm by the first-night audience, and was given the royal seal of approval when the king of Italy called Puccini to his box after the second act to congratulate him. The *Illustrazione italiana* announced that Rome had decreed the new opera a great success, 'without hesitation, without uncertainty, without opposition',[21] although some critics reported hearing negative comments during the intense discussions that took place in the corridors of the Teatro Costanzi during the intervals.[22] The critical reviews that followed included some of the harshest press criticism of Puccini to be penned to date.

According to Puccini's future librettist Giuseppe Adami, *Fanciulla* was a work that was balanced, full of colour, power and fresh inspiration, and above all 'Italian, healthy in an Italian way', its première the most significant event in Italian theatre for years.[23] However, there was a widespread perception that the opera was not a genuinely Italian work at all, with many observers expressing their anxieties about the foreign influences that they detected in it. After operas set in France and Japan, the American subject matter of *Fanciulla* ought to have been relatively untroubling to Italian audiences, although some critics used their reviews to question why Puccini repeatedly refrained from setting Italian subjects, a strand of criticism that would intensify over the coming years. Of more concern was the perception that Puccini's score was 'contaminated' with foreign musical influences. Puccini's supporters praised him (in theory, at least) for keeping abreast of technical developments in modern music, somewhat surprisingly given the hostility such publications customarily expressed towards foreign music.

However, most commentators were critical in practice of what was perceived to be a rather blatant attempt on Puccini's part to imitate the harmonic language and orchestration of his foreign contemporaries, and Debussy in particular. These features were noted by the correspondent for *Musica* immediately after the New York première,[24] and subsequently by many critics in Rome. Other undesirable influences were apparent too: after hearing a revised reprise of *Fanciulla* in Rome in February 1915, the critic for the *Idea nazionale* derided the opera as a 'rather tedious medley of Viennese operetta with a dash of Wagner and authentic North-American film'.[25] The reviewer preferred to remain anonymous but was probably Fausto Torrefranca, who was the *Idea nazionale*'s regular music critic during the mid-1910s; certainly, his comments tally with Torrefranca's disparaging remarks about the 'Esperanto'-like quality of Puccini's musical language. His comments were echoed by Raffaello De Rensis, reviewing the first Italian performance in *Musica*, who wrote that the opera was constructed of a mishmash of dramatic episodes, matched by a hotchpotch of musical styles, ranging from monotonous Debussyisms in the first act to a medley of different melodic and instrumental styles later in the opera, with the result that 'no work has ended up as disconnected as this one, in terms of both words and music'.[26] Ironically, such criticisms mirrored Puccini's own original perception of Belasco's play, of which he wrote: 'I have found only some scenes here and there that are good. There is never a clear, simple line of development; just a hotch-potch and sometimes in very bad taste.'[27] Seemingly this was a reservation even Puccini himself had not been able to overcome.

Many commentators were particularly troubled by what they perceived to be the work's lack of lyricism in comparison with Puccini's earlier works, a point they expressed by arguing that *Fanciulla* was 'devoid of music'. The bafflement felt by some of Puccini's most ardent supporters in the conservative press is palpable. Pozza of the *Corriere della sera* boasted that *Fanciulla* had won a 'magnificent victory', and claimed that the work demonstrated 'a more secure mastery of his art' on Puccini's part.[28] Pozza found words of praise for the opera's form and orchestration, but was forced to admit that it could not surpass Puccini's earlier works in terms of inspiration, and later conceded that 'the music in the first act does not in fact have unity of form or continuity of development. It is often nothing more than a rapid descriptive or imitative commentary.'[29] That crucial 'Italian' quality of lyricism was deemed to be missing.

Thus the opera's music was perceived as 'un-American' by American critics and 'un-Italian' by their colleagues across the Atlantic. To the Americans it sounded resolutely Italian, the critic for the *Evening World* noting that 'the suave, mellifluous Italian phrases fall strangely upon the ears from the mouths of the rough and uncouth miners in a camp of forty-niners in California'.[30] For Italian critics, however, there was nothing discernibly Italian about Puccini's new score. Furthermore, many critics felt that Puccini had acted contrary to his natural instincts once again just as he had in *Tosca*: thus *Fanciulla* compounded the concerns about Puccini's sincerity that had been growing since the turn of the century. De Rensis argued that the opera had many 'deficient aspects' and 'lacked sincerity of expression', due to an 'assault' Puccini had inflicted upon his own temperament.[31] For this critic, Puccini's harmonic skill, such as it was, did not disguise the 'immense poverty of ideas', something that the critic observed with sarcasm had been 'respectable and admirable' when Puccini had expressed his scanty ideas clearly, but detestable when he tried to cloak them ostentatiously in Harlequin-like clothes.[32] In other words, Puccini may not be particularly inspired, but at least previously he had been honest. A lack of talent combined with pretensions to be something he was not, musically and dramatically, had produced a detestable result.

Many of the more conservative critics were evidently perplexed by the consciously modern style Puccini had adopted in his new work. However, even the more progressive critics, whom one might expect to have applauded such an endeavour, were not impressed. Carlo Cordara reviewed a performance of *La fanciulla del West* in Florence in April 1912 in *Il marzocco*, a serious weekly literary journal that included lengthy articles on culture, society, literature and the arts. Cordara refuted the widely held view that *Fanciulla* represented a significantly new style for Puccini, noting that the composer had been interested in exploring novel harmonic effects since his earliest works. Puccini's new opera was part of a gradual evolution rather than a revolution, but it was not an evolution that Cordara found convincing or particularly desirable. He used his article to note two different and almost antagonistic sides to Puccini's style, something that would become the focus of much attention a decade and a half later in the reviews of *Turandot*. On the one hand, Cordara wrote, there was 'the real and best' Puccini, the Puccini of *Manon*, *La bohème* and *Madama Butterfly*, 'the sincere and spontaneous musician' who could translate emotions into notes, who avoided rhetoric and shunned a descriptive, 'symphonic' style in favour of expressing his characters' feelings with sympathy and vivacity.[33] On the other, there was the Puccini of *Tosca* and *La fanciulla del West*, who set subjects too violent for his nature, and ended up producing works that were 'contorted, empty, bombastic, insincere'.[34] Moreover, there was nothing in *Fanciulla* that audiences had not seen and heard in Puccini's earlier, similarly misguided work: the poker game and scene where the blood drips through the ceiling were merely a *Grand-Guignolesque* throwback recalling the torture and shooting scenes in *Tosca*.

Continuing the analogies the critics of *Madama Butterfly* had drawn with the fine arts, Cordara wrote that Puccini had created his score from brief fragments, stuck together like a mosaic, or like an impressionist painting. This comment endorsed Torrefranca's argument that Puccini merely created a collage of modern techniques and devices drawn from his foreign contemporaries, which had little sense or meaning in their new context. Puccini's musical advances in the work were, therefore, purely superficial. Cordara admitted that these 'modern' effects might have persuaded the inexpert commentator that Puccini's style had progressed, but asserted that the reflective listener would find it difficult to see any signs of genuine progress in Puccini's new work. Puccini had attempted to achieve the maximum effect with the minimum inspiration, and written a work whose musical soul was absent. The opera's atmosphere was created purely through its libretto and scenery: Puccini's music had added nothing in terms of local colour. The stage 'effects' predominated to the extent that

Cordara perceived Puccini to have composed an empty music that sought to 'hide behind' the events being depicted in the drama.

Fanciulla was, then, an opera in which Puccini had found it hard to please anyone: for the conservatives his new work was too 'modern' and too much of a departure from the old Puccini whom they knew and loved, whereas more progressive critics could detect nothing new in the opera. There were revivals, but *Fanciulla* never entered the core repertory, even in Italy, and was far from being the 'second *Bohème*' that Puccini had envisaged.[35] Within a few years, critics were more open in acknowledging the weaknesses they perceived in the work. Looking back in 1923 Renzo Bianchi wrote that *Fanciulla* 'is perhaps the Maestro's least assured and least sincere work because the technical innovations he introduces seem to be more a preoccupation than an aspiration, more something he has set out to do than a natural inclination'.[36] The view from abroad was even more damning: in 1920 the Scottish critic Cecil Gray called *Fanciulla* 'one of those works that one could safely assert without contradiction to be one perpetual and unrelieved nausea from start to finish, from its sticky beginning to its sloppy end'.[37] After Puccini's death, even his supporters felt able to concede that *Fanciulla* was a misguided experiment; Arnaldo Bonaventura summed up the early-twentieth-century view of *Fanciulla* in his 1925 biography of the composer: 'By now everybody knows, because it is still repeated today *ad nauseam*, that ... *La fanciulla del West* represented a period of crisis.'[38] In truth, however, the real 'crisis' that this opera represented had little to do with music: the initial reception of *Fanciulla* in New York and Rome tells us far more about the inferiority complexes of contemporary Americans and Italians than it does about Puccini's opera itself.

ATTACKS FROM THE AVANT GARDE

Puccini's period of crisis did not end with *Fanciulla*. After the harsh blow dealt to him by the publication of Torrefranca's book in 1912, Puccini was the victim of a second literary assault in 1914, this time from his fellow composer, Ildebrando Pizzetti. The latter's *Musicisti contemporanei* was a study of selected pan-European musical figures of recent years, including Verdi, Boito, Debussy, Charpentier, Alberic Magnard, Ravel, Bloch and Puccini. Pizzetti's essay on Puccini had already appeared as a journal article in 1910, but reached a wider audience through its publication in this later volume. A postlude (dated 18 October 1913) that appeared when the essay was republished in the book asserted that Pizzetti stood by all the claims he had made in 1910. Hearing *Fanciulla* had not persuaded him to revise his negative opinion of Puccini's œuvre; indeed, he wrote: '[*Fanciulla*] presents characters so weary and impoverished to lead one to fear that Puccini will never again be able to rediscover the congenial freshness of *Manon* or *Bohème*',[39] although comments he had made earlier in the article indicate that his opinion of even these operas was not particularly high.

Pizzetti objected to certain aspects of Puccini's music, writing: 'His nature, the insignificant force of his feelings, the limited size of his intuitive ability, meant that he was only capable of producing little melodies, short-breathed and rather restricted in movement.'[40] For the most part, however, Pizzetti's objection to Puccini was more to do with his social role than with technical aspects of his compositional style. Pizzetti depicted Puccini as the product of a particular historical moment, of whose values the younger composer disapproved. During the last couple of decades of the nineteenth century, according to Pizzetti, there had been a shift in the sort of audience for whom operatic composers were expected to write. As the middle classes gained material wealth and social status, the Italian collective spirit came to be dominated by 'a bourgeoisie of mediocre artistic aspirations' and the prevailing taste was for 'an art of mediocre content and modest aims':[41] operas that were accessible and did nothing more than tug at the heart strings. This was particularly the case, Pizzetti argued, in Milan, where Puccini had spent his student years, and that had become 'the most bourgeois city in all of Italy' since the demise of the *scapigliatura* movement. Shaped by such an environment, Puccini's music was, according to Pizzetti, thoroughly representative of the values of the middle classes.

Pizzetti's article was first published in *La voce* and reflected the tone and stance of that journal.[42] As we have already seen, the *Voce* circle was highly critical of the Giolitti government and the social values it had fostered. Its members felt that the Giolitti era had been characterised by corruption, materialism and pragmatism, and they craved a nation founded upon higher ideals. Idealistic, anti-democratic and pro-aristocratic, the *Voce* circle despised the limited aspirations of the bourgeoisie, and Pizzetti saw a direct reflection of the bourgeois mindset in Puccini's works ('Puccini is a man who in a certain sense can do nothing other than express and live the selfish life of the bourgeoisie, of whom he is the most representative musician').[43] Pizzetti found it humiliating that Puccini's operas had come to represent the aesthetic taste of the Italians. However, for so long as the bourgeois mindset dominated Italian society, Italy could never, in Pizzetti's view, hope to raise the level of its culture and the aesthetic sensibility of the Italian people.

It was Puccini's status as the voice of the bourgeoisie that made him the obvious target for an even more strident attack in the autumn of that same year. The occasion was the first performance of *La fanciulla del West* at Milan's Teatro Dal Verme (the second production in the city, following a relatively successful run at La Scala two years earlier); the agitators were F. T. Marinetti's Futurists. Marinetti was an adept self-publicist, and in part the protest was merely a publicity stunt, using the Futurists' typical shock tactics. Choosing the first night of a run, albeit a reprise, of the most recent work by Italy's most prominent composer was guaranteed to attract press coverage, and the Futurists knew that influential members of Milanese society would be in attendance, along with the composer himself. However, the Futurists also had other agendas. Their first intention was to stage a protest against the Austrians, in order to further their campaign for Italian entry into the First World War: the performance of *Fanciulla* on 15 September 1914 coincided with the Battle of the Marne. Their second aim was to express their hostility towards a composer and an audience that represented everything that they held in contempt. Marinetti's disdain for the past – manifested most vehemently in his instruction to his followers to 'set fire to the bookshelves of the libraries! ... Deviate the route of canals to flood the museums!'[44] – also informed his attitude towards Puccini, the most prominent composer keeping alive an art form that, in the eyes of the Futurists, was nauseating and obsolete. The Futurists were enraged by the fact that Puccini and his audience were able to enjoy a glittering social event without apparent thought for the conflict taking place a few hundred miles away to the north. Once again, Puccini had become embroiled in a political debate despite his intentions.

At the end of the first act of *Fanciulla* the audience at the Dal Verme that night were rising to their feet to applaud the singers and the *maestro* when, suddenly, an uproar was heard from the balcony. Amid loud cries of 'Down with Austria!', 'Down with Puccini!', 'Long live Marinetti!', one man unfurled an Italian flag, whilst another set fire to an Austrian standard. Confusion ensued as the protestors were apprehended and ushered from the theatre; the orchestra struck up the *Marcia reale*, and the rest of the evening's performance passed uneventfully. The incident was reported in the Milanese press, but Puccini's later biographers do not mention it; evidently they felt it to be insignificant or were eager to cover it up. The event may have been glossed over as an embarrassment, but reading Marinetti's own account of the night reveals the strength of the avant garde's contempt for Puccini, for his audience and for opera as an institution. Marinetti painted a heroic picture of the demonstration, using a machine-gun-like style of prose to convey the excitement and dynamism of the occasion:

> 200 500 600 stunned faces. Enough! ... Get out! ... It's the Futurists! ... Long live Marinetti! ... Down with Marinetti! ... Good! ... Get out! ... Desperadoes! ... Dowwwn with Austria! ... Imbeciles! ... Madmen! Madmen! ... Cowards!! ... Silence! ... (deluded Puccini hurtles onto the stage).[45]

Probably the most striking passage in the entire account is the one where Marinetti describes the unfurling of the Italian flag by one of his henchmen:

> From the depths of a box the stomach of Mazza gives birth to an eight-foot-square *tricolore* flag. We attach it to a staff made from two sticks tied together. I lean out waving it. Dowwwwwwn with Austriaaa! ...[46]

In this passage Marinetti reveals that his brand of nationalism was, like Torrefranca's, intrinsically intertwined with a violent misogyny. The image of Mazza's stomach 'giving birth' to an Italian flag recalls a persistent trope in Marinetti's work – the mechanised man who is able to reproduce, rendering women redundant. In his novel *Mafarka le futuriste*, which had been published in French in 1909 and translated into Italian the following year, the male protagonist gives birth, unaided by woman, to an automaton son. But the child to which Mazza was symbolically giving birth at the performance of *La fanciulla del West* was not just any child, but a new Italy, the Italy that would be born if the nation entered what the Futurists hoped would be a great 'cleansing' war. All of Marinetti's theories about creating a reformed nation and his hatred of women coalesce in this one image. Later in the report Marinetti takes particular delight in describing the moment when a flaming strip of flag fell onto the creamy *décolletés* in the stalls below:[47] let Austria and women burn together, he seems to imply.

The audience are depicted by Marinetti as vulgar and ridiculous, their hands clapping 'like the beaks of 3,000 very excited wild geese'.[48] Marinetti's no less offensive depiction of the performers ('moronic singers who demand applause with the smiles of beggars'[49]) demonstrates the fact that he associated opera, like the middle classes, with greed, dishonesty and poverty of talent. His description of Puccini's music is virtually incomprehensible, even to native Italian speakers, thanks to his deliberate disregard for formal syntax, but he describes it being 'served up' by the 'hysterical violins', and refers to swaggering 'lasagne' (a general term not specifically denoting the pasta dish but implying something rich, fatty or servile) and 'pink candy-floss'.[50]

The demonstration of September 1914 was not Marinetti's first assault on Puccini. In November 1901 his review of *Tosca* had been published in the Parisian *Revue d'art dramatique*; this too associated

Puccini's music with a range of cheap, greasy and unpalatable types of food:

> Gingerbread fairs (drums, accordions, organs of breathless barbarism) would never surpass the discordant hubbub and the deafening chanting that the heroes of Sardou–Illica–Giacosa shriek over an orchestration of negroes! One finds in *Tosca* all the hackneyed refrains, the rancid corny old tunes of the fairground, with the nauseating stench of candy-floss, of fried food and – above all – the hopeless odour of intellectual scum![51]

Ridiculous as this may seem, Marinetti was later to publish a manifesto entitled *The Futurist Cookbook* (*La cucina futuristica*, 1932), which proposed a revolution in Italian eating habits and blamed the traditional 'bourgeois' Italian diet for the nation's ills.[52] Futurist recipes included dishes with such imaginatively macho names as 'Atlantic Aerofood', 'Ultravirile', 'Libyan Aeroplane', 'Veal Fuselage', 'The Bombardment of Adrianopolis', not to mention 'Italian Breasts in the Sunshine'. The high-protein diet of its day, Marinetti's nutritional regime banned pasta, labelling it 'unpatriotic' food that supposedly made the Italians sluggish, pessimistic, apathetic and lacking in virility: unsurprisingly the idea never caught on.

Although the publication of the cookbook marked the start of the second wave of Futurism, closely associated with the Fascist regime, it is clear that Marinetti had started to associate food with politics much earlier on in his career. Marinetti's references to Puccini's music in terms of junk food associate it firmly with the bourgeoisie, as is demonstrated by his report of a second protest the following night. This demonstration took place in another temple of bourgeois culture and materialism, the Milan Galleria, and turned into a food fight when a group of young men opposed to Futurism challenged the demonstrators. In his report of the evening Marinetti derides the bourgeoisie by contrasting the 'fat families peacefully enjoying ice-cream sodas' with the havoc that ensued: 'Total ruin. Everything tumbling down and breaking. Shrieks. Elimination of fainting women. Flying ice-creams. Insults[,] challenges[,] squabbles.'[53] The ice-cream becomes an emblem of middle-class triviality, cowardice and comfortable complacency in Marinetti's account, as he sneers at 'two fat neutralists' who cry, 'Hey! Hey! Eat in peace! Eat your ice-creams!' Marinetti, the artist Umberto Boccioni and others were marched off by the police, and the solidly bourgeois newspaper *Il secolo* chastised the protesters for both demonstrations, writing:

> This is not the time for Futurist distractions and hubbubs. Declaring war or deciding to maintain neutrality are not things to consider through a strategy of street demonstrations. Everyone must devote themselves to the task of contemplation and silence while we can find ourselves from one moment to the next in the presence of inevitable events of great severity. The nations who have had to accept the sorry necessity of war have given us in this sense a magnificent example of steadfastness and discipline.[54]

LA RONDINE

By the spring of 1915 Italy had herself 'accepted the sorry necessity of war' and joined the Allied campaign. Meanwhile, the image of Puccini as a cowardly neutralist promoted by Marinetti had not disappeared. Out of a commercially minded desire to avoid alienating German and Austrian audiences, Puccini had refused to sign artists' petitions protesting against German aggression towards Belgium in late 1914 and the bombardment of Reims at the beginning of 1915. The Parisian press, and principally the extreme right-wing Léon Daudet of the Action Française, accused Puccini of disloyalty to the allied cause. Daudet was to attack Puccini again two years later when he produced an 'enemy opera', *La rondine*, originally commissioned as an operetta by the Karltheater in Vienna but moved to neutral Monaco on account of the hostilities. Puccini's new opera once again called into question his status as a national or international composer, not only because, like *Fanciulla*, it was first performed abroad, but also because of the generic questions that it raised.

Monte Carlo had a well-established opera season at the Théâtre du Casino that attracted the cream of French and Italian singers. The opera house had staged the premières of recent new works by Massenet and Fauré, but a Puccini première was a very special coup indeed for its director, Raoul Gunsbourg. The first performance of *La rondine* took place on 27 March 1917 with Gilda Dalla Rizza, who would go on to become one of Puccini's favourite singers, in the lead role. Despite the fact that the Monte Carlo audience had a reputation for being hard to please, those in attendance on the first night, including Prince Albert of Monaco and many French and Italian dignitaries, greeted *La rondine* with exceptional warmth, copious applause and numerous curtain calls.

The reviews, penned by critics who had travelled from all over Europe or even made what was a treacherous journey across the Atlantic in wartime from New York, were universally positive, and predicted a long and happy future for the opera. Even Giannotto Bastianelli, a young musicologist, composer and nationalist who was in many respects similar in his ideological views to Fausto Torrefranca, welcomed what he regarded as a return to pure 'Italian' melody after the foreign novelties of *Fanciulla*. Like Marinetti, the metaphors he chose were culinary ones: 'We are pleased with the sense of satisfaction of this good Tuscan, who seems suddenly to be appeasing his hunger with peasant food, little stews, casseroles, etc., after ruining his stomach with exotic and artificial foods.'[55]

The audience in Monaco was evidently content to accept *La rondine* on its own terms: as a charming and light-hearted work that was a welcome distraction from the events taking place a few hundred miles away in the trenches of northern France. Back on Italian soil, however, where the opera was assessed not only as entertainment but as art, the response was rather different. At the Italian première in Bologna the opera and its star cast (including Aureliano Pertile and Toti Dal Monte) were on the whole greeted warmly by the audience. However, both there and in Milan shortly after, the work met with harsh criticism from the press – at least from those publications that deigned to review it, for the opera attracted considerably less attention than Puccini's earlier works. Doubtless this was in part because arts coverage was a lower priority than usual because of the war, but it also indicates that the première of *La rondine* was not regarded to be as significant an event as the premières of many of Puccini's earlier works.

The principal issue that troubled the critics was Puccini's perceived attempt to compose an operetta (something he himself denied), widely regarded as a bastardised, foreign genre. Although the *Corriere della sera* tried to claim that, in Puccini's hands, even a vulgar genre such as operetta could attain dignity,[56] most other critics were less generous and objected emphatically to the opera's 'hybrid' nature. Alberto Gasco wrote in the *Tribuna* that the common man would judge it 'neither meat nor fish', although his own preferred metaphor was to call it an 'amphibian' opera, capable of adapting itself to any environment, as had been proved by its popularity in Monte Carlo, Buenos Aires and now in Bologna.[57] Such a work was not problematic merely because it defied categorisation; rather, Gasco reiterated the objection that Torrefranca had raised five years earlier about Puccini's apparent desire to write operas that would guarantee him commercial success throughout the world, but that had no authentic roots in a national tradition. *La rondine*, with its fashionable dance rhythms, seemed to epitomise Torrefranca and Pizzetti's concerns about Puccini's desire to pander to the demands of bourgeois audiences, with little apparent concern for artistic integrity.

Gasco even went so far as to accuse Puccini of being unpatriotic in his apparent desire to compose in a 'Germanic' genre, writing: 'It is strange to observe: the Italians are fearless in the fire of the Austrian bombardments and yet give way lazily to the allurements of a Lehár waltz.'[58] The concerns of disloyalty regarding Puccini's actions, as expressed by Daudet, now seemed to have been substantiated in his art. His new work was, for many, out of keeping with the troubled mood of a nation at war, and unacceptable as a serious work of opera. An advance notice announcing Puccini's *Il trittico* in *Musica* in May 1917 attacked Puccini for his persistent choice of frivolous subjects out of keeping with the national mood: 'In the great tragic hour in which our maestri live, rather than amusing themselves with *Rondini*, *Lodolette* [Mascagni's recent opera], *Tabarri* and *Gianni Schicchi* they would be well advised graciously and nobly to feel the raising of the national spirit. Otherwise silence would be preferable and advisable.'[59]

Puccini's supporters were, as ever, determined to portray the première of *La rondine* as a triumph, regardless of the doubts expressed by their colleagues elsewhere in the press. The *Corriere della sera* reported that Puccini's experiment with a new genre had merely consolidated his fame, and that Italian art could justifiably feel proud of itself as a result.[60] Gasco, on the other hand, claimed that one's critical judgement of *La rondine* depended upon the importance one accorded to the work. He had no doubt that the work would become a hit with audiences, thanks to its appealing melodic qualities, but the only way in which it could be judged positively from a critical point of view was if it were detached from the rest of Puccini's œuvre and not assessed in terms of artistic achievement or progress.[61] If it *were* treated as high art, the judgement could be nothing other than negative, for 'in writing *La rondine*, Giacomo Puccini has categorically resigned from being a modern musician'.[62] Gasco wrote that whereas in *La fanciulla del West* (a work this critic personally admired and believed to be gaining some recognition with time) Puccini had demonstrated himself to be *au courant* with the latest musical developments, it now seemed that he had tired of study and the idea of progress, and turned back to the musical world of his youth. Gasco warned of the dangers of 'standing still', and expressed his hope that *Il trittico* would be a more adventurous work. His views were representative of a large part of the serious musical establishment, which dismissed *La rondine* as a second-rate *La traviata*, and a temporary setback in Puccini's career that they hoped would be swiftly forgotten.

Even Puccini's supporters who had portrayed *La rondine* as a triumph admitted certain weaknesses in it. The *Corriere della sera* expressed concern about the repetitiveness of the omnipresent waltz rhythms, the superficiality of the sentimental aspect, and the characterisation. Whereas Puccini had previously shown himself to be so skilled at creating characters with whom the audience wanted to weep, Magda and Ruggero were 'simple silhouettes', designed with precision and grace but lacking in any inner (spiritual) depth.[63] The

Corriere dei teatri, meanwhile, rebutted criticisms of *La rondine* by praising the orchestration and arguing that 'the opera is thoroughly Puccinian, in its conception, in its structure, in its form and especially in its melodic writing'.[64] However, even this critic was forced to concede that the opera was 'certainly no longer in the sparkling and gushing vein of *Manon* and *Bohème*', and 'no longer the passionate, inspired, touching music that thrilled us and made us cry'.[65] Even favourably inclined critics conceded that in order to enjoy this opera the listener had to distance him or herself from Puccini's earlier works, to which *La rondine*, they tacitly implied, could not compare. Franco Raineri of the *Giornale d'Italia*, for example, admitted that this was an opera that needed reviewing with prudence and delicacy, and a different critical stance to Puccini's other operas, for it was in fact 'an operetta through and through'.[66] In making a personal judgement of *La rondine*, this critic sat on the fence, stating that Puccini had not committed 'a huge crime' in writing such a work, but nor was he infallible, as certain quarters of the press made him out to be.

The issue of Puccini's compositional 'sincerity' once again dominated the reviews. In *Musica* Vincenzo Davico (a young composer, critic and admirer of modern music) reported Puccini to have confided in a recent interview that he had been guided by his heart in creating his new opera, and that his intention had been to be 'essentially sincere'.[67] However, Davico questioned Puccini's judgement, writing that being sincere was not simply a matter of writing 'romances of a somewhat questionable sentimentalism', obsessively using waltz rhythms, or doubling vocal lines in the violins. Rather,

> sincerity implies a profound knowledge of and insight into the drama; without such it is impossible for the musician to produce real emotion and effectively achieve the emotive effect capable of raising the dynamic force of the situations depicted. And from the moment when this intimate partnership between music and drama does not exist, art ceases to be truly sincere; the musical language becomes useless, without meaning, and produces the effect of musical twaddle![68]

Davico conceded that this was a work that contained elegant moments, citing the brightness of the orchestral colours and variety of rhythms as pleasing aspects, yet concluded that Puccini had not known how to penetrate the drama in its essence, with the result that the music was too often 'a simple sonic illustration'.[69] Thus he accused Puccini of writing music that did not really connect with the dramatic situation: whereas Verdi achieved real drama in his works, the music in Puccini's operas failed to interact at any deep level with the events on stage and functioned simply as a soundtrack. For this critic, Puccini's famed 'sincerity' was something that existed merely at the most superficial of musical levels, a view he shared with many of the reviewers of Puccini's earlier works.

In response to the mediocre, and at times harsh, reception *La rondine* received in the press, Puccini made substantial revisions to the work for a production in Palermo in 1920, including transpositions, modifications to the plot and the addition of a new tenor aria.[70] That same year also witnessed the long-awaited first performance in Vienna, on 9 October at the Volksoper, but here too the press was largely hostile to the work. Thus Puccini returned to his desk for a third time, partially reverting back to some aspects of the Monte Carlo version, although the autograph score of this edition was to be lost in a Second World War bombing raid. By 1922, Puccini himself was referring to the work as 'this pig of an opera',[71] and he continued to tinker with it up until the final months of his life, making it impossible to speak meaningfully of a definitive version of the work. The opera was not a catastrophic failure, as *Madama Butterfly* had been at its première, but nor did it ever become a staple of the operatic repertory, even in Italy. In 1925, Filippo Brusa dismissed it in the *Rivista musicale italiana* as 'a transitional work between *La fanciulla del West* and *Il trittico*, which reveals nothing of Puccini to us that we didn't already know, with the exception of a few moments in which a comical smile curled upon his lips'.[72] By 1917 it truly seemed that Puccini's star was waning, his reputation as Italy's national composer no longer assured.

IL TRITTICO

Eventually there was to be a ray of light for Puccini at the end of what had been a decade marked by botched experiments (one opera being deemed too progressive, the next too regressive) and harsh criticism. *Il trittico*, his triptych of one-act operas of starkly contrasting moods, had its first performance at the New York Met on 14 December 1918. The sell-out première was generally deemed to have been a sensation, although critical responses to two of the three short operas were mixed. The review by James Huneker of the *New York Times* was typical: he expressed reservations about *Il tabarro* ('the book is better than the music'; 'it will hardly outrival ... *Cavalleria* or *Pagliacci*') and *Suor Angelica* ('the ineffable dullness and silliness of the book is absolutely mirrored in the score'; 'plays fifty minutes but seems double that time'), but was bowled over by *Gianni Schicchi*.[73] 'If Puccini had written nothing else, *Gianni Schicchi* would give him fame because of its staccato, mirthful, brilliant music and happy characterization,' Huneker reported, declaring the opera one in which 'Puccini has achieved unqualified distinction'.[74]

But the 'real' première, as far as Italy was concerned, took place in Rome the following month, on 11 January 1919. Despite the mixed reception that had greeted Puccini's previous two operas, the performance was a glittering social occasion, attended by the Italian royal family, ministers, senators, diplomats and critics from the main national newspapers. Puccini's supporters in the press bandied about their usual words of praise, but in this case their victory cries were justified, at least in the case of *Gianni Schicchi*, which drew praise in unexpected quarters. The three panels of the *Triptych* were conceived by Puccini as a homogeneous and complementary whole, but they were not received as such in practice. Critics found it straightforward to assess each work individually, but difficult to evaluate the three together, because they could see few organic connections between them. Only Mario Incagliati of the *Giornale d'Italia* considered the three works to be connected by their 'shared Italianness', writing: 'It is an ideal bond that unites the three new operas, the flicker, the light, the flame that even today illuminates Italian genius.'[75]

The three works of the *Triptych* were certainly not greeted with equal degrees of enthusiasm. However, the success of *Gianni Schicchi* – hailed as a national triumph and a welcome return to form for Puccini – was sufficient to eclipse the critics' reservations about the other two works. Most reviewers passed swiftly over *Il tabarro* and *Suor Angelica* in order to devote their full attention to the opera that had stolen the show in Rome as it had in New York. On the whole their comments about *Il tabarro* mirrored the scant applause that had greeted the work at the Rome première. The stridently veristic, *Grand-Guignolesque* subject matter alienated audience members and critics alike, as did the unsympathetic characters and musical palette that was too reminiscent of *La fanciulla del West* for most tastes. The episodic nature of the story Puccini had chosen was deemed to have resulted in a fragmented musical style that led critics to reiterate their earlier reservations about Puccini's collage-like, inorganic manner of composition; 'Alastor' in *Musica*, for example, dismissed *Il tabarro* as a disconnected, prolix and boring work 'made up of small pieces'.[76] Harsh criticism also came from a critic identifying himself in the right-wing *Idea nazionale* only as 'a member of the public', who announced that the public's verdict had been that one hearing was sufficient for *Il tabarro*, on account of its episodic nature, grim and emotionless conclusion, use of modern counterpoint and 'forced' singing.[77] Puccini, it seemed, had experimented with a 'modern' musical and dramaturgical approach, and abandoned his characteristic empathy, creating in the process a work that many perceived as soulless. The *Idea nazionale* critic wrote that the opera contained vividly expressive passages here and there, but that for the most part 'the musical drama remains external, without intimacy, without human truth. It is a spectacle.'[78]

Suor Angelica was Puccini's favourite panel of the *Triptych*. It was greeted by the first-night audience with more enthusiasm than *Il tabarro* and drew a certain amount of praise from the press: Incagliati of the *Giornale d'Italia*, for example, depicted the opera as a highly emotional and genuinely moving work in which Puccini had depicted the tragedy of a broken heart as in no previous opera, and 'emulated

Verdi' during Angelica's confrontation with her aunt.[79] Even the *Idea nazionale*, usually so hostile towards Puccini, noted a nobility in the work that had been absent from much recent Italian opera, and found the work pleasing, if not containing any great musical revelations. However, some critics noted that the opera's lack of male voices had given it a 'monotonous quality', and noted an 'excess of details' that were deemed to have weakened the work.[80] As with *Il tabarro*, *Suor Angelica* did not seem to the critics to be a wholeheartedly honest conception, but had an air of falseness about it, this time created by its excessively saccharine nature: Alberto Gasco noted in *La tribuna* that Puccini's score was divided between '*real* music' (the scene with the aunt and the miracle scene) and sections where Puccini had pulled off all his usual lyrical tricks, but where true drama was missing.[81] For 'Alastor', writing in *Musica*, *Suor Angelica* suffered from the same lack of organicism as *Il tabarro*, being merely a series of episodes, 'stuffed with old conventions', and 'more cinematographic than mystical'.[82] Carlo Cordara of *Il marzocco* dismissed *Suor Angelica* as the least interesting of the *Triptych* panels owing to the conventional nature of its action,[83] and ultimately it would go on to be the least frequently staged of the three.

If the first-night critics were reticent about *Suor Angelica* and *Il tabarro*, they were won over by *Gianni Schicchi* from start. For virtually the first time in Puccini's career, this was an opera that provoked no cries of dissent. Gasco wrote in *La tribuna* that whereas many critics were lying in wait for the first two operas with their fists drawn, *Gianni Schicchi* was able to disarm these 'hired assassins' at a single glance.[84] Neither *Il tabarro* nor *Suor Angelica* was reported by the press to be innovative in any significant way: the first had its modern moments, but they seemed little more than tacked-on pastiches of Debussy and Stravinsky; the second was an exaggerated and not entirely convincing throwback to the ultra-sentimental Puccini of old. However, with *Gianni Schicchi*, Puccini had produced something strikingly new.

The opera was hailed as 'a genuine revelation', which showed the signs of a 'second youth' for Puccini,[85] and heralded a new era both for him and for Italy. In a pocket guide to *Gianni Schicchi* published in 1920 – by which time the opera was regularly being performed independently of *Il tabarro* and *Suor Angelica* – Giacomo Setaccioli, a musicologist and professor of composition at the Liceo Musicale di Santa Cecilia in Rome, argued that Puccini had been widely regarded as something of a spent force until the première of *Il trittico*.[86] However, in *Gianni Schicchi* Puccini had answered his detractors back and redeemed himself: 'With his *Schicchi* the Maestro has given a clear and eloquent response, an admonishment to those who inopportunely take delight in expressing catastrophic judgements about his art, not realising, perhaps, that it is never wise to pronounce the last word about the work of an artist who has not yet given up the fight.'[87]

After a war that had left Italy battered and bruised, *Gianni Schicchi* seemed a reaffirmation of a healthy, positive Italianness, a work 'destined joyously to gladden the restless spirits of the twentieth century'.[88] Not only had Puccini produced his sunniest opera to date, composed in a 'single burst of inspiration' in the manner advocated by Verdi (unlike the 'episodic' *Il tabarro* and *Suor Angelica*[89]), but it was the first he had set in Italy since *Tosca*. Furthermore, it was based on a work by Dante, that most iconic of Italian cultural heroes. *Gianni Schicchi* was thus widely hailed as a national masterpiece, even drawing praise from the ultra-nationalistic *Idea nazionale*, which applauded the composer for his return to an Italian subject 'after so many useless Japanese, American, Parisian digressions'.[90] The critic for this newspaper welcomed *Schicchi* as a truly Italian opera, which had emerged from the grey operatic scene of the past few years, and which represented 'our people, our refinement, our accents, clear Italian vivacity': finally, the critic wrote, the Italian people could breathe once more.[91]

Schicchi prompted comparisons with the great *opere buffe* of Rossini and Donizetti. Puccini was deemed to have revived a noble and characteristically Italian genre, but also given it a modern twist through the use of a sophisticated network of orchestral motifs that acted as a commentary on the words and actions. Predictably, many critics also noted a parallel with Verdi's turn to comedy late in life, and *Gianni Schicchi* was hailed as a second *Falstaff*. Gasco wrote in *La tribuna*: 'After 25 years the marvels of *Falstaff* have been repeated: after ten attempts of varying degrees of success, our art rejoices in the birth of a comic opera in which the music and the words are bound together throughout, without uncertainty, without apparent effort.'[92] Some critics even felt Puccini to have bettered Verdi: Giannotto Bastianelli argued in *La nazione* that Puccini's work was perhaps an even more perfect 'miracle of Italian brio and luminosity' than *Falstaff*, combined with a perfect grasp of modern musico-dramatic language.[93] Certainly, in Bastianelli's view, *Gianni Schicchi* was an equally symbolic work: 'I believe that the national significance of *Falstaff* can be repeated today with *Gianni Schicchi*, as the vibrations of its spontaneous, purely Italian beauty reverberate still in my spirit, like an unforgettable sunlight and blue sky.'[94] Such praise was high indeed, for the reviews of Verdi's final work were characterised by patriotic bombast of the most extravagant kind, and as Roger Parker has written, '*Falstaff* was from the start thought of (and in some ways conceived as) a monument to the newly emerged Italian nation, a secular equivalent to Verdi's *Requiem* of some twenty years earlier.'[95] However, as Emanuele Senici has shown, the reception of *Falstaff* was in fact complex: a certain discomfort and embarrassment can be detected in the reviews at the fact that Verdi's advanced musical language had baffled the public, but the press evidently felt that they had no alternative but to depict the première of his final opera as a triumphant moment for the nation.[96] Conversely, there is no evidence in the *Schicchi* reviews of 'the inflated, slightly desperate tone' that Senici detects in the nationalist reception of *Falstaff*,[97] or indeed that is manifest in the reviews of many of Puccini's earlier works.

The fact that *Gianni Schicchi* seemed to embody a genuine sense of shared Italianness is demonstrated by the praise it drew from unexpected quarters; particularly significant are the warm words it drew from the *Idea nazionale* and from Giannotto Bastianelli. Bastianelli was a young, progressive composer, pianist and writer, and a prominent member of the *Voce* circle, whose most significant publication was

La crisi musicale europea (1912), a lengthy and sophisticated treatise on contemporary European music. Like Torrefranca, Bastianelli advocated the revival of a 'purer' Italian music and lamented the fact that the music of the past century had been corrupted by commercial considerations: praise from Bastianelli was therefore high praise indeed, given his opposition to the musical world to which Puccini belonged. His review of *Il trittico* in the Florence newspaper *La nazione* was given front-page billing. This was unusual (opera reviews usually appeared on the third page of newspapers), but in the circumstances hardly surprising, given that *La nazione* was edited by none other than Giovacchino Forzano, who had written the libretti for *Suor Angelica* and *Gianni Schicchi*. One would naturally expect such a review to smack of bias, but in fact Bastianelli was not averse to meting out criticism where he felt it to be due. His assessment of *Il tabarro* was that it was an unsuccessful opera with a few brilliant moments, and in *Suor Angelica* he praised the novelty of the opera's conception although not the quality of the music, singling out the Zia Principessa scene as the only notable moment. However, Bastianelli's admiration for *Gianni Schicchi* was unreserved and he devoted six times as much space to this opera as to the other two combined.

Bastianelli particularly admired Rinuccio's aria 'Firenze è come un albero fiorito', a rather bombastic hymn of praise to the city and all the great artists it had produced. It is unsurprising that a Florentine critic writing in a Florentine newspaper should have praised such sentiments, but Bastianelli went further, according the aria symbolic, patriotic significance, calling it 'a divine, sweet, spontaneous melody that makes us overcome with hope and faith in our great eternal land'.[98] Bastianelli portrayed *Gianni Schicchi* as a work capable of inspiring the sceptical young (himself included), which signalled the fact that Italian culture was entering a new phase. As we have seen, the *Voce* circle, members of the generation born around 1880, had advocated Italy's entry into the First World War, which they hoped would provide the 'struggle' and 'purpose' that they had so long craved, and act as a stimulus for national reinvigoration. In the event, however, the 'great collective war' had not been the glorious Italian victory for which they had hoped: Italy had suffered great losses on the Alpine Front, particularly at the battle of Caporetto. Around the time of the *Trittico* première in Rome, Gabriele D'Annunzio was protesting about what he christened the 'mutilated victory' – the botched peace settlement and dispersal of contested Italian territories – and would stage his famous march on Fiume in September of that same year. However, Bastianelli evidently felt that the war had been a spur to artistic creativity, writing that Italy had risen from blood and sacrifice to rediscover its sunny smile (with *Gianni Schicchi* making the war 'disappear like a nightmare'[99]), much in the way that the Napoleonic occupation had prompted the composition of great comic works by Rossini. After the apathetic years of the Giolitti era, military struggle had finally led to artistic productivity, and Bastianelli urged the disaffected young to look to *Gianni Schicchi* as a model, because it expressed 'the purest word of the [Italian] race'.[100]

In the last work to be premièred during his lifetime, Puccini seemed finally to have produced what his supporters had boasted about all along: an authentically Italian work capable of creating a sense of shared Italian identity. *Gianni Schicchi* had united critics of almost all political colours. Puccini had rarely won such undivided acclaim; expectations for his next opera, *Turandot*, were higher still. In the event, *Turandot* would fail to match *Schicchi*'s immediate critical success; the reception of this opera showed that Puccini's music was still to be the site of attempted political appropriations. But before then an unexpected event would intervene and provoke a show of unanimity that would demonstrate that Puccini's status as an Italian composer, at least, was finally secure.

7 | A suitable ending?

On a grey, drizzling day in late November 1924, 80,000 people lined the streets of Brussels for 'the passing of a triumphant hero'.[1] Among the many wreaths borne upon Puccini's coffin were an immense bouquet of chrysanthemums and lilies bearing the name Benito Mussolini and a wreath of orchids from the king of Italy. When the coffin later arrived in Milan, those waiting to meet the train included Puccini's librettists Simoni and Adami, Toscanini – reportedly 'almost petrified with sorrow'[2] – and the composers Montemezzi and Pizzetti, the latter presumably repenting his attack on Puccini ten years earlier. An overnight vigil was held in the Church of San Fedele before the coffin was moved to the Duomo the following day. The sober candelabras that surrounded Puccini's coffin were placed in an arrangement identical to that which had been used for another national icon, Vittorio Emanuele II.

To read Puccini's obituaries, his status as national hero would seem to be beyond challenge. Although he had been widely criticised for losing his way during the 1910s, this was not alluded to in the grandiose tributes paid to him following his death. In a sixty-page tribute, the Ricordi journal *Musica d'oggi* recounted every stage of Puccini's demise in graphic detail, under such headings as 'First symptoms of the illness', 'The operation', 'The catastrophe', although even at the very end of his life Puccini's physical vigour was emphasised ('Puccini enjoyed very good health; with the exception of his minor diabetic condition, his health was not undermined by physical frailty in the slightest').[3] In reality, of course, Puccini had long suffered from a sore throat, but was oblivious to the fact that its cause was throat cancer, the legacy of a lifetime of heavy smoking. *Musica d'oggi* devoted twenty-seven pages to excerpts reprinted from obituaries that had appeared in other publications, both home-grown and foreign, in which Puccini's Italian qualities were incessantly repeated. Ironically, given the sharp blows Puccini had weathered from the press over the years, *Musica d'oggi* printed a telegram from the President of the Italian Press Association saying, 'The Italian press weeps with you for the irreparable loss of the illustrious and talented Maestro, through whose music our nation continues to be the world's leader in artistic beauty.'[4] Such sentiments demonstrate that the nature of Puccini's status had undergone a significant mutation: now he was being fêted, somewhat hypocritically, as an Italian hero by those at the very centre of institutional power.

From the very start of his career, Puccini's music had been depicted by his supporters as a force for unification, an antidote to the perceived decline of Italian culture and a beacon that would illuminate the continuing greatness of Italian opera to the rest of the world. According to the obituaries, he had succeeded on all three counts, despite the fact that the reviews of his operas published over the previous decades had often told a different story. Even the most cursory glance at the late reviews reveals that critics continued to draw upon the same repertoire of clichés lavished upon Puccini by his patrons during his lifetime: the composer as warrior, statue, everyman, man of the soil and descendant of an ancient race. By this stage, even critics who had been sceptical about Puccini during his lifetime were beginning to realise that he was perhaps the best national composer Italy had to offer, and numerous comparisons were drawn with Verdi, despite the fact that Puccini had patently chosen to follow a rather different stylistic course.

Critics depicted Puccini as a force for unity, who had succeeded in creating a culturally homogeneous Italy. Tancredi Mantovani argued in the *Nuova antologia* that Puccini appealed to all classes, the workers as well as the bourgeoisie with whom he shared a special affinity.[5] This was a point that the official Fascist newspaper *Il popolo d'Italia* was keen to emphasise, its critic 'Raff' writing that whenever a Puccini opera was advertised on a theatre bill, a 'miracle of unity' occurred, and 'all class divisions ceased'.[6] 'Raff' used extravagant references to the Italian landscape in order to depict Puccini's music as the embodiment of a sense of Italianness that was shared by all: 'That stream of melody, gushing from his Italian heart like the purest spring of water from our mountainsides, seemed to have assumed the role of linking heart to heart, drawing them together in indestructible solidarity, of creating understanding between them more effectively than the law, more solemnly than a rite.'[7] Similarly, G. Sommi, writing in *L'impero*, stated that Puccini was 'Italian to his deepest roots' and a 'vessel for the sentiments of our land', which were embodied in his music as much as in pine forests, azure hills and the sparkling and tranquil Mediterranean sea.[8]

Such emotive but impressionistic references to the Italian landscape were reminiscent of those that had characterised the early profiles of Puccini and reviews of his music. The sort of language that critics used about Puccini remained as grandiose, romanticised and obsessed with physiognomy in the 1920s as it had been in the 1890s. However, by this time – the early years of the Fascist regime – a desire for cultural unification had been supplanted by an emphasis upon exporting Italian values to the rest of the world. Writings about Puccini from the final years of his life took on a markedly more imperialistic tone. A prime example was the introduction to Gino Monaldi's *Giacomo Puccini e la sua opera* (1924), written by Fausto Salvatori, upon whose bombastic poem Puccini's 1919 *Inno a Roma* had been based (a work Puccini himself had dismissed as 'a right load of rubbish').[9] Salvatori's introduction was replete with inflated patriotic references, which posited Puccini's music as an emblem of imperialist ambition:

> Giacomo Puccini is a conqueror of multitudes. He has carried, like a flag unfurled in the wind on the day of victory, the *tricolore* of Italy, the name of Italy, the divine melody of Italy, across mountains, torrents, oceans, through noisy cities and savage lands, into theatres of stone and rich gold, and into the tents of nomadic miners.[10]

Salvatori argues here that Puccini's music is omnipresent, capable of entering all spaces from the grandest to the most humble. The sense of the somewhat puzzling remark about 'nomadic miners' is ambiguous, but presumably Salvatori intends it as a metaphor for an impoverished, rootless, theatre-less community, in much the same way as he contrasts 'noisy cities' with 'savage lands'. Whatever the exact sense meant here, the spirit of conquest underpinning the rhetoric is beyond question, reflecting the fact that the Italian drive for empire and attempt to 'pacify' those areas of Libya that remained outside full Italian control had recently been given new impetus by Mussolini with the outbreak of the second Italo-Sanusi War.

Salvatori, like De Amicis a quarter of a century before him, mythologised Puccini by depicting him as a statue, standing firm and proud across the years in the face of adversity: 'his courageous, masculine persona, calm with a confident strength, appears in the pages of this book like a statue swathed in snow that the west wind blows away little by little'.[11] To situate Puccini within a historic Italian lineage, and to emphasise his strength and determination, Salvatori portrayed Puccini-the-statue as having been sculpted from the ancient rock of Etruria, lingering over his 'vast forehead under a crown of thick hair', 'powerful arched eyebrows', 'determined jawbone' and eyes looking into the distance for inspiration.[12] Salvatori's description exuded strength, manliness, determination and purity of race: good Fascist values. Indeed, the techniques used to play up Puccini's manliness were strikingly similar to those used by Mussolini's publicists; visual representations and written descriptions of il Duce frequently likening his physique to that of a classical statue.[13]

For Salvatori, Puccini had the imperialist zeal of a conquering warrior; he likened him to a Tuscan Renaissance commander capturing his rival merchants' cities, and turned a series of potentially feminised musical attributes into masculine, military qualities: 'Melody is his might; grace his power; elegance his weapon.'[14] The tone of Salvatori's explicitly militaristic comments was echoed with even more vehemence in some of the obituaries, L. Parodi for example writing in the Genovese newspaper *Il caffaro*: 'Italy has been successful once again in giving the world an operatic composer who has triumphed without arms and without treaties: ambassador of eternal Latin beauty. On his glorious tomb I raise the sacred Italian flag and repeat again: blessed nationalism!'[15]

For Torrefranca, Puccini's international appeal had been proof of the composer's wilful renunciation of distinctively national traits in a spirit of cheap opportunism, signalling the decisive loss of an Italian identity in music and an enfeebled national culture. However, commentators of the 1920s such as Salvatori regarded Puccini's exportability as a virtue, proof of the hegemony of Italian culture and values. Nationalism and internationalism were thus happily reconciled. Comments such as 'his work knows no borders'[16] were near ubiquitous in the obituaries and Puccini was depicted in numerous papers and journals aimed at different readerships as an ambassador of Italian culture overseas. Arnaldo Fraccaroli wrote in the *Corriere della sera*: 'The good that this man has done for Italian art throughout the world! The good that he has done for Italy! Puccini was ... the best known, the most loved propagandist of Italianness abroad: if music had a diplomatic hierarchy, Puccini should have been the ambassador of ambassadors.'[17] Similarly, Mantovani of the *Nuova antologia* called Puccini 'the most powerful and successful ambassador for Italy in lands beyond the Alps and overseas, where he knew how to win so much sympathy and support for our country, keeping the prevailing prestige of the Italian musical tradition alive and well in every foreign land',[18] while Sommi wrote in *L'impero*: 'There isn't a metropolis, city, town or village in the civilised world that hasn't been inundated by his music; in twenty years there cannot be a person in the world who has not got to know Italy through his melodious language, and who hasn't imagined the colour and the scent of our great blessed land, through the music he has written, the finest reflection of Italy.'[19] A critic signing himself 'Gajanus' in *Il resto del Carlino* boasted that 'Puccini represented for we Italians the intoxicating and glorious certainty of being the world's pre-eminent musical race'.[20]

It was of considerable chagrin to many obituarists that Puccini had died in Brussels, so far from the fatherland, but the *Illustrazione italiana* managed to turn this unhappy accident into proof of Puccini's status as a cultural imperialist. Its critic associated him with another recently deceased national treasure, the actress Eleonora Duse, writing:

> Theirs were perhaps the two voices that resonated most loudly beyond the nation's boundaries, and both these great figures died beyond the nation's boundaries, almost as if to confirm that their glory wasn't restricted to within the confines of our Alps. ... They were voices of our race in the opinion of other nations, heralds of our art throughout the world, champions, triumphant preachers of our supremacy that we don't want to renounce, because even in times of slavery that supremacy was our main qualification to rise again as a nation.[21]

In addition to reprinting reviews, the *Musica d'oggi* supplement also printed tributes and speeches about Puccini by public figures, some of whom were official spokesmen for the Fascist regime. These too made much of Puccini's success in exporting his music abroad, and the fact that he was at once the embodiment of Italianness and yet able to speak a language that was universal. Rocco, President of the Chamber of Deputies, called Puccini 'the illustrious artist who gloriously spread the name of Italy throughout the world',[22] while the statesman Clausetti said in his speech: 'If music is a universal language, nobody knew how to speak it better than Puccini. His melodies revealed to the furthest flung people what their souls had in common, whether of sorrow or of joy.'[23] The composer and critic Adriano Lualdi wrote in *Il secolo*: 'He is dead, a Man who truly rendered our Fatherland illustrious, and whose name and whose music resounded in every land, even the farthest flung,'[24] while his fellow reviewer Alceo Toni wrote: 'The most representative and the most universal of our musicians is no more. His loss is a blow for Italy and a source of sorrow for the whole world.'[25]

Not all the critics who praised Puccini in extravagantly imperialist terms were card-carrying Fascists, although most were pragmatically minded enough to toe the party line, for press censorship was heavy-handed from 1922 onwards. However, the allegiance of Lualdi and Toni to the regime cannot be disputed. Along with Giuseppe Mulè, they were the most important Fascist music bureaucrats, playing a key role in running national musical organisations during the *ventennio*. Toni was music critic for Mussolini's *Il popolo d'Italia* from 1920 to 1943 and director of the Milan Conservatorio from 1926 to 1943 – two key positions that allowed him to exert considerable influence over the promotion and programming of the nation's music and in shaping public taste. Lualdi, meanwhile, wrote for *Il secolo* from 1923, then *La sera*, and from 1936 *Il giornale d'Italia*. In 1929 he was elected a deputy to the National Parliament as representative of the Sindacato Fascista dei Musicisti. Both writers were themselves composers, but were conventional and unadventurous in their own music and in that of other composers that they chose to promote; Lualdi in particular was a staunch defender of a rather conservative model of 'Italianness' in music, opposing the efforts of Casella and Malipiero to create a more modern brand of Italian music. Both were staunch supporters of Puccini.

One might have expected a continuation of the anti-Puccini rhetoric of Torrefranca and the *Voce* circle in the Fascist era, given their use of a proto-Fascistic language of virility, misogyny, imperialism and opposition to the bourgeoisie. Rather than emulating such thinkers, however, the most prominent Fascist critics drew instead upon the nationalist hagiography favoured by Puccini's patrons and magnified it. This seeming contradiction is explained by the fact that Torrefranca was an intellectual with progressive artistic ideas, whereas critics such as Toni and Lualdi were conservative pragmatists; Antonio Trudu writes that as a critic Toni 'displayed a totally closed mind towards twentieth-century musical developments',[26] while Harvey Sachs depicts Lualdi as a Mussolini sycophant who was 'full of hot air'.[27] Mussolini himself expressed official state approval for Puccini in a telegram to Ricordi in which he referred to him as 'one of the nation's purest and most resplendent glories',[28] and also in his address to the Chamber of Deputies on 29 November 1924, in which he praised the composer as a national treasure, who 'occupies an extremely eminent position in the history of Italian music and the history of the Italian spirit'.[29] The dictator had publically stated on several occasions that Puccini was one of his favourite composers (along with Mascagni) because of the 'popular and national' qualities of his music.[30] Furthermore, *Il popolo d'Italia*, the official mouthpiece of Fascism, demonstrated its acknowledgement of Puccini's status as Italy's national composer by reproducing a wide range of patriotically inspired comments from other newspapers.

Puccini had greeted the advent of Fascism with some enthusiasm, believing the regime would bring what he perceived to be much-needed order and discipline to his country.[31] 'Mussolini was undoubtedly sent by God for the salvation of Italy,' he wrote to his librettist Adami on the day after the March on Rome.[32] Il Duce claimed in his parliamentary speech on Puccini's death that the composer had explicitly requested membership of the Fascist party a few months earlier,[33] although this has recently been disputed by Michele Girardi, who writes that 'the officials of the Viareggio branch of the Partito Nazionale Fascista sent [Puccini] an honorary membership card, and for the sake of a quiet life he did not refuse it'.[34] Whatever the true extent of Puccini's involvement with the fledgling Fascist regime, Mussolini was keen to have the composer on side and made Puccini a senator shortly before his death, an honour that reportedly brought the composer much delight.

However, the Fascists' interest in Puccini was probably essentially pragmatic. Their embrace of Puccini as a national icon may seem somewhat surprising, but Fascist cultural policy at this time was characterised by confusion and contradiction. Fascist Italy was far more tolerant of artistic experimentation than was Nazi Germany, but was also content to embrace pre-existing artistic movements. Mussolini was actively involved in promoting new music, declaring in 1927: 'We must reawaken the public's interest in new music; at the moment they like nothing except the music they hear in the street, played on barrel organs. The public must also appreciate and learn to love the music that they do not know off by heart.'[35] Both modernist and more conservative artistic tendencies could happily be accommodated so long as all art acted in the service of *italianità*; indeed, Fascism put forward many apparently contradictory faces in order to guarantee the widest possible appeal.[36] Early Fascism did not seek to develop its own cultural policy; as Lino Pertile writes, 'Fascism did not initially need a cultural policy: what it found was already good enough.'[37] The Puccini myth was therefore a convenient, pre-established bandwagon onto which the Fascists were more than happy to leap. In death as much as in life, then, Puccini's music and persona acted as blank canvases onto which any number of ideological ambitions could be projected. *Turandot*, a work that looks simultaneously forwards and backwards, was thus a fitting emblem for Fascist Italy, caught between presenting itself to the world as modern and keeping faith with tradition.

TURANDOT

So ostentatious were the tributes paid to Puccini in his obituaries that the anticipation prior to the posthumous première of his last work was more intense than ever. Renzo Bianchi wrote: 'The expectations surrounding this new opera – composed by the popular maestro in a marvellous totality of thought, enthusiasm and physical power – are enormous; and everybody wholeheartedly hopes that the author of *La bohème* will create another fine victory for Italian opera.'[38] The first performance of *Turandot*, on 25 April 1926, was, without doubt, the operatic event of the season; indeed, it was widely felt that there had never been a performance of such significance in La Scala's entire illustrious history. The première was deemed even more important than that of another work recently invested with much nationalist symbolism – Boito's *Nerone*, first performed posthumously at La Scala just under two years earlier, on 1 May 1924. Anybody who was anybody was there; Mussolini himself refrained from attending only after Toscanini threatened to stand down when instructed that he would be required to conduct the Fascist hymn 'Giovinezza' in il Duce's honour before the curtain rose. Rosa Raisa, the Polish soprano who sang the title role, reported an atmosphere in the auditorium more electrified than any she had previously experienced.[39] There was much to surprise and delight the audience: the staging was unprecedentedly lavish for a Puccini opera and the chorus impressively large. And added to these striking scenographic aspects was a marked change in dramatic mood, for the composer had abandoned his customary humble characters sketched from real life for a cruel fantasy world on a much more ambitious scale than anything he had previously attempted.

The performance was not merely a glittering social occasion, but a highly symbolic event. It was Milan's way of making amends, if posthumously, with a composer whose last opera to receive its première at La Scala, *Madama Butterfly*, had been mercilessly booed off the stage. In sharp contrast to that disorderly and disastrous night, the *Turandot* première was characterised by a reverential, quasi-religious mood, with many critics making reference to the opera's 'baptism' and 'consecration', and even reporting Puccini's ghostly presence to be with them in spirit in the auditorium.[40] The evening, then, took on the atmosphere of a wake, but if this was in a sense a memorial service, it was one particularly charged with significance, for Puccini was a national composer with no obvious successor. His status as heir to Verdi remained unchallenged; the generation that followed was for the most part more interested in founding a new school of Italian instrumental music than in writing operas with wide popular appeal. Aware that an era was at an end, the audience at the *Turandot* première had come to commemorate not merely the passing of a composer but that of an entire tradition. *Turandot* was expected to be a fitting tribute to both – but was it?

After its long-awaited première, delayed for seventeen months after Puccini's death whilst Alfano completed the final act, *Turandot* was widely hailed as a sensation.[41] Given the hype that surrounded it, it could hardly be anything less; however, strip this away and complex subtexts underpinning the encomia emerge. *Turandot* was greeted with a certain amount of nervous misapprehension, with some critics devoting large parts of their reviews to celebrating Puccini's life and earlier works in what turned into a second round of obituaries, in order to avoid commenting explicitly on a score that many of them found perplexing. The music itself was frequently overlooked, as critics confounded by it dwelt upon discussing its composer's personality. Reading between the lines, it seems unlikely that the first-night audience genuinely believed *Turandot* to be the monument to Puccini for which they had so desperately longed.

The aspect of the opera deemed to be most problematic was its eponymous heroine, a character Puccini's supporters seem to have been reluctant to discuss. 'Turandot does not exist,' sing the three Masks in Act I, and as far as many of the contemporary critics set on portraying the opera as an unequivocal success were concerned, this might as well have been true. 'Turandot,' wrote Raffaello de Rensis in *Il giornale d'Italia*, 'with her regal mantles, her tiaras, her beauty, was forgotten. Not one member of the public, in our view, wanted to see her again.'[42] Those few critics who were prepared to talk about Turandot consistently emphasised her resemblance to a puppet, robot or mask. At first glance this might be taken as an indictment of a stilted interpretation on the part of the prima donna, yet in fact several critics praised Rosa Raisa for her valiant execution of a thankless role. The antipathy that greeted Turandot transcended considerations of performance; what troubled the critics so profoundly was the wider shift in cultural values that this mechanistic figure seemed to represent.

By the mid 1920s, puppets, robots and masked figures had become emblems of the avant garde, icons of a moment of cultural crisis,[43] and the critics' hostile and fearful response to Turandot can be viewed as encapsulating their anxieties about the social and aesthetic implications of the apparent decline of the human in a machine age. As part of a deliberate process of distancing and detachment, many modernist artists consciously attempted to place a barrier between the characters and the audience, often literally concealing the performers' faces behind masks so they wore an expression that was fixed. Metaphorically speaking, Turandot seemed to many early listeners to have the same sort of 'blank face', an idea contemporary musicologist Antonio Capri conveyed vividly when he wrote, 'More than a character [Turandot] is a mask underneath which one feels emptiness and inconsistency'.[44] In contrast to the near silence that greeted Turandot, the chorus of adoration with which Puccini's supporters responded to the ultra-sentimental, self-sacrificing slave girl Liù was ecstatic. The critics depicted the opera as a battle for supremacy between the two female protagonists, which naturally was won by Liù. Indeed, Puccini had surely misnamed his opera, for the common consensus among critics was that 'to all intents and purposes the opera ends evocatively with the death of Liù. She becomes the real lead. . . . In *Turandot* Liù triumphs.'[45]

A similarly fraught battle was played out in the reviews between those critics who wanted to dispense with operatic sentimentality and those who sought desperately to preserve it. My contention in this chapter is that Puccini himself was caught somewhere midway between these two poles. *Turandot* engaged in a reflexive dialogue about the merits of the old and the new; the creation of a mechanical Turandot was to some degree a deliberate, if tentative, move on Puccini's part towards updating his operatic style, an exploration of the ways in which opera might engage with modernist preoccupations in the other arts. The debates that surrounded Puccini's two heroines resurrected long-standing anxieties about a perceived dichotomy in Puccini's style and his compositional 'sincerity' – the vexed question of locating a composer's personal voice. These in turn raised generic questions about changing notions of authorship, character and theatricality in the modern age. The reception of *Turandot*, and the response to its two heroines in particular, provides a vital key to understanding the ambivalent Italian relationship with modernism (and the related negotiation between 'high' and 'popular' culture) in the 1920s.

GREAT EXPECTATIONS

Looking back in 1927, the year after the *Turandot* première, Guido Pannain wrote in the progressive music journal *Il pianoforte* that 'nineteenth-century Italian opera was sentimental opera. Impulsive art, without intellectual reflection, without cerebral complications.'[46] In Puccini's music these characteristics were seemingly preserved well into the twentieth century; as earlier chapters have illustrated, emotional directness and an ability to create a special bond of trust with the listener – posited as dearly cherished national character traits – were the key qualities upon which his reputation as a truly Italian composer had been built. Even as late as the 1920s, when, as we shall see, moving the spectator was no longer necessarily a criterion for theatrical success, music that 'penetrated straight to the heart' was still what Puccini's supporters in the press and the majority of listeners expected and demanded from him.

Arnaldo Bonaventura, in his 1925 biography of Puccini, praised the special bond of trust that had been established between Puccini and his listeners:

> He knew how to express himself with that simplicity and sincerity that ... were features of his moral character. Now, he is always very successful in endearing himself to those who speak simply and sincerely; for his simplicity he is easily understood, for his sincerity he is easily believed. Thus a current of attraction is established between composer and public: and Giacomo Puccini was, undoubtedly, a very attractive composer. This was his artistic *Credo*.[47]

'Intellectual' music was still actively disparaged by the majority of Italian critics towards the end of Puccini's life; Lualdi, for instance, was typical in lauding *La bohème* in 1923 for being 'a work of theatre and not a university thesis'.[48] Meanwhile, Bonaventura wrote that a beautiful and admirable work of art is born only when an artist allows instinct to guide him, when he gives his imagination free rein, and most of all when he 'sets the beating of his own heart to music'.[49] He confidently assumed that *Turandot* would be another such work based on emotion rather than intellect, in which the composer whom he called 'the pride and glory of Italian art and the Italian nation' would once again appeal directly to the sentimental Latin spirit.[50]

The key Italian qualities Puccini's music seemed to his admirers to exemplify – sincerity, humanity and sentiment – were widely regarded as being most effectively communicated through his female characters. While Puccini's heroes attracted scant attention, his suffering heroines – frequently referred to fondly by critics as his 'daughters' – had come to epitomise the very essence of Puccini's aesthetic, and were routinely presented as vessels for the expression of their creator's 'true voice'. It is unsurprising therefore that Puccini's obituaries in 1924 should have been devoted in large part to his female figures, with whom the composer was closely identified and effectively conflated. To cite just one example of many, Cesare Brighenti-Rosa wrote in *Il pensiero musicale* that Puccini's imagination was coloured 'by an almost feminine grace' and that the composer's best-delineated characters were his heroines. He concluded his obituary by urging readers to imagine 'the sweet figures of [Puccini's] heroines surrounding his airborne spirit, holding him aloft in his flight to heaven'.[51] Likewise, Franco Salerno wrote in a 1928 pamphlet entirely devoted to Puccini's heroines that 'ultra-human as he was, Giacomo Puccini could not shine except in the presence of characters in harmony with his sensibility', characters who were exclusively female.[52]

Among the lavish wreaths embellishing Puccini's coffin in Brussels were two rather more humble ones from anonymous members of the public that alluded to the composer's special affinity with female characters, characters with whom, according to several of his biographers, he had 'fallen in love'.[53] One was a small posy of violets bearing the words 'En souvenir de Musette' the other was two roses tied with a piece of coarse string, bearing the message 'Une pauvre Mimì'.[54] Puccini's works were deemed to have particular appeal to women: *Il popolo d'Italia* wrote, 'How many women, especially those who are weeping, have found in Butterfly their hopes and expectations, in Mimì their sorrowful love, in Minnie and Tosca their right to decisively affirmed happiness, and in Manon the sin that is redeemed through the grace of sincere sentiment?'[55] When Puccini's coffin was moved to Milan, the crowds who had waited for two hours outside the Duomo were dominated by women.[56] Puccini had only one genuine voice, it would seem, and this is what listeners hoped to hear in his final opera: ironically, given Torrefranca's earlier criticisms, it was the voice of gentle feminine sentiment.

Puccini's supporters approached *Turandot* with uncompromising expectations of what a composer's last work ought to do: numerous critics referred to the opera as Puccini's 'artistic testament', his last will and testament, and the point up to which his entire career had been building. In fact the composer had several future projects in the pipeline, and throughout much of *Turandot*'s composition was unaware that it was to be his last work. The mythology surrounding late works dictated that Puccini was expected to be ultra-sincere, to express his personal voice most clearly in his last, presumed to be summative, opera. And sincerity, in Puccini's case, was widely perceived to equate to what critics called his 'first manner', for as Renzo Bianchi observed in *L'Avanti!*: 'the public, as always happens, has fixed the personality of the musician in those operas that made him famous, disregarding the entire rest of his œuvre'.[57]

Thus although Puccini's endeavour to update his style was in principle welcomed by his patrons, they were ultimately discomfited by the result. Many commentaries on Puccini's music from around this time reveal that critics in 1920s Italy remained wedded to nineteenth-century teleological ideals. Adami boasted that in striving for artistic self-renewal late in life, Puccini was following in the footsteps of a much-fêted predecessor, writing: 'He demonstrated that musical evolution that would have set him on the road to a second manner, as had happened to Verdi after *Aida*.'[58] Lualdi, meanwhile, presented Puccini as a composer forever seeking to renew his style:

> With *Turandot*, Giacomo Puccini has provided the last, unfortunately, and most significant proof of his qualities as an artist of his race, and of good Italian stock. As an artist, that is, for whom the concept 'life' was indissolubly linked to the concept of 'movement'. To move, for him as for everyone, could not and cannot mean anything other than renewal. And so, in the posthumous *Turandot* the aspiration and striving for the new is obvious and tangible in every passage to a greater extent than in any of his other late works.[59]

Yet in truth, what most critics wanted from Puccini in *Turandot* were reminiscences of his much-loved works of the turn of the century, despite the accusation frequently levelled at him earlier in his career (and most vehemently after the première of *Madama Butterfly*) of 'repeating himself'.

Turandot was certainly not a wholesale attempt upon Puccini's part to liberate himself from old models, and sections of the opera did indeed fulfil the critics' hopes, particularly the music of the slave girl Liù, to which we will return later. However, other sections of the score, and most notably Turandot's music, were characteristic of the more modern style that Puccini had been developing since the 1910s. These may justifiably be viewed as his response to a shifting artistic climate, which might have pointed the way forward to even more adventurous experimentation had death not intervened. Discussions of Liù and Turandot were a way of articulating debates about the merits of the first and second 'manners' that were felt to have characterised Puccini's career.

Turandot is an opera that plays out a discursive dialogue with itself, in which Puccini attempts to reassess his own artistic œuvre past and present. One contemporary critic labelled Turandot a work that 'bears witness to the entire musical life of its author, in the sense that it recapitulates all the evolutionary phases of [its] composer'.[60] In this sense Puccini seemed almost to be writing his own epitaph, although it was not the one his advocates desired. Puccini's patrons evidently assumed the relationship between the composer and his loyal audience to be a static one, and many must have felt that in Turandot Puccini had reneged on his side of the deal. However, the reception of this opera and indeed the often rather complex responses to his earlier works illuminate the fact that this was a relationship that in fact had to be renegotiated constantly. The gap between expectation and practice was to prove problematic in the debates that followed the première of Turandot. And yet relatively recent experience had shown that composers did not always produce the last works expected of them. As we have already seen, Verdi's Falstaff, an even more progressive and self-interrogatory work, had also seemed perplexing to the critics set on portraying it as a national triumph. Although Puccini's commitment to artistic renewal was more equivocal than Verdi's, and his anxiety to court popular appeal more intense, Turandot, like Falstaff before it, illustrates the fact that the new relationship between artist, artwork and audience that modernism demanded was unworkable within the traditional paradigms of Italian opera. The critics' puzzled reaction to both works raised questions about the extent to which artistic renewal was in fact any longer possible within the Italian operatic tradition, and whether, indeed, this tradition was fundamentally incompatible with modernism.

A MECHANICAL HEROINE

Turandot was interpreted by the press as representing a retreat from the emotionalism that was, for many of the critics, not only Puccini's most characteristic and attractive asset but also an integral aspect of Italian opera. Puccini's supporters laid the blame vehemently at Gozzi's door, for creating a cruel, perverse, frozen, insensible creature impossible to set to music.[61] Such attempts on the part of Puccini's supporters to defend his compositional skills by dismissively attributing an opera's deficiencies to a poor choice of plot were common. Many wrote that *Turandot*, like *Tosca* before it, was an opera 'unsuited to Puccini's temperament',[62] although such excuses would not have impressed Croce, whose theories were still highly influential in 1920s Italy. He had written in 1902 that 'when art critics point out that a subject is ill-chosen, then, when that assertion has some foundation, it is not really a matter of blaming the subject-matter but of blaming the way in which the artist has dealt with it, of blaming an expression which is unsuccessful by virtue of the contradictions it contains'.[63] Furthermore the *femme fatale* was an operatic commonplace – not to mention a staple of the most popular silent movies of the time, starring such divas as Lyda Borelli and Francesca Bertini – and other composers had succeeded in creating heroines whose wickedness was offset by a compelling allure. But Puccini had captured nothing of this. It was not so much Turandot's malice that disturbed the critics as her mechanicalism, as Antonio Capri explained by way of comparison with recent operas by Strauss and Pizzetti:

> In short Turandot should resemble Salome, Phaedra, Elektra; should be all flaming passion; have in her an implacable power of domination

and destruction; be the centre of and motive for the drama. Instead she occupies only a relatively quite small part of the opera; remains a background figure, who presents herself only half way through the second act, with rigid and cold features.[64]

Writing in 1931, Capri's comments echoed those made five years earlier by the first-night critics. Turandot was a heroine who seemed bewilderingly inexpressive from the moment the curtain rose. Whereas Puccini's heroines were customarily perceived as the bearers of Puccini's genuine feelings, the critics' overriding impression was that Turandot was a character who 'said nothing'. This was, of course, quite literally the case during Act I, where Turandot remained vocally mute, a gesture that had dramatic logic but undoubtedly compounded the character's perceived inhumanity. But in Act II, when Turandot finally did sing, her music still seemed to reveal nothing of her character. 'Musically,' noted Michele Lessona in the *Rivista musicale italiana*, 'Turandot does not live: she merely sings, or hums; she speaks without saying anything, or says too little.'[65] And the dramatic inadequacy of Turandot's music was apparent not only to those, like Lessona, who analysed the score in some detail in the specialist music press, but also to those writing in the daily press. Gaetano Cesari, customarily Puccini's staunch supporter, grudgingly admitted in the *Corriere della sera* (by this time edited by Puccini's friend Ugo Ojetti) that 'the music does not succeed in making manifest the sphinx that is in Turandot, that is, in translating into sensations, and even less into emotions, her obscure and immovable states of mind'.[66]

Like one of Turandot's unfortunate suitors, Puccini had been confounded, reduced to a state of impotence by the princess, as Raffaello De Rensis explained: 'The exquisitely delicate femininity of Puccini's art, which created characters whose names alone are enough to move us, was shattered when faced with the marmoreal and, we might add, anything but attractive Turandot.'[67] Puccini's death had, of course, robbed the work of its crucial dénouement, but the first-night critics had little confidence that he would have been up to the task of effecting Turandot's transformation from icy disdain to flaming passion even had he survived to complete the work, as De Rensis suggested:

> Turandot the cruel should have been transformed through fiery love. The cold and dry theme with which Puccini characterised her should have warmed up, sparkled, taken flame; should have taken on vast and infinite proportions and left its mark on the entire opera. Because without the redemption of Turandot the entire structure crumbles. But this redemption appears to have been a riddle even more difficult to solve than those set by the Princess for her suitors, and Puccini did not solve it, nor do we know whether he would have succeeded in solving it. The heroine so loved by him is of an icy, perfidious nature, quite beyond redemption.[68]

Puccini himself was, indeed, unconfident that he would succeed in 'solving the riddle of Princess Turandot'; he wrote in March 1923: 'This infamous *Turandot* terrifies me and I shan't finish it, or if I finish it it will be a fiasco.'[69]

Commentators agreed that it was the second act – the one dominated by Turandot – that had proved Puccini's greatest challenge in the opera. Pino Valmarana complained that the atmosphere of the enigma scene was 'too cold and decorative', that it had sapped Puccini of his creative energy.[70] Lessona alluded to the shallowness of the work by suggesting that all that remained of Gozzi's original tale in Simoni and Adami's libretto was merely the 'decorative' aspect.[71] (Such comments were ominously reminiscent of the charges levelled at *Madama Butterfly*.) The Ricordi camp may have claimed that in *Turandot* Puccini 'had said not merely his last word but his best word',[72] but to many listeners this was an opera in which he did not seem to have said very much at all. Rather than bearing his soul, as the critics expected him to do in his final opera, Puccini seemed to have concealed genuine feeling behind a number of deceitful masks.

MACHINES AND THE MODERN THEATRE

Aware of the commercial importance of an alluring heroine, Puccini expressed to his librettist Simoni his desire to create a flesh-and-blood

Turandot, writing: 'With luck we will succeed in modernising the old cardboard cut-out, in humanising her with new feeling,'[73] and 'Our Princess ... will be delighted to see us united to subject her soul to extensive examination.'[74] On the surface, his avowed aim was to contrast the mechanicalism of the Masks – whose artificial nature he enhanced by giving them literally machine-made music borrowed from a Chinese music box[75] – with what he saw as the psychodrama of Princess Turandot. Whereas earlier settings of the Turandot story had presented the heroine as purely malicious, the story about Turandot's ancestress that Puccini's librettists invented for Act II was intended to give justification to her behaviour and render her increasingly sympathetic as the opera progresses. But the great difficulties Puccini experienced in composing Turandot's music have been well documented,[76] and, as we have seen, his supposedly 'human' heroine failed to convince the critics.

The challenge that faced Puccini was an exacting one, for there was something innately mechanistic about the Turandot subject. His librettists would have been familiar with Schiller's version of *Turandot* (*Turandot, Prinzessin von China*), which had been translated into Italian by Andrea Maffei.[77] Schiller had noted a puppet-like quality common to all the characters in Gozzi's play, not merely the Masks: 'The figures have the appearance of marionettes operated by wires; there is a certain pedantic stiffness running through the whole thing which will have to be overcome.'[78] But later renderings of the Turandot story had failed to surmount this apparently inherent mechanicalism. In 1867, the opera *Turanda* by Antonio Bazzini (later to be Puccini's composition teacher at the Milan Conservatorio) prompted the following disparaging comment from the *Gazzetta musicale di Milano*: 'The libretto is a dramatic absurdity – a fairy tale, which wants to give the appearance of an episode from real life, and precisely for this reason, by trying to be lifelike, self-destructs. Not one interesting character, not one moving scene.'[79]

Fifty years later, it was precisely the robotic nature of the *Turandot* characters that was to draw Busoni to the subject when he was searching for a suitably 'mechanical' work as a companion piece for his *commedia-dell'arte*-derived *Arlecchino* of 1917. Could this aspect of the Turandot story also have been a positive stimulus for Puccini, who by the early 1920s was consciously striving for a way in which to update his style, desirous of a break with realism after the indifferent reception that had greeted *Il tabarro* in 1918? For all Puccini's protestations about creating a human heroine, the robotic Turandot actually offered him a means of experimenting with an entirely new approach to operatic character and dramaturgy.

Ever eager to keep up with the latest trends, Puccini would have known that in the late 1910s and early 1920s to be 'mechanical' was to be modern. Puccini's more progressive contemporaries, from Stravinsky to Schoenberg to Strauss, whose works he observed with interest, were all inspired by the marionette-like figures of the *commedia dell'arte*. Furthermore, puppets, both literal and metaphorical, were omnipresent on the spoken stage of the late 1910s and early 1920s, from the theatres of Moscow to the cabarets of Barcelona. After watching Vittorio Podrecca's Teatro dei Piccoli, an Italian puppet troupe which enjoyed international acclaim performing comic operas throughout the 1920s, one critic observed: 'The fact is that while Dr Podrecca's puppets are more lifelike than any before him, our present ballets, and some modern acting come nearer to marionette movements than ever before.'[80] Podrecca's puppets, given voice by professional opera singers, performed *opere buffe* by Mozart, Rossini, Paisiello, and Pergolesi, as well as specially composed contemporary works such as Respighi's *La bella addormentata* (1922), and were watched by, amongst others, Puccini, Busoni and Stravinsky. The troupe, founded in Rome in 1914, developed out of a long and prestigious tradition of Italian puppeteering, led by the Lupi family in Turin and the Colla family in Milan, whose companies operated in lavish permanent theatres, attracted a middle-class audience, and parodied the repertory staged in the mainstream theatres and opera houses.

While Podrecca's puppets provided popular entertainment, puppet theatre had also come to form the core of highbrow, avant-garde theatre. The fusion of men with machines offered a vehicle through which a number of modernist preoccupations could be expressed: the falseness of contemporary society, the perceived loss of the individual in the modern faceless crowd, the implications of a post-Nietzschean godless world and (in Italy at least) concern about the 'machinations' of an increasingly autocratic state. Puppet theatre offered an opportunity not merely for social commentary but for an aesthetic re-evaluation of traditional perceptions of the boundary between reality and illusion. Such experiments were a reaction against bourgeois theatre, against psychological realism and against sentimentality: in short, against everything that Puccini's operas might at first seem to represent. And yet the questioning of what constituted artistic 'truth' that was promulgated in these works and, indeed, their quest for a new sort of truth was a dialogue that was played out in Puccini's last opera as much as in the criticism surrounding it.

The use of puppet-like figures, masks or robots as theatrical protagonists constituted a profound reappraisal of the nature of theatrical character and traditional ideas of performativity. In Italy, the disparate theatrical experiments of the 1910s and 1920s shared a common aesthetic aim: to demonstrate that dramatic 'realism' was in fact an illusion, and the puppet the only 'sincere' theatrical protagonist. Thus, unlike Podrecca, the avant garde did not use puppets to mimic humans; rather, the artificiality of the marionette was its very authenticity, and a puppet-like style of delivery and gesture became an ideal towards which progressive actors should strive. Let us briefly consider a number of manifestations of this new approach to theatricality, and Puccini's response to them.

Puccini can hardly have been unaware of the new machine aesthetic, which was all-pervading by the early 1920s, both on the stage and off it, such as in the robotic mannerisms – thrust-out chest, tensed jaws, and bellicose voice – cultivated by Mussolini. Indeed, there is evidence to suggest that Puccini was attracted by it. He was drawn to the Turandot subject after hearing accounts of a production of Gozzi's play in Berlin directed by Max Reinhardt. Significantly, what interested him most were the staging techniques Reinhardt had used. He wrote to Simoni:

> Yesterday I was speaking to a foreign lady, who told me about a production of this work given in Germany with very strange and

original staging by Max Reinhardt. She will write and get photographs of this 'mise en scène', and then we can see for ourselves what it's all about.[81]

The accounts Puccini heard of Reinhardt's production of *Turandot* must surely have dwelt upon the actors' robotic movements and impassive expressions, a style of acting that enhanced the mechanicalism of the characters. Reinhardt trained his actors to move and behave like puppets, in order to render them completely subordinate to his directorial will. In so doing he worked along similar lines to those advocated by the Florence-based director and designer Edward Gordon Craig, who between 1908 and 1929 used his journal *The Mask* and his progressive theatre school at the Arena Goldoni to expound his radical theory that puppets should be substituted for live actors. Craig advocated the use of puppets in order to effect a complete break with realism, which he dismissed in an article entitled 'Some Evil Tendencies of the Modern Theatre' as mere 'caricature'.[82] Craig's contention was that acting, inferior even to photography as an art form, was 'a poor art and a poor cleverness, which cannot convey the spirit and essence of an idea to an audience, but can only show an artless copy, a facsimile of the thing itself', and suggested that the theatre banish 'this idea of impersonation, this idea of reproducing nature', which Craig called 'the flashiness of displayed personality'.[83] Directors should replace the actor with the marionette, which 'will not compete with life – but will rather go beyond it',[84] becoming the superhuman *Übermarionette*, an idea inspired both by Nietzsche and by Kleist's *Über das Marionettentheater* of 1810.

Craig's promotion of the puppet as protagonist found echoes in contemporary Italian dramatic practices and debates. Most significantly, the concept of the synthesis of man and machine lay at the heart of the Futurist aesthetic. Paraphrasing Craig, Marinetti protested that 'the dramatic art ought not to concern itself with psychological photography' and advocated that actors be subordinated entirely to the writer's or director's will.[85] Futurist artworks were preoccupied both with machine-like characters and with a mechanistic style of declamation from which all human emotion should be purged. Marinetti instructed performers to 'dehumanise completely the voice, systematically doing away with every modulation and nuance', to 'dehumanise the face completely, avoiding every grimace', and to adopt a 'geometric' manner of gesticulation.[86] Marinetti's theories were applied not only to spoken theatre but to dance, which should be characterised by geometric gestures, as outlined in his 'Manifesto of the Futurist Dance' of 8 July 1917 and manifested in Depero's *Balli Plastici* of 1918, performed by cubistic marionettes, and Ivo Pannaggi and Vinicio Paladini's *Futurist Mechanical Ballet*, performed in Rome in 1922.

As we have seen, the Futurist aesthetic was at odds with everything for which Puccini's operas stood; it is therefore hardly surprising that this was a movement with which he never felt inclined to ally himself. He did, however, toy with the idea of setting a work by one of the avant-garde Italian playwrights of the post-First World War era whose works, while less radical than those of the Futurists, nevertheless envisioned a new type of theatrical character. In 1920, despairing at the slow progress that Adami and Simoni were making with the *Turandot* libretto, Puccini wrote to Renzo Valcarenghi: 'Should I look for something else? Bring myself up to date and devote myself to some big new genius with a bit of style and a bit of imagination? Who? Pirandello? Rosso di San Secondo? Someone else? There are dozens.'[87] We can only guess at what sort of an opera such a partnership would have produced, but *Turandot*, with its mechanical antiheroine, may provide some clues.

Pirandello's celebrated *Sei personaggi in cerca d'autore* (1921) explored such issues as the nature of character, acting and authorship, and the boundaries of reality and illusion. The now less-well-remembered Piermaria Rosso di San Secondo, along with his contemporaries Luigi Chiarelli and Massimo Bontempelli, created a genre known as the *Teatro grottesco*, in which they aspired to parody the hypocrisy and shallowness of pre-war society and theatre, often using the image of a mask to demonstrate that true humanity existed only beneath the surface of bourgeois conventions. Their plays reflect upon the fact that an entire generation seemed to have been reduced to the status of puppets manipulated by the hand of fate. Chiarelli's *La maschera e il volto* (*The Mask and the Face*), which established the *grottesco* genre in 1916, was described thus by the author of a book on contemporary Italian drama in 1927: 'All this play's originality lies precisely in the way in which, by treating the old protagonists of bourgeois drama ironically, it has been able to render them human: the deformed artifice that humanity has turned into.'[88] In order to accentuate this sense of 'deformed artifice', the protagonists of the *grottesco* plays were portrayed as impersonal blank canvases, such as the 'the man in grey' and 'the woman in the blue fox' in Rosso di San Secondo's *Marionette, che passione!* (1918). Bontempelli, the founder of the influential literary journal '900, went a step further in critiquing both traditional gender representations and the very nature of theatricality in *Nostra Dea*. In this play, he created a heroine who is a living doll, whose actions and voices are determined by the different outfits she wears and who acquires a new personality with each dress she dons – a striking gesture in a country where the whole theatrical system was dominated by star actresses and the cult of personality. First performed in 1925, the play came too late to have been seen by Puccini, but nevertheless sums up the new theatrical ethos of the age – that character was all artifice.

All these experiments, then, envisioned a new sort of character, and most particularly a new sort of *female* character, the sentimental heroine having come to epitomise the effeminate, bourgeois theatre that the avant garde wanted to jettison. The contemporary Italian machine plays, many of which were highly misogynistic, strove to purge society and culture of all traces of the 'degenerate' carnal woman and of romantic sentimentality. A new type of metallic and mechanistic heroine became a key part of the modernist renunciation of sentimental excess, a particularly effective vehicle through which to sever links with the art of the past. This trend is exemplified particularly clearly by the works of 'Fillia' (Luigi Colombo), such as *Sensualità* (1923), *Adulterio futurista* (1925), *Il sesso di metallo* (1925), and *La morte della donna* (1925), which were concerned with the synthesis of women with machines, a concept taken to literal extremes in *L'uomo senza sesso* (1927), in which a female racing driver fuses her body with the metal of her car. Furthermore, mechanistic women were not confined to the stage. The critics watching and listening to what they perceived to be the 'robotic' Turandot would also have found her echo in the automaton-like heroines of numerous international films of the 1920s, including Fritz Lang's *Metropolis* (1926), and, even more striking, Marcel L'Herbier's *L'Inhumaine* (1924) set to music by Darius Milhaud, which concerns the transformation of an 'inhuman' *femme fatale* – an opera singer – into a loving woman. In the visual arts, too, mechanistic women were a dominant motif, as seen in the mannequin-like female figures of Mario Sironi, Giorgio De Chirico, Carlo Carrà and Giorgio Morandi.

Turandot seemed to some reviewers to be more akin to the protagonists of the contemporary experimental plays than a traditional operatic heroine. She was a character to whom one could not relate – indeed to whom one did not seem to be meant to relate. As such she was, in a way, a highly fitting emblem of her era, the heroine Puccini had promised when he wrote of his ambition to create 'a Turandot filtered through the modern mind'.[89] But this was of course highly problematic, for the modernist eschewal of sentiment and empathy was profoundly at odds with the Italian operatic tradition, a tradition in which popular approval and instant emotional appeal were essential criteria for a work's success. As Emanuele Senici has noted: 'empathy, identification with the characters, is precisely what the nineteenth-century tradition of Italian opera ... considered its highest goal, its very raison d'être, what the audience expected and longed for'.[90]

CONTESTING *TURANDOT*'S MODERNITY

But what was the response to Puccini's latest work by the more progressive critics, those less attached to affective empathy as the lynchpin of Italian opera? While traditionalists found Turandot objectionable because she seemed representative of an emotionally sterile modernism at odds with the entire Italian operatic tradition, the progressive critics responded equally coldly because they saw Puccini's efforts to update his style as unconvincing. Just as Stravinsky's stylistically eclectic works were attacked for being, in W. Anthony Sheppard's words, 'parodistic masks, casually assumed',[91] so too did Puccini appear to be simply playing with a range of superficial musical masks, not perceived to be sincerely felt. He seemed to critics to have engaged with a more modern style of composition at only the most cursory of levels, an attack that arguably seems justified given the rather nonchalant tone of the letter about Reinhardt's production of *Turandot* cited above. If artistic renewal were to take place it must be honest rather than forced, whereas Renzo Bianchi hinted that Puccini was merely going through the motions: 'At the age of fifty an artist can achieve any evolution – a revolution, even – but must succeed in achieving it solely in himself: in his own brain, in his own blood, in his own nerves.'[92]

For Guido M. Gatti, a committed champion of the modernist movement who founded and edited the progressive *Il pianoforte* (from 1920) and its successor, the *Rassegna musicale* (from 1928), and was the secretary-general of the first Maggio Musicale Fiorentino, *Turandot* represented 'the torment of an artist who wants to transform himself'.[93] Gatti felt that Puccini, incapable of assimilating the musical language of Debussy, Stravinsky and Schoenberg, had merely peppered his score with a few quasi-modern phrases. Indeed, for Gatti, *Turandot* marked a veritable stylistic regression: '[Puccini's] language did not substantially change or become richer between *Manon* and *Turandot*: on the contrary, one might say that in certain respects it became more impoverished.'[94] Nor was it only in Italy that objections were being made to Puccini's attempts to update his style. As early as 1920, Cecil Gray, for example, had attacked Puccini in the English journal *The Sackbut* for trying to escape from the past 'to which he naturally belongs' and for incorporating more modern elements into his music 'in the spirit of disagreeable necessity' – to the extent that 'we almost see him setting his teeth as he writes them'.[95]

Thus, for the modernist critics as much as for Puccini's supporters, *Turandot* represented a compromised vision. Puccini had not fully liberated himself from the past and some critics felt that he ought to have embraced the machine aesthetic more wholeheartedly. Vittorio Gui, writing with hindsight in the 1940s, argued that Busoni had handled the Turandot subject more effectively precisely because he had emphasised the intentionally 'robotic' aspect of Gozzi's play, retaining 'the caustic, satirical, humorous flavour, the "mechanicalism" of the characters, who are and want to be artificial, symbols of life more than images of real life'.[96] Gui was not ill disposed towards Puccini; indeed, he had conducted *Fanciulla* at the Teatro Regio in Turin in November 1911 and the première of the second version of *La rondine* in Palermo in April 1920. However, he mocked Puccini for his attempt to humanise Turandot, demanding: 'How can one think of taking a character as grotesque and absurdly fictitious seriously? ... As a ludicrous symbol of female frigidity, combined with physical beauty, she might have existed; as a living woman, never.'[97]

The message that critics such as Gui were trying to articulate was that Puccini had engaged with the fantasy world of the Turandot legend at only the most shallow of levels. Puccini was ever drawn to the visual; when asked by Ugo Ojetti whether he heard the music or saw the images on stage when he composed, Puccini replied: 'I see, above all I see. I see the characters and the colours and gestures of the characters.'[98] Thus, Puccini had been attracted to the Turandot subject by dint of its picturesque atmosphere and colour, but had failed to take account of its more profound complexities; Gatti accused Puccini of 'seeing the scene but not seeing the characters'.[99]

Just like Bazzini, Puccini had attempted to treat the fairy tale as realism, and thereby created a character who, far from being lifelike, had become the least human of all operatic heroines. Saverio Procida argued in the *Nuova antologia* that 'materially and psychologically the Maestro belongs to that realistic world of which he is the faithful echo', and that Puccini's music was informed by his own subjectivity to such an extent that he was unable to step outside himself, to 'split himself in two'.[100] Michele Lessona argued that whereas the central scene of Act II ought to be 'where the essence of Turandot's soul is situated', the music did not fit the drama: Puccini had simply lapsed into his usual trivial realist vein. 'In questa reggia' began in a 'sing-song manner, like a lullaby', and

> the thought that Turandot addresses to her unfortunate ancestress does not transport us into the world of fairy tale, nor into that of tragedy; that invocation to her 'sweet and serene ancestress' could be, in an opera with a contemporary subject and realistic treatment, the memory a good girl has for her affectionate grandmother.[101]

And of 'Mai nessun m'avrà', arguably the most sensuous passage in the score, Lessona wrote: 'The musical phrase is warm, strong, rising, but reveals to us nothing specific; it is the sort of phrase that one can very well imagine in many love duets; and because there is such a duet at the end of the opera, sure enough it's found there.'[102]

This, then, was what made Turandot so profoundly contradictory – the dislocation between her music and what it was apparently intended to express. Puccini's attempt to update his musical style was presented in the reviews not as spontaneous, but as something that had simply been tacked on to his existing aesthetic. Lessona's compliment that 'in this opera the technique is almost perfect, always' was therefore backhanded, as his subsequent words reveal: 'it is of no use insisting upon the particular merits of the technique, when the opera in its entirety lives only a false and wretched existence, doesn't touch us, and adds nothing either to our artistic heritage in general, or to the preceding output of the same author'.[103] In other words, the substance of the work was dislocated from the technique with which it had been elaborated. Domenico De Paoli, doubtless aware of Croce's theories about technique and expression (as discussed in chapter 4), singled out *Turandot* for particular attack in his study of the 'crisis' that had befallen Italian music in the first three decades of the twentieth century:

> Every technical renewal not accompanied by a corresponding evolution in feeling has the sole result of accentuating the contrast between the new form and the substance that no longer corresponds

to it (from this point of view a study of the posthumous *Turandot* is particularly revealing).[104]

Turandot seemed to be a work divided into two parts: one looking backwards (widely perceived as honest), the other looking forwards (perceived as dishonest). For the more conservative commentators, the very act of attempting to 'split himself in two' was seen as undermining Puccini's sincerity. The simultaneous coexistence within one text of two apparently irreconcilable manners was inimical to the critics' enduring attachment to the idea of organicism as a marker of musical beauty. Furthermore, the persistence of a quasi-Romantic faith in the inseparability of an artist from his art meant that a composer was expected to speak in a single 'voice', to have a distinct musical 'physiognomy', an idea that Puccini's critics and biographers had stressed repeatedly throughout his career. Puccini's blending of familiar and more adventurous styles of music made it impossible to ascertain which parts of the score represented the 'authentic' Puccini, with the result that those sections that did not conform to expectations were discreetly ignored in the reviews. Critics eager to depict *Turandot* as an unmitigated success and Puccini's œuvre as homogeneous called the work '*puccinianissimo* among Puccini operas', an opera that 'the public greeted like a dear old friend' and a work in which Puccini had 'remained faithful to himself', but such approving comments were based on a highly selective – arguably insincere – reading of the score.[105]

LA DONNA VERAMENTE DONNA

Thankfully, there was another character in *Turandot* who fulfilled the critics' criteria for an acceptable operatic heroine. In Liù, Puccini had created a character who provided a refuge for those critics reluctant to accept the abandonment of feeling that being modern seemed to necessitate. At the dramatic level, Adriano Lualdi argued that it was only by becoming a sacrificial victim along the same lines as Liù that Turandot stood any chance of making herself acceptable to audiences:

> The Prince does not know what to do except embrace and touch the beautiful body of this snake-tongued woman. He should have slapped her, beaten her. Some women enjoy this means of gentle persuasion. Perhaps Turandot was one of them. As a victim in turn, it might have finally been possible to foster a little sympathy for her.[106]

And at the musical level, Liù's music provided the lyricism that nostalgic reviewers craved: one referred to 'Signore ascolta' as a refreshing stream that 'moistens the arid earth' of the surrounding pages of music.[107]

Liù was repeatedly referred to as 'the most Puccinian character of the opera',[108] a claim that is unsurprising given that the character does not appear in earlier versions of the Turandot story and was invented specially for Puccini by his librettists. The inclusion of such a character, the self-sacrificial heroine *par excellence*, suggests a reluctance on Puccini's part to forsake his old sentimental world altogether, demonstrated in his instruction to Adami in 1919 that he and Simoni must

> put all your strength into [the *Turandot* libretto], all the resources of your heads and hearts, and create for me something that will make the world weep. They say that emotionalism is a sign of weakness, but I like to be weak! To the *strong*, so-called, I leave the triumphs that fade; for us, those that endure.[109]

Liù seemed to provide a link to the 'real' Puccini because she provided a connection both dramatically and musically to what critics called Puccini's 'first manner'. Even a progressive reviewer largely critical of *Turandot* such as Michele Lessona, writing only the second review of a Puccini opera that the *Rivista musicale italiana* had deigned to publish, rejoiced in the fact that Puccini had at least created one *creatura umana* in his opera, whose music was the 'spontaneous and sincere expression of the Maestro's soul'.[110] Liù was depicted by the press as the most Puccinian of the Puccini women – a model for *all* women, even, with one critic calling her *la donna veramente donna*[111] – a high accolade given what his heroines had come to embody.

How convenient for the hagiographers, then, that the last page of music that Puccini had reputedly written was Liù's death scene, the pathos of which was intensified for many by memories of Puccini's own recent demise. Character and composer were depicted as virtually synonymous in most of the reviews, yet there was no Torrefranca-style approbation here. Lualdi mused: 'The soul of Liù. Or perhaps the soul of Giacomo Puccini who, having taken his last little creature by the hand, and accompanied her piously to rest, expired upon her tomb.'[112] Almost all first-night reviews recounted the anecdote of Toscanini laying down his baton after Liù's funeral, at the precise point where Puccini was reported to have laid down his pen. A few days after the première *Turandot* was staged with Alfano's ending in Rome, but the performance was halted once again after Liù's death, as the result of a supposedly spontaneous reaction from the audience:

> At the end of Liù's scene, just after the funeral, the audience, as if obeying a command, fell silent and rose to its feet, remaining for a moment in collective silence, thus greeting with regret the moment at which the author had been forced to break off from orchestrating the work. A voice, from a box, exclaimed: 'Peace and glory to the Italian soul of Giacomo Puccini!'[113]

Through Liù's music, then, the critics claimed, Puccini had remained himself to the end. According to Salerno, it was through Liù's music that Puccini had revealed himself in his last opera as 'the most sincere, human, and above all Italian Puccini we have hitherto known'.[114]

SENTIMENT AND SINCERITY

For the conservative critics, 'sincerity' and 'sentiment' were terms used interchangeably, but, according to their ideological opponents, their failure to understand Turandot was attributable to an unwillingness to engage with a changing understanding of the notion of sentiment. According to Domenico De Paoli, these 'zealous conservatives' had failed to take account of the fact that 'during the war (even before this, to tell the truth) human "sentiment" had changed character considerably – and that the notions "sentiment" and "expression" did *not*, necessarily, any longer have a *sentimental* value'.[115] Sentiment, regarded as a praiseworthy artistic quality in earlier eras, had indeed taken on a new character during the first decades of the twentieth century; now being widely interpreted as more self-indulgent and manipulative than 'sincere'. Modernist artists were increasingly contemptuous of the instant popular appeal cultivated by most nineteenth-century dramatists, Marinetti declaring 'disdain for the public' and writing that 'we despise all those works that merely want to make people weep or to move them'.[116] Times were changing, and by the 1920s sentiment occupied an uneasy position in the Italian spoken theatre. Although the avant garde had by and large rejected it, the shapers of Fascist cultural policy were aware of the political expediency of appealing to the irrational instincts of the masses, with Mussolini calling the theatre 'one of the most direct means of getting through to the hearts of the people'.[117]

An Italian opera without feeling might seem to be an anomaly, yet in 1923 Gino Roncaglia cited the 'superficial and effeminate sentimentality of certain Puccini melodies' in the progressive journal *Il pianoforte* as evidence that 'sentimentalism is the degeneration of sentiment'.[118] Thus, the reviews of *Turandot* reveal a profound divide among contemporary music critics between those who regarded the ability to move the audience not as sincere but as mawkish and those who continued to be guided by public taste when judging a work of art, claiming that unschooled audiences were the best critics. By the time of *Turandot* the more progressive critics seemed to be winning out, to the extent that one Puccini-loving commentator wrote bitterly that listening to his music in the 1920s had become an indulgence to be enjoyed only in secret.[119]

Perhaps even Puccini's old model of sentimentality, as represented by Liù, was not sincere but something feigned. After all the label 'sentimentalist' can be used pejoratively, to denote one who *affects* sentimentality, who indulges in an exaggerated, inappropriate or *insincere* display of feeling. *Suor Angelica* had received a mediocre reception and failed to become a staple of the operatic repertory because its sentimentality was widely perceived to be so overstated as to be unconvincing. Seen in this light one might regard Liù rather than Turandot as the real 'puppet', created especially to indulge Puccini's most sentimental and anachronistic side. One contemporary critic did, after all, call her 'a simple, attractive figurine', a comment doubtless intended to suggest that she was decorative, fragile, charming, but one that also conveys a sense of inanimacy – that she was a mere plaything, cynically manipulated by her creators in order to stir the audience's feelings.[120] That Puccini regarded Liù as a 'type' is revealed by the fact that in the early stages of the compositional process he referred to her simply as the 'piccola donna'.[121]

In common with virtually all of the critics, the modernist Guido Gatti likened Liù to Puccini's earlier heroines; however, unlike the majority, his aim was to condemn rather than to praise. He argued that Mimì, Manon and Butterfly were 'poetic' figures only in a deceptive sense: 'They place the spectator in that state of "sensiblerie" that is close to emotion, to that emotion, you understand, that has nothing to do with art, and that manifests itself with tears and sighs, above all among the female public.'[122] For Gatti, the moments in Puccini's works that moved the listener to tears were in fact the least successful aspects of his operas, in which Puccini the musician gave way to Puccini the man of the theatre, putting in the minimum effort to gain the maximum effect. This Puccini would be applauded by all the audiences in the world, but would be of no significance in the history of music. In Gatti's opinion this Puccini was not sincere.

Sentimentality seemed no longer to equate to sincerity by the late 1920s; perhaps in truth it never really had. The critics' quest for artistic sincerity in Puccini's last opera reopened old anxieties about the honesty and homogeneity of his earlier works. Puccini's supporters had long boasted of his 'sincerity', and yet paradoxically an insincere streak, apparent even to his champions, had long been heard in his music, as chapters 3 and 4 have revealed. Puccini, whose reputation had been built on his sincerity, had in fact been regarded by some as a puppet-master from the outset, but for such concerns to re-emerge in 1926 at what should have been a moment of national celebration was little short of disastrous. Only some years after the *Turandot* première would the Italian critics – and even then only the most forward-thinking – be prepared to accept that the cold, mechanical Turandot might actually represent the new 'real' Puccini. Writing in the forward-looking *Rassegna musicale* a decade later, Renato Mariani proposed an alternative reading of Puccini's work. Despite the fact that 'it was always asserted and it is still asserted that the real Puccini, the best Puccini, the authentic Puccini is expressed completely only in *Manon*, in *Bohème*, and in *Butterfly*',[123] Mariani's personal, controversial, opinion was that Puccini's ignored, criticised and misunderstood late style – as found in *La fanciulla del West*, the first two operas of *Il trittico* and *Turandot* – was the composer at his most sincere:

> The authentic musician is here: the artistic and human toil that led him from Mimì to Turandot was necessary and urgent; without such labour his œuvre would have appeared, today, decidedly incomplete. ... To deny this Puccini, to deny in *Turandot* the positive values of healthy, living modernity, of absolute indisputable contemporaneousness, is to fail to appreciate the best of his art.[124]

Amid the fanfares that surrounded *Turandot* in 1926, it seemed that Puccini had in fact pleased few listeners with his much-hyped, supposedly most 'sincere' work. Rather, it was an opera characterised by tensions and dichotomies at every level, between the two heroines, between the human and the machine, between the two stylistic manners, between past and present, between what Puccini intended and what the critics perceived: more of a transitional work than the decisive end-point that the critics expected. They fought over which of Puccini's 'voices' in his last opera was 'sincere', but both female principals in *Turandot* were, in their own way, different sorts of masks, used by Puccini as part of a cautious re-evaluation of his aesthetic approach, a critique of his own artistic strategies in a work of stylised gestures that seemed to send up the very excesses of opera itself. *Turandot* can be seen both as a re-evaluation of the aesthetics of opera in the twentieth century and as an illustration of the contingent, constructed nature of modernity. Multivalent conceptions of what it meant to be modern jumbled together both in the reception of *Turandot* and in the opera itself, with Puccini's use of several different musical voices destabilising the idea that there was one particular way in which 'modern' ideas might be expressed. Within such a work, any quest to find the 'real' Puccini was futile.

EPILOGUE

The responses that greeted *Turandot* marked a turning-point in its composer's reception history. After Puccini's death, even his enemies were prepared to acknowledge him as *the* Italian artist of his day. His status as national composer was now finally secure – to the extent that Renato Mariani would go so far as to write in 1939 that 'Italy and Puccini are one and the same'[1] – and the Fascist regime sought to appropriate his music for its own political ends. Adriano Lualdi would write in the 1950s: 'as far as the theatre is concerned, Puccini's œuvre in fact represents Italian music in the period 1880–1910 much more truthfully than the masterwork *Falstaff* and much more faithfully than *Cavalleria rusticana*'.[2] Finally, or so it seems, Puccini had won unequivocal endorsement from the majority of the critics; even if they were baffled by *Turandot* itself, there can be no doubt that its composer was now seen as one of Italy's most significant creative figures. The question of Puccini's Italianness – for so long a bone of contention among writers and musicologists of all political persuasions – was settled.

However, as this particular issue receded into the background, other problems came to the fore. *Turandot* prompted such questions: Puccini's conscious attempt to renew his style had thrown into relief the very irreconcilability of modern compositional styles with the basic aesthetic premises of Italian opera. 'Modern' though *Turandot* undoubtedly was, both in terms of Puccini's own output and Italian opera more generally, many people (then as now) would nevertheless claim that it cuts a very traditional figure indeed when compared, say, with the roughly contemporaneous *Wozzeck* or *Oedipus Rex*. The Puccini problem was changing: whereas the central dispute surrounding him had previously concerned his status as a national composer, it now concerned his status as either a progressive or reactionary.[3] Critics both in Italy and abroad became increasingly preoccupied with the issue of what Puccini's historical standing would be in the longer term, and how he would rank alongside composers from neighbouring countries. National acclaim and international status merely provoked historiographical anxiety: this was, if anything, an even bigger problem, and in one form or another it has dogged Puccini ever since his death.

Put bluntly, the point was this: the reviews of *Turandot* questioned whether pandering to the sentimental tastes of middle-class audiences was a sufficient ambition for a composer of Italian opera, or whether artistic progress (however that might be defined) ought to be a greater priority. This was an exceptionally sensitive issue, given that the emergent modernisms in the Austro-German traditions were explicitly antagonistic to bourgeois consumption; the very popularity and acclaim that Puccini had long courted (often successfully) threw him into a direct conflict with what would later be viewed by some as the mainstream of twentieth-century music. The terms of this debate have remained remarkably unchanged since Puccini's death: Guido M. Gatti wrote in 1927, for instance, that 'Puccini as a man of the theatre may be applauded by all the audiences in the world, but he is of no interest to the history of music',[4] and a brief survey of histories of twentieth-century music reveals that most scholars outside of Italy have taken their cue from such assessments. In *Giacomo Puccini: The Man, His Life, His Work* (1932), for example, Richard Specht wrote that in Germany, and even in Italy, Puccini 'has been represented as the great corruptor, the very negation of an artist, a merely theatrical composer striving after nothing but effectiveness, and the incarnation of modern degeneration and insincerity'.[5] Although Specht's book was intended as 'an act of atonement and expiation' for the harsh comments he himself had made in the past about 'the problem presented by Giacomo Puccini',[6] it is by no means free of approbation. He writes of the (supposed) indistinguishability of Puccini's music and characters from opera to opera, the superficiality of the local colour in his works, the lack of impact of his melodies and the fact that 'he produces his effects by crudities of the most brutal sort' – factors that make it understandable that 'some should have been of the opinion that he appeals solely to the evil instincts of the masses, to those who find satisfaction in the sensationalism of film, the "shocker", and the popular melodrama'.[7]

More recent writers have echoed the tone of such criticism. Particularly dismissive is Donald J. Grout (1947), who criticises the 'perpetual pregnancy' in Puccini's melodies and the reminiscence or mood-invoking motifs that 'do not serve as generating themes for musical development'.[8] Grout concludes that Puccini was 'not one of the great composers' and that 'Puccini's music often sounds better than it is, owing to the perfect adjustment of means to ends'.[9] Similarly, William W. Austin, in a key study of twentieth-century music (1966), criticises *Tosca* (an opera he sees as 'typical of Puccini's work in the twentieth century') for its trite rhythms, frequent use of climactic phrases that 'never compose a satisfying melodic whole to compare with Verdi', absorption of more progressive harmonic moments into an overall harmonic framework that is thoroughly conventional and leitmotifs that 'assure an obvious sort of unity without development'.[10] Although Austin admits that Puccini's success cannot be denied, his conclusion is that 'only naïve or corrupt tastes could rank Puccini with Mozart, Verdi and Wagner, ahead of Debussy or Stravinsky'.[11]

Indeed, many musicologists have argued (questionably) that Puccini did not advance Italian music beyond the achievements of Verdi; his music has, in fact, often been condemned as marking a veritable regression. David Ewen (1968), for example, writes that Puccini had 'little of Verdi's nobility and grandeur and sustained inspiration' and that 'the blemishes in Puccini's operas (which even his most enthusiastic admirers will not deny) could never have been perpetrated by Verdi: the excessive sentimentality; the often thin material with which he worked; the comparatively weak counterpoint; the excessive love for the voice which made him inflate an aria out of proportion to the requirements of the drama'.[12]

As recently as 2005 Richard Taruskin has attributed Puccini's maltreatment at the hands of historians to a growing separation during the twentieth century of repertoire and canon, a tendency he attributes to a prevailing historicist viewpoint 'according to which history is conceived in terms not only of events but also of goals'.[13] He continues: 'Accordingly, the historiography of music in the twentieth century has been fundamentally skewed, on the one hand, by the failure of actual events to conform to the purposes historicists have envisioned, and on the other, by the loyalty not only of many historians but also of many greatly talented and interesting composers to historicist principles.'[14] The apparent refusal of Puccini at his most crowd-pleasing to adhere to these principles has been, naturally, to the detriment of his historical standing, and rendered him a problematic figure in the history of music. As Taruskin notes: 'From the very beginning of his career there were some who called [Puccini] Verdi's legitimate heir and others who refused to take him seriously as a composer at all. What is remarkable is that the dispute remains heated even now, more than three-quarters of a century after his death, despite Puccini's long-since settled place in the active repertoire and in the hearts of opera lovers.'[15] But while Taruskin laments musicology's neglect of Puccini,[16] even he – tellingly – relegates Puccini to the nineteenth-century volume of his study. Thus even Taruskin denies Puccini full acceptance into the canon of modern composers, despite the fact that the majority of his operas were composed after 1900, and despite the strikingly innovative features of *La fanciulla del West* or *Turandot*.

And this, indeed, is perhaps the crux of the Puccini problem as it exists today. Even though it is now obvious that progress and reaction can be configured in ways that do not depend, say, on the rejection or otherwise of tonality, or the conscious gratification of middle-class audiences, these prejudices are so entrenched that it is still difficult to see how Puccini might be viewed as in some way modern and/or progressive. Indeed, one might wonder whether he does even need (or demand) to be seen in this way? After all, whenever Puccini obviously did try to be modern, he was heavily criticised and assumed to be insincere. This was a recurring rhetorical motif from almost the start of his career to the end, but the argument became more pressing as the twentieth century went on, exemplified by Torrefranca's claim that Puccini had pasted together a collage of modern effects, by the widely held contention that *Fanciulla* represented a moment of 'crisis', by Cecil Gray's claim that Puccini was writing in a modern style 'in the spirit of disagreeable necessity', by the view that Puccini had merely donned a modern 'mask' in *Turandot* and so on.

Nevertheless, it is possible to envisage one way in which Puccini might be viewed as modern or progressive that most critics have largely overlooked. This concerns the music itself: front-line Anglo-American music theory has devoted only the most cursory attention to Puccini. Moreover, when Puccini has attracted analysis, established methodologies have been applied with only limited success; as William Drabkin writes: 'The occasions on which his music has been subjected to serious investigation have often pointed up the shortcomings in applying analytical methods or systems which have met with success elsewhere.'[17] This is, of course, a very common problem when dealing with tonal repertories from around the turn of the twentieth century: the viability of the most widely accepted analytical methodology, Schenkerian voice-leading analysis, has not always been self-evident for this body of music, or, indeed, for opera in general. But it is striking that few coherent alternatives have been proposed, and as a result, Puccini's scores remain largely untouched by systematic formal analyses.

However, this presents an opportunity of a rather different nature. Rather than belatedly attempting to subject Puccini's music to methodologies that were not designed for it, this may well be the moment to begin a more radical reassessment of the nature of Puccini's music. One plausible direction that this might take would be to consider Puccini in the light of a development that seems more significant now than it perhaps did at the time when musicologists such as Grout were penning their disparaging comments – film music. This intriguing possibility of re-evaluating Puccini's aesthetic positively might even emerge from early-twentieth-century criticism that was hostile to precisely this aspect of his music. A handful of critics perceived similarities between the experience of listening to Puccini's music of the 1910s and watching a film; such analogies occasioned disparaging remarks at the time, as Chapter 6 illustrated, but it is possible that these critics had alighted on something fundamental to the way in which Puccini crafted his musical structures. As we have seen repeatedly in this study, critics objected to Puccini's mosaic-like way of stitching together a scene from lots of diverse fragments – *La bohème*, *Madama Butterfly*, and *Fanciulla* ('No work has ended up as disconnected as this one'[18]) were particularly criticised in this respect – and it was felt that this was a technique more suited to cinema than opera. As Stephen Banfield has claimed: 'Nothing went on for more than a few bars; film music later learnt much from such effectiveness. This was musical drama for an audience without a connoisseur's ability to savour and concentrate.'[19] Or as Specht put it: '[Puccini] offers us film drama in its frankest and most uncompromising form, yet justifies it by the subtle eroticism of his music.'[20]

In another sense, too, this analogy with the filmic is promising. One of the principal ways in which film music has been subjected to criticism has been through its supposed 'manipulation' of its listeners' emotions. The point, of course, is not just that the music creates particular emotional effects, or that it complements the visual images, but that it somehow underlines these images and evokes a response in its listeners that is beyond their immediate control. In other words, the music is felt to be manipulative because it accomplishes a powerful, almost instinctive, response that has been theorised to be beyond the consciousness of its auditors. This is the basis of Adorno and Eisler's well-known critique in *Composing for the Films*, for they see such blind submission to be brazenly ideological; the sophisticated mechanisms by which the 'culture industry' placates and pleases its consumers carry a chilling echo of the mass responses to the Fascisms of the 1920s and 1930s.[21]

There is a sense in which this is directly relevant to Puccini: he has long been regarded as a manipulative composer; such a suspicion is surely encoded in the view that we have already heard and shall shortly analyse in which self-proclaimed arbiters of taste decide that the popularity of his music does not underwrite its quality. The implication is that the masses are being hoodwinked by music that more intellectually sophisticated listeners can see to be using (cheap) underhand tactics to elicit emotional responses. *Madama Butterfly*, we might recall, was criticised for simply going through the motions, using a stock of preformed musical clichés 'guaranteed' to win over its audience (without success, ironically, in that particular case). Rather than prioritising the voice, as Italian opera had traditionally done, Puccini's operas seemed to function in a new way – as a 'soundtrack' to a series of visual images.

It is thus possible, with a little imagination, to come up with alternatives to the damning judgements of yesterday's critics and musicologists. Their writing, one suspects, in some cases served few other purposes than simply securing their own disdain for (and distance from) what audiences enjoyed. It is hard nowadays to believe that this is anything other than a rather shallow consequence of the hardened modernist belief in the idea that true artistic progress depends on the few rather than the many. While musicologists today might trace the lineage of such a position to Theodor Adorno, these ideas might just as easily result from a reading of Torrefranca – despite the fact that the two thinkers hailed from opposing ends of the political spectrum.

Indeed, it is essential to realise that it was criticism in Puccini's own time that laid the path for his negative reputation later in the twentieth century. The critics who fought over Puccini's Italianness manipulated his image and œuvre to suit their own ideological ends, but later dismissals of Puccini by supposedly more unbiased and objective music historians can hardly be seen as any less ideologically driven. In fact, the Puccini problem offers a particularly clear example of the way in which supposedly unarguable aesthetic judgements – in this case, that Puccini is not progressive – are supported by often questionable or even distasteful critical frameworks, for who could not believe that, on some level, Puccini's customary role in music history is filling a slot designated 'tub-thumping heart-on-sleeve Italian opera'? And can there be much doubt that such a categorisation (indeed, a pigeon-holing) results from a continued ethnic stereotyping that unfortunately remains much bandied-about in Britain, at least, today – namely, the association of Italianness with an impetuous mediocrity: good food and great lovers, but politically shambolic and culturally declining?

This is the point at which, surprisingly, the second (and later) dimension of the Puccini problem returns us to the first: the nature of national identity, and, more pointedly, Puccini's role in any notion of what it meant to be an Italian composer. It is possible that his critics were too successful in making him an emblem of Italianness – because this image has stuck and degenerated into a shallow stereotype. This book has shown that a lot was at stake for Puccini's critics: his music was central to their quest to provide a body of cultural products that would support a nation whose identity was yet to be securely established. Their success bred their failure: Puccini became the very paradigm of popular Italian opera, but at a time when this popularity was increasingly little valued; Puccini himself might nowadays be more commonly regarded as the culmination of an operatic tradition that was seen to have ended – hence its historical marginalisation. Hindsight, however, should not diminish the importance of Puccini in his own time; moreover, until we can better grasp the nature of the composer's historical and enduring appeal, we shall continue to mistake him for an aesthetically insignificant figure.

In the introduction to an anthology of writings published around the time of Puccini's centenary, Claudio Sartori wrote: 'the Puccini problem, if a problem exists, doesn't concern so much the Maestro's life and works as the critical method used to evaluate his œuvre'.[22] The simplest response to this is: quite. And as I hope this book has demonstrated, the need for new methods to re-evaluate the work of this key cultural figure has never been so pressing. Thus, the Puccini problem may, as Sartori suspected, be one of our own making, but it is also one that it might be within our powers to solve.

APPENDIX 1: SELECTED NEWSPAPERS AND JOURNALS

NEWSPAPERS

L'Avanti! (Rome) Socialist daily, founded 1896.

Il caffaro (Genoa) Founded 1876 by pro-Garibaldi writer Anton Giulio Barrili.

Corriere della sera (Milan) Conservative daily, founded 1876 by E. Torelli-Viollier; edited by aristocratic, moralistic Luigi Albertini at the turn of the century. Circulation of 100,000 by 1900; approaching 200,000 by 1910. Supported the liberal establishment. Favoured strong government, colonies and would later endorse war in Libya. Important *terza pagina* appeared from 1905, with contributions from Italy's foremost writers, including D'Annunzio, Ojetti, Simoni, Verga, Giacosa, Ada Negri and Pirandello. Music critics included Giovanni Pozza (also the paper's literary critic), Alfredo Colombani and Gaetano Cesari. Opera reviews attempted to analyse the music and its appropriateness to the drama, while using descriptive language accessible to a general audience.

Fanfulla (Rome) Daily paper, founded 1871. Tradition of satire.

Fanfulla della domenica (Rome) Indexed Sunday broadsheet, founded 1879; renowned for its arts coverage. Specialised in serious articles on cultural and social issues; claimed to be Italy's oldest literary periodical. Opera critics included 'Diapason' and Giorgio Barini. Coverage: literary criticism, history, geography and biography, poetry, archaeology, painting and sculpture, music, drama, short stories, reviews of new books.

Gazzetta del popolo (Turin) Daily paper, founded 1848. Pro-Crispi. Accused of provincialism. Later incorporated into the *Gazzetta piemontese*, then in 1895 *La stampa*.

Gazzetta di Venezia (Venice) Daily newspaper, founded 1741; came under intransigent conservative editorship from 1866. Best-selling Venice paper with circulation of about 10,000 copies.

Il giornale d'Italia (Rome) Nationalist daily paper, founded 1901; voice of the conservative right, speaking for the landed bourgeoisie and aristocracy. Roman equivalent of the *Corriere della sera*. Edited by Alberto Bergamini, the paper was opposed to Giolitti but gave enthusiastic support to authoritarian politics, to the policies of Sonnini and Salandra, to war in Libya, and became more explicitly nationalist from 1913. Important *terza pagina* to which Croce contributed until 1902, and the paper devoted space to the writings of D'Annunzio. Followed the standard newspaper opera review format in providing a brief commentary upon the plot, the music, the audience, the performance and the views of other critics, although occasionally more detailed reviews appeared.

L'idea nazionale (Rome) Most important voice of pre-war Italian nationalism, founded 1911 (ran until 1927), and edited by Enrico Corradini. Weekly; then daily from 1914, when provided with funding from the steel and armaments industries. Influenced by French nationalist movements such as the Action Française. Credo of authoritarian imperialism and bellicosity. Opposed to democracy, Giolitti's government and socialism. Typical article titles included 'Cultura nazionalista', 'Verità nazionale', 'La patria' and 'Gli italiani per l'Italia'. Published the manifesto of the Associazione Nazionalista Italiana, 4 June 1911. Enthusiastic readership in central and southern Italy and among city-dwellers fearing socialism. Initially strictly political; later extended remit to articles on art, archaeology, theatre, literature, music. Contributors included D'Annunzio, Grazia Deledda, Giovanni Gentile, Domenico Oliva, Marco Praga, Scipio Sighele. Torrefranca contributed music reviews from October 1914 to December 1915.

La Lombardia (Turin) Moderate, liberal newspaper, founded 1859 and directed by the centre-left ex-republican Emilio Broglio, and by Fratelli Civelli from 1876.

Il mattino (Naples) Founded 1891. Conservative.

Il messaggero (Rome) Founded 1878 by Luigi Cesana. Moderate, democratic.

La nazione (Florence) Founded 1859 by Bettino Ricasoli and the Barbera publishing house. Short, unattributed opera reviews; also published serialised stories.

La perseveranza (Milan) Morning newspaper, founded 1859. Politically and culturally conservative; devoted to the monarchy and to Cavourian principles. Spoke for the agrarian aristocracy. Modest circulation but political gravitas. Sister paper: *La perseveranza di domenica*. Music critics included Filippi and Nappi. Artistically progressive in being pro-Wagner.

Il popolo d'Italia (Milan) Established by Mussolini. Ran 1914–1943. Became official organ of the Fascist regime. Its sister publication was the *Rivista illustrata del Popolo d'Italia*.

Il popolo romano (Rome) Founded 1873; ceased publication 1922.

La prensa (Buenos Aires) Leading Argentinean newspaper, based in Avenida de Mayo. Editorial team at turn of the century included Ezechiele Paz, Eriberto Lopez, Evaristo Gismondi.

Il pungolo (Milan) Founded 1859 (absorbed Treves's left-wing *Corriere di Milano* in 1874); directed by Leone Fortis. Best-selling Milanese paper until the foundation of *Il secolo*; spoke for the *media borghesia*. Anti-Wagnerian.

Il resto del Carlino (Bologna) Daily, founded 1885. Represented the Emilian agrarian bourgeoisie. Originally not averse to Giolitti and reform; became increasingly nationalist after 1909 and was strongly in favour of war in Libya. D'Annunzio and Torrefranca contributed articles.

La riforma (Rome) Founded 1867. Left wing.

Il secolo (Milan) Daily, founded by Sonzogno publishing house in 1866 and became Italy's best-selling paper by the early 1870s. Published until 1927. Circulation of 45,000 copies in 1880; c.100,000 by 1900. Moderate liberal and democratic in stance; represented the interests of the newly expanded electorate: new urban and rural middle classes, including professionals, industrialists, shopkeepers, small tenants, peasant landowners and those who would later join the socialist movement. Contained serialised novels and monthly illustrated supplements. Music critics included Amintore Galli and, from 1910, Gaetano Cesari. Puccini reviews limited in detail, merely summarising plot, music and audience response. Anti-Wagnerian.

Il secolo XIX (Genoa) Founded 1886 by the industrialist Ferdinando Maria Perrone of the shipbuilding and iron and steel industry Ansaldo. Protectionist interests.

La stampa (Turin) Daily paper, founded 1861, absorbing the older *Gazzetta piemontese*. Edited by Alfredo Frassati at the turn of the century; adopted a moderate, pro-Giolitti stance. Music critics included Giuseppe Depanis (to 1896), Luigi Alberto Villanis and Vittorio Gui.

La tribuna (Rome) Daily newspaper, founded by the left-wing opposition in 1883. (Its sister paper, the *Tribuna illustrata*, edited by Vincenzo Morello, was founded in 1890.) Sales figures of 200,000 by 1900. Supported the drive for colonies and Giolitti's involvement in Libya. Music critics included 'Max' and the noted polemicist 'Rastignac' (Vincenzo Morello).

PERIODICALS

Ars et labor (Milan) Ricordi house journal from 1906. Monthly, small-format, lavishly illustrated review; little detailed music criticism.

Il corriere dei teatri (Milan) Organ of the theatrical agency De Born and Co., based in via San Paolo, founded 1898. Format: audience members, description of the opera, audience response, critic's assessment, appraisal of the singers' performance.

Il cosmorama (Milan) *Giornale letterario, artistico, teatrale*, founded 1835, published three times monthly. Short reviews, notices, articles, lists of singers.

La critica (Rome) *Rivista settimanale d'arte*, 1894–1896, published weekly, three volumes. Crocean. Anti-positivist.

Cronaca musicale (Pesaro) Scholarly journal, founded by Tancredi Mantovani, 1896; published monthly until 1917. Contributors included Arnaldo Bonaventura.

Cronache musicali illustrate (Rome) Published 1 January 1900 to 30 December 1903. Covered opera, concerts, church music, Italian, French and German music. Articles on Berlioz, Massenet and so on. Theatre reviews of Wilde, Bernard Shaw and the like. Contributors included Giorgio Barini, Alfredo Colombani, Romain Rolland, Eugenio Checchi, Oscar Chilesotti.

La frusta teatrale (Milan) *Giornale artistico teatrale, con annessa agenzia*, published fortnightly from office in Via San Paolo. Detailed front-page review of a recent work performed in Milan, followed by shorter reviews and listings.

Gazzetta dei teatri (Milan) Originally founded 1836 as *La moda: giornale dedicato al bel sesso* (concentrating on fashion, theatre, parties, balls, gossip); became the *Gazzetta dei teatri* on 20 April 1850 (anno XIII, no. 24). From then on no longer targeted a female readership, and became a theatrical bulletin. Published twice weekly, later six times a month, ran to 1924. Edited Carlo D'Ormerville. Specialised in articles on singers.

Gazzetta musicale di Milano (Milan) Ricordi house journal. Published weekly, 1842–1848, 1850–1862, and 1866–1902 (thereafter monthly *Musica e musicisti*). Broadsheet format; through-numbered and indexed. Detailed music reviews and articles.

Gazzetta teatrale italiana (Milan) Broadsheet, founded 1871, published on the 10th, 20th, 30th of each month. Organ of the Agenzia Teatrale Internazionale based in Piazza del Duomo (later Via Dogana). Combined lists of singers, conductors, choreographers and dancers (giving place of abode and availability) with articles on new works, correspondence and obituaries.

L'illustrazione italiana (Milan) Weekly, through-numbered, indexed illustrated journal; published by Fratelli Treves from 1875. Modelled on the French *L'Illustration*. Coverage included contemporary events and personalities, science, the fine arts, travel, theatre, music, fashion and serialised stories. Target audience composed of the families of professionals, industrialists, large shopkeepers, senior civil servants and politicians. Subjects covered reflected aspirations of middle and upper bourgeoisie who frequented La Scala. Illustrations of carnivals, exotic foreign locations, royal weddings, the Paris International Exhibition of 1900 and so on. Advertisements for eau de cologne, ice skates, the Printemps store in Paris, slimming pills, toothpaste, hotels on the Venice Lido. Contributors included Ada Negri, Matilde Serao, Scipio Sighele. Music critics included Achille Tedeschi ('Leporello').

L'illustrazione popolare (Milan) Illustrated cultural review, published by Fratelli Treves. Aimed at petit bourgeoisie. Celebrated great Italian figures of the past.

La lanterna (Milan) *Giornale artistico-teatrale-letterario*; organ of theatrical agency based on the Via San Pietro all'Orto. Typically featured front-page article on an issue such as Wagnerism or theatrical reform, followed by shorter listings.

Leonardo (Florence) Florentine avant-garde journal, published 1903–1907; similar in remit to *La voce*. Founded by Papini and Prezzolini.

La lettura (Milan) Monthly literary journal published from 1901 in conjunction with the *Corriere della sera*. Founded and initially edited by Giacosa. Similar format and appearance to *Musica e musicisti* but more literary, with fewer illustrations. Articles on literature, science, social issues, culture, wildlife, plus book reviews, serialised stories, summaries of contents of periodicals.

Il marzocco (Florence) Weekly literary journal (broadsheet format), published Sundays, 1896–1932. Briefly edited by Corradini, later by Angelo and Adolfo Orvieto. Articles on culture, society, literature, arts. Contributors included D'Annunzio, Pascoli and Pirandello. Aesthetic, anti-positivist stance. Music critics included Carlo Cordara and Giacomo Orefice in the 1910s.

The Mask (Florence) Avant-garde theatrical journal founded by the director and designer Edward Gordon Craig. Monthly; ran 1908 to 1929.

Il mondo artistico (Milan) *Giornale di musica, dei teatri e delle belle arti*. Illustrated journal, published weekly 1867–1914; organ of a theatrical agency based at Via Pietro All'Orto. Covered music, theatre and the fine arts. In addition to a front-page review and listings, included reviews of foreign performances of operas and summarised articles published in other journals. Fairly lengthy reviews of Puccini's operas, largely unsigned (Rome review by G. Macchi).

Musica (Rome) *Rivista della cultura e del movimento musicale*; later *settimanale di cultura e di cronaca*. Weekly broadsheet (later semi-monthly), founded 1907 by Raffaele De Rensis; published until 1929.

Musica d'oggi (Milan) Ricordi house Journal 1919–1942.

Musica e musicisti (Milan) Ricordi house journal, superseding the *Gazzetta musicale di Milano* in 1903. Small-format illustrated journal.

Musica nuova (Milan) *Rivista artistica*; appeared twice monthly in 1903–1904; edited by Romeo Carugati. Contained serious, lengthy articles, about both works and wider musical issues. Contributors included Luigi Alberto Villanis of *La stampa*.

Nuova antologia (Florence, later Rome) Serious, through-numbered journal, founded 1866 (moving to Rome in 1878). For many years edited by Maggiorino Ferraris. Covered eclectic range of artistic and social issues. Of a liberal, secular persuasion, expressing moderate patriotism while not aligning itself with any particular political grouping. Independence attracted notable writers, politicians and philosophers. Music critics included Ippolito Valetta.

Il palcoscenico (Milan) *Giornale d'arte, lettere e teatri*. Founded 1863 or 1864 by Luigi Grabinski Broglio (ran to 1907). Originally published three times a month, later weekly. Organ of the Agenzia G. Broglio. Included lengthy opera reviews giving serious consideration to both music and drama. Reviewers included Broglio, E. A. Marescotti, C. Gabardini and 'Metronomo'.

Il pensiero musicale (Bologna) Monthly, 1921–1929. Edited by F. Balilla Pratella.

Il pianoforte (Turin) *Rivista di cultura musicale*. Monthly. Founded 1920 by Guido Maria Gatti (later *Rassegna musicale* – see below).

La rassegna musicale Progressive music journal, 1928–1962, founded and edited by Gatti.

Il regno (Florence) Cultural review, 1903–1906; founded and edited by Corradini. Nationalist; opposed to Giolitti governments. Pro-expansionism.

La riforma musicale (Alessandria, later Turin) Weekly journal, founded 1913, edited Carlo Scaglia. Similar in format to *Musica*. Objective: to present *serena discussione e critica educata, ma ferma e severa*. Contained lengthy philosophical articles on the state of contemporary music culture, including contributions by Torrefranca and Casella. Anti-Puccini stance, indicative of growing dissatisfaction with the composer post-1910.

Rivista d'Italia: lettere, scienze ed arti (Rome) Published 15 January 1898–15 December 1928. Aimed at a wide public who wanted to learn about many areas of Italian and foreign cultural life. Contributors included Edmondo De Amicis, Cesare Lombroso, Ugo Ojetti, Luigi Pirandello, Paolo Mantegazza, Antonio Salandra. Edited by G. Chiarini. Originally published by the Società Editrice Dante Alighieri. Covered literature, history, philosophy, science, social sciences, archaeology, geography, music and drama.

Rivista musicale italiana (Turin, later Milan) Italy's most serious music journal, founded 1894 by Luigi Torchi. Published by Fratelli Bocca

1894–1932, 1936–43, 1946–55; revived as the *Nuova rivista musicale italiana* in 1967. Accommodated both positivist approaches and more idealist, Crocean approaches, similar to those adopted in the Florentine avant-garde journals. Darwin- and Spencer-inspired articles about origins of music. Dedicated to rediscovery of early Italian music and to detailed criticism of modern works (mainly German and French). Pro-Wagner. Opposed to *verismo*. Attracted the cream of serious music critics.

Il teatro illustrato (Milan) 1905–1914. Focus mainly on singers. Lavishly illustrated, with colour photographs.

Il teatro illustrato e la musica popolare (Milan) Sonzogno, founded 1881. Incorporated *La musica popolare* in 1886. Monthly.

Il trovatore (Turin, Milan from 1859) *Giornale letterario, artistico, teatrale*. Agency journal, published weekly, 1854–1913. Lengthy front-page reviews followed by short notices on Milanese theatres, concerts, events in other cities, specific singers and foreign news. Ensured a wide readership by diversifying out from music to a wide range of artistic topics.

Vita musicale (Cusano, nr Milan) Organ of the Associazione Italiana degli Amici della Musica. Published monthly, 1911–1913.

La voce (Florence) Influential avant-garde cultural review, founded by Giuseppe Prezzolini in 1908. Published weekly until 1913 (a second incarnation appeared in 1914 – almost entirely literary, ed. Giuseppe De Robertis, and two different *La voces* – one literary and one political – appeared in 1915 and 1916). Initial print-run of 2,000 copies, reaching a peak of 5,000 in 1911, and regularly attracted between 1,000 and 2,000 subscribers. Influenced by early Florentine reviews such as *Leonardo*, but accommodated contradictory intellectual approaches. Devoted space to all aspects of contemporary culture, including fine art, sculpture, music, politics and institutions such as libraries and universities. Openly élitist; opposed to Giolitti governments, to positivism and materialism. Responded to growing dissatisfaction among intelligentsia. Contributors included Benedetto Croce, Arturo Graf, Giovanni Gentile, Alfredo Oriani, Giovanni Papini, Romain Rolland and Ardengo Soffici. Articles on music supplied by Romain Rolland, Torrefranca, Bastianelli and Pizzetti.

APPENDIX 2: PERSONALIA

Major composers (Puccini, Verdi, Wagner, Beethoven, Bach etc.) and political figures (Mussolini etc.) have been omitted from this list on the assumption that they need no introduction. Critics and writers who used short pseudonyms are listed under the name by which they were most commonly identified. Some critics, alas, remain untraceable.

Giuseppe ADAMI   Writer, librettist and critic, 1878–1946. Met Puccini in 1912 and wrote libretti for *La rondine, Il tabarro* and *Turandot* (with Simoni). Edited a collection of Puccini's letters and wrote several biographies about him. Also librettist for Zandonai and Mulè, author of comedies in Italian and Venetian dialect, screenwriter and reviewer for *La sera* and *La lettura*.

Domenico ALALEONA   Musicologist, composer and conductor, 1881–1928. Trained Milan Conservatory; chair of music history there from 1916. Advocate for the rebirth of Italian music.

Sibilla ALERAMO (Pseudonym of Rina FACCIO)   Novelist and feminist, 1876–1960. Edited *L'Italia femminile* in Milan from 1899. Influenced by Ibsen and D'Annunzio. Her most famous novel was *Una donna* (1906).

Franco ALFANO   Composer, 1875–1954. Completed Puccini's *Turandot*. Director of the Bologna Conservatory and the Liceo Musicale di Torino. Wrote operas (most famously *La leggenda di Sakuntala*), orchestral works and chamber pieces.

Giorgio BARINI   Composer and music critic, 1864–1944. Composed songs, piano works, string quartets. Secretary of the assembly of the Accademia Filarmonica Romana from 1883. Helped to establish the Scuola Nazionale di Musica di Roma, where he taught music history. Critic for *La tribuna, Fanfulla della domenica, Il Giornale d'Italia, Il messaggero, L'epoca* and the *Nuova antologia* (to which he contributed for twenty years).

Giannotto BASTIANELLI   Tuscan composer, pianist and critic, 1883–1927. A self-taught musician, he taught harmony, composition, aesthetics and history at the Istituto Musicale Libero di Firenze. Founded the journal *Dissonanza* with Pizzetti to promote the music of young avant-garde musicians. Books included *La crisi musicale italiana* (Pistoia, Paganini Editore, 1912) and studies of Mascagni, Wagner and Liszt. Prominent music critic for *La voce* (1909–1915); also wrote for *Il marzocco*, *La nuova musica*, *La nazione* (1915–1918) and *Il resto del Carlino* (1919–1923). Committed suicide.

Antonio BAZZINI   Composer, violinist and teacher, 1818–1897. Composed *Turanda* (1867), overtures, symphonic poems and sacred works. Taught composition at the Milan Conservatory, where his pupils included Puccini and Catalani.

David BELASCO   American actor and playwright, 1853–1931. Plays included *Madame Butterfly* (1900, based on a story by John Luther Long) and *The Girl of the Golden West* (1905), both set by Puccini.

Silvio BENCO   Poet, journalist, novelist and historian, 1874–1949. Besides writing historical and political works, the author of libretti for operas by Smareglia and Malipiero. Wrote on politics, history, art, theatre and music, as well as on the works of Shakespeare, Goethe, Baudelaire and others. Editor of two Trieste newspapers, the *Independente* and the *Piccolo della sera*. Later joint editor of *La nazione*. Pro-Wagnerian.

Carlo BERSEZIO   Torinese composer, b. 1871. Music critic for *La stampa* 1895–1900.

Edoardo Augusto BERTA ('Doctor Alfa')   Torinese scholar and poet, 1855–1923. Trained in law. Wrote novels, stories, comedies, lyrics, libretti. Founded the *Gazzetta del popolo della domenica* in 1883.

Francesca BERTINI   Actress, 1888–1985. Italian film star of the 1910s – gained international recognition.

Renzo BIANCHI   Critic, composer and conductor, 1887–1972. Studied Milan Conservatory. Composer of operas including *Fausta* (1916), *Ghismonda* (1918) and *La Ghibellina* (1924). Author of a 1923 pocket guide to *La bohème*.

Umberto BOCCIONI   Painter, 1882–1916. Futurist artist.

Arrigo BOITO   Poet, librettist, critic and composer, 1842–1918. Member of the *scapigliatura* movement. Wrote libretti for Ponchielli's

La Gioconda and Verdi's Otello and Falstaff, and revised Piave's libretto for the second (1881) version of Simon Boccanegra. Composer of Mefistofele and Nerone. Helped to arrange the first performance of Le villi.

Massimo BONTEMPELLI   Playwright, 1884–1960. Founded the Teatro grottesco genre. Established the Novecento movement when he founded the journal '900 in 1926. Interested in unifying the arts.

Lyda BORELLI   Actress, 1887–1959. Italian stage actress and celebrated film star of the 1910s, specialising in femme fatale roles.

Antonio CAPRI   Writer and composer, dates not known. Based in Milan. Author of Musica e musicisti d'Europa dal 1800 al 1930 (1931), a history of chamber music (La musica da camera dai clavicembalisti a Debussy, 1925), and of commemorative articles about Puccini during the 1940s and 1950s.

Giosuè CARDUCCI   Poet, 1835–1907. Held chair in Italian literature at the University of Bologna 1860–1903. Made senator in 1890 and received the Nobel prize for literature in 1906. Opposed to the new Italy which had renounced the values of the Risorgimento.

Carlo CARRÀ   Futurist painter, 1881–1966. Founded the Scuola metafisica with De Chirico (see below) in 1917.

Albert CARRÉ   French stage director, 1852–1938. Took over direction of the Opéra Comique in 1898 and staged the first productions of Charpentier's Louise, Debussy's Pelléas et Mélisande and Dukas's L'Ariane et Barbe-bleue. Staged the first French production of Madama Butterfly in 1906, with his wife Marguerite (1880–1947) in the lead role.

Romeo CARUGATI   Veronese novelist and critic, 1870–1920. Art and theatre critic for La Lombardia, editor of Musica nuova and the Rivista per tutti. Conservative nationalist, opposed to Wagner, Ibsen, Maeterlinck, Debussy.

Enrico CARUSO   Tenor, 1873–1921. Studied in Naples. Sang Puccini roles throughout Italy, before finding fame in New York in 1903. Created the role of Johnson in Fanciulla.

Alfredo CATALANI   Composer, 1854–1893. Born, like Puccini, in Lucca, and also studied at the Milan Conservatory. His most famous works are Dejanice (1883), Loreley (1890) and La Wally (1892). Died of TB.

Gaetano CESARI   Cremonese musicologist, critic, librarian, 1870–1934. Trained Milan Conservatory, then studied musicology in Munich. Later librarian of the Milan Conservatory; taught music at the Milan State University (1924–1934). Contributor to the *RMI*, *Il secolo* (from 1910), *Illustrazione italiana*, *Corriere della sera*. Wrote on sixteenth- and seventeenth-century music; transcribed the music of Monteverdi. Helped to found the Scuola di Palaegrafia Musicale at Cremona.

Eugenio CHECCHI ('Tom'; 'Caliban')   Critic, poet, freelance journalist, teacher, 1838–1932. Volunteer in Garibaldi's campaign of 1866. Taught literature at the Istituto Tecnico di Roma. Editor of the *Fanfulla della domenica*, music critic for the *Fanfulla*, drama critic for the *Giornale d'Italia*. Wrote books on Verdi and Rossini, and libretti for Spinelli, Bustini and Tasca.

Luigi CHIARELLI   Playwright, 1880–1947. Established the *Teatro grottesco* genre with *La maschera e il volto* (1916).

Oscar CHILESOTTI   Musicologist and critic, 1848–1916. Read law at Padua. Wrote for the *GMM* and the *RMI*. Worked on transcribing early lute music; wrote on sixteenth- and seventeenth-century music. Promoted positivist musicology in Italy.

Guelfo CIVININI   Writer, journalist and librettist, 1873–1954. Collaborated with Zangarini on the libretto for *Fanciulla*. Foreign correspondent for various newspapers including the *Corriere della sera* and *Il giornale d'Italia*. Fought in the wars in Libya and Ethiopia.

Alfredo COLOMBANI   Music scholar and journalist, 1869–1900. Wrote for the *Corriere della sera*. Books included *L'opera italiana nel secolo XIX* (Milan: Corriere della Sera, 1900) and *Le nove sinfonie di Beethoven* (Turin: Bocca, 1897).

Luigi COLOMBO   Painter, sculptor and playwright, 1904–1936. Leader of the Torinese second wave of Futurism; communist. Wrote under the pseudonym 'Fillia'.

Enrico CORRADINI   Florentine writer, politician, nationalist, 1865–1931. Follower of D'Annunzio in his literary writings (novels, stories, plays). One of the founders of *Il marzocco*. Founded *Il regno* in 1903. Also wrote for the *Giornale d'Italia* and the *Nuova antologia*. Founded the Associazione Nazionalista Italiana in 1910 and launched the nationalist journal *L'idea nazionale* the following year. Made senator in 1923 and minister of state in 1928.

Alessandro CORTELLA   Writer and librettist, d. Milan, 30 October 1926. Employed for many years at Casa Ricordi. Wrote for *Ars et labor*.

Benedetto CROCE   Prominent Italian philosopher, critic, historian and politician, 1866–1952. Particularly well known for his *Estetica come scienza dell'espressione e linguistica generale* (1902). Founded and edited the journal *Critica* (1903).

Gilda DALLA RIZZA   Soprano, 1892–1975. Created the roles of Magda (*La rondine*) in Monte Carlo, Suor Angelica in Rome and Lauretta (*Gianni Schicchi*) in Rome. Puccini wrote the part of Liù with her in mind, although in the end the part was created by Maria Zamboni.

Cesare DALL'OLIO   Bolognese composer and writer, 1849–1906. German-influenced operas unsuccessful. Expressed his dissatisfaction in periodicals such as *Scaramuccia* (Florence). Wrote theoretical works.

Gabriele D'ANNUNZIO   Novelist, poet, dramatist and political activist, 1863–1938. Collaborator on and later director of Sommaruga's *Cronaca bizantina* in Rome. Most famous works included *Il piacere* (1889), *Trionfo della morte* (1894) and *Il fuoco* (1898). Influenced by Nietzsche; admirer of Wagner. Supplied libretti for Mascagni, Zandonai, Franchetti, Pizzetti and Montemezzi. Approached to supply a libretto for Puccini. Supporter of Mussolini. His aesthetic centred upon heroic myths, the idea of the superman, imperialism and eroticism.

Francesco D'ARCAIS (Marquis of Valverde)   Critic and composer, 1830–1890. Studied Law in Turin. Composed comic operas. Music critic for the *Rivista contemporanea* (Turin, from 1853), *Nuova antologia*, *GMM*; edited *L'opinione* (Rome) for thirty-six years. Came to admire Wagner and Boito after early hostility.

Hariclea DARCLÉE   Romanian soprano, 1868–1939. Studied in Paris. The first Tosca. Also created eponymous heroines of *La Wally* (Catalani) and *Iris* (Mascagni). Retired 1918.

Nicola D'ATRI   Critic, 1866–1955. Wrote for the *Giornale d'Italia*, 1901–1924.

Léon DAUDET   French critic and author, 1867–1942. Son of the writer Alphonse Daudet. Conservative royalist and critic of democracy; founded the Action Française with Charles Maurras.

Vincenzo DAVICO Critic, composer and conductor, 1889–1969. Studied in Turin and Leipzig. Conductor and critic for *Musica* in Rome during the 1910s, then resident in Paris from 1918 to 1940. Promoted modern Italian music. Composed predominantly miniaturist works.

Massimo D'AZEGLIO Statesman, 1798–1866, moderate politician, painter and historical novelist. Prime minister of Piedmont from 1849 to 1852.

Edmondo DE AMICIS Writer, 1846–1908. Combatant in Battle of Custoza in 1866. Made his name with *Vita militare* (1869). Also wrote travel literature, recounting visits to Spain, France, England, Holland, Morocco, South America. Supporter of socialism from 1891. Famed for his novel *Cuore* (1866), translated into numerous languages.

Giorgio DE CHIRICO Painter, 1888–1978. Influenced by Symbolists and Surrealists. Specialised during the 1920s in painting faceless mannequins.

Giuseppe DEPANIS Torinese art and music critic, b. 1853. Studied law. Art critic for the *Gazzetta piemontese* from 1883. Edited the *Gazzetta letteraria*. Abandoned journalism in 1896 when elected consigliere comunale di Torino. Assisted his father with the management of the Teatro Regio, 1876–81; from 1884 director of the Liceo Musicale. President of the Società di Concerti and founder of the Società di musica di Camera. Wrote (favourable) books on Wagner.

Domenico DE PAOLI Musicologist and composer (1894–1984). Author of *La crisi musicale italiana*, written in 1939 when De Paoli was resident in Paris. Also wrote a biography of Monteverdi (1979) and edited a collection of Monteverdi's letters (1973).

Raffaele DE RENSIS Critic, b. 1882. Founded *Musica*, of which he was editor from 1907–1918. Music critic for *Il messaggero* from 1916.

Emmy DESTINN Czech soprano, 1878–1930. Created the role of Minnie (*Fanciulla*) in New York. Also sang Wagner, Mozart and Verdi roles.

Eleonora DUSE Actress, c.1858–1924. Considered one of the greatest actresses of the nineteenth century. Had a relationship with D'Annunzio, who wrote several plays for her.

Giulio FARA Musician and writer, b. 1880. Teacher of harmony, solfege and singing in Cagliari; from 1923 Professor of Aesthetics and

Music History at the Liceo Rossini di Pesaro. Articles on music in Sardinia and on popular song published in the *RMI*.

Geraldine FARRAR   American soprano, 1882–1967. Created the role of Suor Angelica in New York. Puccini heard her in the definitive version of *Madama Butterfly* at the Met in 1907.

Cesira FERRANI   Italian soprano, 1863–1943. The first Mimì.

Filippo FILIPPI ('Dott. F. F.')   Highly esteemed music critic, 1830–1887. Read law at Padua; studied music in Venice and Vienna. Assistant editor of Ricordi's *GMM* 1859–1860; editor 1860–1862. Wrote for *La perseveranza* 1862–1887. Wagnerian; also admirer of Verdi. Wrote about his musical travels and about composers. Study on Wagner, *Un viaggio musicale nel regno dell'avvenire*, translated into German in 1876. Author of *Musica e musicisti* (Milan, Brigola, 1876).

Ferdinando FONTANA   Milanese poet, journalist, scholar, librettist, 1850–1919. Wrote for the *Gazzetta piemontese*, *Il pungolo* and many other daily newspapers. Member of the *scapigliatura* movement. Wrote about the arts, science, music, poetry, politics. Wrote libretti for *Le villi* and *Edgar*. Radical republican; banished to Switzerland after riots of 1898.

Cecil FORSYTH   English composer and writer on music, 1870–1941. Studied with Parry and Stanford. Author of a respected orchestration manual.

Leone FORTIS   Trieste scholar, critic, dramatic author, 1828–1898. Studied medicine. Editor of *Il pungolo* for almost thirty years. Later artistic and literary editor of the *Gazzetta ufficiale* (Rome). Wrote under the pseudonym 'Dottor Veritas' for the *Illustrazione italiana*; also contributed to *Il mondo musicale* and *GMM*.

Giovacchino FORZANO   Librettist, director and journalist, 1883–1970. Wrote libretti for *Suor Angelica* and *Gianni Schicchi*. Also wrote libretti for Franchetti, Mascagni, Wolf-Ferrari and Giordano. Critic for *La stampa*, *Corriere della sera*, *Il giornale d'Italia* and editor of *La nazione*. Later wrote propaganda plays for Mussolini.

Arnaldo FRACCAROLI   Journalist and author, b. 1883. Edited *La provincia di Padova*, and wrote for the *Corriere della sera* from 1909.

Amintore GALLI   Composer, theorist and critic, 1845–1919. Trained Milan Conservatory. Critic for *Il secolo*, *Il teatro illustrato*, *Euterpe*, *La musica popolare* and the *RMI*. Taught harmony, history and aesthetics at the Milan Conservatory.

Riccardo GANDOLFI Musicologist, composer, 1839–1920. Trained Naples Conservatory; later based in Florence. Wrote operas, sacred works, orchestral works and chamber music, as well as works of music history. Librarian at the R. Istituto Musicale di Firenze from 1889.

Alberto GASCO Critic and composer, b. 1879. Author of the opera *La leggenda delle sette torri*, chamber music and orchestral music. Signed Toni's 1932 conservative *Manifesto di musicisti italiani per la tradizione dell'arte romantica dell'Ottocento*.

Guido GASPERINI Musicologist and composer, 1865–1942. Gave celebrated lectures in Florence, Rome and Parma, 1899–1903. From 1902, librarian and teacher of music history at the Parma Conservatory; later librarian at the Naples Conservatory. Founded the Associazione dei Musicologi Italiani in Parma in 1908, devoted to cataloguing archives and publishing reproductions of rare works. Specialised in sixteenth-century vocal music.

Guido M. GATTI Musicologist, 1892–1973. Founded the forward-looking music journal *Il pianoforte* in 1920 and its successor the *Rassegna musicale* in 1928. Published books on modern music.

Giuseppe GIACOSA Librettist, dramatist and poet, 1847–1906. Studied law at Turin University. Taught literature and dramatic art at Milan Conservatory, 1888–1894. Wrote libretti with Illica for *La bohème*, *Tosca*, *Madama Butterfly* (taking special responsibility for versification). Founded and edited *La lettura*. Friends with Boito and Verga; wrote plays for Sarah Bernhardt and Eleonora Duse.

Giovanni GIOLITTI Statesman, 1842–1928. Italian prime minister five times between 1892 and 1921. Brought about social reforms, including national insurance (1911) and universal male suffrage (1912).

Edward GORDON CRAIG English actor, theatre director, critic and designer, 1872–1966. Son of celebrated actress Ellen Terry. Founded the Gordon Craig School for the Art of the Theatre in Florence in 1913. Edited *The Mask* (1908–1929).

Cecil GRAY Scottish critic and composer, 1895–1951. Founded *The Sackbut* with Peter Warlock in 1920.

Vittorio GUI   Composer, conductor and critic, 1885–1975. Studied Rome University. Conducted in the most important Italian and European opera houses (including at Covent Garden and Glyndebourne). Directed *Fanciulla* at the Teatro Regio in Turin on 11 November 1911 and the second version of *La rondine* in Palermo on 10 April 1920. Conducted works by Verdi, Gluck, Strauss, Rossini, Puccini in 1930s London. Wrote for *Il pianoforte* in 1920s. Composer of a fairy opera, *La fata malerba*, and orchestral music.

Raoul GUNSBOURG   Impresario and composer, 1859–1955. Directed the Saint Petersburg Opera House, theatres in Lille, Nice and Lyon, and ultimately (from 1893) the Opéra di Monte Carlo, where *La rondine* was premièred in 1917.

Joris-Karl HUYSMANS   French writer, art critic and decadent, 1848–1907. Author of *A rebours*.

Luigi ILLICA   Librettist and playwright, 1857–1919. Wrote for the *Corriere della sera*. Ardent republican, associated with the *scapigliatura* movement. With Giacosa, wrote librettos for *La bohème*, *Tosca*, *Madama Butterfly* (taking particular responsibility for devising scenarios and stage directions); also provided librettos for Catalani, Franchetti, Giordano, Mascagni, Zandonai.

Salomea KRUSCENISKI   Polish soprano, 1872–1952. Sang the role of Cio-Cio-San in the revised production of *Madama Butterfly* in Brescia on 28 May 1904.

Anna KULISCIOFF   Russian revolutionary socialist, 1857–1925. Based in Switzerland from 1877 and in Milan from 1885, where she edited *Critica sociale* with Filippo Turati.

Ruggero LEONCAVALLO   Composer, 1857–1919. Studied in Naples and Bologna. Gained great success with *I pagliacci* (1892). Dispute with Puccini over the rights to Murger's *La bohème* – Leoncavallo's version premiered in 1897. Also wrote songs and piano works.

Primo LEVI   Journalist and critic, 1853–1917. Wrote for *Il messaggero* under the pseudonym 'L'Italico'.

Cesare LOMBROSO   Psychiatrist and anthropologist, 1835–1909. Creator of the discipline of criminal anthropology. Sought to explain the moral degeneration of the delinquent through the study of physical anomalies. Author of the widely read *Genio e follia* and *La donna delinquente*, co-authored with his son-in-law, Guglielmo Ferrero.

Adolf LOOS   Austrian architect and writer on art, 1870–1933. Studied in Dresden and the United States, based in Vienna from 1896. Opponent of the Jugendstil movement; opposed decoration and ornament. Father of Modernist architecture.

Pierre LOUŸS   Belgian writer, 1870–1925. Refined, sensual, decadent style. Author of *Chansons de Bilitis* (1894), and novels *Aphrodite* (1896), *La femme et le pantin* (1898) and *Les aventures du roi Pausole* (1901).

Adriano LUALDI   Critic, composer and conductor, 1885–1971. Studied in Rome and Venice with Wolf-Ferrari. Committed Fascist. Sat in parliament as representative of the Sindacato Nazionale dei Musicisti. Admirer of Puccini.

Gustavo MACCHI   Librettist and freelance journalist, based in Milan. Wrote and translated libretti; wrote books on Beethoven and Wagner. Critic for *La Lombardia*, *Corriere della sera*, *Il tempo*.

Luigi MANCINELLI   Composer and conductor, 1848–1921. Studied music in Florence. Conducted in Bologna, London (Drury Lane 1886–1888, Covent Garden 1888–1905), Spain, the United States and Argentina. Founder of the Bologna Società del Quartetto. Conducted many works by Wagner and was influenced by Wagner and late Verdi in his compositions.

Paolo MANTEGAZZA   Anthropologist, pathologist, writer, 1831–1910. Taught pathology at the University of Pavia. Awarded the first Italian chair of pathology (Florence, 1870). Fervent follower of Darwinian theories. Worked on atavism, sexual selection, physiology and physiognomy. Member of parliament and senator.

Tancredi MANTOVANI   Musicologist, b. 1864. Studied with Alessandro Busi and Luigi Torchi in Bologna. Taught music history and aesthetics at the Liceo Rossini, Pesaro, from 1894. Founded *La cronaca musicale* in 1896. From 1919 taught at the R. Liceo di Santa Cecilia in Rome.

Ercole Arturo MARESCOTTI   Composer and critic, b. 1866. Editor in chief of Ricordi's *Ars et labor*. One of the main advocates of the Milan festivities to mark the Verdi centenary, 1913. Secretary of the Congresso Didattico for the centenary of the Milan Conservatory. Wrote the opera *Amleto* (Siena, 1894).

Filippo Tommaso MARINETTI   Poet, dramatist, political activist, 1876–1944. Founded the review *Poesia* in Milan in 1905. Published the Futurist manifesto in *Le Figaro* (1909). Exalted youth, speed, action, sacrifice, violence, warfare, misogyny. Renounced grammar and syntax in his poems. Author of the novel *Mafarka le futuriste* (*Mafarka il futurista*). Member of the Accademia d'Italia. Supporter of Mussolini from the early days of Fascism.

Pietro MASCAGNI   Composer, 1863–1945. Studied with Ponchielli at the Milan Conservatory from 1882. Won first prize in the Concorso Sonzogno with *Cavalleria rusticana* (1890), which went on to enjoy huge international success. Later operas such as *Le maschere* (1901) were less successful. Supporter of the Fascist regime, which staged his final opera *Nerone* (1935) with great pomp.

Edoardo MASCHERONI   Conductor, 1859–1941. Conducted first performance of *Falstaff* and made Wagner's works better known in Italy. Composed sacred music, operas, instrumental works.

Gino MONALDI (Marquis)   Critic, impresario, composer, 1847–1932. Trained Milan Conservatory. Critic for the *Gazzetta d'Italia* from 1870; also for *La critica* and *Il popolo romano* and later for the *RMI*. Wrote books on Verdi, Wagner and Puccini.

Giorgio MORANDI   Painter, 1890–1964. Associated with Novecento circle.

Vincenzo MORELLO ('Rastignac')   Journalist, critic, lawyer and playwright, 1862–1933. Trained in Law. Wrote on foreign and domestic politics in addition to theatrical and literary reviews. Editor of *Piccolo* and *Corriere di Napoli*; wrote for *Fracassa*, *Il messaggero*, *Don Chisciotte* and *La tribuna*. Numerous writings, including novels and plays. Friend of D'Annunzio, whose work he published in *Il piccolo*. Founded short-lived *La tribuna illustrata* with D'Annunzio and Giulio Aristide in 1890. Founded *Il giornale* in 1894.

Leopoldo MUGNONE   Conductor and composer, 1858–1941. Trained at the Conservatorio di S. Pietro, Majella. Conductor at the Teatro Costanzi, Rome. Conducted the premières of *Cavalleria rusticana* and *Tosca*. Conducted in Paris (1889) and London (1905–1906). Promoted French music in Italy. In dispute with Puccini in 1908 over the musical direction of *Madama Butterfly* in Rome, but later conducted first Italian performance of *La rondine*. Composer of *verismo* operas.

Giovanni Battista NAPPI   Critic, writer and composer, b. 1857. Music critic for *L'Araldo* (Como), *L'illustrazione italiana*, *GMM* (1885–1887), *La perseveranza* (from 1885, after Filippi).

Max NORDAU (Pseudonym of Max Simon Südfeld)   German writer, 1849–1923. Best-selling author of *Entartung* (*Degeneration*) (1893). Opponent of Wagner.

Ugo OJETTI   Journalist, 1871–1946. Art critic for the *Corriere della sera* from 1898; editor 1926–1927. Important figure in shaping Italian taste for thirty years.

Rocco PAGLIARA   Poet, librettist, librarian, 1857–1914. For many years music critic for *Il mattino* and *Corriere del mattino* (Naples) and librarian of the R. Conservatorio Musicale, Naples. Pro-Wagner.

Guido PANNAIN   Critic, musicologist and composer, 1891–1977. Studied composition in his native Naples. Wrote for many daily newspapers; contributed to the *RMI* from 1914 and the *Rassegna musicale* from 1928. Wrote numerous books on music; special interests in aesthetics, Neapolitan music and Monteverdi. Composed chamber and orchestral music.

Giovanni PAPINI   Florentine writer, 1881–1956. Founded *Leonardo* with Prezzolini in 1903; edited *Il regno* with Corradini; editor of *La voce* from 1908; founded *Lacerba* with Soffici in 1913. Promoted the modernisation of Italian culture.

G. C. PARIBENI   Professor of Music, composer, teacher and critic, b. 1881. Trained Rome Conservatory; teacher of harmony and counterpoint at Milan Conservatory 1914–1951. Writings included books on ancient Greek music and on Clementi. Contributor to *Musicisti d'Italia* in 1920s. Composed chamber and instrumental music.

Lorenzo PARODI   Genovese composer, theorist and critic, 1856–1926. Studied with Massenet in Paris. From 1906, director and Professor of Aesthetics and Music History at the Civico Istituto Musicale Paganini, Genoa. Composed sacred works, operas, orchestral and chamber works. Wrote for *Il caffaro*.

Ildebrando PIZZETTI   Composer, conductor, critic, 1880–1968. Trained Parma Conservatory. Held teaching posts at Florence (1908–1924), Milan Conservatory (director from 1924) and Accademia S. Cecilia, Rome (from 1936). Involved in revival of Italian instrumental music; initially very hostile to Puccini but radically reassessed his opinion later. Collaborated with D'Annunzio. Personally associated with Papini, Prezzolini, Soffici and Bastianelli, but more conservative than other *vociani*. Contributed to the *RMI* (1906–1908), *La voce* and *Il marzocco* (1909–1913), *Il secolo* (1910–1911), *La nazione* (1916–1920), *Il pianoforte* (1923). Writings included *Musicisti contemporanei* (1914) and *Intermezzi critici* (1921). Wrote the operas *Fedra* (1915) and *Debora e Jaele* (1922).

Vittorio PODRECCA   Puppeteer, 1883–1959. Founder of the Teatro dei Piccoli, Rome, 1914.

Amilcare PONCHIELLI   Composer, teacher, 1834–1886. Best known for his opera *La Gioconda* (1876). Taught composition at the Milan Conservatory from 1880, where his pupils included Puccini and Mascagni.

Giovanni POZZA   Critic and journalist, 1852–1914. For many years highly regarded theatre and opera critic at the *Corriere della sera*. Translated libretto of *Parsifal* for Ricordi. Collaborated on libretto of Puccini's *Manon Lescaut*.

Francesco Balilla PRATELLA   Futurist composer and critic, 1880–1955. Studied with Mascagni in Pesaro. Advocated use of atonality, microtones, whole tone scales, rhythmic irregularity. Works included the Futurist opera *L'aviatore Dro*. Also interested in folk music and early music. Writings included the *Manifesto dei musicisti futuristi* (1910). Director from 1922 to 1924 of *Il pensiero musicale* (Bologna).

Gaetano PREVIATI   Painter, 1852–1920. Champion of divisionist painting in Italy.

Giuseppe PREZZOLINI   Writer, b. 1882. Founded *Leonardo* with Papini in 1903. Collaborated on Corradini's *Il regno* from 1903 to 1905. Followed an anti-rationalistic, mystical philosophical orientation. Supporter of the nationalist movement. Adherent of Croce's idealistic philosophy. Founded *La voce* in 1908; editor until 1914. Later Professor of Italian Literature at Columbia University.

Rosa RAISA   Polish soprano, 1893–1963. Created the role of *Turandot*.

Luigi RAVA   Lawyer and politician, 1860–1938. Taught philosophy at the universities of Siena and Pavia. Parliamentary deputy, 1890–1897 and 1900–1919, holding various ministerial positions.

Max REINHARDT   Austrian theatre director and actor, 1873–1943. Worked for many years in Berlin. Directed his actors to move and behave like puppets, in order to render them completely subordinate to his directorial will.

Giulio RICORDI   Publisher, writer and composer, 1840–1912. Joined Ricordi firm in 1863, assuming directorship of the firm in 1888 after death of his father, Tito, at which point the company acqired the Lucca publishing firm. Revived the *Gazzetta musicale di Milano* in 1866 (suppressed by his father in 1862). Composed under the pseudonym 'J. Burgmein'. Originally a staunch anti-Wagnerian. Encouraged Puccini as a composer and close confidante of the composer. The Ricordi house published all Puccini's works except *La rondine* (pub. Sonzogno).

Tito RICORDI   Son of Giulio, publisher, 1865–1933. Involved in first productions of *Tosca* and *Madama Butterfly*. Took over direction of the Ricordi firm on death of his father in 1912. Authoritarian figure; disliked by Puccini. Resigned from Ricordi firm in 1919; directorship passed to Renzo Valcarenghi and Carlo Clausetti.

Romain ROLLAND   French man of letters and writer on music, 1866–1944. Studied at the Ecole Normale Supérieure, at the Sorbonne and in Rome. Appointed to first chair of music history at the Sorbonne in 1903. Historian, critic, biographer, playwright and novelist.

Gino RONCAGLIA   Composer, musicologist and journalist, 1883–1968. Wrote for *Il pianoforte* in 1920s. Published writings on Verdi and Rossini.

Pier Maria ROSSO DI SAN SECONDO   Sicilian playwright, 1887–1956. Co-founder of the *Teatro grottesco* genre.

Fausto SALVATORI   Poet, librettist and writer, 1870–1929. Won the Sonzogno libretto prize in 1906. Wrote an epic biblical poem, 'La terra promessa', in 1907. Worked on cinematographic projects. Author of the *Inno a Roma*. Wrote the prologue to Monaldi's *Giacomo Puccini e la sua opera*, using exaggerated fascistic language.

Victorien SARDOU   French playwright, 1831–1908. Achieved great success in Second Empire and Third Republic France. Author of *La Tosca* (1887), *Thermidor* (1891), *Madame Sans-Gêne* (1893) and many other works.

Giovanni SEGANTINI   Painter, 1858–1899. Studied originally at the Brera (1877), then self-taught. Follower of the Divisionist school, influenced by Millet and Seurat. Best known for depictions of Alpine landscapes, also for mystical and symbolist works.

Sybil SELIGMAN   Puccini's friend and correspondent, 1878–1931. Met Puccini in 1904. Gave Puccini much personal support and advised him on choice of operatic subjects.

Giacomo SETACCIOLI   Composer, theorist and critic, 1868–1925. Author of a short guide to Puccini's *Gianni Schicchi*, a book on Debussy and a treatise on modern harmony. Translated Riemann's *Handbuch der Harmonielehre* into Italian, 1906. Successful composer 1910–1925; much of his music is now forgotten or lost.

Scipio SIGHELE   Sociologist, 1868–1913. Follower of Lombroso, wrote on criminology, crowd psychology, women. Taught at the universities of Rome and Pisa (1899–1902) and at the University of Brussels. Irredentist and activist for the Associazione Nazionalista Italiana in its early years.

Renato SIMONI   Librettist and journalist, 1875–1952. Wrote libretto for *Turandot* with Adami. Wrote for the *Corriere della sera*. Edited *La lettura* after Giacosa (1906–1924). Also wrote libretti for Cilea and Giordano.

Mario SIRONI   Sardinian modern artist, 1885–1961. Involved with Futurists but broke with them in early 1920s; leading artist of the Novecento movement in the 1920s. Later a pioneer of abstract expressionism.

Ardengo SOFFICI   Painter, writer, art critic, b. 1879. Studied in Paris. Upon returning to Paris, founded *La voce* with Prezzolini and Papini, then *Lacerba* with Papini.

Angelo SOLERTI   Italian musicologist and philologist, 1865–1907. Documented the origins of early opera. Contributor to the *RMI*.

Edoardo SONZOGNO   Publisher, 1836–1920. Took over the Sonzogno firm (founded 1797) in 1861. Founded *Il secolo* in 1866. Secured the Italian rights for works by Adam, Auber, Bizet, Thomas, Halévy, Massenet, Offenbach and so on. Founded *Il teatro illustrato* in 1881.

Lorenzo SONZOGNO   Publisher, 1871–1920. Took over music publishing at Sonzogno after his uncle Edoardo's retirement in 1909. Collaborated with Puccini on *La rondine*.

Rosina STORCHIO Italian soprano, 1872–1945. The first Madama Butterfly. Found fame after playing Micaela in *Carmen* at the Teatro Dal Verme in Milan in 1892; joined the La Scala company in 1895.

Giovanni TEBALDINI Composer, conductor and musicologist, 1864–1952. Studied with Ponchielli. Choral director, for some time *vice maestro di cappella* at St Mark's, Venice. Director of the Parma Conservatory. Wrote for the *RMI*, mainly on sacred music. Promoter of the Cecilian Movement for the reform of church music.

Achille TEDESCHI ('Leporello') Scholar and journalist, 1859–1911. Editor of *Giornale dei fanciulli*; wrote for *Corriere della sera*. Edited *Il secolo XX* and was for many years drama critic for the *Illustrazione italiana*.

Enrico THOVEZ Critic, writer, painter, 1869–1926. Studied mathematics and engineering, later specialising in archaeology. Literary and art critic for the *Corriere della sera*, *La stampa*, *L'illustrazione italiana*, *Nuova antologia* and for foreign periodicals. Published poetry. Translated the works of Mark Twain. His paintings were displayed in Milan and Venice. Wrote *La leggenda del Wagner* in 1896. Helped to organise the Esposizione Internazionale d'Arte Decorativa Moderna (Turin, 1902).

Alceo TONI Writer and composer, 1884–1969. Studied with Torchi at Bologna. Music critic for *Il popolo d'Italia*, the official Fascist newspaper. Member of the national directorate of Fascist musicians. President of the Milan Conservatory, 1936–1940. Opponent of modernism.

Luigi TORCHI Critic, musicologist, historian, teacher, librarian, 1858–1920. Pioneer of Italian musicology. Studied in Bologna, Naples and Germany, where introduced to positivism. Promoted knowledge of Wagner's theoretical works in Italy. Detested contemporary Italian opera and sought the creation of a new Italian *opera nazionale*. Librarian and Professor of Music History and Aesthetics at the Liceo Musicale di Pesaro (1885–1891); later taught composition at the Liceo Musicale di Bologna (1891–1914). Named president of the R. Accademia Filarmonica Bolognese, 1894. Contributed to the *Gazzetta musicale di Milano* in 1880s. Founded the *RMI* in 1894; edited the journal until 1904; lifelong contributor. Writings included *L'arte musicale in Italia* (Ricordi), *Riccardo Wagner* (Bologna, Zanichelli, 1890) and translations of Hanslick and Wagner's prose works.

Fausto TORREFRANCA (Fausto Acanfora Sansone dei duchi di Porta e dei duchi di Torrefranca)   Musicologist and critic, 1883–1955. Trained in engineering; studied music in Turin. Taught music history at Rome University from 1913; librarian at Naples Conservatory 1915–1923; at Milan Conservatory 1924–1940; taught at Milan Catholic University 1930–1935; appointed to a chair at Florence University in 1941. Nationalist. Influenced by neo-idealistic philosophy of Croce. Contributed to the *Nuova antologia, RMI, Critica musicale, Rassegna contemporanea, La lettura, Il resto del Carlino, La tribuna, L'idea nazionale,* etc. Writings included *La vita musicale dello spirito* (1910) and *Giacomo Puccini e l'opera internazionale* (Turin, Bocca, 1912).

Arturo TOSCANINI   Conductor, 1867–1957. Conducted premières of *La bohème, Fanciulla* (New York and Rome) and *Turandot*.

Ippolitto VALETTA (Pseudonym for Giuseppe Ippolitto Franchi-Verney)   Musicologist, 1848–1911. Studied Turin. Founded concert societies. Music critic for the *Gazzetta del popolo*. Writings included *F. Chopin* (1910).

Giovanni VERGA   Realist writer, 1840–1922. Wrote short stories set in his native Sicily. One of his *Vita dei campi* stories (1880) was adapted by Mascagni as *Cavalleria rusticana*. Puccini considered setting another, *La lupa*.

Luigi Alberto VILLANIS   Critic, musicologist, librettist, 1863–1906. Taught music history and aesthetics at the Liceo Rossini, Pesaro (1891–1892), at Turin University (1894–1896), and Pesaro Conservatory (from 1905). Music critic for *GMM, La stampa, Musica nuova*. Writings included books on Beethoven and music psychology.

Otto WEININGER   Austrian philosopher and psychologist, 1880–1903. Attempted to found a psychology of sex, allying the masculine with objectivity, truth and goodness, and depicting women as a malign influence, in *Geschlecht und Charakter* (1903). Of Jewish origin, but expressed anti-Semitic theories. Tormented by his own homosexuality; committed suicide in 1903.

Carlo ZANGARINI   Journalist and librettist, 1874–1943. Wrote libretto for *Fanciulla* with Civinini. Translated libretto of *Pelléas et Mélisande* into Italian.

NOTES

INTRODUCTION

1 Joseph Kerman, *Opera As Drama*, new and revised edn. (London: Faber and Faber, 1989), p. 206.
2 Vittorio Gui, 'Puccini', *Il pianoforte* 3/6–7 (June–July 1922), 172–8, 172.
3 Guido M. Gatti, 'Rileggendo le opere di Puccini', *Il pianoforte* 8/8 (15 August 1927), 257–71, 257.
4 Anon., *Gazzetta ferrarese*, cited in *Il teatro illustrato e la musica popolare* 12/134 (February 1892).
5 Fausto Torrefranca, *Giacomo Puccini e l'opera internazionale* (Turin: Bocca, 1912), p. 9.
6 Anthony Arblaster entitles his chapter on Puccini and Strauss in *Viva la libertà! Politics in Opera* (New York: Verso, 1992) 'Interlude – Opera without Politics' and refers to Puccini as a 'determinedly non-political composer' and *Tosca* as 'an essentially political story ... emptied of political content' (p. 245). Helen Greenwald writes: 'Puccini was more likely to equate power with sex than to explore a political issue. In general, Puccini considered politics an accessory.' Helen Greenwald, 'Verdi's Patriarch and Puccini's Matriarch: "Through the Looking-Glass and What Puccini Found There"', *Nineteenth-Century Music* 17/3 (Spring 1994), 220–36, 222.
7 Cited in Richard Drake, *Byzantium for Rome: The Politics of Nostalgia in Umbertian Italy, 1878–1900* (Chapel Hill, NC: University of North Carolina Press, 1980), p. 21.
8 Tancredi Mantovani, 'Giacomo Puccini', *Nuova antologia* 237/6 (November–December 1924), 429–36, 429.
9 See for example Robert P. Morgan, *Twentieth-Century Music: A History of Musical Style in Modern Europe and America* (New York and London: Norton, 1991), p. 114.
10 Julian Budden, *Puccini: His Life and Works* (Oxford: Oxford University Press, 2002). See also Dieter Schickling, *Giacomo Puccini: Biographie*

(Stuttgart: Deutsche Verlags-Anstalt, 1989), Michele Girardi, *Puccini: His International Art*, trans. Laura Basini (Chicago, IL, and London: University of Chicago Press, 2000), and Mary-Jane Phillips-Matz, *Puccini: A Biography* (Boston, MA: Northeastern University Press, 2002).

11 Linda B. Fairtile, *Giacomo Puccini: A Guide to Research* (New York and London: Garland, 1999).

12 Dieter Schickling and Michael Kaye, *Giacomo Puccini: Catalogue of the Works* (Kassel: Bärenreiter, 2003).

13 *Studi pucciniani*, I (1998). The journal is published by the Centro Studi Giacomo Puccini, a research centre established in the composer's home town of Lucca by an international group of scholars in 1996.

1 INVENTING AN ITALIAN COMPOSER

1 Luigi Rava, speech delivered as Ministro della Pubblica Istruzione, at the inauguration of the twentieth Dante Conference, Brescia, 22 September 1909, in Luigi Rava, *Per la 'Dante Alighieri' (trenta anni di propaganda): discorsi e ricordi, 1900–1931* (Rome: Società Nazionale Dante Alighieri, 1932), p. 63.

2 Luigi Rava, 'Il saluto di Ravenna', speech given at the eleventh Dante Conference, 27 September 1900, cited in ibid., p. 2.

3 Richard Drake writes: 'the almost complete lack of international recognition for Italy's foremost poet tells us something about the continued decline of Italian cultural prestige in Europe, a process that had been going on for a long time and had made the country a literary graveyard'. Drake, *Byzantium for Rome*, pp. 3–4.

4 Cited in G. C. Paribeni, 'Giacomo Puccini', *Musicisti d'Italia: organo della federazione dei professionisti di musica* 4/11–12 (1924), 93–6, 95.

5 See Roger Parker, 'Arpa d'or dei fatidici vati': The Verdian Patriotic Chorus in the 1840s (Parma: Istituto Nazionale di Studi Verdiani, 1997), and Mary Ann Smart, 'Verdi, Italian Romanticism, and the Risorgimento', in Scott L. Balthazar (ed.), *The Cambridge Companion to Verdi* (Cambridge: Cambridge University Press, 2005), pp. 29–45.

6 Giacomo Leopardi, *Discorso sopra lo stato presente dei costumi degl'italiani*, Maurizio Moncagatta (ed.) (Milan: Feltrinelli, 1991).

7 Massimo D'Azeglio, cited in Emilio Gentile, *La Grande Italia: ascesa e declino del mito della nazione nel ventesimo secolo* (Milan: Mondadori, 1997), p. 40.
8 Drake, *Byzantium for Rome*, p. xxii.
9 Published in Italian as *Degenerazione* (Turin: Bocca, 1896).
10 Anon., 'Wagnerismo per forza!', *La lanterna* 19/1 (10 January 1896), 1–2, 1.
11 For a fuller consideration of the institutions which were founded in order to foster a national music in England, see Meirion Hughes and Robert Stradling, *The English Musical Renaissance 1860–1940: Constructing a National Music*, 2nd edn. (Manchester and New York: Manchester University Press, 2001), and Maria McHale, 'A Singing People: English Vocal Music and Nationalist Debate, 1880–1920', unpublished doctoral thesis, Royal Holloway, University of London (2002).
12 Cited in Drake, *Byzantium for Rome*, p. 21.
13 Anon., 'Dalle riviste', *La lettura* 1/2 (February 1901), 153.
14 Cited in Walter L. Adamson, *Avant-Garde Florence: From Modernism to Fascism* (Cambridge, MA, and London: Harvard University Press, 1993), p. 25.
15 Performance statistics drawn from Giampiero Tintori, *Teatro alla Scala: cronologia opere–balletti–concerti 1778–1977* (Gorle: Grafica Gutenberg Editrice, 1979).
16 See Roger Parker, '"Classical" Music in Milan during Verdi's Formative Years', *Studi musicali* 13/2 (1984), 259–73.
17 Cesare Dall'Olio, *La musica e la civiltà: pensieri di una musicista* (Bologna: Tipografia di G. Cenerelli, 1897), p. 11.
18 Riccardo Gandolfi, 'Utilità e danno dell'influenza straniera sulla musica italiana', *Gazzetta musicale di Milano* 39/32 (10 August 1884), 295–8, 295; continued in 39/33 (17 August 1884), 303–4.
19 Anon., *La cronaca musicale*, 2/1 (1897).
20 *Gazzetta musicale di Milano* 39/1 (6 January 1884), 1.
21 Letter of 14 April 1892 to Hans von Bülow, in Charles Osborne (ed.), *Letters of Giuseppe Verdi* (London: Gollancz, 1971), p. 249.
22 Anon. (presumed to be Tancredi Mantovani), *La cronaca musicale* 1/1 (18 February 1896), 1.

23 Enrico di San Martino, *Saggio critico sopra alcune cause di decadenza nella musica italiana alla fine del secolo XIX* (Rome: Tipografia della Pace di Filippo Cuggiani, 1897), p. 38.
24 Michele Virgilio, *Della decadenza dell'opera in Italia: a proposito di 'Tosca'* (Milan: Gattinoni, 1900), p. 13.
25 Cited in Arnaldo Marchetti (ed.), *Puccini com'era* (Milan: Edizioni Curci, 1973), p. 67n.
26 Cited in Ildebrando Pizzetti, *Musicisti contemporanei: saggi critici* (Milan: Treves, 1914), p. 66.
27 Guido Pannain, 'Il cinquantenario di un successo: *Cavalleria rusticana*', in *Rivista italiana del dramma* (1949), reproduced in Piero Ostali and Nandi Ostali (eds.), *Cavalleria rusticana 1890–1990: cento anni di un capolavoro* (Milan: Sonzogno, 1990), p. 155.
28 Francesco D'Arcais, 'La musica italiana e la *Cavalleria rusticana* del M. Mascagni', *Nuova antologia* (June 1890), reproduced in Ostali and Ostali (eds.), *Cavalleria rusticana 1890–1990*, p. 128.
29 Pannain, 'Il cinquantenario di un successo', p. 157.
30 D'Arcais, 'La musica italiana' p. 128.
31 Lorenzo Parodi, 'Sulla "giovane scuola" francese. Studio critico-biografico. Introduzione', *Il teatro illustrato* 10/1 (10 February 1890), 20–1, cited in Marco Capra, 'Tra wagnerismo, sinfonismo e Giovane Scuola: gli inizi della carriera di Puccini nel racconto della stampa periodica', in Gabriella Biagi Ravenni and Carolyn Gianturco (eds.), *Giacomo Puccini: l'uomo, il musicista, il panorama europeo. Atti del convegno internazionale di studi su Giacomo Puccini nel 70° anniversario della morte (Lucca, 25–29 novembre 1994)* (Lucca: Libreria Musicale Italiana, 1997), pp. 23–48, p. 33.
32 Letter of 20 August 1889 to Giuseppe Depanis (music critic of the Turin-based *Gazzetta piemontese*), in Richard M. Berrong (ed.), *The Politics of Opera in Turn-of-the-Century Italy, As Seen through the Letters of Alfredo Catalani* (Lewiston, Queenston and Lampeter: The Edwin Mellen Press, 1992), p. 65. Puccini occasionally signed his own letters 'The Successor', but the reference was very much tongue-in-cheek. See, for example, letter of 22 June 1906 to Sybil Seligman, signed 'Yours very affectionately, THE SUCCESSOR (Naughty!)', in Vincent Seligman, *Puccini among Friends* (London: Macmillan, 1938), p. 81.

33 Soffredini, 'Edgar, dramma lirico in 4 atti di Ferdinando Fontana, musica di Giacomo Puccini', *Gazzetta musicale di Milano* 44/17 (28 April 1889), 267–70, 267.
34 Letter of 10 June 1884 to O. Arrivabene, in Annibale Alberti, *Verdi intimo: carteggio di Giuseppe Verdi con il Conte Opprandino Arrivabene (1861–1886)* (Verona: Mondadori, 1931), pp. 311–15.
35 Cited in Budden, *Puccini: His Life and Works*, p. 66.
36 Pizzetti, *Musicisti contemporanei*, p. 70.
37 Letter of 15 May 1889 to Giulio Ricordi, in Eugenio Gara (ed.), *Carteggi Pucciniani* (Milan: Ricordi, 1958), p. 161.
38 Anon., *Gazzetta del popolo*, cited in *Gazzetta musicale di Milano* 48/6 (5 February 1893), 86.
39 Ibid.
40 't', *Il Parlamento*, cited in *Gazzetta musicale di Milano* 48/47 (19 November 1893), 774.
41 Cited in Budden, *Puccini: His Life and Works*, p. 106.
42 Giovanni Pozza, *Corriere della sera*, cited in *Gazzetta musicale di Milano* 48/6 (5 February 1893), 88.
43 Verdi to Francesco Florimo, in Gaetano Cesari and Alessandro Luzio (eds.), *I copialettere di Giuseppe Verdi* (Bologna: Forni, 1968), pp. 232–3.
44 Tancredi Mantovani, '*Manon Lescaut* di Giacomo Puccini al comunale di Bologna', cited in *Gazzetta musicale di Milano* 48/46 (12 November 1893), 750.
45 Eugenio Checchi, 'Giacomo Puccini e la sua nuova opera', *Fanfulla della domenica* 32/51 (18 December 1910), 1–2, 1.
46 Arnaldo Bonaventura, *Giacomo Puccini: l'uomo – l'artista* (Livorno: Raffaello Giusti, 1925).
47 F. Fontana, 'Giacomo Puccini', *Gazzetta musicale di Milano* 39/42 (19 October 1884), 381–2, 381.
48 Giorgio Vasari, *Lives of the Most Excellent Painters, Sculptors and Architects*, 1550, cited in Ernst Kris and Oto Kurz, *Legend, Myth, and Magic in the Image of the Artist* (New Haven, CT, and London: Yale University Press, 1979), p. 52.
49 Fontana, 'Giacomo Puccini', 381.
50 See for example 'Dr V', *Il pungolo* (25–6 January 1885), reprinted in *Gazzetta musicale di Milano* 40/5 (1 February 1885), 45. Michele Girardi opens his recent biography of Puccini with the same metaphor: 'The

impressive musical lineage of the Puccini family is surpassed only by that of the Bachs' (Girardi, *Puccini: His International Art*, p. 1).
51 Alessandro Cortella, *Il teatro illustrato e la musica popolare* 9/101 (May 1889).
52 Letter of 23 February 1896 to Mascheroni (conductor of the Rome première of *La bohème*), *Gazzetta musicale di Milano* 51/10 (5 March 1896), 172.
53 'A', 'Musicali allegrezze', *Rivista politica e letteraria*, cited in 'Bibliografia', *Gazzetta musicale di Milano* 55/10 (8 March 1900), 140.
54 Cited in Jeremy Crump, 'The Identity of English Music: The Reception of Elgar 1898–1935', in Robert Colls and Philip Dodd (eds.), *Englishness: Politics and Culture, 1880–1920* (London, Sydney and Dover, NH: Croom Helm, 1986), pp. 164–90, p. 167.
55 Giulio Fara, 'Genio e ingegno musicale: Riccardo Wagner – Giuseppe Verdi', *La cronaca musicale* 16/11 (1912), 207–18, 208. (The earlier parts of this serialised article appeared in *La cronaca musicale* 16/7–8, 143–61, and 16/9–10, 175–92.)
56 Gandolfi, 'Utilità e danno dell'influenza straniera sulla musica italiana', 296.
57 See Nina Maria Athanassoglou-Kallmyer, *Cézanne and Provence: The Painter in His Culture* (Chicago, IL, and London: University of Chicago Press, 2003).
58 Guido Pannain, 'Il cinquantenario di un successo', 157.
59 Eugenio Checchi ['Tom'], 'Giacomo Puccini: le sue ville, le sue folaghe, le sue opere', *La Tosca (supplemento straordinario alla Gazzetta musicale ed al Palcoscenico)* (January 1900), 11–12, 11.
60 Ibid.
61 Ibid.
62 Ibid.
63 'I nostri operisti: Giacomo Puccini ritratto da Edmondo De Amicis', *La prensa* (n.d.), reprinted in *L'illustrazione popolare* (May 1900).
64 Ibid.
65 As reported in Vincent Seligman, *Puccini among Friends*, p. 68.
66 Anthony Smith, *National Identity* (London: Penguin, 1991), p. 91.
67 Reproduced in Wakeling Dry, *Giacomo Puccini* (London and New York: John Lane, 1906).
68 Cesare Lombroso, *Genio e follia* (Milan: Tipografica Chiusi, 1864).

69 Mussolini would later employ a similar publicity tactic, decreeing that he must always be depicted engaged in virile pursuits such as riding, flying or motorcycling, and banning the publication of all photographs of himself in domestic settings. As discussed in Barbara Spackman, *Fascist Virilities: Rhetoric, Ideology and Social Fantasy in Italy* (Minneapolis, MN, and London: University of Minnesota Press, 1996), p. 3.
70 *Musica e musicisti* 58/3 (March 1903), 227–32.
71 *Ars et labor* 64/1 (May 1909), 362.
72 See *Musica e musicisti* 60/9 (15 September 1905), 565.
73 Checchi, 'Giacomo Puccini: le sue ville, le sue folaghe, le sue opere', 11.
74 Dry, *Giacomo Puccini*.
75 Roland Barthes, 'The Writer on Holiday', in *Mythologies*, trans. Annette Lavers (London: Vintage, 1993), pp. 29–31, 30–1.
76 Ibid., p. 29.
77 Fontana, 'Giacomo Puccini', 382.
78 Ugo Ojetti, 'Puccini' (30 September 1923), in *As They Seemed to Me*, trans. Henry Furst (London: Methuen, 1928), p. 158.

2 LA BOHÈME: ORGANICISM, PROGRESS AND THE PRESS

1 L'infognato, 'La "Boheme" di Giacomo Puccini', *La cronaca musicale* 1/1 (18 February 1896), 15.
2 Giulio Ricordi, *Gazzetta musicale di Milano* 40/5 (1 February 1885).
3 Filippo Filippi, *Musica e musicisti* (Milan: Brigola, 1876), p. 210.
4 Virgilio, *Della decadenza dell'opera in Italia*, p. 9.
5 Anon., 'Wagnerismo per forza!', 1.
6 Ibid.
7 Ibid.
8 See Guido Salvetti, 'Come Puccini si aprì un sentiero nell'aspra selva del wagnerismo italiano', in Biagi Ravenni and Gianturco (eds.), *Giacomo Puccini: l'uomo, il musicista, il panorama europeo*, pp. 49–79.
9 'Diapason', *Fanfulla della domenica* (9 February 1896).
10 Ippolito Valetta, 'Rassegna Musicale', *Nuova antologia* 61/4 (15 February 1896), 755–62, 755.
11 Ibid., 756.
12 Anon., 'Wagnerismo per forza!', 1.

13 'Diapason', *Fanfulla di domenica* (9 February 1896).
14 Cited in Arnaldo Fraccaroli, *Giacomo Puccini si confida e racconta* (Milan: Ricordi, 1957), p. 108.
15 Carlo Bersezio, review of *La bohème* in *La stampa*, cited in *La nazione* (3–4 February 1896).
16 'Leporello', *L'illustrazione italiana* 23/6 (9 February 1896), 87.
17 Puccini's youthful enthusiasm for Wagner is documented in Dieter Schickling, 'Giacomo Puccini and Richard Wagner: A Little-Known Chapter in Music History', in Biagi Ravenni and Gianturco (eds.), *Giacomo Puccini: l'uomo, il musicista, il panorama europeo*, pp. 517–28.
18 Valetta, 'Rassegna Musicale', 756.
19 Ruth A. Solie, 'The Living Work: Organicism and Musical Analysis', *Nineteenth-Century Music* 4/2 (Fall 1980), 147–56, 148.
20 Cited in Gilles de Van, *Verdi's Theater: Creating Drama through Music* (Chicago, IL, and London: University of Chicago Press, 1998), p. 315.
21 Katharine Ellis, *Music Criticism in Nineteenth-Century France: La Revue et Gazette Musicale de Paris, 1834–80* (Cambridge: Cambridge University Press, 1995), p. 207.
22 Enrico Thovez, *La leggenda del Wagner*, 1896, cited in Adriana Guarnieri Corazzol, *Tristano, mio Tristano: gli scrittori italiani e il caso Wagner* (Bologna: Il Mulino, 1988), p. 64.
23 E. A. Berta, review of the Turin première of *La bohème*, *La gazzetta del popolo*, cited in *Il secolo* (3–4 February 1896).
24 Anon., *Corriere di Napoli* (16 March 1896), reproduced in *Gazzetta musicale di Milano* 51/13 (26 March 1896), 221.
25 'Clm' (Colombani), *Corriere della sera* (2–3 February 1896).
26 'Veritas', '*La bohème* di Puccini', *Il secolo* (3–4 February 1896).
27 'Diapason', *Fanfulla di domenica* (9 February 1896).
28 Ibid.
29 Ibid.
30 Cited in Arthur Groos and Roger Parker (eds.), *Giacomo Puccini: La bohème* (Cambridge: Cambridge University Press, 1986), p. 134.
31 A. Morandi, review of the Turin première of *La bohème*, *Frusta teatrale* 32/8 (13 February 1896).
32 Colombani, *Corriere della sera* (2–3 February 1896).

33 *La bohème*, Ricordi vocal score, Act III, rehearsal number 20: 'In van, in van nascondo la mia vera tortura. Amo Mimì sovra ogni cosa al mondo, io l'amo, ma ho paura, ma ho paura.'
34 Pizzetti, *Musicisti contemporanei*, pp. 83–4.
35 Lawrence Kramer, *Franz Schubert: Sexuality, Subjectivity, Song* (Cambridge: Cambridge University Press, 1998), p. 95.
36 Gustavo Macchi, *La sera* (3–4 February 1896), 85–6, reproduced in *Gazzetta musicale di Milano*, 51/6 (6 February 1896), 86.
37 Ibid.
38 Anon., '*La bohème*, opera del Maestro Puccini al Regio di Torino', *Perseveranza di domenica* (2 February 1896).
39 Gino Monaldi, *La critica* (27 February 1896), reproduced in *Gazzetta musicale di Milano* 51/10 (5 March 1896), 169.
40 Gino Monaldi, *Il popolo romano* (24 February 1896), reproduced in *Gazzetta musicale di Milano* 51/10 (5 March 1896), 175.
41 Pizzetti, *Musicisti contemporanei*, pp. 80–1.
42 Ibid., p. 103.
43 Cited in Gregory Moore, *Nietzsche, Biology and Metaphor* (Cambridge: Cambridge University Press, 2002), p. 29.
44 Carlo Bersezio, review of the Turin première of *La bohème*, *La stampa*, cited in *La nazione* (3–4 February 1896).
45 Fabrizio della Seta, 'Some Difficulties in the Historiography of Italian Opera', *Cambridge Opera Journal* 10/1 (1998), 3–13, 3.
46 Gatti, 'Rileggendo le opere di Puccini', 258.
47 Leone Fortis, *Gazzetta ufficiale del regno d'Italia* (26 February 1896), reproduced in *Gazzetta musicale di Milano* 51/10 (5 March 1896), 172.
48 Valetta, 'Rassegna Musicale', 759.
49 Ibid., 760.
50 Rocco Pagliara, review of the Naples première of *La bohème*, *Il mattino* (15–16 March 1896), reproduced in *Gazzetta musicale di Milano* 51/13 (26 March 1896), 220.
51 'Tom' (Eugenio Checchi), Review of the Turin première of *La bohème*, *La fanfulla* (4 February 1896), reproduced in *Gazzetta musicale di Milano* 51/6 (6 February 1896), 81–2, 82.
52 Colombani, *Corriere della sera* (2–3 February 1896).
53 Anon., *Corriere di Napoli* (15 March 1896), reproduced in *Gazzetta musicale di Milano* 51/13 (26 March 1896), 220.

54 Gino Monaldi, *La critica* (27 February 1896), reproduced in *Gazzetta musicale di Milano* 51/10 (5 March 1896), 169.
55 Ibid., 170.
56 Gino Monaldi, *Il popolo romano* (24 February 1896), reproduced in *Gazzetta musicale di Milano* 51/10 (5 March 1896), 175.
57 Ibid.
58 E. A. Marescotti, 'La bohème', *Il palcoscenico* 1/9 (25 March 1897), 1.
59 Ibid.
60 Statistic taken from John Rosselli, *Singers of Italian Opera: The History of a Profession* (Cambridge: Cambridge University Press, 1992), p. 118.
61 'Dottor Libertà', 'La critica odierna', *Gazzetta musicale di Milano* 41/10 (7 March 1886), 71–2, 71.
62 Virgilio, *Della decadenza dell'opera in Italia*, p. 15.
63 Gino Monaldi, *Verdi e le sue opere* (Florence: n.p., 1878).
64 John Rosselli, 'Music and Nationalism in Italy', in Harry White and Michael Murphy (eds.), *Musical Constructions of Nationalism: Essays on the History and Ideology of European Musical Culture, 1800–1945* (Cork: Cork University Press, 2001), pp. 181–96, 184.
65 Frank Walker, *The Man Verdi* (London: Dent, 1962), p. 395.
66 Filippi, *Musica e musicisti*, p. 222.
67 Luigi Torchi, *Riccardo Wagner* (Bologna: Zanichelli, 1890).
68 G. Conrado, 'A proposito della *Tosca*', *Gazzetta musicale di Milano* 55/22 (31 May 1900), 302–3, 302.
69 Fara, 'Genio e ingegno musicale', 213, 218.
70 Benedetto Croce, *Aesthetic As Science of Expression and General Linguistic*, cited in Solie, 'The Living Work', p. 150.
71 Eugenio Checchi, *La fanfulla* (4 February 1896), reproduced in *Gazzetta musicale di Milano* 51/6 (6 February 1896), 81–2.
72 Anon., *La tribuna* (4 February 1896), reproduced in *Gazzetta musicale di Milano* 51/6 (6 February 1896), 91.
73 'Piero', 'La prima della *Bohème* a Torino', *La tribuna* (3 February 1896).
74 Ibid.
75 'Quirite', 'Nostre corrispondenze', *La lanterna* 23/3 (25 January 1900), 1.
76 Gino Monaldi, *Giacomo Puccini e la sua opera* (Rome: Mantegazza, 1924).
77 Virgilio, *Gazzetta teatrale italiana* 25/5 (7 Feburary 1896).
78 Ibid.

79 Jim Samson, 'Nations and Nationalism', in Jim Samson (ed.), *The Cambridge History of Nineteenth-Century Music* (Cambridge: Cambridge University Press, 2002), p. 583.
80 Luigi Alberto Villanis, review of the Turin première of *La Bohème*, *Gazzetta di Torino*, cited in Fraccaroli, *Puccini si confida e racconta*, p. 108.
81 Richard Taruskin, *The Oxford History of Western Music*, 6 vols. (Oxford: Oxford University Press, 2005), Vol. 3, p. 666.
82 Anon., *La perseveranza* (2 February 1896).

3 TOSCA: TRUTH AND LIES

1 See in particular Kerman, *Opera As Drama*, p. 206.
2 Luigi Torchi, '*Tosca*', *Rivista musicale italiana* 7 (1900), 78–114, 84.
3 Ibid., 78.
4 G. Conrado, 'A proposito della *Tosca*', supplement to *Caffaro*, reproduced in the *Gazzetta musicale di Milano* 55/22 (31 May 1900), 302–3, 302.
5 Virgilio, *Della decadenza dell'opera in Italia*.
6 Letter of 23 August 1896 to Giulio Ricordi, in Gara (ed.), *Carteggi Pucciniani*, pp. 150–1.
7 Letter of 10 October 1899 to Puccini, ibid., p. 177.
8 Virgilio, *Della decadenza dell'opera in Italia*, p. 25.
9 Anon., 'Giacomo Puccini', *Tosca: supplemento straordinario alla 'Gazzetta musicale' ed al 'Palcoscenico'* (January 1900), 3.
10 Anon., 'La prima della *Tosca* al Teatro Costanzi di Roma', *Il messaggero* 22/15 (15 January 1900).
11 Virgilio, *Della decadenza dell'opera in Italia*, p. 25.
12 Alfredo Colombani. 'La *Tosca* del maestro Giacomo Puccini al Teatro Costanzi di Roma', *Corriere della sera* (15–16 January 1900). 'L'atmosfera tinta di sanguigno che tutto pervade e circonda'. Virgilio, *Della decadenza dell'opera in Italia*, p. 21.
13 G. Macchi, 'La prima della *Tosca* di Puccini a Roma', *Il mondo artistico* 34/4–5 (21 January 1900), 1.
14 G. B. Nappi, 'La *Tosca* di Puccini alla Scala', *La perseveranza di domenica* (18 March 1900). Nappi was music critic for *L'araldo* (Como),

L'illustrazione italiana, Gazzetta musicale di Milano (1885–1887) and La perseveranza (from 1885, after Filippi).
15 Virgilio, Della decadenza dell'opera in Italia, p. 18.
16 Torchi, 'Tosca', 113–14.
17 Virgilio, Della decadenza dell'opera in Italia, p. 25.
18 The obituarist for the Corriere della sera, for example, wrote of the young Puccini 'dying of cold and misery' in Milan. Anon., 'La vita e le opere del Maestro', Corriere della sera (30 November 1924).
19 Virgilio, Della decadenza dell'opera in Italia, p. 20.
20 Ibid., p. 21.
21 'Quirite', 'Nostre corrispondenze', 1.
22 Giorgio Barini, 'Tosca melodramma di Giacomo Puccini', Fanfulla della domenica 22/3 (21 January 1900).
23 Torchi, 'Tosca', 86.
24 Ibid., 80, 92.
25 Ibid., 80.
26 Ibid., 85.
27 Ibid., 109.
28 Pizzetti, Musicisti contemporanei in Italia, p. 92.
29 Torchi, 'Tosca', 88.
30 Virgilio, Della decadenza dell'opera in Italia, p. 30.
31 Nappi, 'La Tosca di Puccini alla Scala'.
32 See Torchi, 'Tosca', 88, and the review of Tosca in La nazione (Anon., 15–16 January 1900).
33 Virgilio, Della decadenza dell'opera in Italia, pp. 30–1.
34 Mario Thermignon, 'La "brutalità" in Puccini', Musica 5/42 (1911).
35 Barini, 'Tosca melodramma di Giacomo Puccini'.
36 'Rastignac', La tribuna (16 January 1900).
37 Torchi, 'Tosca', 99.
38 Anon., 'Tosca. Teatro Costanzi in Roma. Prima Rappresentazione: 14 gennaio', Gazzetta musicale di Milano 55/3 (18 January 1900), 33.
39 Il secolo (15–16 January 1900); La nazione (15–16 January 1900); Il messaggero 22/15 (15 January 1900).
40 Virgilio, Della decadenza dell'opera in Italia, p. 30.
41 Macchi, 'La prima della Tosca di Puccini a Roma', 1.
42 Letter of 27 January 1900 to Luigi Illica, in Mario Morini, Roberto Iovino and Alberto Paloscia (eds.), Pietro Mascagni: epistolario, 2 vols.

(Lucca: Libreria musicale italiana, 1996), Vol. 1, p. 226. It is likely that Mascagni felt a certain amount of *Schadenfreude* at Puccini's misfortune: as early as 1896 he had complained that the papers were 'full of *Tosca*' and asked 'what about *Iris*?' Mascagni to Illica, ibid., p. 179.

43 Anon., *Il mondo artistico* 34/3 (11 January 1900), 1.
44 'Rastignac', *La tribuna* (16 January 1900).
45 Kerman, *Opera As Drama*, p. xiii.
46 Primo Levi, 'In difesa di un libretto', essay written in Rome on 22 January 1900, in *Paesaggi e figure musicali* (Milan: Treves, 1913), pp. 334–9, 335.
47 Torchi, '*Tosca*', 91.
48 'Rastignac', *La tribuna* (16 January 1900).
49 According to Gino Monaldi's sometimes unreliable biography of Verdi, the composer had himself expressed an interest in setting Sardou's *La Tosca*. Cited in Mosco Carner, *Puccini: A Critical Biography*, 3rd edn. (London: Duckworth, 1992), p. 109.
50 Kerman, *Opera As Drama*, p. x.
51 'Rastignac', *La tribuna* (16 January 1900).
52 Colombani, 'La *Tosca* del maestro Giacomo Puccini'.
53 Virgilio, *Della decadenza dell'opera in Italia*, p. 28.
54 Barini, '*Tosca* melodramma di Giacomo Puccini'.
55 Colombani, 'La *Tosca* del maestro Giacomo Puccini'.
56 Barini, '*Tosca* melodramma di Giacomo Puccini'.
57 Virgilio, *Della decadenza dell'opera in Italia*, pp. 25–6.
58 Torchi, '*Tosca*', p. 82.
59 'Rastignac', *La tribuna* (16 January 1900).
60 Ibid.
61 Torchi, '*Tosca*', 109, 104.
62 Ibid., 78, 90.
63 Ibid., 114.
64 Paraphrased in Virgilio, *Della decadenza dell'opera in Italia*, p. 9.
65 Barini, '*Tosca* melodramma di Giacomo Puccini'.
66 Torchi, '*Tosca*', 85.
67 Barini, '*Tosca* melodramma di Giacomo Puccini'.
68 Torchi, '*Tosca*', 100.
69 Virgilio, *Della decadenza dell'opera in Italia*, p. 5.

70 Ibid., p. 8.
71 Ibid., p. 13.
72 Ibid., p. 7.
73 Ibid., p. 8.
74 Ibid., p. 7.
75 Ibid., p. 31.
76 'A', 'Musicali allegrezze', *Rivista politica e letteraria*, cited in 'Bibliografia', *Gazzetta musicale di Milano* 55/10 (8 March 1900), 140.
77 Anon., 'Tosca. Teatro Costanzi in Roma. Prima Rappresentazione: 14 gennaio', 33.
78 'A', 'Musicali allegrezze'.
79 Carlo Nasi, '*Tosca*: impressioni e divagazioni', *Gazzetta musicale di Milano* 55/10 (8 March 1990), 133–5, 133.
80 Anon., 'La prima di *Tosca* al Teatro Costanzi di Roma'.
81 'Quirite', 'Nostre corrispondenze', 1.
82 Ibid.
83 Ibid.
84 Ibid.
85 Ibid.
86 Ibid.
87 Ibid., 2.
88 Virgilio, *Della decadenza dell'opera in Italia*, pp. 16–17.
89 Barini, '*Tosca* melodramma di Giacomo Puccini'.
90 G. P. Fanciano Gangemi, 'L'Opera', *Ars nova* 3/5 (May 1903), 5–6, 5.

4 A FRAME WITHOUT A CANVAS *MADAMA BUTTERFLY* AND THE SUPERCIAL

1 Nicola d'Atri, 'La prima rappresentazione di *Madama Butterfly* alla Scala di Milano', *Il giornale d'Italia* (19 February 1904).
2 Giulio Ricordi, 'Il giro del mondo in un mese', *Musica e musicisti* 59/3 (15 March 1904), 189. The review is reproduced in full in Arthur Groos (ed.), *Madama Butterfly. Fonti e documenti della genesi* (Lucca: Centro Studi Giacomo Puccini, 2005), p. 455, along with other reviews of the Milan and Brescia premières and the first performances in London and Paris.
3 David Kimbell, *Italian Opera* (Cambridge: Cambridge University Press, 1991), p. 627.

4 See for example the discussion in Charles S. Brauner, 'The Rossini Renaissance', in Emanuele Senici (ed.), *The Cambridge Companion to Rossini* (Cambridge: Cambridge University Press, 2004), pp. 37–47.
5 For example Walter Crane objected to art nouveau's tendency 'to adopt forms and lines for the sake of the forms and lines, irrespective of their adaptation to particular materials and uses; to gather from every kind without giving time to digest and assimilate; to imitate superficial or artificial mannerisms in all sorts of ways; to use material simply to display material and skill of hand, without thought of the harmonising sense of its beauty'. Walter Crane, 'Modern Decorative Art at Turin: General Impressions', *The Magazine of Art* (September 1902), part 263, 488–93, 489.
6 Anon., 'Cronaca Milanese', *Frusta teatrale* 42/6 (24 February 1904).
7 Letter of 1869 to Toni Gallo, in Franco Abbiati, *Giuseppe Verdi*, 2nd edn., 4 vols. (Milan: Ricordi, 1963), Vol. 3, p. 253. I am very grateful to James Hepokoski for drawing this reference to my attention and for sharing with me his illuminating thoughts on the different possible readings of Verdi's highly ambiguous letter.
8 The archetypal 'decadent' novel was undoubtely Joris-Karl Huysmans's *A Rebours* of 1884, which devotes numerous pages to intricate descriptions of sounds, tastes, jewels, sensations and colours. Huysmans' anti-hero, the ennui-ridden aristocrat Des Esseintes, who retreats from the public world to an inner sanctum of heightened pleasure and pain, was clearly the model for Count Andrea Sperelli-Fieschi d'Ugenta, the immoral, narcissistic, over-refined protagonist of D'Annunzio's *Il piacere* (1889).
9 Paul Bourget, *Essais de psychologie contemporaine* (Paris: Lemerre, 1883), p. 25.
10 Cited in John Woodhouse, *Gabriele D'Annunzio: Defiant Archangel* (Oxford: Clarendon Press, 1998), p. 61.
11 Adolf Loos, *Ornament and Crime: Selected Essays*, trans. Michael Mitchell (Riverside, CA: Ariadne Press, 1998), p. 170.
12 Ibid., p. 175.
13 Rae Beth Gordon, *Ornament, Fantasy, and Desire in Nineteenth-Century French Literature* (Princeton, NJ: Princeton University Press, 1992), p. 3.
14 Reported in Pizzetti, *Musicisti contemporanei*, p. 51.

15 Illica's scenario for the opera included an act set at the American consulate, during which Butterfly and Kate Pinkerton would meet. Puccini ultimately decided to cut the act so as to emphasise Cio-Cio-San's psychological situation at the expense of the stark confrontation of Eastern and Western values that Illica originally hoped to stage. See Arthur Groos, 'Madama Butterfly: il perduto atto del consolato americano', in Biagi Ravenni and Gianturco (eds.), *Giacomo Puccini: l'uomo, il musicista, il panorama europeo*, pp. 147–58, and Groos, *Madama Butterfly. Fonti e documenti della genesi*, pp. 119–35.

16 'Mos', 'La prima di Madama Butterfly alla Scala', *Il marzocco* 9/8 (21 February 1904).

17 See Philip Gossett, 'Compositional Methods', in Senici (ed.), *The Cambridge Companion to Rossini*, p. 80.

18 Verdi to Camille Du Locle, 6 October 1869, in Abbiati, *Giuseppe Verdi*, Vol. 3, pp. 324–5.

19 Almost all critics noted the fact that the music with which Butterfly was introduced recalled 'Mi chiamano Mimì'.

20 G. B. Nappi, 'Madama Butterfly di Puccini alla Scala', *La perseveranza* (18 February 1904).

21 'Max', 'La prima di Madama Butterfly alla Scala: l'opera', *La tribuna* (19 February 1904). Full review reproduced in Groos, *Madama Butterfly. Fonti e documenti della genesi*, pp. 467–9.

22 Anon., 'Madama Butterfly di G. Puccini', *Il secolo* (18–19 February 1904).

23 Giovanni Pozza, 'La prima di Madama Butterfly alla Scala', *Corriere della sera* (18 February 1904). Full review reproduced in Groos, *Madama Butterfly. Fonti e documenti della genesi*, pp. 456–60.

24 Anon., 'Cronaca Milanese'; Nicola d'Atri, 'La prima rappresentazione di Madama Butterfly'.

25 'Max', 'La prima di Madama Butterfly alla Scala: l'opera'.

26 Marcia Citron writes that the crafts were 'strongly functional, and produced and consumed in the home. The fine arts, in contrast, have purported to be functionless, originated in more formal circumstances, resided in the public sphere for their consumption, and existed largely for aesthetic purposes'. Marcia J. Citron, *Gender and the Musical Canon* (Cambridge: Cambridge University Press, 1993), p. 129.

27 Camaroni, *La lega lombarda*, quoted in Nicola d'Atri, 'La prima rappresentazione di Madama Butterfly'.

28 Pizzetti, *Musicisti contemporanei*, p. 101.
29 Monaldi, *Giacomo Puccini e la sua opera*, p. 64.
30 Anon., 'Intervista con Puccini', *La perseveranza* (30 January 1904).
31 Altini, *Il tempo* (18 February 1904). Full review reproduced in Groos, *Madama Butterfly. Fonti e documenti della genesi*, pp. 473-4.
32 'Mos', 'La prima di MB alla Scala', *Il marzocco* 9/8 (21 February 1904). Full review reproduced in Groos, *Madama Butterfly. Fonti e documenti della genesi*, pp. 475-7.
33 'Max', 'La prima di Madama Butterfly alla Scala: l'opera'.
34 Benedetto Croce, *The Aesthetic As the Science of Expression*, trans. Colin Lyas (Cambridge: Cambridge University Press, 1992), pp. 9, 25.
35 Torrefranca, *Giacomo Puccini*, p. 26.
36 Ippolitto Valetta, 'Madama Butterfly a Milano', *Nuova antologia* (March–April 1904), 142-6, 146. Full review reproduced in Groos, *Madama Butterfly. Fonti e documenti della genesi*, pp. 477-82.
37 Letter of February 1904 to Antonio Bettolacci, in Gara (ed.), *Carteggi Pucciniani*, p. 264.
38 Valetta, 'Madama Butterfly a Milano', 146.
39 Ibid.
40 Ibid.
41 For a full discussion of the reception of Verdi's late works, see James A. Hepokoski, *Giuseppe Verdi: Falstaff* (Cambridge: Cambridge University Press, 1983), and Hepokoski, *Giuseppe Verdi: Otello* (Cambridge: Cambridge University Press, 1987).
42 Pizzetti, *Musicisti contemporanei*, p. 83.
43 Anon, 'Il grande avvenimento di Torino. Alla vigilia dell'apertura dell'Esposizione', *Corriere della sera*, Milan (5-6 March 1902), cited in Francesca R. Fratini (ed.), *Torino 1902: polemiche in Italia sull'Arte Nuova* (Turin: Martano, 1970), p. 148
44 G. Beltrami, 'L'arte nuova all'Esposizione di Torino', *La lettura* 2/7 (July 1902), 599-607, 607.
45 W. Fred, 'The International Exhibition of Decorative Art at Turin – the Italian Section', *The Studio* 27/118 (15 January 1903), 273-9.
46 Arthur Groos, 'Cio-Cio-San and Sadayakko: Japanese Music-Theatre in *Madama Butterfly*', *Monumenta Nipponica* 54/1 (Spring 1999), 41-73, 47-53.

47 Romeo Carugati, *La Lombardia* (18 February 1904). Full review reproduced in Groos, *Madama Butterfly. Fonti e documenti della genesi*, pp. 470–2.
48 Huysmans, *Against Nature (A rebours)*, trans. Margaret Mauldon (Oxford and New York: Oxford University Press, 1998), p. 114.
49 Helen Greenwald, 'Picturing Cio-Cio-San: House, Screen, and Ceremony in Puccini's *Madama Butterfly*', *Cambridge Opera Journal* 12/3 (November 2000), 237–59, 243.
50 Groos, 'Cio-Cio-San and Sadayakko', 44.
51 Luigi Torchi, '*Iris*', *Rivista musicale italiana*, 6 (1899), 71–118, 74–5.
52 Ibid., 113.
53 Pizzetti, *Musicisti contemporanei*, pp. 95, 100.
54 Ibid., p. 96.
55 M. Incagliati, *Il giornale d'Italia*, cited in Puccini tribute supplement, *Musica d'oggi* 7/3 (March 1925), 27.
56 For further reading, see Klaus Berger, *Japonisme in Western Painting from Whistler to Matisse* (Cambridge: Cambridge University Press, 1992).
57 J. Jackson Jarves, 'A Genuine Artistic Race', part IV, *The Art Journal* 33 (1 June 1871), 161–2, 161.
58 As discussed in Linda Fairtile, 'Giacomo Puccini's Operatic Revisions As Manifestations of His Compositional Priorities', unpublished PhD dissertation, New York University (1996), pp. 168, 217. The result of these cuts was that, as Fairtile notes, 'the contrast between Eastern and Western cultures faded into the background in later versions of the opera' (p. 215). For a full consideration of the revisions Puccini made to *Madama Butterfly*, see Schickling and Kaye, *Giacomo Puccini: Catalogue of the Works*, pp. 322–35.
59 See letter of 16 November 1902 to Illica in which Puccini wrote 'Niente entr'acte e arrivare alla fine tenendo inchiodato per un'ora e mezzo il pubblico!' in Gara (ed.), *Carteggi pucciniani*, p. 225.
60 Giovanni Pozza, '*Madama Butterfly* di Giacomo Puccini al Teatro Grande di Brescia', *Corriere della sera* (29 May 1904).
61 Naomi Schor traces the historical links in literature and philosophy between femininity and detail in *Reading in Detail: Aesthetics and the Feminine* (New York and London: Methuen, 1987).

62 Luigi Alberto Villanis, 'Il segreto dell'arte pucciniana', *Musica nuova* (16 February 1904), 6–8.
63 *L'estetica e la psiche moderna nella musica contemporanea* (Turin: Lattes, 1895), *Come si sente e come si dovrebbe sentire la musica* (Turin: Lattes, 1896), *Lo spirito moderno nella musica* (1903), and *Beethoven e le Sonate per pianoforte* (1904).
64 Villanis, 'Il segreto dell'arte pucciniana', 6.
65 Ibid.
66 Ibid.
67 Ibid., 7.
68 As discussed in Steven Huebner, *French Opera at the Fin de Siècle: Wagnerism, Nationalism and Style* (Oxford: Oxford University Press, 1999).
69 Villanis, 'Il segreto dell'arte pucciniana', 7.
70 Ibid.
71 Ibid., 8.
72 Ravel in particular seems to have been accorded a similar ranking in the history of twentieth-century music to Puccini, being traditionally viewed as a composer who juxtaposed modern harmonies onto an essentially conservative harmonic language, and as a composer whose music straddled an uncomfortable divide between art and entertainment. On the reception of Ravel's music, see Roger Nichols, 'Ravel and the Twentieth Century', in Deborah Mawer (ed.), *The Cambridge Companion to Ravel* (Cambridge: Cambridge University Press, 2000), pp. 240–50.
73 In a comment strikingly reminiscent of our anonymous critic's metaphor of a frame without a canvas, Robert Fink observes that in minimalist music, for example, 'the backdrop has become the curtain'. Robert Fink, 'Going Flat: Post Hierarchical Music Theory and the Musical Surface', in Nicholas Cook and Mark Everist (eds.), *Rethinking Music* (Oxford and New York: Oxford University Press, 1999), p. 127. Fink borrows this expression from Clement Greenberg, who in 1954 summed up modern abstract art as being like a stage in which the backdrop has become the same as the curtain. Greenberg wrote that 'pictorial space has lost its "inside" and become all "outside"'. Clement Greenberg, 'Abstract, Representational, and So Forth', *Arts Digest*, 29 (November 1954), 6–8, cited in Fink, 'Going Flat', p. 121.

5 TORREFRANCA VERSUS PUCCINI

1. Torrefranca, *Giacomo Puccini*, p. vii.
2. Ibid., p. viii.
3. The Bocca firm was founded in Turin in 1775 and became one of the most influential publishers of the late nineteenth century. Many of the key philosophical and scientific texts of the age were first introduced to Italian audiences by Bocca, notably the works of Nietzsche, Schopenhauer and Spencer.
4. Groos and Parker (eds.), *Giacomo Puccini: La Bohème*, p. 131.
5. See for example Leonardo Pinzauti, 'Memoria di Fausto Torrefranca', *L'approdo musicale, quaderni di musica* (1966), 169.
6. Torrefranca, *Giacomo Puccini*, pp. 12–13.
7. Giuseppe Prezzolini, 'La nostra promessa', *La voce* (27 December 1908), cited in Prezzolini, *La voce 1908–1913: cronaca, antologia e fortuna di una rivista* (Milan: Rusconi Editore, 1974), p. 239.
8. Letter of 11 July 1908 to Romain in Rolland, in Prezzolini, *La voce 1908–1913*, p. 44.
9. See George L. Mosse, *Nationalism and Sexuality: Middle-Class Morality and Sexual Norms in Modern Europe* (Madison, WI, and London: University of Wisconsin Press, 1985).
10. F. T. Marinetti, *Fondazione e manifesto del Futurismo* (1909), reprinted in Marinetti, *Teoria e invenzione futurista* (Milan: Mandadori, 1968), p. 10.
11. Marinetti, *Manifesto del partito futurista italiana*, in *Teoria e invenzione futurista*, p. 132
12. Giovanni Papini, 'Il nostro impegno', *Lacerba* (15 November 1914), reprinted in Roger Griffin (ed.), *Fascism* (Oxford and New York: Oxford University Press, 1995), pp. 23–4.
13. Torrefranca, *Giacomo Puccini*, p. 76.
14. Ibid., p. 31.
15. Ibid., p. 78.
16. Otto Weininger, *Sex and Character* (London and New York: Heinemann and G.P. Putnam's Sons, 1906), p. 56.
17. Ibid., p. 346.
18. Papini, 'Il massacro delle donne', *Lacerba* 7 (1 April 1914), 97–9.
19. *La voce* 2/9 (10 February 1910).
20. Scipio Sighele, *Eva moderna* (Milan: Treves, 1910), pp. 45–57.

21 Otto Weininger, *Sesso e carattere*, trans. G. Fenoglio (Turin: Bocca, 1912).
22 Cesare Lombroso and Guglielmo Ferrero, *La donna delinquente* (Turin and Rome: L. Roux, 1893).
23 Ibid., pp. 95–6.
24 See Giorgio Colombo, *La scienza infelice: il museo di antropologia criminale di Cesare Lombroso*, 2nd edn. (Turin: Editore Boringhieri, 2000).
25 Weininger, *Sex and Character*, p. 73.
26 Torrefranca, *Giacomo Puccini*, p. 3.
27 Ibid., p. 3.
28 Mosse, *Nationalism and Sexuality*, p. 11. For further reading on Italian attitudes towards homosexuality at the *fin de siècle*, see Bruno P. F. Wanrooij, 'Crisi dei generi', in *Storia del pudore: la questione sessuale in Italia, 1860–1949* (Venice: Marsilio Editori, 1990), pp. 191–225.
29 P.-J. Proudhon, *La Pornocratie ou les femmes dans les temps modernes* (Paris: Librairie Internationale A. Lacroix, 1875), p. 85.
30 Paolo Mantegazza, *Fisiologia della donna*, 3rd edn., 2 vols. (Milan and Rome: Fratelli Treves, 1893), Vol. 2, p. 201.
31 Weininger, *Sex and Character*, pp. 118–19.
32 Ibid., p. 191.
33 Torrefranca, *Giacomo Puccini*, p. 4.
34 P.-J. Proudhon, *De la Justice dans la Révolution et dans l'Eglise*, 3 vols. (Paris: Librairie de Garnier Frères, 1858), Vol. 3, p. 372.
35 Torrefranca, *Giacomo Puccini*, pp. 5, 31.
36 Ibid., p. 77. Torrefranca counterpoints 'the heroes whom fashion exalts and history demolishes' with historical figures of true quality and endurance who received little recognition during their lifetimes, setting Marini against Dante, Vogler or Wölfl against Beethoven (p. 1).
37 Ibid., pp. 2, 24.
38 Steven Huebner, *French Opera at the Fin de Siècle*, p. 165. Massenet's personality was also deemed to be particularly attractive to women, and contemporary reports emphasise the fact that on public appearances he was invariably surrounded by adoring female admirers (p. 160).
39 Torrefranca, *Giacomo Puccini*, p. 27.
40 Ibid., pp. 27–8.

41 Ibid., p. 34.
42 Ibid., p. 28.
43 Weininger, *Sex and Character*, p. 273.
44 Michela De Giorgio, *Le italiane dall'unità a oggi*, 2nd edn. (Rome and Bari: Laterza, 1993), p. 174.
45 Torrefranca, *Giacomo Puccini*, p. 27. Torrefranca uses the phrase *arte riflessa*, an alternative translation for which would be the equally pejorative 'reflex art', suggesting Puccini's perceived lack of critical judgement.
46 Mantegazza, *Fisiologia della donna*, Vol. 1, p. 292.
47 Weininger, *Sex and Character*, pp. 210, 262.
48 Torrefranca, *Giacomo Puccini*, pp. 3, 94.
49 Mantegazza, *Fisiologia della donna*, Vol. 1, p. 292 and Vol. 2, p. 207.
50 Cesare Lombroso and Guglielmo Ferrero, *The Female Offender* (London: T. Fisher Unwin, 1895), p. 151.
51 Torrefranca, *Giacomo Puccini*, p. 32.
52 Ibid., pp. 25, 8, 81, 10.
53 Arnold Whittall, *Romantic Music: A Concise History from Schubert to Sibelius* (London: Thames and Hudson, 1987), p. 179.
54 Torrefranca, *Giacomo Puccini*, pp. 89, 54.
55 Valeria P. Babini, Fernanda Muniz and Annamaria Tagliavini, *La donna delle scienze dell'uomo: immagini del femminile nella cultura scientifica italiana di fine secolo* (Milan: Franco Angeli, 1989), p. 127.
56 Torrefranca, *Giacomo Puccini*, p. 5.
57 'A nation in dissolution is like a body attacked by gangrene: only the toe seems afflicted, and the surgeon cuts off the foot. Six months later the gangrene reappears in the leg and it is necessary to remove the thigh; finally it reaches the stomach and all is lost' (Proudhon, *Pornocratie*, p. 258).
58 Sander L. Gilman explains that Jews had been associated with disease across Europe since Medieval times and that 'by the time Heine penned his lines on the founding of the Jewish hospital in 1842 the association of the Jew with illness had become a complex anti-Semitic commonplace'. Sander L. Gilman, *Difference and Pathology: Stereotypes of Sexuality, Race, and Madness* (Ithaca, NY, and London: Cornell University Press, 1985), p. 151.

59 Weininger, *Sex and Character*, pp. 306, 320. For a wider European perspective on the association of Jews and women, see Mireille Dottin-Orsini, 'La femme, le juif', in *Cette Femme qu'ils disent fatale* (Paris: Bernard Grasset, 1993), pp. 306–33.
60 Quoted in Nancy A. Harrowitz, *Antisemitism, Misogyny, and the Logic of Cultural Difference: Cesare Lombroso and Matilde Serao* (Lincoln, NE, and London: University of Nebraska Press, 1994), p. 70.
61 See Jane F. Fulcher, *French Cultural Politics and Music: From the Dreyfus Affair to the First World War* (New York and Oxford: Oxford University Press, 1999), p. 32.
62 Torrefranca, *Giacomo Puccini*, p. 8.
63 Ibid.
64 Ibid., p. 42.
65 Ibid., p. 124.
66 Cecil Forsyth, *Music and Nationalism: A Study of English Opera* (London: Macmillan, 1911), p. 119.
67 Richard Wagner, 'Il Giudaismo nella musica', *Rivista Musicale Italiana* 4 (1897), 95–113.
68 Richard Wagner, *Judaism in Music*, trans. Edwin Evans (London: William Reeves, 1910), pp. 11–12.
69 Ibid., pp. 29–30.
70 See Lynn M. Gunzberg, *Strangers at Home: Jews in the Italian Literary Imagination* (Berkeley, Los Angeles, CA, and Oxford: University of California Press, 1992).
71 As discussed by Roberto Maiocchi, *Scienza italiana e razzismo fascista* (Florence: La Nuova Italia Editrice, 1999), p. 188.
72 Scipio Sighele, *Il nazionalismo e i partiti politici* (Milan: Treves, 1911), pp. 29–30.
73 Mazzini, cited in Gentile, *La Grande Italia*, p. 26.
74 Jeffrey Kallberg, *Chopin at the Boundaries: Sex, History, and Musical Genre* (Cambridge, MA, and London: Harvard University Press, 1996).
75 Torrefranca, *Giacomo Puccini*, p. 10.
76 Ibid., pp. 9, 11.
77 Ibid., p. 30.
78 Richard Wagner, *Opera and Drama*, trans. Edwin Evans, 2 vols. (London: William Reeves, 1913), Vol. 1, pp. 187–8.
79 Torrefranca, *Giacomo Puccini*, p. 6.

80 On the Italian early music movement, see Tim Carter, *Monteverdi's Musical Theatre* (New Haven, CT, and London: Yale University Press, 2002), pp. 5–7.
81 Torrefranca, *Giacomo Puccini*, pp. ix, 19.
82 Ibid., p. 20.
83 Ibid., p. xi.
84 Ibid., pp. 15–16. Similar endeavours were taking place elsewhere in Europe. In England in 1881 the Duke of Albany had made a fund-raising speech for the Royal College of Music in which he said of 'Sumer is icumen in': 'this tiny glee, which is the germ of modern music, the direct and absolute progenitor to the oratorios of Handel, the symphonies of Beethoven, the operas of Wagner is a purely English creation, dealing with English sights and sounds – the cuckoo, the blooming meadow ... the pastures of Berkshire.' Cited in Hughes and Stradling, *The English Musical Renaissance 1860–1940*, p. 28.
85 See also Fausto Torrefranca, 'La creazione della Sonata drammatica moderna rivendicata all'Italia', *Rivista musicale italiana* 17 (1910), 309–58.
86 Torrefranca, *Giacomo Puccini*, p. 30.
87 De Giorgio, *Le italiane dall'unità a oggi*, p. 498.
88 Ibid., p. 502.
89 Ibid., p. 503.
90 Arrigo Plinio Pagliaini (ed.), *Catalogo generale della libreria italiana dall'anno 1900 a tutto il 1920: Indice per materie A–D* (Milan Associazione Tipografica Libraria, 1933), pp. 871–7.
91 Torrefranca, *Giacomo Puccini*, p. 5.
92 De Giorgio, *Le italiane dall'unità a oggi*, p. 353.
93 Victoria de Grazia, *How Fascism Ruled Women: Italy, 1922–1945* (Berkeley, Los Angeles, CA, and London: University of California Press, 1992), p. 4.
94 Kate Flint, 'Blood and Milk: Painting and the State in Late Nineteenth-Century Italy', in Kathleen Adler and Marcia Pointon (eds.), *The Body Imaged: The Human Form and Visual Culture* (Cambridge: Cambridge University Press, 1993), pp. 109–23, 112.
95 De Giorgio, *Le italiane dall'unità a oggi*, pp. 6–7.
96 Ibid., p. 18.
97 Mantegazza called woman 'the vestal virgin of morality and human idealism'. Mantegazza, *Fisiologia della donna*, Vol. 1, pp. 316, 321–2.

98 As discussed by De Giorgio, *Le italiane dall'unità a oggi*, p. 7.
99 Letter of 14 June 1910 to Sybil Seligman, Seligman, *Puccini Among Friends*, p. 191.
100 Puccini cited in Dante Del Fiorentino, *Immortal Bohemian: An Intimate Memoir of Giacomo Puccini* (London: Victor Gollancz, 1952), p. 144.
101 Letter of 11 February 1915 to Alfredo Vandini, in Gara (ed.), *Carteggi pucciniani*, pp. 432–3.
102 Nevertheless, copies of Torrefranca's book have been found in some far-flung places, such as Buenos Aires (I should like to thank Eduardo Benarroch for providing this information).
103 Mario Ferraguti, 'Tra i libri musicali: *Giacomo Puccini e l'opera internazionale*', *Vita musicale: giornale dell'Associazione italiana di amici della musica* 1/6–7 (May–June 1912), 95–6, 95.
104 Ferraguti, 'Tra i libri musicali', 95–6; Anon., 'Fausto Torrefranca. *Giacomo Puccini e l'opera internazionale*', *Rivista teatrale italiana* 5/17 (1913), 28–31.
105 Domenico De Paoli, *La crisi musicale italiana (1900–1930)* (Milan: Hoepli, 1939), p. 55.
106 Anon., 'Fausto Torrefranca. *Giacomo Puccini e l'opera internazionale*', 31.
107 Ferraguti, 'Tra i libri musicali', 95.
108 Raymond O'Neil, '"Et tu, Brute", Murmurs the Heckled Puccini as an Italian Critic Drives a Long Dagger into Him While His Countrymen Flock to Read the Subsequent Antony Orations in the Newspapers', *The Cleveland Leader* (4 August 1912). I should like to thank Linda Fairtile for drawing my attention to this article.
109 Ibid.
110 Ibid.
111 Ferruccio Vecchi, 'Il melodramma e Giacomo Puccini', *Il Trovatore* 59/16–17 (15 July 1912), 1–2.
112 Filippo Brusa, 'Una violenta aggressione a Puccini', *Musica* 6/27 (21 July 1912), 1–2. Brusa's review responded more overtly to the book's musical analysis than was typical, and claimed that Torrefranca exposed his own weaknesses by attacking music which his derisory knowledge of harmony did not equip him to understand.
113 Silvio Benco, 'Giacomo Puccini e un suo critico', *Il mondo artistico* 46/36–37 (21 August 1912), 1–3.
114 Benco, 'Giacomo Puccini e un suo critico', pp. 1, 2.

6 THE ITALIAN COMPOSER AS INTERNATIONALIST

1 F. Balilla Pratella, *Evoluzione della musica dal 1910 al 1917*, 2 vols. (Milan: Istituto Editoriale Italiano, 1918), Vol. I, p. 93. This entry in Pratella's collection of essays was dated 6 April 1913.
2 Cited in Gentile, *La Grande Italia*, p. 60.
3 Sighele, *Il nazionalismo e i partiti politici*, p. 27.
4 Ibid., p. 98.
5 Checchi, 'Giacomo Puccini e la sua nuova opera'.
6 Torrefranca, *Giacomo Puccini*, p. 24.
7 Sighele, *Pagine nazionaliste* (Milan: Treves, 1910), p. 208.
8 Pratella, *Evoluzione della musica*, Vol. I, p. 11; this section signed Milan, 11 October 1910. Pratella cited Strauss, Debussy, Elgar, Mussorgsky and Sibelius as more praiseworthy foreign models, although his own Futurist music would be considerably more consciously avant-garde than that of any of the composers on his list.
9 Letter of 15 May 1912 to Egon Petri, in Antony Beaumont (ed.), *Ferruccio Busoni: Selected Letters* (London and Boston, MA: Faber and Faber, 1987), p. 147.
10 D'Indy letters, BN Mus l.a., No. 210, 25 September 1911, to Gabriel Marie. I should like to thank Katharine Ellis for drawing my attention to this reference.
11 Mantovani, 'Giacomo Puccini', 434.
12 Annie J. Randall and Rosalind Gray Davis, *Puccini and the Girl: History and Reception of The Girl of the Golden West* (Chicago, IL, and London: University of Chicago Press, 2005), p. 96.
13 Discussed in ibid., pp. 97, 133–6, 147.
14 Ibid., p. 97.
15 As reported by Gustavo Macchi, 'Il successo della *Fanciulla del West* al Costanzi', *La Lombardia* (13 June 1911). Macchi lamented the fact that Mascagni's *Isabeau* and the most recent works by Giordano, Franchetti and Leoncavallo (the now-long-forgotten *Mese Mariano*, *La figlia di Jorio*, and *Maià*) were not also paraded in front of the international audience.
16 Ettore Alessio, 'Da Roma: la prima della *Fanciulla del West*', *La frusta teatrale* 49/13 (12 July 1911).

17 'Vice', 'La vittoria della Fanciulla del West', *Lirica* 4/16 (20 June 1911), 7–8, 7.
18 F. Checchini, 'Corrispondenze', *Il trovatore* 58/19 (15 June 1911).
19 Leporello, 'La *Fanciulla del West* al Costanzi di Roma', *L'illustrazione italiana*, 38/25 (18 June 1911), 610.
20 Letter of 15 August 1910 to Sybil Seligman, in Seligman, *Puccini among Friends*, p. 192.
21 Leporello, 'La *Fanciulla del West* al Costanzi di Roma', 610.
22 Reported in Anon., 'La *Fanciulla del West* di G. Puccini al Costanzi', *La sera* (13–14 June 1911).
23 Giuseppe Adami, 'Il grande successo della *Fanciulla del West* al Costanzi', *La perseveranza* (13 June 1911), 2.
24 E. Begni, 'La Fanciulla del West a New York', *Musica* 4/39 (18 December 1910), 2.
25 Anon., 'La Fanciulla del West al Costanzi', *L'idea nazionale* (20 February 1915).
26 r.d.r., 'L'incerta fortuna della "Fanciulla del West"', *Musica* 5/25 (18 June 1911).
27 Letter to Adami, cited in Randall and Gray Davis, *Puccini and the Girl*, p. 45.
28 Giovanni Pozza, '*La Fanciulla del West* di Puccini a Roma: il successo della prima rappresentazione', *Corriere della sera* (13 June 1911), 2.
29 Ibid.
30 '*Girl of the Golden West* Given a Rousing Reception', *The Evening World* (12 December 1910), cited in Randall and Gray Davis, *Puccini and the Girl*, p. 134.
31 r.d.r., 'L'incerta fortuna della "Fanciulla del West"'.
32 Ibid.
33 Carlo Cordara, 'La Fanciulla del West', *Il marzocco* 17/16 (21 April 1912), 3.
34 Ibid.
35 'I am thinking of [the opera] constantly and I am certain that it will prove to be a second *Bohème*, unless my brain and energy fail me'. Letter of 14 September 1907 to Giulio Ricordi, in Adami (ed.), *Letters of Giacomo Puccini*, trans. Ena Makin (New York: Vienna House, 1973), pp. 175–6.
36 Renzo Bianchi (ed.), *Giacomo Puccini, La bohème: guida attraverso il dramma e la musica* (Milan: Presso Bottega di Poesia, 1923), p. 31.

37 Gray, 'Three Modern 284–8, 284.
38 Bonaventura, *Giacomo Puccini: l'uomo – l'artista*, p. 31.
39 Pizzetti, *Musicisti contemporanei*, p. 105.
40 Ibid., p. 65.
41 Ibid., p. 74.
42 Ildebrando Pizzetti, 'Giacomo Puccini', *La voce* 3/5–7 (1911), 497–9, 502–3, 508–9.
43 Pizzetti, *Musicisti contemporanei*, p. 83.
44 Marinetti, 'Fondazione e manifesto del Futurismo', in *Teoria e invenzione futurista* (Milan: Mondadori, 1968), p. 12.
45 Marinetti, 'Marinetti e il futurismo', in *Teoria e invenzione futurista*, p. 520. Marinetti's original text reads: 'Urlooooo. Gesticulazione. Gorgo. Risacca. 200 500 600 facce inebitite. Basta! ... Fuori! ... Sono i futuristi! ... Viva Marinetti! ... Abbasso Marinetti! ... Bene! ... Fuori! ... Bravi! ... Abbassooo l'Austria! ... Imbecili! ... Pazzi! Pazzi! ... Vigliacchi! ... Silenzio! ... (Puccini illuso si precipita alla ribalta).'
46 Ibid. Original text: 'Nel fondo del palco la pancia di Mazza partorisce una bandiera tricolore di 8 metri quadrati. L'attachiamo all'asta di 2 bastoni legati. Mi sporgo agitandola: Abbassoooo l'Austriaaa! ....'
47 Ibid.
48 Ibid.
49 Ibid. Original text: 'Cantanti che domandano applausi con sorrisi da mendicanti.'
50 Ibid. Original text: 'Forbiciano la musica di Puccini: strascichi arpeggiati, lasagne scodinzolanti nervi isterici violinati e zuccherifilati rosa.'
51 Marinetti, 'Teatro Dal Verme', *La Revue d'art dramatique* 636 (November 1901), 118. Original text: 'Jamais les foires aux pains d'épices (tambours, accordéons, orgues de barbarie essoufflés) ne surpasseront le discordant brouhaha et les mélopées abrutissantes que les héros de Sardou–Illica–Giacosa glapissent sur une orchestration de nègres! On retrouve dans *La Tosca* tous les refrains usés, les rengaines rances des fêtes foraines, avec le relent nauséabond du sucre filé, des fritures et – surtout – la désespérante odeur de la crasse intellectuelle!'
52 Lesley Chamberlain (ed.), *Marinetti: The Futurist Cookbook*, trans. Suzanne Brill (London: Trefoil Publications, 1989).

53 Marinetti, 'Marinetti e il futurismo', in *Teoria e invenzione futurista*, p. 521. Original reads: 'Gioia pacifica di grasse famiglie intorno ai gelati centellinati'; 'Crollo universale. Tutto ruzzola e si schianta. Urli. Liquidazione di donne che svengono. Gelateria volante. Insulti sfide battibecchi.'

54 Anon., *Il secolo* (17 September 1914).

55 Giannotto Bastianelli, *La nazione* (28 and 29 March 1917), cited in Girardi, *Puccini: His International Art*, p. 338.

56 Anon., 'La *Rondine* di Puccini. Il successo al Comunale di Bologna', *Corriere della sera* (6 June 1917).

57 Alberto Gasco, 'La rondine di Puccini a Bologna', *La tribuna* (7 June 1917).

58 Ibid.

59 Anon., *Musica* 11/10 (31 May 1917).

60 Anon., 'La *Rondine* di Puccini.

61 Gasco, 'La rondine di Puccini a Bologna'.

62 Ibid.

63 Anon., 'La *Rondine* di Puccini. Il successo al Comunale di Bologna'.

64 Ferrante Mecenati, 'La prima rappresentazione della Rondine di Giacomo Puccini al Teatro Comunale di Bologna', *Corriere dei teatri* 38 (23 June 1917).

65 Ibid.

66 Franco Raineri, 'La prima della Rondine di Puccini a Bologna', *Giornale d'Italia* (7 June 1917).

67 Vincenzo Davico, '*La rondine* di Giacomo Puccini: impressioni critiche', *Musica* 11/6 (30 March 1917), 1.

68 Ibid.

69 Ibid.

70 For a full consideration of the revisions Puccini made to *La rondine*, see Schickling and Kaye, *Giacomo Puccini: Catalogue of the Works*, pp. 322–35.

71 Budden, *Puccini: His Life and Works*, p. 352.

72 Filippo Brusa, 'Giacomo Puccini', *Rivista musicale italiana* 32 (1925), 98–101, 101.

73 James Gibbons Huneker, 'A World Premier of Puccini Operas', *The New York Times* (15 December 1918), 22.

74 Ibid.

75 Incagliati, 'L'arte di Puccini canta e trionfa tre volte'.

76 Alastor, 'Le tre nuove opere di Giacomo Puccini', *Musica* 13/2 (15 January 1919).
77 'Uno del pubblico', 'Il successo di Puccini al Costanzi: Il Tabarro – Suor Angelica – Gianni Schicchi', *L'idea nazionale* (13 January 1919).
78 Ibid.
79 M. Incagliati, 'L'arte di Puccini canta e trionfa tre volte', *Giornale d'Italia* (13 January 1919).
80 Alberto Gasco, 'Le nuove opere di Puccini al Costanzi', *La tribuna* (13 January 1919).
81 Ibid.
82 Alastor, 'Le tre nuove opere di Giacomo Puccini'.
83 Carlo Cordara, 'Il "Trittico" di G. Puccini', *Il marzocco* 24/20 (18 May 1919), 2–3, 3.
84 Gasco, 'Le nuove opere di Puccini al Costanzi'.
85 Ibid.
86 Giacomo Setaccioli, *Il contenuto musicale del Gianni Schicchi di Giacomo Puccini con la esposizione e la illustrazione dei motivi tematici* (Rome: Fratelli De Santis, 1920), p. 10.
87 Ibid., p. 45.
88 Incagliati, 'L'arte di Puccini canta e trionfa tre volte'.
89 Setaccioli, *Il contenuto musicale del Gianni Schicchi*, p. 29.
90 'Uno del pubblico', 'Il successo di Puccini al Costanzi'.
91 Ibid.
92 Gasco, 'Le nuove opere di Puccini al Costanzi'.
93 Giannotto Bastianelli, 'La prima rappresentazione delle nuove opere di Giacomo Puccini', *La nazione* (11 January 1919).
94 Ibid.
95 Roger Parker, *Gianni Schicchi* house programme essay, Glyndebourne Festival Opera, 2004.
96 Emanuele Senici, 'Verdi's *Falstaff* at Italy's *Fin de Siècle*', *Musical Quarterly* 85/2 (Summer 2001), 274–310.
97 Ibid., 279.
98 Bastianelli, 'La prima rappresentazione delle nuove opere di Giacomo Puccini'.
99 Ibid.
100 Ibid.

7 A SUITABLE ENDING?

1 Puccini tribute supplement, *Musica d'oggi* 7/3 (March 1925), 10.
2 Ibid., 12.
3 Ibid., 6.
4 Ibid., 21.
5 Mantovani, 'Giacomo Puccini', 429.
6 Raff, *Il popolo d'Italia*, cited in Puccini tribute supplement, *Musica d'oggi*, 29.
7 Ibid.
8 G. Sommi, *L'impero*, cited in Puccini tribute supplement, *Musica d'oggi*, 30.
9 'Una bella porcheria'. Letter of 26 March 1919 to Elvira Puccini, in Gara (ed.), *Carteggi Pucciniani*, p. 483.
10 Fausto Salvatori, introduction to Monaldi, *Giacomo Puccini e la sua opera*, p. 4.
11 Ibid.
12 Ibid., pp. 3–4.
13 For a selection of photographs of Mussolini in iconic poses designed to show his many-faceted personality (with a lion cub, with his horse, playing the violin), see Denis Mack Smith, *Mussolini il duce: quattrocento immagini deall vita di un uomo e di vent'anni di storia italiana* (Milan: Gruppo editoriale Fabbri, 1983).
14 Salvatori, introduction to Monaldi, *Giacomo Puccini e la sua opera*, p. 4.
15 L. Parodi writing in *Il caffaro*, cited in *Musica d'oggi*, supplement to issue 3 (March 1925), 33.
16 Quotation from *Il giornale d'Italia*, cited in Alceo Toni, 'La morte di Giacomo Puccini', *Il popolo d'Italia* (30 November 1924).
17 Arnaldo Fraccaroli, *Il corriere della sera*, cited in Puccini tribute supplement, *Musica d'oggi*, 25.
18 Mantovani, 'Giacomo Puccini', 429.
19 G. Sommi, *L'impero*, cited in Puccini tribute supplement, *Musica d'oggi*, 30.
20 Gajanus, *Il resto del Carlino*, cited in *Musica d'oggi*, supplement to issue 3 (March 1925), 34.
21 Tartaglia, 'Giacomo Puccini: una recita e un monologo', *L'illustrazione italiana* 51/49 (7 December 1924), 728–9, 728.

22 Puccini tribute supplement, *Musica d'oggi*, 19.
23 Ibid., 18.
24 Adriano Lualdi, *Il secolo*, cited in Puccini tribute supplement, *Musica d'oggi*, 25.
25 Toni, 'La morte di Giacomo Puccini'.
26 Antonio Trudu, 'Toni, Alceo', in Stanley Sadie and John Tyrrell (eds.), *The New Grove Dictionary of Music and Musicians*, 2nd edn., 29 vols. (London: Macmillan, 2001), Vol. 25, p. 602.
27 Harvey Sachs, *Music in Fascist Italy* (London: Weidenfeld and Nicolson, 1987), p. 23.
28 Cited in Puccini tribute supplement, *Musica d'oggi*, 19.
29 Cited in *Musica d'oggi*, supplement to issue 3 (March 1925), 48.
30 Michela Niccolai, '"La Scala sotto la tenda". *La bohème* inaugura il Carro di Tespi lirico', in Roberto Illiano (ed.), *Italian Music during the Fascist Period* (Turnhout: Brepols, 2004), p. 268.
31 'What do you think of Mussolini? I hope he will prove to be the man we need. Good luck to him if he will cleanse and give a little peace to our country!' Letter of 30 October 1922 to Adami, cited in Adami (ed.), *Letters of Giacomo Puccini*, trans Ena Makin (New York: Vienna House, 1973), p. 289.
32 Cited in Giuseppe Adami, *Puccini*, 2nd edn. (Milan: Treves, 1938), p. 207.
33 Edoardo and Duilio Susmel (eds.), *Opera omnia di Benito Mussolini*, 44 vols. (Florence: La Fenice, 1956), Vol. 21, p. 189.
34 Girardi, *Puccini: His International Art*, p. 436.
35 Fiamma Nicolodi, 'Aspetti di politica culturale nel ventennio fascista', in Illiano (ed.), *Italian Music during the Fascist Period*, p. 27.
36 For further discussion of this issue, see Emily Braun, 'The Visual Arts: Modernism and Fascism', and Bruno P. F. Wanrooij, 'Italian Society under Fascism', in Adrian Lyttelton (ed.), *Liberal and Fascist Italy* (Oxford: Oxford University Press, 2002).
37 Lino Pertile, 'Fascism and Literature', in David Forgacs (ed.), *Rethinking Italian Fascism: Capitalism, Populism and Culture* (London: Lawrence and Wishart, 1986), p. 170.
38 Bianchi (ed.), *Giacomo Puccini, La bohème*, pp. 33–4.
39 Charles Mintzer, *Rosa Raisa: A Biography of a Diva with Selections from Her Memoirs* (Boston, MA: Northeastern University Press, 2001), p. 130.

40 See for example Anon., 'Il trionfale successo di *Turandot*', *Musica d'oggi* 8/5 (May 1926), 141–51, 141; Raffaello De Rensis, 'La prima rappresentazione di *Turandot* di Puccini alla Scala', *Il giornale d'Italia* (27 April 1926); and Pino di Valmarana, '*Turandot* di G. Puccini alla Scala', *Musica e scena* 3/4 (April 1926), 16–17, 16.

41 *Musica d'oggi* proudly declared: 'The night of 25 April will undoubtedly remain a memorable one for Italian music. That night, *Turandot*, the posthumous opera of Giacomo Puccini, the most glorious and most popular composer of our times, had its triumphal baptism at La Scala in Milan'. Anon., 'Il trionfale successo di *Turandot*', 141.

42 Raffaello de Rensis, 'La prima rappresentazione di *Turandot*'.

43 A discussion of modernist puppet theatre in Italy, France, Spain, Austria, Poland, Germany, Russia and Czechoslovakia may be found in Harold B. Segel, *Pinocchio's Progeny: Puppets, Marionettes, Automatons, and Robots in Modernist and Avant-Garde Drama* (Baltimore, MD, and London: Johns Hopkins University Press, 1995). Over 200 twentieth-century plays which use masks as an integral part of the drama are considered in Susan Valeria Harris Smith, *Masks in Modern Drama* (Berkeley, Los Angeles, CA, and London: University of California Press, 1984).

44 Antonio Capri, *Musica e musicisti d'Europa dal 1800 al 1930* (Milan: Hoepli, 1931), p. 54.

45 De Rensis, 'La prima rappresentazione di *Turandot*'.

46 Guido Pannain, 'L'opera italiana dell'ottocento', *Il pianoforte* 8/5–6 (15 May–15 June 1927), 166–74, 166.

47 Bonaventura, *Giacomo Puccini: l'uomo – l'artista*, pp. 5–6.

48 Adriano Lualdi, *Serate musicali* (Milan: Fratelli Treves Editori, 1928), p. 51.

49 Bonaventura, *Giacomo Puccini: l'uomo – l'artista*, p. 45.

50 Ibid.

51 Cesare Brighenti-Rosa, 'Giacomo Puccini', *Il pensiero musicale* 4/11–12 (November–December 1924), 170–2, 172.

52 Franco Salerno, *Le donne pucciniane* (Palermo: Casa Editrice Ant. Trimarchi, 1928), p. 8.

53 Monaldi refers to Puccini as 'innamorato come sempre delle sue eroine'. Monaldi, *Giacomo Puccini e la sua opera*, p. 33. The curious mixture of sentimentality and veiled eroticism that characterised the

way in which critics wrote about Puccini's heroines would endure long after the composer's death, demonstrated most strikingly by Mosco Carner's questionable attempt at amateur psychoanalysis: 'It was with these creatures of fantasy that Puccini formed the close attachments which were absent from his life in the real world. Manon, Mimì, Tosca, Cio-Cio-San, Angelica and Liù – these were his true loves, and on his own confession he wept with "nostalgia, tenderness and pain" while composing their music'. Carner, *Puccini: A Critical Biography*, p. 188.

54 Reported in Puccini tribute supplement, *Musica d'oggi*, 10.
55 Cited in ibid., 30.
56 As reported in ibid., 16.
57 Renzo Bianchi, *L'Avanti!*, cited in Anon., 'Il trionfale successo di *Turandot*', 145.
58 Giuseppe Adami, *Il romanzo della vita di Giacomo Puccini* (Milan and Rome: Rizzoli, 1942), pp. 197–8.
59 Adriano Lualdi, *Il secolo*, cited in Anon., 'Il trionfale successo di *Turandot*', 144.
60 G. C. Paribeni, *L'ambrosiano*, cited in ibid., 145.
61 See Salerno, *Le donne pucciniane*, p. 18.
62 For example De Rensis, 'La prima rappresentazione di *Turandot*'.
63 Croce, *The Aesthetic As the Science of Expression*, p. 58.
64 Capri, *Musica e musicisti d'Europa*, p. 54.
65 Michele Lessona, '*Turandot* di Giacomo Puccini', *Rivista musicale italiana* (1926), 239–47, 244.
66 Gaetano Cesari, 'La prima della *Turandot* di Puccini alla Scala', *Corriere della sera* (27 April 1926).
67 De Rensis, 'La prima rappresentazione di *Turandot*'.
68 Ibid.
69 Letter of 20 March 1923 to Sybil Seligman, in Seligman, *Puccini among Friends*, p. 346.
70 Di Valmarana, '*Turandot* di G. Puccini alla Scala', 16.
71 Lessona, '*Turandot* di Giacomo Puccini', 241.
72 Anon., 'Il trionfale successo di *Turandot*', 141.
73 Letter to Simoni, cited in Adami, *Il romanzo della vita di Giacomo Puccini*, p. 225.

74 Letter of 28 July 1920 to Simoni, in Gara (ed.), *Carteggi Pucciniani*, p. 492.
75 See the Masks' entrance ('Ferma! Che fai?'). The music box also provided the 'Mo-li-hua' theme sung by the children's chorus, and the 'Imperial hymn'. Discussed in William Ashbrook and Harold Powers, *Puccini's Turandot: The End of the Great Tradition* (Princeton, NJ: Princeton University Press, 1991), pp. 94–6.
76 See for example the chapter on the opera's genesis in Ashbrook and Powers, *Puccini's Turandot*.
77 Carner, *Puccini: A Critical Biography*, p. 511.
78 Cited in Antony Beaumont, *Busoni the Composer* (London and Boston, MA: Faber and Faber, 1985), p. 80.
79 Antonio Ghislanzoni, *Gazzetta musicale di Milano* 22/3 (20 January 1867), cited in Kii-Ming Lo, *'Turandot' auf der Opernbühne* (Frankfurt am Main: Peter Lang, 1996), p. 206.
80 G. A. Pfister, 'The Marionettes at the New Scala', *The Sackbut* 3/11 (June 1923), 344–6, 346.
81 Letter of 18 March 1920 to Simoni, in Gara (ed.), *Carteggi pucciniani*, p. 490.
82 Edward Gordon Craig, 'Some Evil Tendencies of the Modern Theatre', *The Mask* 1/8 (October 1908), 153.
83 Craig, 'The Actor and the Übermarionette', *The Mask* 1/2 (April 1908), 3–15, 5, 9, 11.
84 Ibid., 12.
85 Marinetti, 'The Pleasure of Being Booed', from *War, the World's Only Hygiene* (1911–1915), cited in Filippo Tommaso Marinetti, *Let's Murder the Moonshine: Selected Writings*, trans. R. W. Flint and Arthur A. Coppotelli (Los Angeles: Sun and Moon Classics, 1991), pp. 122–3.
86 From *Dynamic and Synoptic Declamation*, 11 March 1916, reproduced in Marinetti, *Let's Murder the Moonshine*, pp. 150–5, p. 152.
87 Letter of 17 September 1920 to Renzo Valcarenghi, in Lo, *"Turandot" auf der Opernbühne*, p. 294.
88 Giacomo Antonini, *Il teatro contemporaneo in Italia* (Milan: Corbaccio, 1927), p. 107.
89 Letter of 18 March 1920 to Renato Simoni.
90 Senici, 'Verdi's *Falstaff* at Italy's *Fin de Siècle*', 298.

91 W. Anthony Sheppard, *Revealing Masks: Exotic Influences and Ritualised Performance in Modernist Music Theater* (Berkeley, Los Angeles, CA, and London: University of California Press, 2001), p. 59.
92 Renzo Bianchi, 'L'ultima opera di Giacomo Puccini: *Turandot*', *La fiera letteraria* (2 May 1926), 3.
93 Gatti, 'Rileggendo le opere di Puccini', 268.
94 Ibid.
95 Gray, 'Three Modern Italian Composers', 284.
96 Vittorio Gui, 'Le due *Turandot*', in *Battute d'aspetto: meditazioni di un musicista militante* (Florence: Monsalvato, 1944), p. 156.
97 Ibid., pp. 150–1.
98 Ugo Ojetti, *Cose viste*, 3 vols. (Milan: Treves, 1923), Vol. 2, p. 122.
99 Gatti, 'Rileggendo le opere di Puccini', 268.
100 Saverio Procida, '*Turandot* nel teatro di Puccini', *Nuova antologia* 61 (May 1926), 180–8, 183.
101 Lessona, '*Turandot* di Giacomo Puccini', 244.
102 Ibid.
103 Ibid., 246.
104 De Paoli, *La crisi musicale italiana*, p. 182.
105 Anon, 'La prima di *Turandot* alla Scala', *Il teatro* 6/3–4 (1 March–30 April 1926), 17; Anon., 'Gli avvenimenti scaligeri', *Musicisti d'Italia* 6/5 (30 May 1926), 4–8, 4; Innocenzo Cappa, '*Turandot* alla Scala', *La rivista illustrata del Popolo d'Italia* 4/5 (May 1926), 58–61, 59.
106 Lualdi, *Serate musicali*, p. 248.
107 Ettore Montanaro, '*Turandot* di Giacomo Puccini al "Costanzi" di Roma', *Musica* 20/7–8 (30 April–15 May 1926).
108 See for example Di Valmarana, '*Turandot* di G. Puccini alla Scala', 17.
109 Letter of 23 October 1919 to Adami, in Adami, *Letters of Giacomo Puccini*, p. 260.
110 Lessona, '*Turandot* di Giacomo Puccini', 243, 245.
111 Giulio Mario Ciampelli, 'Ricordi e rimpianti: Puccini e la *Turandot*', *Il teatro* 6/3–4 (1 March–30 April 1926), 12–17, 15.
112 Lualdi, *Serate musicali*, p. 261.
113 Anon., 'Il trionfale successo di *Turandot*', 143.
114 Salerno, *Le donne pucciniane*, p. 17.
115 De Paoli, *La crisi musicale italiana*, p. 124.

116 Marinetti, 'The Pleasure of Being Booed', cited in Marinetti, *Let's Murder the Moonshine*, pp. 122, 121.
117 Letter of 22 June 1927 to Gastone Monaldi, cited in Günther Berghaus, 'The Ritual Core of Fascist Theatre: An Anthropological Perspective', in Berghaus ed., *Fascism and Theatre: Comparative Studies on the Aesthetics and Politics of Performance in Europe, 1925–1945* (Providence, RI, and Oxford: Berghahn Books, 1996), p 97.
118 Gino Roncaglia, 'Il problema dell'arte dal punto di vista musicale', *Il pianoforte*, 4/7–8 (July–August 1923), 169–73, 171.
119 Anon., 'Gli avvenimenti scaligeri', 8.
120 Cesari, 'La prima della *Turandot* di Puccini alla Scala'.
121 See for example letter of 28 August 1920 to Simoni, in Gara (ed.), *Carteggi Pucciniani*, p. 495.
122 Gatti, 'Rileggendo le opere di Puccini', 265.
123 Renato Mariani, 'L'ultimo Puccini', *La rassegna musicale* 9/4 (April 1936), 133–40, 134.
124 Ibid., 139–40.

EPILOGUE

1 Renato Mariani, *Giacomo Puccini* (Turin: Edizioni Arione, 1939), p. 34.
2 Adriano Lualdi, 'Giacomo Puccini, i suoi detrattori e l'Opera nazionale del '900', estratto dal volume V di *Piazza delle Belle Arti*, Rassegna 1957–1958 dell'Accademia Nazionale Luigi Cherubini, 20.
3 The 'modernity' (or otherwise) of Puccini's harmonic language had been a subject of growing interest to serious music critics during the 1910s, reaching a peak during the early 1920s. See Giorgio Sanguinetti, 'Puccini's Music in the Italian Theoretical Literature of Its Day', in Deborah Burton, Susan Vandiver Nicassio and Agostino Ziino (eds.), *Tosca's Prism: Three Moments of Western Cultural History* (Boston, MA: Northeastern University Press, 2004), pp. 221–45.
4 Gatti, 'Rileggendo le opere di Puccini', 269.
5 Richard Specht, *Giacomo Puccini: The Man, his Life, his Work*, trans. Catherine Alison Phillips (London and Toronto: Dent, 1933), p. ix. (First published in German 1932.)
6 Ibid.
7 Ibid., pp. 2, 3.

8 Donald J. Grout, *A Short History of Opera*, 2 vols. (London: Oxford University Press, 1947), Vol. 2, pp. 438–9.
9 Ibid., p. 441.
10 William W. Austin, *Music in the 20th Century: from Debussy through Stravinsky* (London: Dent, 1966), p. 108. Austin was echoing criticisms from Puccini's own time. In 1911, for example, Domenico Alaleona criticised Puccini for juxtaposing whole tone chords with an essentially traditional harmonic language. Domenico Alaleona, 'L'armonia modernissima: le tonalità neutre e l'arte di stupore', *Rivista musicale italiana* 18 (1911), 769–838, 821.
11 Austin, *Music in the 20th Century*, p. 109.
12 David Ewen (ed.), *The World of Twentieth-Century Music*, 2nd edn., rev. Stephen J. Pettitt (London: Robert Hale, 1991), pp. 601–2. (Originally published 1968).
13 Taruskin, *The Oxford History of Western Music*, Vol. 3, p. 665.
14 Ibid.
15 Ibid., p. 664.
16 '[Puccini] is usually barely mentioned in books like this (that is, general histories of "art music"), even though his commanding stature within the world of opera has been a historical fact for more than one hundred years and thus would seem to constitute a robust claim to the composer's historical significance.' Ibid.
17 William Drabkin, 'The Musical Language of *La bohème*', in Groos and Parker (eds.), *Giacomo Puccini: La bohème*, p. 80.
18 r.d.r., 'L'incerta fortuna della "Fanciulla del West"'. As discussed in chapter 6.
19 Stephen Banfield, 'Music, Text, and Stage: Bourgeois Tonality to the Second World War', in Nicholas Cook and Anthony Pople (eds.), *The Cambridge History of Twentieth-Century Music* (Cambridge: Cambridge University Press, 2004), pp. 90–122, 100.
20 Specht, *Giacomo Puccini*, p. 4.
21 Theodor Adorno and Hans Eisler, *Composing for the Films* (London: Oxford University Press, 1947).
22 Claudio Sartori (ed.), *Giacomo Puccini* (Milan: Ricordi, 1959), p. vii.

BIBLIOGRAPHY

SELECT NINETEENTH- AND EARLY-TWENTIETH-CENTURY NEWSPAPERS

L'avanti!
Il caffaro
Corriere della sera
Corriere di Napoli
The Evening World
Fanfulla
Fanfulla della domenica
Gazzetta del popolo
Gazzetta di Torino
Gazzetta piemontese
Gazzetta ufficiale del regno d'Italia
Giornale d'Italia
L'idea nazionale
L'impero
La lega lombarda
La Lombardia
Il mattino
Il messaggero
La nazione
The New York Times
La perseveranza
Perseveranza di domenica
Il popolo d'Italia
Il popolo romano
La prensa
Il pungolo
Rivista politica e letteraria
Il secolo
Il secolo XIX

La sera
La stampa
Il tempo
La tribuna

SELECT NINETEENTH- AND EARLY-TWENTIETH-CENTURY PERIODICALS

Ars et labor
The Art Journal
Il caffaro
La critica
Corriere dei teatri
Cronaca musicale
L'edilizia moderna
La fiera letteraria
La frusta teatrale
Gazzetta musicale di Milano
Gazzetta teatrale italiana
L'illustrazione italiana
L'illustrazione popolare
Lacerba
La lanterna
Leonardo
La lettura
Lirica
The Magazine of Art
Il marzocco
The Mask
Il mondo artistico
Musica
Musica d'Oggi
Musica e musicisti
Musica e scena
Musica nuova
Musicisti d'Italia
Nuova antologia
Il palcoscenico

Il pensiero musicale
Il pianoforte
La rassegna musicale
Il regno
La revue d'art dramatique
La riforma musicale
La rivista illustrata del Popolo d'Italia
The Sackbut
The Studio
Il teatro
Il teatro illustrato e la musica popolare
Rivista musicale italiana
Rivista teatrale italiana
La Tosca (supplemento straordinario alla *Gazzetta musicale* ed al *Palcoscenico*, Milan, January 1900)
Il trovatore
Vita musicale
La voce

BOOKS AND SECONDARY ARTICLES

Abbiati, Franco, *Giuseppe Verdi*, 2nd edn., 4 vols. (Milan: Ricordi, 1963).

Adami, Giuseppe, *Puccini*, 2nd edn. (Milan: Fratelli Treves, 1938).

Adami, Giuseppe, *Il romanzo della vita di Giacomo Puccini* (Milan and Rome: Rizzoli, 1942).

Adami, Giuseppe (ed.), *Letters of Giacomo Puccini*, trans. Ena Makin (New York: Vienna House 1973).

Adamson, Walter L., *Avant-Garde Florence: From Modernism to Fascism* (Cambridge, MA, and London: Harvard University Press, 1993).

Adorno, Theodor and Eisler, Hans, *Composing for the Films* (London: Oxford University Press, 1947).

Affron, Matthew and Antliff, Mark (eds.), *Fascist Visions: Art and Ideology in France and Italy* (Princeton, NJ: Princeton University Press, 1997).

Alberti, Annibale, *Verdi intimo: carteggio di Giuseppe Verdi con il Conte Opprandino Arrivabene (1861–1886)* (Verona: Mondadori, 1931).

Alloway, Lawrence, *The Venice Biennale, 1895–1968: From Salon to Goldfish Bowl* (London: Faber, 1969).

Anderson, Benedict, *Imagined Communities: Reflections on the Origin and Spread of Nationalism* (London: Verso, 1983).

Antolini, Bianca Maria (ed.), *Milano musicale: 1861–1897, Quaderni del Corso di Musicologia del Conservatorio 'G. Verdi' di Milano* (Lucca and Milan: Libreria Musicale Italiana, 1999).

Antonini, Giacomo, *Il teatro contemporaneo in Italia* (Milan: Corbaccio, 1927).

Arblaster, Anthony, *Viva la libertà! Politics in Opera* (New York: Verso, 1992).

Ashbrook, William and Powers, Harold, *Puccini's Turandot: The End of the Great Tradition* (Princeton, NJ: Princeton University Press, 1991).

Athanassoglou-Kallmyer, Nina Maria, *Cézanne and Provence: The Painter in His Culture* (Chicago, IL, and London: University of Chicago Press, 2003).

Austin, William W., *Music in the 20th Century: From Debussy through Stravinsky* (London: Dent, 1966).

Babini, Valeria P., Muniz, Fernanda and Tagliavini, Annamaria, *La donna delle scienze dell'uomo: immagini del femminile nella cultura scientifica italiana di fine secolo* (Milan: Franco Angeli, 1989).

Balilla Pratella, F., *Musica italiana: per una cultura della sensibilità musicale italiana* (Bologna: Francesco Bongiovanni Editore, 1915).

Balilla Pratella, F., *Evoluzione della musica dal 1910 al 1917*, 2 vols. (Milan: Istituto Editoriale Italiano, 1918).

Banfield, Stephen, 'Music, Text, and Stage: Bourgeois Tonality to the Second World War', in Nicholas Cook and Anthony Pople (eds.), *The Cambridge History of Twentieth-Century Music* (Cambridge: Cambridge University Press, 2004, pp. 90–122).

Barrows, Susanna, *Distorting Mirrors: Visions of the Crowd in Late Nineteenth-Century France* (New Haven, CT, and London: Yale University Press, 1981).

Barthes, Roland, *Mythologies*, trans. Annette Lavers (London: Vintage, 1993).

Battersby, Christine, *Gender and Genius: Towards a Feminist Aesthetics* (London: The Women's Press, 1989).

Beaumont, Antony, *Busoni the Composer* (London and Boston, MA: Faber and Faber, 1985).

Beaumont, Antony (ed.), *Ferruccio Busoni: Selected Letters* (London and Boston, MA: Faber and Faber, 1987).

Berger, Klaus, *Japonisme in Western Painting from Whistler to Matisse* (Cambridge: Cambridge University Press, 1992).

Berghaus, Günther (ed.), *Fascism and Theatre: Comparative Studies on the Aesthetics and Politics of Performance in Europe, 1925–1945* (Providence, RI, and Oxford: Berghahn Books, 1996).

Bernheimer, Charles, *Figures of Ill Repute: Representing Prostitution in Nineteenth-Century France* (Cambridge, MA, and London: Harvard University Press, 1989).

Berrong, Richard M. (ed.), *The Politics of Opera in Turn-of-the-Century Italy, As Seen through the Letters of Alfredo Catalani* (Lewiston, Queenston and Lampeter: The Edwin Mellen Press, 1992).

Biagi Ravenni, Gabriella, and Gianturco, Carolyn (eds.), *Giacomo Puccini: l'uomo, il musicista, il panorama europeo. Atti del convegno internazionale di studi su Giacomo Puccini nel 70° anniversario della morte (Lucca, 25–29 novembre 1994)* (Lucca: Libreria Musicale Italiana, 1997).

Bianchi, Renzo, *Giacomo Puccini, La bohème: guida attraverso il dramma e la musica* (Milan: Presso Bottega di Poesia, 1923).

Bonaventura, Arnaldo, *Giacomo Puccini: l'uomo – l'artista* (Livorno: Raffaello Giusti, 1925).

Bossaglia, Rossana, Godoli, Ezio and Rosci, Marco (eds.), *Torino 1902: le arti decorativi internazionali del nuovo secolo* (Milan: Fabbri Editori, 1994).

Bosworth, R. J. B, *Italy and the Wider World, 1860–1960* (London and New York: Routledge, 1996).

Bourget, Paul, *Essais de psychologie contemporaine* (Paris: Lemerre, 1883).

Brand, Peter and Pertile, Lino (eds.), *The Cambridge History of Italian Literature* (Cambridge: Cambridge University Press, 1996).

Briganti, Alessandra, *Intellettuali e cultura tra ottocento e novecento: nascita e storia della terza pagina* (Padua: Liviana, 1972).

Budden, Julian, *Puccini: His Life and Works* (Oxford: Oxford University Press, 2002).

Campana, Alessandra, review of Michele Girardi, *Puccini: His International Art, Cambridge Opera Journal* 12/3 (2001), 261–6.

Capra, Marco, 'Bohème nei giudizi della stampa periodica', in *La Bohème* house programme, Teatro Regio, Città di Parma, stagione lirica 1988–1989.
Capri, Antonio, *Musica e musicisti d'Europa dal 1800 al 1930* (Milan: Hoepli, 1931).
Carner, Mosco, *Giacomo Puccini: Tosca* (Cambridge: Cambridge University Press, 1985).
Carner, Mosco, *Puccini: A Critical Biography*, 3rd edn. (London: Duckworth, 1992).
Carter, Tim, *Monteverdi's Musical Theatre* (New Haven, CT, and London: Yale University Press, 2002).
Castronovo, Valerio, *La stampa italiana dall'unità al fascismo* (Bari: Laterza, 1970).
Castronovo, Valerio and Fossati, Luciana Giacheri, *Storia della stampa italiana*, 6 vols. (Rome and Bari: Laterza, 1979), Vol. III, *La stampa italiana nell'età liberale*, ed. Valeria Castronovo and Nicola Tranfaglia.
Cesari, Gaetano and Luzio, Alessandro (eds.), *I copialettere di Giuseppe Verdi* (Bologna: Forni, 1968).
Chamberlain, Lesley (ed.), *Marinetti: The Futurist Cookbook*, trans. Suzanne Brill (London: Trefoil Publications, 1989).
Citron, Marcia J., *Gender and the Musical Canon* (Cambridge: Cambridge University Press, 1993).
Colls, Robert and Dodd, Philip (eds.), *Englishness: Politics and Culture, 1880–1920* (London, Sydney and Dover, NH: Croom Helm, 1986).
Colombo, Giorgio, *La scienza infelice: Il museo di antropologia criminale di Cesare Lombroso*, 2nd edn. (Turin: Editore Boringhieri, 2000).
Cook, Nicholas and Pople, Anthony (eds.), *The Cambridge History of Twentieth-Century Music* (Cambridge: Cambridge University Press, 2004).
Criscione, Caterina, *Luigi Torchi: un musicologo tra otto e novecento* (Imola: Editrice La Mandragora, 1997).
Croce, Benedetto, *The Aesthetic As the Science of Expression*, trans. Colin Lyas (Cambridge: Cambridge University Press, 1992).
Cubitt, Geoffrey, *Imagining Nations* (Manchester and New York: Manchester University Press, 1998).

Cubitt, Geoffrey and Warren, Allen (eds.), *Heroic Reputations and Exemplary Lives* (Manchester and New York: Manchester University Press, 2000).

Cunsolo, Ronald S., 'Italian Nationalism in Historical Perspective', *History of European Ideas* 16/4–6 (1993), 759–66.

Dall'Olio, Cesare, *La musica e la civiltà: pensieri di una musicista* (Bologna: Tipografia di G. Cenerelli, 1897).

Davis, John A. (ed.), *Italy in the Nineteenth Century* (Oxford: Oxford University Press, 2000).

De-Bernardis, Lazzaro Maria, *La leggenda di Turandot: note di storia letteraria* (Genova: Marsano, 1932).

De Giorgio, Michela, *Le italiane dall'unità a oggi*, 2nd edn. (Rome and Bari: Laterza, 1993).

De Grazia, Victoria, *How Fascism Ruled Women: Italy, 1922–1945* (Berkeley, Los Angeles, CA, and London: University of California Press, 1992).

Del Fiorentino, Dante, *Immortal Bohemian: An Intimate Memoir of Giacomo Puccini* (London: Victor Gollancz, 1952).

Della Corte, Andrea, *La critica musicale e i critici* (Turin: Unione Tipografico-Editrice Torinese, 1961).

Della Seta, Fabrizio, 'Some Difficulties in the Historiography of Italian Opera', *Cambridge Opera Journal* 10/1 (March 1998), 3–13.

De Paoli, Domenico, *La crisi musicale italiana (1900–1930)* (Milan: Hoepli, 1939).

De Van, Gilles, *Verdi's Theater: Creating Drama through Music* (Chicago, IL, and London: University of Chicago Press, 1998).

Di Francia, Letterio, *La leggenda di Turandot nella novellistica e nel teatro* (Trieste: CELVI, 1932).

Dijkstra, Bram, *Idols of Perversity: Fantasies of Feminine Evil in Fin-de-Siècle Culture* (New York and Oxford: Oxford University Press, 1986).

Di San Martino, Enrico, *Saggio critico sopra alcune cause di decadenza nella musica italiana alla fine del secolo XIX* (Rome: Tipografia della Pace di Filippo Cuggiani, 1897).

Dottin-Orsini, Mireille, *Cette Femme qu'ils disent fatale* (Paris: Bernard Grasset, 1993).

Drake, Richard, *Byzantium for Rome: The Politics of Nostalgia in Umbertian Italy, 1878–1900* (Chapel Hill, NC: University of North Carolina Press, 1980).

Drake, Richard, 'Decadence, Decadentism and Decadent Romanticism in Italy: Towards a Theory of *Décadence*', *Journal of Contemporary History* 17 (1982), 69–92.

Dry, Wakeling, *Giacomo Puccini* (London and New York: John Lane, 1906).

Duggan, Christopher, *Francesco Crispi 1818–1901: From Nation to Nationalism* (Oxford: Oxford University Press, 2002).

Ellis, Katharine, *Music Criticism in Nineteenth-Century France: La Revue et Gazette Musicale de Paris, 1834–1880* (Cambridge: Cambridge University Press, 1995).

Ewen, David (ed.), *The World of Twentieth-Century Music*, 2nd edn., rev. Stephen J. Pettitt (London: Robert Hale, 1991).

Fairtile, Linda B., 'Giacomo Puccini's Operatic Revisions As Manifestations of His Compositional Priorities', unpublished PhD thesis, New York University (1996).

Fairtile, Linda B., *Giacomo Puccini: A Guide to Research* (New York and London: Garland, 1999).

Falasca-Zamponi, Simonetta, *Fascist Spectacle: The Aesthetics of Power in Mussolini's Italy* (Berkeley, Los Angeles, CA, and London: University of California Press, 1997).

Ferraro, Giuseppe and Pugliese, Annunziato (eds.), *Fausto Torrefranca: l'uomo, il suo tempo, la sua opera. Atti del convegno internazionale di studi Vibo Valentia, 15–17 dicembre 1983* (Vibo Valentia: Istituto di Bibliografia Musicale Calabrese, 1993).

Filippi, Filippo, *Musica e musicisti* (Milan: Brigola, 1876).

Fink, Robert, 'Going Flat: Post-Hierarchical Music Theory and the Musical Surface', in Nicholas Cook and Mark Everist (eds.), *Rethinking Music* (Oxford and New York: Oxford University Press, 1999), 102–37.

Flint, Kate, 'Blood and Milk: Painting and the State in Late Nineteenth-Century Italy', in Kathleen Adler and Marcia Pointon (eds.), *The Body Imaged: The Human Form and Visual Culture* (Cambridge: Cambridge University Press, 1993), pp. 109–23.

Forgacs, David (ed.), *Rethinking Italian Fascism: Capitalism, Populism and Culture* (London: Lawrence and Wishart, 1986).

Forsyth, Cecil, *Music and Nationalism: A Study of English Opera* (London: Macmillan, 1911).

Fraccaroli, Arnaldo, *Giacomo Puccini si confida e racconta* (Milan: Ricordi, 1957).

Fratini, Francesca R. (ed.), *Torino 1902: polemiche in Italia sull'Arte Nuova* (Turin: Martano, 1970).

Fulcher, Jane F., *French Cultural Politics and Music: From the Dreyfus Affair to the First World War* (New York and Oxford: Oxford University Press, 1999).

Gara, Eugenio (ed.), *Carteggi Pucciniani* (Milan: Ricordi, 1958).

Garb, Tamar, *Bodies of Modernity: Figure and Flesh in Fin-de-Siècle France* (London: Thames and Hudson, 1998).

Gentile, Emilio, 'The Conquest of Modernity: From Modernist Nationalism to Fascism', trans. Lawrence Rainey, in *Modernism/Modernity* 1/3 (September 1994), 55–87.

Gentile, Emilio, *La Grande Italia: ascesa e declino del mito della nazione nel ventesimo secolo* (Milan: Mondadori, 1997).

Gilman, Sander L., *Difference and Pathology: Stereotypes of Sexuality, Race, and Madness* (Ithaca, NY, and London: Cornell University Press, 1985).

Girardi, Michele, *Puccini: His International Art*, trans. Laura Basini (Chicago, IL, and London: University of Chicago Press, 2000).

Gordon, Rae Beth, *Ornament, Fantasy, and Desire in Nineteenth-Century French Literature* (Princeton, NJ: Princeton University Press, 1992).

Greenwald, Helen, 'Verdi's Patriarch and Puccini's Matriarch: "Through the Looking-Glass and What Puccini Found There"', *Nineteenth-Century Music* 17/3 (Spring 1994), 220–36.

Greenwald, Helen, 'Picturing Cio-Cio-San: House, Screen, and Ceremony in Puccini's *Madama Butterfly*', *Cambridge Opera Journal* 12/3 (November 2000), 237–59.

Griffin, Roger (ed.), *Fascism* (Oxford and New York: Oxford University Press, 1995).

Groos, Arthur and Parker, Roger (eds.), *Giacomo Puccini: La bohème* (Cambridge: Cambridge University Press, 1986).

Groos, Arthur, 'Cio-Cio-San and Sadayakko: Japanese Music-Theatre in *Madama Butterfly*', *Monumenta Nipponica* 54/1 (Spring 1999), 41–73.

Groos, Arthur (ed.), *Madama Butterfly. Fonti e documenti della genesi* (Lucca: Centro Studi Giacomo Puccini, 2005).

Grout, Donald J., *A Short History of Opera* (London: Oxford University Press, 1947).

Guarnieri Corazzol, Adriana, *Tristano, mio Tristano: gli scrittori italiani e il caso Wagner* (Bologna: Il Mulino, 1988).
Gui, Vittorio, *Battute d'aspetto: meditazioni di un musicista militante* (Florence: Monsalvato, 1944).
Guiot, Lorenza and Maehder, Jürgen (eds.), *Nazionalismo e cosmopolitismo nell'opera fra '800 e '900: Atti del 3° convegno internazionale 'Ruggero Leoncavallo nel suo tempo', Locarno, Biblioteca Cantonale, 6–7 October 1995* (Milan: Casa Musicale Sonzogno di Piero Ostali, 1998).
Gunzberg, Lynn M., *Strangers at Home: Jews in the Italian Literary Imagination* (Berkeley, Los Angeles, CA, and Oxford: University of California Press, 1992).
Harris Smith, Susan Valeria, *Masks in Modern Drama* (Berkeley, Los Angeles, CA, and London: University of California Press, 1984).
Harrowitz, Nancy A., *Antisemitism, Misogyny, and the Logic of Cultural Difference: Cesare Lombroso and Matilde Serao* (Lincoln, NE, and London: University of Nebraska Press, 1994).
Haskell, Francis, *The Ephemeral Museum: Old Master Paintings and the Rise of the Art Exhibition* (New Haven, CT, and London: Yale University Press, 2000).
Hepokoski, James A., *Giuseppe Verdi: Falstaff* (Cambridge: Cambridge University Press, 1983).
Hepokoski, James A., *Giuseppe Verdi: Otello* (Cambridge: Cambridge University Press, 1987).
House, Jane and Attisani, Antonio (eds.), *Twentieth-Century Italian Drama: An Anthology. The First Fifty Years* (New York: Columbia University Press, 1995).
Huebner, Steven, *French Opera at the Fin de Siècle: Wagnerism, Nationalism and Style* (Oxford: Oxford University Press, 1999).
Hughes, Meirion and Stradling, Robert, *The English Musical Renaissance 1860–1940: Constructing a National Music*, 2nd edn. (Manchester and New York: Manchester University Press, 2001).
Huysmans, Joris-Karl, *Against Nature (A rebours)*, trans. Margaret Mauldon (Oxford and New York: Oxford University Press, 1998).
Illiano, Roberto (ed.), *Italian Music during the Fascist Period* (Turnhout: Brepols, 2004).
Kallberg, Jeffrey, *Chopin at the Boundaries: Sex, History, and Musical Genre* (Cambridge, MA, and London: Harvard University Press, 1996).

Kerman, Joseph, *Opera As Drama*, new and revised edn. (London and Boston, MA: Faber and Faber, 1989).
Kimbell, David, *Italian Opera* (Cambridge: Cambridge University Press, 1991).
Kramer, Lawrence, *Franz Schubert: Sexuality, Subjectivity, Song* (Cambridge: Cambridge University Press, 1998).
Kris, Ernst and Kurz, Oto, *Legend, Myth, and Magic in the Image of the Artist* (New Haven, CT, and London: Yale University Press, 1979).
Leopardi, Giacomo, *Discorso sopra lo stato presente dei costumi degl'italiani*, ed. Maurizio Moncagatta (Milan: Feltrinelli, 1991).
Lo, Kii-Ming, *'Turandot' auf der Opernbühne* (Frankfurt am Main: Peter Lang, 1996).
Lombroso, Cesare, *Genio e follia* (Milan: Tipografica Chiusi, 1864).
Lombroso, Cesare and Ferrero, Guglielmo, *La donna delinquente* (Turin and Rome: L. Roux, 1893).
Lombroso, Cesare and Ferrero, Guglielmo, *The Female Offender* (London: T. Fisher Unwin, 1895).
Loos, Adolf, *Ornament and Crime: Selected Essays*, trans. Michael Mitchell (Riverside, CA: Ariadne Press, 1998).
Lualdi, Adriano, *Serate musicali* (Milan: Treves, 1928).
Lualdi, Adriano, 'Giacomo Puccini, i suoi detrattori e l'opera nazionale del '900', estratto dal volume V di *Piazza delle Belle Arti*, Rassegna 1957–1958 dell'Accademia Nazionale Luigi Cherubini.
Lyttelton, Adrian (ed.), *Liberal and Fascist Italy* (Oxford: Oxford University Press, 2002).
Mack Smith, Denis, *Mussolini il Duce: quattrocento immagini della vita di un uomo e di vent'anni di storia italiana* (Milan: Gruppo Editoriale Fabbri, 1983).
Mack Smith, Denis, 'Documentary Falsification and Italian Biography', in T. C. W. Blanning and David Cannadine (eds.), *History and Biography: Essays in Honour of Derek Beales* (Cambridge: Cambridge University Press, 1996), pp. 173–87.
Maiocchi, Roberto, *Scienza italiana e razzismo fascista* (Florence: La Nuova Italia Editrice, 1999).
Mantegazza, Paolo, *Fisiologia della donna*, 3rd edn., 2 vols. (Milan and Rome: Treves, 1893).
Marchetti, Arnaldo (ed.), *Puccini com'era* (Milan: Edizioni Curci, 1973).

Marchicelli, Graziella, 'Futurism and Fascism: The Politicization of Art and the Aestheticization of Politics', unpublished doctoral dissertation, University of Iowa (1996).

Mariani, Renato, *Giacomo Puccini* (Turin: Edizioni Arione, 1939).

Marinetti, Filippo Tommaso, *Teoria e invenzione futurista* (Milan: Mandadori, 1968).

Marinetti, Filippo Tommaso, *Let's Murder the Moonshine: Selected Writings*, trans. R. W. Flint and Arthur A. Coppotelli (Los Angeles, CA: Sun and Moon Classics, 1991).

Mawer, Deborah (ed.), *The Cambridge Companion to Ravel* (Cambridge: Cambridge University Press, 2000).

McCrone, David, *The Sociology of Nationalism* (London and New York: Routledge, 1998).

McHale, Maria, 'A Singing People: English Vocal Music and Nationalist Debate, 1880–1920', unpublished doctoral thesis, Royal Holloway, University of London (2002).

Miller, Marion S., 'Wagnerism, Wagnerians, and Italian Identity', in David C. Large and William Weber (eds.), *Wagnerism in European Culture and Politics* (Ithaca, NY, and London: Cornell University Press, 1984), pp. 167–97.

Mintzer, Charles, *Rosa Raisa: A Biography of a Diva with Selections from Her Memoirs* (Boston, MA: Northeastern University Press, 2001).

Monaldi, Gino, *Verdi e le sue opere* (Florence: n.p. 1878).

Monaldi, Gino, *Giacomo Puccini e la sua opera* (Rome: Libreria Editrice Mantegazza, 1924).

Mondello, Elisabetta, *La nuova italiana: la donna nella stampa e nella cultura del ventennio* (Rome: Editori Riuniti, 1987).

Moore, Gregory, *Nietzsche, Biology and Metaphor* (Cambridge: Cambridge University Press, 2002).

Morgan, Robert P., *Twentieth-Century Music: A History of Musical Style in Modern Europe and America* (New York and London: Norton, 1991).

Morini, Mario, Iovino, Roberto and Paloscia, Alberto (eds.), *Pietro Mascagni: Epistolario*, 2 vols. (Lucca: Libreria Musicale Italiana, 1996).

Mosse, George L., *Nationalism and Sexuality: Middle-Class Morality and Sexual Norms in Modern Europe* (Madison, WI, and London: University of Wisconsin Press, 1985).

Murialdi, Paolo, *Storia del giornalismo italiano: dalle prime gazzette ai telegiornali* (Turin: Gutenberg 2000, 1986).

Nicassio, Susan Vandiver, *Tosca's Rome: The Play and the Opera in Historical Perspective* (Chicago, IL, and London: University of Chicago Press, 1999).

Niceforo, Alfredo, *Italiani del nord e italiani del sud* (Turin: Bocca, 1901).

Nicolodi, Fiamma, 'Parigi e l'opera verista: dibattiti, riflessioni, polemiche', *Nuova rivista musicale italiana* 15/4 (October–December 1981), 577–623.

Nicolodi, Fiamma (ed.), *Musica italiana del primo novecento: 'La generazione dell'ottanta' (atti di convegno Firenze 9–10–11 maggio 1980)* (Florence: Leo S. Olschki Editore, 1981).

Nicolodi, Fiamma, 'Il teatro lirico e il suo pubblico' in Simonetta Soldani and Gabriele Turi (eds.), *Fare gli italiani: scuola e cultura nell'Italia contemporanea, I, La nascita dello Stato nazionale* (Bologna, Il Mulino, 1993).

Nicolodi, Fiamma, 'Opera Production from Italian Unification to the Present', in Lorenzo Bianconi and Giorgio Pestelli (eds.), *Opera Production and Its Resources* (Chicago, IL, and London: Chicago University Press, 1998).

Nietzsche, Friedrich, *The Birth of Tragedy and The Case of Wagner*, trans. Walter Kaufman (New York: Vintage Books, 1967).

Nordau, Max, *Degenerazione* (Turin: Bocca, 1896).

Nordau, Max, *Degeneration* (London: Heinemann, 1913).

Ojetti, Ugo, *Cose viste*, 7 vols. (Milan: Treves, 1923), Vol. II.

Ojetti, Ugo, *As They Seemed to Me*, trans. Henry Furst (London: Methuen, 1928).

Osborne, Charles (ed.), *Letters of Giuseppe Verdi* (London: Gollancz, 1971).

Ostali, Piero and Ostali, Nandi (eds.), *Cavalleria rusticana 1890–1990: cento anni di un capolavoro* (Milan: Sonzogno, 1990).

Pagliaini, Arrigo Plinio (ed.), *Catalogo generale della libreria italiana dall'anno 1900 a tutto il 1920: indice per materie A–D* (Milan: Associazione Tipografica Libraria, 1933).

Parker, Roger '"Classical" Music in Milan during Verdi's Formative Years', *Studi musicali* 13/2 (1984), 259–73.

Parker, Roger, *Leonora's Last Act: Essays in Verdian Discourse* (Princeton, NJ: Princeton University Press, 1997).

Parker, Roger, *'Arpa d'or dei fatidici vati': The Verdian Patriotic Chorus in the 1840s* (Parma: Istituto Nazionale di Studi Verdiani, 1997).

Parker, Roger, *Gianni Schicchi* house programme essay, Glyndebourne Festival Opera (2004).

Pasley, Malcolm (ed.), *Nietzsche: Imagery and Thought. A Collection of Essays* (London: Methuen, 1978).

Phillips-Matz, Mary-Jane, *Puccini: A Biography* (Boston, MA: Northeastern University Press, 2002)

Pick, Daniel, *Faces of Degeneration: A European Disorder, c.1848–c.1918* (Cambridge: Cambridge University Press, 1989).

Pierrot, Jean, *The Decadent Imagination, 1880–1900*, trans. Derek Coltman (Chicago, IL, and London: Chicago University Press, 1981).

Pinzauti, Leonardo, 'Memoria di Fausto Torrefranca', *L'approdo musicale, quaderni di musica* (1966).

Pisa, Beatrice, *Nazione e politica nella Società 'Dante Alighieri'* (Rome: Bonacci Editore, 1995).

Pizzetti, Ildebrando, *Musicisti contemporanei: saggi critici* (Milan: Treves, 1914).

Porter, James I. (ed.), *Constructions of the Classical Body* (Ann Arbor, MI: University of Michigan Press, 1999).

Prezzolini, Giuseppe, *La voce 1908–1913: cronaca, antologia e fortuna di una rivista* (Milan: Rusconi Editore, 1974).

Proudhon, P.-J., *De la Justice dans la Révolution et dans l'Eglise*, 3 vols. (Paris: Librairie de Garnier Frères, 1858).

Proudhon, P.-J., *La Pornocratie ou les femmes dans les temps modernes* (Paris: Librairie Internationale A. Lacroix, 1875).

Randall, Annie J. and Gray Davis, Rosalind, *Puccini and the Girl: History and Reception of The Girl of the Golden West* (Chicago, IL, and London: University of Chicago Press, 2005).

Rava, Luigi, *Per la 'Dante Alighieri' (trenta anni di propaganda): discorsi e ricordi, 1900–1931* (Rome: Società Nazionale Dante Alighieri, 1932).

Rescigno, Eduardo, *Dizionario pucciniano* (Milan: Ricordi, 2004).

Rosselli, John, *Music and Musicians in Nineteenth-Century Italy* (London: Batsford, 1991).

Rosselli, John, *Singers of Italian Opera: The History of a Profession* (Cambridge: Cambridge University Press, 1992).

Roth, Cecil, *The History of the Jews of Italy* (Farnborough, Hants. Gregg International Publishers, 1969).

Rovito, Teodoro, *Letterati e giornalisti italiani contemporanei. Dizionario bio-bibliografico*, 2nd edn. (Naples: Teodoro Rovito ed., 1922).

Sachs, Harvey, *Music in Fascist Italy* (London: Weidenfeld and Nicolson, 1987).

Salerno, Franco, *Le donne pucciniane* (Palermo: Casa Editrice Ant. Trimarchi, 1928).

Samson, Jim (ed.), *The Cambridge History of Nineteenth-Century Music* (Cambridge: Cambridge University Press, 2002).

Sanguinetti, Giorgio, 'Puccini's Music in the Italian Theoretical Literature of Its Day', in Deborah Burton, Susan Vandiver Nicassio and Agostino Ziino (eds.), *Tosca's Prism: Three Moments of Western Cultural History* (Boston, MA: Northeastern University Press, 2004), pp. 221–45.

Sartori, Claudio (ed.), *Casa Ricordi: 1908–1958* (Milan: Ricordi, 1958).

Sartori, Claudio (ed.), *Giacomo Puccini* (Milan: Ricordi, 1959).

Schickling, Dieter, *Giacomo Puccini: Biographie* (Stuttgart: Deutsche Verlags-Anstalt, 1989).

Schickling, Dieter and Kaye, Michael, *Giacomo Puccini: Catalogue of the Works* (Kassel: Bärenreiter, 2003).

Schmidl, Carlo, *Dizionario universale dei musicisti*, 2 vols. (Milan: Sonzogno, 1937).

Schor, Naomi, *Reading in Detail: Aesthetics and the Feminine* (New York and London: Methuen, 1987).

Schumacher, Claude (ed.), *Naturalism and Symbolism in European Theatre, 1850–1918* (Cambridge: Cambridge University Press, 1996).

Segel, Harold B., *Pinocchio's Progeny: Puppets, Marionettes, Automatons, and Robots in Modernist and Avant-Garde Drama* (Baltimore, MD, and London: John Hopkins University Press, 1995).

Seligman, Vincent, *Puccini among Friends* (London: Macmillan, 1938).

Senici, Emanuele, 'Verdi's *Falstaff* at Italy's Fin de Siècle', *Musical Quarterly* 85/2 (Summer 2001), 274–310.

Senici, Emanuele (ed.), *The Cambridge Companion to Rossini* (Cambridge: Cambridge University Press, 2004).

Setaccioli, Giacomo, *Il contenuto musicale del Gianni Schicchi di Giacomo Puccini con la esposizione e la illustrazione dei motivi tematici* (Rome: Fratelli De Santis, 1920).
Sheppard, W. Anthony, *Revealing Masks: Exotic Influences and Ritualised Performance in Modernist Music Theater* (Berkeley, Los Angeles, CA, and London: University of California Press, 2001).
Sighele, Scipio, *Eva moderna* (Milan: Treves, 1910).
Sighele, Scipio, *Pagine nazionaliste* (Milan: Treves, 1910).
Sighele, Scipio, *Il nazionalismo e i partiti politici* (Milan: Treves, 1911).
Sighele, Scipio, *La donna e l'amore* (Milan: Treves, 1913).
Smart, Mary Ann, 'Verdi, Italian Romanticism, and the Risorgimento', in Scott L. Balthazar (ed.), *The Cambridge Companion to Verdi* (Cambridge: Cambridge University Press, 2005), pp. 29–45.
Smith, Anthony, *National Identity* (London: Penguin, 1991).
Soldani, Simonetta and Turi, Gabriele (eds.), *Fare gli italiani: scuola e cultura nell'Italia contemporanea, I, La nascita dello Stato nazionale* (Bologna: Il Mulino, 1993).
Solie, Ruth A., 'The Living Work: Organicism and Musical Analysis', *Nineteenth-Century Music* 4/2 (Fall 1980), 147–56.
Spackman, Barbara, *Decadent Genealogies: The Rhetoric of Sickness from Baudelaire to D'Annunzio* (Ithaca, NY: Cornell University Press, 1989).
Spackman, Barbara, *Fascist Virilities: Rhetoric, Ideology and Social Fantasy in Italy* (Minneapolis, MN, and London: University of Minnesota Press, 1996).
Specht, Richard, *Giacomo Puccini: The Man, His Life, His Work*, trans. Catherine Alison Phillips (London and Toronto: Dent, 1933).
Susmel, Edoardo and Susmel, Duilio (eds.), *Opera omnia di Benito Mussolini*, 44 vols. (Florence: La Fenice, 1956), vol. XXI (14 June 1924–4 November 1925).
Tannenbaum, Edward R., *The Fascist Experience: Italian Society and Culture, 1922–1945* (New York and London: Basic Books, 1972).
Taruskin, Richard, *The Oxford History of Western Music*, 6 vols. (Oxford: Oxford University Press, 2005), Vol. III, *The Nineteenth Century*.
Tintori, Giampiero, *Teatro alla Scala: cronologia opere–balletti–concerti 1778–1977* (Gorle: Grafica Gutenberg Editrice, 1979).
Torchi, Luigi, *Riccardo Wagner* (Bologna: Zanichelli, 1890).

Torrefranca, Fausto, *Giacomo Puccini e l'opera internazionale* (Turin: Bocca, 1912).

Tranfaglia, Nicola and Vittoria, Albertina, *Storia degli editori italiani: Dall'unità alla fine degli anni sessanta* (Rome and Bari: Laterza, 2000).

Trudu, Antonio, 'Toni, Alceo', in Stanley Sadie and John Tyrrell (eds.), *The New Grove Dictionary of Music and Musicians*, 2nd edn., 29 vols. (London: Macmillan, 2001), Vol. 25, p. 602.

Turi, Gabriele (ed.), *Storia dell'editoria nell'Italia contemporanea* (Florence: Giunti, 1997).

Virgilio, Michele, *Della decadenza dell'opera in Italia: a proposito di 'Tosca'* (Milan: Gattinoni, 1900).

Wanger, Richard, *Judaism in Music*, trans. Edwin Evans (London: William Reeves, 1910).

Wagner, Richard, *Opera and Drama*, trans. Edwin Evans, 2 vols. (London: William Reeves, 1913).

Walker, Frank, *The Man Verdi* (London: Dent, 1962).

Wanrooij, Bruno P. F., *Storia del pudore: la questione sessuale in Italia, 1860–1949* (Venice: Marsilio Editori, 1990).

Weaver, William and Puccini, Simonetta (eds.), *The Puccini Companion* (New York and London: Norton, 1994).

Weininger, Otto, *Sex and Character* (London and New York: Heinemann and G.P. Putnam's Sons, 1906).

Weininger, Otto, *Sesso e carattere* (Turin: Bocca, 1912).

Weininger, Otto, *Sesso e carattere* (Pordenone: Edizioni Studio Tesi, 1992).

Weir, David, *Decadence and the Making of Modernism* (Amherst, MA: University of Massachusetts Press, 1995).

Weissmann, Adolf, *The Problems of Modern Music*, trans. M. M. Bozman (London: Dent, 1925).

White, Harry and Murphy, Michael (eds.), *Musical Constructions of Nationalism: Essays on the History and Ideology of European Musical Culture 1800–1945* (Cork: Cork University Press, 2001).

Whittall, Arnold, *Romantic Music: A Concise History from Schubert to Sibelius* (London: Thames and Hudson, 1987).

Wilson, Alexandra, 'Torrefranca vs. Puccini: Embodying a Decadent Italy', *Cambridge Opera Journal* 13/1 (March 2001), 29–53.

Wilson, Alexandra, 'Modernism and the Machine Woman in Puccini's *Turandot*', *Music & Letters* 86/3 (August 2005), 432–51.

Woodhouse, John, *Gabriele D'Annunzio: Defiant Archangel* (Oxford: Clarendon Press, 1998).

Wyke, Maria, *Projecting the Past: Ancient Rome, Cinema, and History* (New York and London: Routledge, 1997).

Wyke, Maria (ed.), *Gender and the Body in the Ancient Mediterranean* (Oxford: Blackwell, 1998).

INDEX

Action française, 129, 172
Adami, Giuseppe, 162, 185, 192, 199, 203, 208, 215, 237
Adorno, Theodor, 226
Adua, military defeat at, 129
'Alastor', 179, 180
Aleramo, Sibilla, 148, 237
Alexandria, 40
Alfano, Franco, 194, 216, 237
'Altini', 110, 121
America, United States of, 17, 72, 114, 117, 118, 159–61, 162, 163, 164, 166, 181, 224
anti-Semitism, 4, 127, 140–4, 152
Argentina, 24
Arnstadt, 27
Ars et labor, 36, 60, 61, 232
Ars nova, 95
Art nouveau, 103, 108, 113, 114, 118, 120, 136, 147
Associazione Nazionalista Italiana, 129, 156
Auber, Daniel-François-Esprit, 18
Austin, William W., 223
L'Avanti, 199, 229

Bach, family of musicians, 26
Bach, Johann Sebastian, 27, 90
Balbo, Cesare, 15
Banfield, Stephen, 225
Barcelona, 205
Barini, Giorgio, 77, 82, 86, 89, 95, 237
Barthes, Roland, 38
Bastianelli, Giannotto, 129, 173, 182–4, 238
    La crisi musicale europea, 182–3
Baudelaire, Charles, 103

Bayreuth Festival, 45
Bazzini, Antonio, 204, 212, 238
    Turanda, 204
Beethoven, Ludwig Van, 19, 27, 51–2, 90, 104, 120, 142, 146
    Eroica Symphony, 27
Belasco, David, 109, 118, 163, 238
Bellini, Vincenzo, 44, 56, 72
Benco, Silvio, 153–4, 238
Berg, Alban
    Wozzeck, 221
Berlin, 40, 206
Berlioz, Hector, 18, 93
    La Damnation de Faust, 18
Bernhardt, Sarah, 77
Bersezio, Carlo, 44, 54–5, 238
Berta, Edoardo Augusto, 49, 238
Bertini, Francesca, 201, 238
Bianchi, Renzo, 166, 193, 199, 211, 238
Bizet, Georges
    Carmen, 18
    Les Pêcheurs des perles, 18
Bloch, Ernest, 167
Bocca (publishing house), 125, 126, 128
Boccioni, Umberto, 172, 238
Boito, Arrigo, 42, 167, 238–9
    Nerone, 193
Bologna
    Bolognese school of music, 28
    First Italian performance of *La rondine*, 173, 174
    Staging of The *Ring*, 43
    And Wagnerism, 44

310

Bonaventura, Arnaldo, 166, 197
Bontempelli, Massimo, 208, 209, 239
    Nostra Dea, 209
Borelli, Lyda, 201, 239
Bourget, Paul, 103
Brazil, 24
Brescia, 102, 119
Brighenti-Rosa, Cesare, 198
Bruckner, Anton, 159
Brusa, Filippo, 177
Brussels, 185, 189, 198
Buenos Aires, 32, 37, 38, 40, 174
Bülow, Hans, 21
Busoni, Ferruccio, 158, 204, 205, 212
    Arlecchino, 204
Buxtehude, Dietrich, 27

Caesar, Julius, 13, 152
Il caffaro, 188, 229
Calabria, 29
Camaroni, 108
Caporetto, Battle of, 184
Capri, Antonio, 195, 201–2, 239
Capuana, Luigi, 15
Carducci, Giosuè, 4, 13, 15, 17, 18, 239
Carrà, Carlo, 210, 239
Carré, Albert, 119, 239
Carugati, Romeo, 114, 239
Caruso, Enrico, 160, 239
Casella, Alfredo, 145, 191
Cassatt, Mary, 118
Catalani, Alfredo, 23, 112, 239
Catholicism, 148, 150, 156
Cavour, Camillo Benso, Conte di, 12, 13
Cesari, Gaetano, 202, 240
Cézanne, Paul, 29
Charpentier, Gustave, 167
Checchi, Eugenio, 30–1, 37, 57, 64, 157, 240
Chiarelli, Luigi, 208, 240
    La maschera e il volto, 209

Chilesotti, Oscar, 240
China, 204
Chopin, Fryderyk, 144
Cilea, Francesco, 72
Cimarosa, Domenico
    Il matrimonio segreto, 153
Civinini, Guelfo, 240
Clausetti, 190
Cleveland Leader, 152
Coleridge, Samuel Taylor, 47
Colla family, 205
Colombani, Alfredo, 49, 51, 57, 74, 86, 240
Colombo, Luigi, 209–10, 240
commedia dell'arte, 204, 205
Conrado, G., 63–64, 70
Cordara, Carlo, 164–6, 180
Corelli, Arcangelo, 146
La cornelia, 148
Corradini, Enrico, 81, 128, 240
Corriere dei teatri, 176, 232
Corriere della sera, 17, 25, 51, 57, 74, 86, 107,
    113, 119, 163, 174, 175, 189, 202, 229
Corriere di Napoli, 49, 57
Cortella, Alessandro, 27, 241
Croce, Benedetto, 64, 110–11, 129, 156, 201,
    213, 241
    Estetica, 110–11
Cronaca musicale, 20, 21, 28, 64, 232

Dal Monte, Toti, 173
Dalla Rizza, Gilda, 173, 241
Dall'Olio, Cesare, 19, 241
Dante Alighieri, 12, 28, 29, 90, 181
    Società "Dante Alighieri", 12, 32
D'Annunzio, Gabriele, 13, 15, 42, 81, 82, 103,
    131, 145, 184, 241
    Il fuoco, 42
    Il trionfo della morte, 42
D'Arcais, Francesco, 23, 241
Darclée, Hariclea, 77, 78, 241

Darwin, Charles, 47, 67, 129, 149
D'Atri, Nicola, 108, 241
Daudet, Léon, 172, 174, 241
Davico, Vincenzo, 176–7, 242
Da Vinci, Leonardo, 13
d'Azeglio, Massimo, 11, 15, 242
De Amicis, Edmondo, 31, 32, 188, 242
Debussy, Claude, 63, 137, 142, 163, 167, 180, 211, 223
De Chirico, Giorgio, 210, 242
decadence, 2, 14–17, 22, 24, 47, 70, 90, 96, 103–4, 111, 122, 124, 125, 126, 137
Degas, Edgar, 118
del Fiorentino, Dante, 151
Della Seta, Fabrizio, 55
Depanis, Giuseppe, 24, 242
De Paoli, Domenico, 152, 213, 217, 242
Depero, Fortunato, 208
De Rensis, Raffaello, 163, 164, 195, 202–3, 242
Destinn, Emmy, 160, 242
'Diapason', 43, 44, 50
d'Indy, Vincent, 141, 145, 146, 159
Di San Martino, Enrico, 22
Divisionist movement, 102
Donizetti, Gaetano, 56, 72, 181
La favorite, 153
La donna, 148
'Dottor Libertà', 60
Drabkin, William, 224
Drake, Richard, 15
Dry, Wakeling, 37
Du Locle, Camille, 106
Dupuis, Albert, 159
Duse, Eleonora, 190, 242
Dvořák, Antonín, 160

Egypt, 116
Eisler, Hans, 226
Elgar, Edward, 27
England, 17, 27, 33, 115, 116, 161
Etruria, 188

eugenics, 16
Evening World, 164
Ewen, David, 223

Fanfulla della domenica, 43, 44, 50, 61, 77, 82, 86, 95, 229
Fara, Giulio, 64, 242
Farrar, Geraldine, 243
Fascism, 9, 10, 33, 81, 122, 132, 171, 186, 187, 188, 190–3, 217, 221, 226
Fauré, Gabriel, 173
feminism, 131, 148
Ferraguti, Mario, 152
Ferrani, Cesira, 243
Ferrero, Guglielmo, 134, 138
'Filia' *see* Colombo, Luigi
Filippi, Filippo, 41, 62–3, 243
film, 33, 163, 201, 210, 222, 225–6
Finzi, Gerald, 27
First World War, 9, 10, 131, 147, 168–9, 172, 173, 181, 183, 208, 217
Fiume, March on, 184
Florence, 29, 118, 128, 152, 164, 183, 207
  avant-garde journals, 29, 129–30
  Dante festivities of 1865, 12
  Maggio Musicale Fiorentino, 211
  University, 135
Florimo, Francesco, 25
Fontana, Ferdinando, 26, 39, 243
Forsyth, Cecil, 142, 243
Fortis, Leone, 56, 243
Forzano, Giovacchino, 183, 243
Foscolo, Ugo, 28
Fraccaroli, Arnaldo, 189, 243
France, 29, 33, 41, 116, 130, 141, 143, 145, 149, 162, 173
  French drama, 18, 74
  French literature, 18, 74, 104
  French music, 18, 20, 27, 89, 101, 106–7, 112, 130
  French music criticism, 48

Franchetti, Alberto, 23, 112
Fratelli Bocca *see* Bocca
Freud, Sigmund, 133
Frusta teatrale, 51, 60, 100–101, 108, 161, 232
Futurist movement, 10, 34, 81, 122, 131, 158, 168–72, 207, 208

'Gajanus', 189
Galli, Amintore, 243–4
Gallo, Toni, 101
Gandolfi, Riccardo, 19–20, 28, 244
Gasco, Alberto, 174, 175, 180, 182, 244
Gatti, Guido M., 1, 55, 211, 212, 218, 222, 244
La gazzetta del popolo, 24, 49, 229
Gazzetta di Torino, 66
Gazzetta musicale di Milano, 20, 24, 26, 30, 41, 55, 60–1, 63, 72, 73, 83, 92, 120, 204, 233
Gazzetta teatrale italiana, 66, 233
Gazzetta ufficiale del regno d'Italia, 56
generazione dell'ottanta, 158
Genoa, 188
Germany, 15, 17, 28, 33, 62, 192, 206, 222
   German music, 18, 19, 20, 27, 41–2, 43, 46, 48, 63–5, 66, 67, 89, 112, 146
Giacosa, Giuseppe, 17, 49–50, 61, 71, 86, 171, 244
Gide, André, 38
Gilson, Paul, 159
Gioberti, Vincenzo, 15
Giolitti, Giovanni, 4, 81, 122, 129, 156, 168, 184, 230, 244
Giordano, Umberto, 243
   Andrea Chénier, 18
   La mala vita, 30
Giornale d'Italia, 108, 176, 178, 179, 191, 195, 230
Girardi, Michele, 192
Goethe, Johann Wolfgang Von, 47, 90
Gordon, Rae Beth, 104
Gordon Craig, Edward, 207, 244

Gounod, Charles-François, 18, 46, 89
   Roméo et Juliette, 46
Gozzi, Carlo, 201, 203, 206, 212
   Turandot, 207, 211
Grand Guignol, 69, 165, 179
Gray, Cecil, 166, 211, 224, 244
Gray Davis, Rosalind, 160
Greenwald, Helen, 116
Groos, Arthur, 127
Grout, Donald J., 222–3, 225
Gunsbourg, Raoul, 173, 245
Gui, Vittorio, 1, 212, 245

Hague, The, 40
Halévy, Fromental, 18
Handel, George Frideric, 142
Hanslick, Eduard, 50
Haydn, Joseph, 142, 146
Herder, Johann Gottfried Von, 47
Hervé, Louis, 18
homosexuality, 4, 132, 134, 141, 147, 152
Huebner, Steven, 136
Huneker, James, 178
Huysmans, Joris-Karl, 103, 245
   A rebours, 115
L'idea nazionale, 128, 129, 163, 179, 180, 181, 182, 230

Illica, Luigi, 49–50, 83, 86, 149, 171, 245
Illustrazione italiana, 45, 61, 81, 162, 189, 233
L'impero, 187, 189
Impressionist movement, 116, 118
Incagliati, Mario, 178, 179
India, 30, 117
instrumental music, 19, 63, 145, 146, 194
internationalism, 2, 5, 17, 20, 75, 88, 100, 112–13, 114, 120, 124, 125, 126, 143–4, 155, 156–8, 159, 160, 161, 189
L'Italia, 22

Italy
　bourgeoisie *see* Italy, middle
　　classes cultural decline, 2, 3, 11, 14–20,
　　　21–22, 23, 24, 34, 40, 43, 49, 54–5, 66–7,
　　　68, 70, 72, 73, 84, 87, 88, 89–92, 95, 96,
　　　101, 111, 112, 113, 120, 121, 122, 123, 124,
　　　125–6, 127, 130, 131–2, 134, 135–47, 153,
　　　154, 155, 156–9, 163–6, 167–8, 174–7,
　　　223, 227
　cultural unification, 3, 11, 12–14, 25–34,
　　35–9, 150, 186–90
　giubileo of 1911, 155–6, 161
　and heroism, 16, 80–82, 131
　and imperialism, 33, 91, 116, 129, 156, 187,
　　191
　landscape and climate, 27–9, 30, 32, 90–1,
　　92, 182, 186–7
　language and dialects, 11–12, 13, 29
　middle classes, 4, 35, 38, 42, 45, 46, 81, 82,
　　84, 100, 113, 116, 122, 124, 129, 130, 143,
　　167, 168, 170, 171, 172, 174, 186, 191, 205,
　　206, 208, 209, 222, 224
　Militarism, 22, 23, 33, 129, 130, 131, 146, 149,
　　184, 188
　nationalist movement, 9, 42, 81, 82, 122,
　　128–31, 132, 147, 155, 156, 170
　north-south divide, 11, 130–1
　patriotic education, 12, 31, 94
　regionalism, 11, 28–31, 32, 90
　social unrest, 11, 72–3, 81
　Unification, 11, 12, 13, 14, 15, 26, 29, 33, 143,
　　156
　urbanisation and industrialisation, 5, 11,
　　16, 27, 113
Italian Press Association, 186
Italo-Sanusi War, 188

Jackson Jarves, James, 118
Japan, 30, 98, 103, 105, 106, 114, 115–19,
　162, 181

Journalism, 7–8, 19, 21, 25, 33, 41, 43, 48,
　59–67, 70, 73, 100–101, 151–2, 168, 183,
　229–36 *see also* references to individual
　newspapers and periodicals
Journals, avant-garde *see* under-Florence
Jugendstil, 103

Kant, Immanuel, 47
Kerman, Joseph, 1, 84, 85
Kimbell, David, 98
Kleist, Heinrich Von
　Über das Marionettentheater, 207
Klimt, Gustav, 118, 147
Krafft-Ebing, Richard Freiherr Von
　Psychopathia Sexualis, 126
Kramer, Lawrence, 51
Krusceniski, Salomea, 245
Kuliscioff, Anna, 148, 245

Labriola, Teresa, 148
Lacerba, 133
Lalo, Edouard, 18
Lang, Fritz, 210
La lanterna, 42, 44, 60, 65, 77, 93–4, 233–4
Lecocq, Charles, 18
La lega lombarda, 108
Lehár, Franz, 174
Leonardo, 129, 133, 234
Leoncavallo, Ruggero, 72, 112, 130, 245
　I pagliacci, 178
Leoni, Michele, 47
Leopardi, Giacomo, 15, 28
'Leporello' *see* Tedeschi, Achille
Lessona, Michele, 202, 203, 212–3, 215
La lettura, 17, 61, 116, 234
Levi, Primo, 84, 92, 245
L'Herbier, Marcel, 210
Libya, 156, 188
Ligue de la Patrie française, 145
Lirica, 161

Lisbon, 40
La lombardia, 22, 24, 114, 230
Lombroso, Cesare, 16, 34, 104, 126, 134, 138, 141, 245
   L'antisemitismo e le scienze moderne, 141
   La donna delinquente, 133–4
   Genio e follia, 34
London, 16, 40, 115
   first performance of *Tosca*, 73
   Covent Garden, 161
   Performance of Belasco's *Madame Butterfly*, 109, 118
Long, John Luther, 116
Loos, Adolf, 104, 246
Los Angeles, 40
Louÿs, Pierre, 246
Lualdi, Adriano, 190–1, 197, 199, 214, 216, 221, 246
Lübeck, 27
Lucca, 26, 27, 31, 39
Lucca (publishing house), 41
Lupi family, 205

Macchi, Gustavo, 52, 74, 246
Macchiaioli movement, 116
machine aesthetic, 195, 201, 204–10, 212, 219
Maffei, Andrea, 204
Magnard, Alberic, 167
Mahler, Gustav, 159
Malipiero, Gian Francesco, 145, 153, 191
Manchester, 40
Mancinelli, Luigi, 23, 246
Manet, Edouard, 118
Mantegazza, Paolo, 16, 126, 133, 135, 138, 150, 246
Mantovani, Tancredi, 21, 186, 189, 246
Manzoni, Alessandro, 31
   I promessi sposi, 13
Marcello, Benedetto, 25
Mareira, 159

Marescotti, Ercole Arturo, 58–9, 246
Mariani, Renato, 219, 221
Marie, Gabriel, 159
Marinetti, Filippo Tommaso, 10, 131, 168–72, 173, 207–8, 217, 247
   The Futurist Cookbook, 171
   Mafarka le futuriste, 170
Marne, Battle of the, 168
Martucci, Giuseppe, 23
Marx, Adolf Bernhard, 146
Il marzocco, 106, 110, 124, 164, 180, 234
Mascagni, Pietro, 22, 29, 30, 72, 74, 83, 112, 192, 247
   Cavalleria rusticana, 22–3, 30, 85, 153, 158, 178, 221
   Guglielmo Ratcliffe, 18
   Iris, 83, 117
   Lodoletta, 174
   Nerone, 32
   Zanetto, 18
The Mask, 207, 234
Massenet, Jules, 18, 88, 89, 93, 107, 121, 136, 137, 144, 173
   La Navarraise, 18
Il mattino, 56, 230
'Max' (*see* Roux, Mario)
Mazza, Armando, 170
Mazzini, Giuseppe, 144
Mendelssohn, Felix Bartholdy-, 142
Il messaggero, 73, 83, 92, 230
Meyerbeer, Giacomo, 18
Mexico, 40
Michelangelo Buonarroti, 26, 90
Milan, 16, 19, 30, 44, 59, 73, 74, 98, 100, 128, 148, 152, 167, 169, 173, 185, 194, 198, 205
   Church of San Fedele, 185
   Conservatoire, 76, 191, 204
   Duomo, 185, 198
   Galleria, 81, 171
   and industrialisation, 11

Milan *cont.*
   Lombardian school of music, 28
   Quartet Society, 19
   Teatro alla Scala, 18, 41, 45, 97, 107, 168, 193, 194
   Teatro dal Verme, 168, 169
   Triennale, second, 149
Milhaud, Darius, 210
misogyny, 127, 130, 132, 138, 140–1, 147–50, 152, 170, 191, 209
modernism, 1, 6, 8, 10, 16, 196, 200, 201, 205, 210, 211, 217, 220, 221, 222
Monaco, 172, 173
Monaco, Albert Prince of, 173
Monaldi, Gino, 53, 57–8, 59, 62, 65, 109, 187, 247
Il mondo artistico, 60, 74, 83, 153, 234
Monet, Claude, 118
Monte Carlo, 172–3, 174, 177
   Théâtre du Casino, 172–3
Monteleone Calabro (now Vibo Valentia), 128
Montemezzi, Italo, 185
Monteverdi, Claudio, 145
Morandi (critic), 50
Morandi, Giorgio, 210, 247
Morbelli, Angelo, 102
Morello, Vincenzo, 82, 84, 85, 87, 247
Moreau, Gustave, 144
'Mos', 106, 110
Mosca, Gaetano, 129
Moscow, 40, 205
Mozart, Wolfgang Amadeus, 18, 146, 205, 223
Mozzoni, Anna Maria, 148
Mugnone, Leopoldo, 72, 247
Mulè, Giuseppe, 190
Murger, Henri, 49–50
Musica, 80, 163, 174, 176, 179, 180, 234
Musica d'oggi, 60, 185, 186, 190, 234
Musica e Musicisti, 35, 60, 61, 97, 116, 234

Musica nuova, 120, 234
The Musical Times, 27
Mussolini, Benito, 128, 185, 188, 191, 192, 193, 206, 217

Naples, 30, 41, 128
   Conservatoire, 25
   Neapolitan school of music, 28
Napoleon Bonaparte, 184
Nappi, Giovanni Battista, 74, 80, 107, 248
Nasi, 92
La nazione, 83, 182, 183, 230
Neumann, Angelo, 43
New York, 159–60, 163, 166, 173, 179
   Metropolitan Opera House, 159–60, 161, 178
New York Times, 178
Nicefero, Alfredo, 16
Nietzsche, Friedrich, 81, 131, 206, 207
Nordau, Max, 120, 121, 248
   Degeneration, 16, 120, 126
Nuova antologia, 23, 43–4, 56, 111, 124, 159, 186, 189, 212, 234

Offenbach, Jacques, 18
Ojetti, Ugo, 39, 202, 212, 248
O'Neil, Raymond, 152
operetta, 10, 18, 163, 172, 174, 176
Orefice, Giacomo, 145
organicism, 3, 9, 40, 46–54, 55, 64, 67, 68, 73, 86, 156, 178, 179, 180, 214

Pagliara, Rocco, 56, 248
Paisiello, Giovanni, 205
Paladini, Vinicio, 208
Il palcoscenico, 58, 235
Palermo, 177, 212
Palestrina, Giovanni Pierluigi da, 25
Pannaggi, Ivo, 208
Pannain, Guido, 23, 30, 196, 248

Papini, Giovanni, 130, 131, 133, 150, 248
Pareto, Vilfredo, 129
Paribeni, G. C., 248
Paris, 16, 114, 115, 151, 170, 172, 181
  Albert Carré's production of *Madama Butterfly* in 1906, 119
  artists' departure of for the provinces, 29
  Exposition Universelle, 113
  first performance of *Tosca*, 73
Parker, Roger, 127, 182
Il parlamento, 24
Parodi, Lorenzo, 23, 188, 248
Pasquini, Bernardo, 146
Pellizza da Volpedo, Giuseppe, 102
Il pensiero musicale, 198, 235
Pergolesi, Giovanni Battista, 205
La perseveranza, 67, 74, 107, 231
La perseverenza di domenica, 53, 80
Pertile, Aureliano, 173
Pertile, Lino, 193
Pesaro
  Conservatoire, 120
  Liceo Rossini, 120
Petrarch, Francesco, 28
physiognomy, 20, 55, 56, 187, 214
Il pianoforte, 196, 211, 217, 235
Pirandello, Luigi, 208
  Sei personaggi in cerca d'autore, 208
Pisa, 27
Pizzetti, Ildebrando, 10, 24, 51, 54, 79, 108, 112, 117, 129, 145, 166–8, 174, 185, 201, 248–9
Plato, 47
Platti, Giovanni Benedetto, 146
Podrecca, Vittorio, 205, 206, 249
Poliziano, Angelo Ambrogini, 90
Pompeii, 34
Pompeii, Last Days of, 32
Ponchielli, Amilcare, 72, 95, 249
Il popolo d'Italia, 186, 191, 192, 198, 231

Il popolo romano, 53, 92, 231
Post-Impressionist movement, 118
Pozza, Giovanni, 24–5, 107, 119, 163, 249
Pratella, Francesco Balilla, 155, 158, 249
La prensa, 31–2, 231
Previati, Gaetano, 102, 249
Prezzolini, Giuseppe, 130, 131, 249
Procida, Saverio, 212
Proudhon, Pierre-Joseph, 135, 140
Puccini, family of composers, 26
Puccini, Giacomo, 18, 41, 43, 62, 104, 128, 151, 153, 169, 170–1, 207, 209
  academic disparagement of, 1, 6, 7, 69–70, 221–5, 226–8
  biographers of, 6, 14, 25, 26, 27, 37, 65, 75, 76, 125, 132, 151, 166, 169, 197, 198, 214
  and boats, 35–7
  and cars, 35–7
  as Classical hero, 32–4, 37, 139, 147, 154, 186, 188
  death, 10, 185, 221, 222
  as emblem of Italy's modernity, 34–8
  and gendered discourses, 4, 9, 31, 34, 52, 84, 93, 95, 100, 113, 119–22, 124, 126–7, 130, 132–40, 144–5, 146–7, 150, 152, 154, 188, 198, 216
  and hunting, 37, 38
  and internationalism, 2, 5, 7, 9, 17, 75, 88, 100, 112–14, 120, 124, 125, 126, 141–2, 143, 144, 154, 155, 157–8, 160, 161, 172, 189, 222
  lack of originality, 55–7, 66, 75, 88–9, 107–8, 112–13, 137, 141–2, 155, 162–3, 165, 199
  and modernism, 1, 3, 4, 5–6, 7, 8, 10, 40, 57–9, 67, 68, 87, 122, 161–3, 164, 165, 166, 179, 180, 195, 196, 199–201, 204–5, 206–7, 208, 210–12, 213, 214, 220, 221–4
  and national identity, 1, 2, 3, 4–5, 6, 8, 9, 10, 14, 22, 23, 24, 25, 26–7, 29, 30–2, 34, 37, 38, 43, 46, 55, 58, 63, 65, 67, 69, 70–2

318 | Index

Puccini, Giacomo *cont.*
    75, 88–9, 90–1, 92–4, 95–6, 106–7, 111, 112–3, 114, 120–1, 122, 124, 125, 126, 127, 134, 135, 140, 141–2, 144, 145, 147, 150, 152–3, 154, 155, 157–9, 161, 162, 163, 164, 166, 167–8, 172, 173, 174–5, 177, 178, 181–2, 183–4, 185, 186–90, 191, 192, 193, 196–7, 201, 210, 213, 217, 221, 227
  obituaries, 4, 10, 76, 117, 127, 185–7, 189–91, 192, 193, 194
  ordinariness of, 34, 37–9, 186
  political convictions, 3, 192
  physique, 25, 32, 34
  and sincerity, 9, 49, 68, 69, 74–5, 76, 80, 84–5, 89, 94, 111, 114, 117, 125, 137, 152, 155, 165, 176–7, 196, 197–8, 199, 214, 216–20
  Tuscan origins, 29–32, 173, 188
  Works,
    La bohème, 1, 3, 9, 27, 40, 43, 44–5, 46, 49, 50–1, 52, 53, 54–5, 56, 57, 58, 59, 64–5, 66, 67, 68, 71, 72, 73, 75, 76, 84, 95, 98, 100, 105, 107, 109, 112, 114, 165, 166, 167, 176, 193, 197, 219, 225
    Edgar, 24, 27
    La fanciulla del West, 5, 10, 155, 157, 159–66, 167, 168, 170, 172, 173, 175, 177, 179, 212, 219, 224, 225
    Gianni Schicchi, 5, 10, 30, 174, 178, 179, 180, 181, 182, 183, 184
    Inno a Roma, 187
    Madama Butterfly, 9, 49, 51, 52, 68, 84, 88, 97–101, 102, 105–6, 107–13, 114–24, 159, 165, 177, 194, 199, 203, 219, 225, 226
    Manon Lescaut, 3, 24, 25, 55, 71, 95, 108, 114, 151, 165, 167, 176, 211, 219
    La rondine, 5, 10, 155, 172–7, 212
    Suor Angelica, 106, 178, 179, 180, 181, 183, 218
    Il tabarro, 174, 178, 179, 180, 181, 183, 205
    Tosca, 1, 9, 27, 30, 49, 63, 65, 66, 68, 69–75, 76–80, 81, 82–90, 91, 92–6, 98, 100, 114, 161, 164, 165, 170, 181, 223
    Il trittico, 5, 174, 175, 177, 178–84, 219
    Turandot, 6, 10, 55, 80, 165, 184, 193–6, 198–205, 206, 208, 210–20, 221, 224
    Le villi, 20, 22, 24, 95

Puccini, Michele, 32

'Quirite', 65, 77, 93–4

Rachmaninov, Serge, 159
'Raff', 186
Raffaello Santi, 90
Raineri, Franco, 176
Raisa, Rosa, 193, 195, 249
Randall, Annie J., 160
La rassegna musicale, 211, 235
'Rastignac' *see* Morello, Vincenzo
Rava, Luigi, 11–12, 249
Ravel, Maurice, 123, 167
Il regno, 81, 129, 235
Reims, 172
Reinhardt, Max, 206–7, 211, 250
Renaissance, 12, 13, 15, 90, 188
Rennie Mackintosh, Charles, 118
Respighi, Ottorino
  La bella addormentata, 205
Il resto del Carlino, 189, 231
Revue d'art dramatique, 170
Ricordi (publishing house), 10, 14, 18, 20, 23, 24, 25, 27, 34, 35, 36, 42, 49, 55, 60–1, 72, 97, 107, 116, 125, 150, 185, 203
Ricordi, Giulio, 27, 41, 71, 72, 73, 250
Ricordi, Tito, 191, 250
La riforma musicale, 235
Rimsky-Korsakov, Nikolai, 159
Rio de Janeiro, 32, 40
Risorgimento, 10, 11, 12, 14, 16, 31, 33, 81, 128, 130
Rivista musicale italiana, 62, 63–4, 70, 75, 117, 124, 128, 142, 177, 202, 215, 235–6
Rivista politica e letteraria, 27, 92
Rivista teatrale italiana, 152
Rocco (President of the Chamber of Deputies), 190

Rolland, Romain, 130, 250
romanità, cult of, 32–4
Romanticism, 66, 138
Rome, 29, 40, 50, 73, 83, 92, 114, 128, 148, 152, 159, 163, 205, 208
    first performance of *La fanciulla del West*, 159, 161–3, 166
    first performance of *Il trittico*, 178–9, 184
    first Rome performance of *La bohème*, 56
    first Rome performance of *Turandot*, 216
    Liceo musicale di Santa Cecilia, 181
    performance of *Roméo et Juliette*, 46
    political demonstrations in, 72–3
    Roman school of music, 28
    Teatro Costanzi, 72, 159, 162
    Vittorio Emanuele monument, 155
Roncaglia, Gino, 217, 250
Rosselli, John, 62
Rossini, Gioachino, 47, 100, 106, 181, 184. 205
    Guglielmo Tell, 153
Rosso di San Secondo, Piermaria, 208, 250
    Marionette, che passione, 209
Rousseau, Jean-Jacques, 135
Roux, Mario ('Max'), 107, 108

Sachs, Harvey, 191
The Sackbut, 211
Sadayakko, Madam, 114, 116
Saint-Saëns, Camille, 18
    Henry VIII, 18
    Samson et Dalila, 18
Sala, Marco, 22
Salerno, Franco, 198, 216
Salvatori, Fausto, 187–8, 189, 250
Samson, Jim, 66
San Francisco, 1
Sardou, Victorien, 71, 73, 74, 75, 76, 77, 82, 86, 171, 250
Sartori, Claudio, 227–8
scapigliatura movement, 42, 129, 167

Schenkerian voice-leading analysis, 225
Schiller, Friedrich, 90, 204
Schoenberg, Arnold, 205, 211
Schopenhauer, 90
Schubert, Franz, 51–2
Secession movement, 103
Il secolo, 49, 61, 83, 107, 172, 190, 191, 231
Second World War, 177
Segantini, Giovanni, 102, 251
    Le cattive madri, 149
    La vanità (La fonte del male), 138
Seligman, Sybil, 32, 151, 251
Senici, Emanuele, 182, 210
La sera, 52, 191
Sergi, Giuseppe, 16
Setaccioli, Giacomo, 181, 251
Sgambati, Giovanni, 23
Sheppard, W. Anthony, 211
Sicily, 30, 37, 128
Sighele, Scipio, 126, 143, 156–7, 158, 251
    Eva moderna, 133
    La folla delinquente, 129
Simoni, Renato, 185, 203, 206, 208, 215, 251
Sinding, Christian, 159
Sironi, Mario, 210, 251
Smareglia, Antonio, 153
Smith, Anthony, 32
socialism, 17, 135, 148, 156
Soffici, Ardengo, 130, 251
Solerti, Angelo, 145, 251
Solie, Ruth, 47
Sommi, G., 187, 189
Sonzogno (publishing house), 18, 22, 23, 49, 97, 107
Sonzogno, Edoardo, 251
Sonzogno, Lorenzo, 251
Specht, Richard, 222, 225
Spencer, Herbert, 47
Spontini, Luigi
    La vestale, 153

La stampa, 44, 54, 120, 232
Stile floreale, 103
Stile liberty, 103
Storchio, Rosina, 97, 98, 99, 252
Strauss, Richard, 63, 123, 137, 142, 144, 159, 201, 205
Stravinsky, Igor, 180, 205, 211, 223
  Oedipus Rex, 221
The Studio, 114
Sydney, 1
Symbolist movement, 118

Taruskin, Richard, 223-4
Tchaikovsky, Pyotr Il'yich, 142
Teatro dei Piccoli, 205
Teatro grottesco, 208-9
Il teatro illustrato e la musica popolare, 23, 236
Tedeschi, Achille, 45, 252
Il tempo, 110
Thermignon, Mario, 80
Thomas, Ambroise, 18
  Hamlet, 18
Thovez, Enrico, 48, 113, 252
Toni, Alceo, 190-1, 252
Torchi, Luigi, 63, 67, 70, 75, 77, 79, 83, 85, 87, 88, 89, 92, 93, 117, 252-3
Torre del Lago, 30-1, 76
Torrefranca, Fausto, 4-5, 9, 95, 98, 111, 113, 120, 124, 125-8, 129, 130, 131, 132, 133, 134, 135-7, 138-40, 141-3, 144-7, 149, 150-4, 155, 157-8, 163, 165, 166, 170, 174, 183, 189, 191, 198, 216, 224, 226, 253
Toscanini, Arturo, 160, 185, 193, 216, 253
Toulouse Lautrec, Henri de, 118
La tribuna, 64, 82, 107, 108, 153, 174, 180, 182, 232
La tribuna illustrata, 82
Triple Alliance, 33
Il trovatore, 153, 161, 236
Trudu, Antonio, 191

Turin, 29, 31, 44, 45, 49, 53, 54, 63, 64, 73, 125, 152, 205
  Esposizione Internazionale d'Arte Decorativa Moderna, 113-14
  first performance of a Beethoven symphony, 19
  Fratelli Bocca publishing house *see* Bocca
  and industrialisation, 11
  Lombroso's Museum of Criminal Anthropology, 134
  Lombroso's psychiatric clinic, 34
  Politecnico, 128
  première of *Götterdämmerung*, 40, 43, 44
  Teatro Regio, 40, 44, 64, 212,
  University, 120
Tuscany, 29-32, 173, 188

Umberto I, King of Italy, 16, 81

Valcarenghi, Renzo, 208
Valetta, Ippolito, 43-4, 56, 111, 112, 253
Valmarana, Pino, 203
Vandini, Alfredo, 151
Van Gogh, Vincent, 118
Vasari, Giorgio, 26
Vaughan Williams, Ralph, 27
Vecchi, Ferruccio, 153
Venice
  Biennale exhibition, 13
  Staging of The *Ring*, 43
  Venetian school of music, 28
Veracini, Franceso Maria, 146
Verdi, Giuseppe, 6, 13-14, 21, 24, 25, 31, 41, 44, 46, 48, 50, 51, 54, 57, 58, 62, 63, 64, 68, 72, 77, 85, 88, 101-2, 106, 112, 139, 153, 155, 167, 177, 182, 186, 200, 223
  Aida, 27, 199
  Falstaff, 21, 25, 58, 158, 182, 200, 221
  La forza del destino, 101
  Nabucco, 47

Verdi, Giuseppe *Cont.*
  Otello, 21, 48
  Requiem, 182
  La traviata, 175
  succession to, 8, 20–1, 22, 23–4, 125, 194, 224
Verga, Giovanni, 15, 253
  Cavalleria rusticana, 75
  La lupa, 30
verismo, 29, 45, 69, 71, 85, 86
'Veritas' see Fortis, Leone
Viareggio, 192
Vicenza, 101
Vienna, 16, 40, 104, 163
  Karltheater, 172
  Viennese Classical tradition, 19
  Volksoper, 177
Villanis, Luigi Alberto, 66, 120–2, 253
Virgilio, Michele, 22, 42, 60, 66, 70, 71, 73, 74, 76, 79, 80, 83, 86, 87, 90–2, 95
La vita musicale, 152, 236
Vitali, Giovanni Battista, 146
Vittorio Emanuele II, King of Italy, 185
Vivaldi, Antonio, 146
La voce, 29, 129, 130, 131, 133, 168, 182, 183, 191, 236
Vreuls, Victor, 159

Wagner, Richard, 3, 18, 19, 27, 39, 40–4, 45, 46, 47, 48, 49, 53, 54, 56, 59, 63, 64, 65, 67, 68, 88, 89, 93, 94, 112, 117, 121, 136, 142, 153, 154, 163, 223
  anti-Wagnerism, 17, 41–4, 46
  Das Rheingold, 41
  Die Meistersinger von Nürnberg, 40, 42
  Die Walküre, 41, 46
  Götterdämmerung, 40, 43, 44, 45, 47
  Lohengrin, 40, 41, 42
  Parsifal, 41
  prose works, 63, 142–3, 144
  Ride of the Valkyries, 42
  Tannhäuser, 42
  The *Ring*, 43, 52
  Tristan und Isolde, 40
Wagner, Siegfried, 72
Walker, Frank, 62
Weininger, Otto, 132–3, 134, 135, 137, 138, 140–1, 150, 253
  Geschlecht und Charakter, 132–3
Whistler, James McNeill, 118
Whittall, Arnold, 139
Wilde, Oscar, 134, 144

Zangarini, 253